Basic Economics for Business

Basic Economics for Business

Ken HOYLE BSc (Econ)

and

Geoffrey WHITEHEAD BSc (Econ)

Stanley Thornes (Publishers) Ltd

First published in 1990 by:
Stanley Thornes (Publishers) Ltd
Old Station Drive
Leckhampton
CHELTENHAM GL53 0DN
England

British Library Cataloguing in Publication Data
Hoyle, Ken
  Basic economics for business.
  1. Economics
  I. Title   II. Whitehead, Geoffrey
  330

  ISBN 0–7487–0411–6

Typeset in 10/12 Plantin by ⫪\ Tek Art Ltd, Croydon, Surrey
Printed and bound in Great Britain at The Bath Press, Avon

Contents

9   The national income   257

PART 4   Macro-economics – the study of the whole economy

10   The background to practical macro-economics   281

11   Keynesian economics   295

12   Supply-side economics and monetarism   320

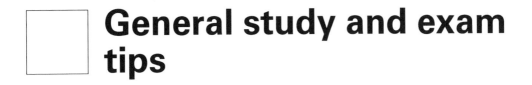

General study and exam tips

'*In many situations information is so great a part of effectiveness that without information a really clever person cannot get started. With information a much less clever person can get very far.*'

Dr Edward De Bono

Being successful on a course does not simply result from listening to lectures or reading a textbook. You must become actively involved in the learning process in order to acquire knowledge and skills and perform well in assessments.

There is no reason why you cannot achieve this aim. After all you are on a course of study because an examining authority believes that you have the necessary ability to complete the course successfully. If you are prepared to become actively involved and do the work required, you have every right to feel confident that you can succeed in the final examinations.

These notes are designed to make your study more efficient, to ensure that you use this manual to best advantage and to help you improve both your coursework and your examination techniques. They have been divided into four parts:
1 general study tips
2 improving the quality of your work
3 examination technique
4 studying with this text.

1 GENERAL STUDY TIPS

An eminent physicist once said: 'Thinking is 99 per cent perspiration and 1 per cent inspiration'. Take his advice and that of most of us who have had the benefit of a good education. Ignore the advice of those who believe you can prepare yourself for the examination in one or two weeks. Knowledge and skills of any value are not easily learned. For most of us it takes time to understand and permanently remember the content of a subject; instead of forgetting everything immediately the examinations are over. Therefore start working at studying right at the very start of your course and continue at a steady pace until the examinations. Do all the work expected of you by your tutor including homework and mock/mid term examinations. Homework is good practice and the mock exams simulate aspects of the final examination. Doing them as well as you can makes your tutor more willing to help you, as he or she will see that you are playing your part in the learning process.

The knowledge and skills you will gain on your course of study are precisely the kind needed by professional business people. So approach the study of each subject as if you were in real life a business man or woman, or a person following a profession such as accountancy or law. In this way the subject should come alive for you, and your motivation to learn should increase.

To help realise this objective, read a quality daily and Sunday newspaper that has a good business section. By doing this you will discover what is happening on a day-to-day basis and be in a better position to understand the topics you are studying on the course. You will also broaden and deepen your knowledge of the subject. Professional people at work usually read a quality newspaper and monthly or quarterly periodical related directly to their discipline in order to keep abreast of the latest developments. You will probably wish to do the same when you commence work, so why not start now?

Carry a pocket dictionary with you and look up words you hear or read but do not understand. None of us has a complete vocabulary but we can improve it if we really want to be able to read and study more effectively. In the case of students it is even more important because words used in lectures, textbooks or newspapers often become misused in examinations. Some words which cause problems with their meaning or spelling are:

aggregate	disseminate	heterogeneous
antithesis	distinguish	homogeneous
constituent	evaluate	panacea
discipline	facsimile	prognosis

Do you fully understand how these words may be used in the context of your subject? Use a dictionary.

As soon as you start your course, find out if you are going to be given past examination reports for your subject, examiners' reports, specimen answers to previous examination questions and a work scheme. It is probable that they will not all be available at your school, college or university or even from the examining authority. You should, however, obtain as much information about your course of study and the examinations as possible so you know exactly what amount of work lies ahead of you and the academic standard you are expected to reach. This will help in planning your personal workload for the period of your course.

If you do not understand something ask your tutor. Do not assume that you are inadequate because you did not understand something that other students seemed to appreciate. They may be having difficulties too or your lecturer may simply not have explained the point to everyone's satisfaction. If something is overlooked by the tutor, don't be afraid to bring it to his/her attention.

Personal health is something that many students dismiss with comments such as: 'what has health got to do with ability to think?' Studies on the topic have now clearly indicated that general health and mental performance are statistically related. Within four weeks of being given multi vitamin and mineral tablets students in two separate controlled studies improved upon their written performance in intelligence tests by approximately ten points. Your commonsense alone should tell you that you cannot perform at your best if you continually feel tired or have flu or a heavy cold in an examination. Eat a varied diet that includes protein foods, vegetables and fruit, and get some daily exercise even if it is only a good brisk walk home after your day's study.

Contrary to the belief of many students, the best academic work is not done at night-time. Once again research shows that students perform better in the early part of the week, in the daytime – particularly mornings – and in a place where there is natural daylight to read and write by. Therefore plan your study schedule so that it is completed in the day. This will also leave you the evenings and weekends free to relax and enjoy yourself.

2   IMPROVING THE QUALITY OF YOUR WORK

The earlier in the course you bring your work to a satisfactory standard the more likely you are to exhibit a good standard of work in the examinations. Obviously, academic standards do relate to the thinking abilities of the student but they also depend on motivation, and a logical approach to one's work if effective presentation at the appropriate academic standard is to be achieved. Here are three tips that will help you develop a logical approach to the presentation of your work.

Read the question carefully

When undertaking essay or numerical work make sure you read the question very carefully. Underline the key words in the question so that your mind is concentrated on the essential aspects. For example, distinguish between the two main types of question.

DESCRIPTIVE QUESTIONS

A descriptive question is one in which you will be expected to describe or explain something and possibly distinguish it from alternative or similar items or ideas. Two examples are:

a) *Describe* and *distinguish above-the-line advertising* from other forms of *advertising*.

b) *Explain* with the *aid of graphs, how the price* of a product is *determined* in a highly *competitive economy*.

Some of the key words have been emphasised in italics to give you an idea of which words are at the heart of the question. Always underline or highlight the key words yourself before attempting to answer.

ANALYTICAL QUESTIONS

These include the purely analytical question, or the analytical question that requires you to evaluate a statement (indicate your level of support for an idea/ give it a value) or only to present your own ideas. Examples of these are:

a) *Solely analytical*: Analyse the contention that there is no such thing as fixed costs.

b) *Analytical and Evaluative*: How far do you support the idea that adult behaviour is predominantly related to one's early childhood experiences?

If you have been presented with a minicase (short story) or case study (extended story) detailing opposing opinions regarding a problem a company is faced with, you may be requested to offer your own solution. In this event your answer should analyse the value of all the opinions offered in the case as well as possibly suggesting your own.

Consider also the way a question is structured. If it is in two or more parts give equal time to each if equal marks are awarded to each part. If more marks are awarded to one part than another, allocate your time in the same proportions as the marks awarded. For example, if a Question has marks awarded: part (a) 5 marks, part (b) 15 marks (total 20 marks), you should spend a quarter (5/20) of your time answering (a) and three quarters (15/20) on (b).

Sometimes the time you should allocate to a part of a question is indicated by the implied requirements of the question, rather than by marks. For example

Q1 (a) Briefly outline 'actual' and 'ostensible' authority.

(b) Brown and Brown Ltd contracted with a married woman for the laying of new carpets. After the work had been done, the woman's husband refuted the contract and refused to pay for the carpets. Advise Brown and Brown Ltd and the woman on their legal position.

By using the words 'briefly outline' the examiner is indicating that much less time should be spent on answering part (a). The question requires more marks to be awarded to part (b) as the analytical and applied nature of this part indicates that it is more difficult to answer.

With numerical type questions, such as in accountancy and statistics, do not assume that all you have to do is arrive at the right answer. Your tutor – or an examiner – will expect you to explain what you are doing as you introduce each set of workings, graphs, illustrations or tables. After all, how is your tutor to know how you arrived at the right answer if you do not explain? Even more importantly, even if you give the wrong answer, at least you will be given some marks for those parts of your calculation which are correct. Such subjects involve a large element of communication and if you do not communicate effectively in your answer what you are doing you will lose marks.

Construct an essay plan

Always spend a few minutes constructing an essay plan before answering a question. This only requires jotting down a few notes for each paragraph which indicates the approach you will take to your answer and the points you will include. This will make sure that you construct your essay in a logical manner and that you keep to a target when writing your answer.

Follow up with your tutor

To understand fully what is required when answering questions, ask your tutor about the work you have handed in and had marked if he or she has not commented sufficiently on your script, informing you of where you were right and wrong and why.

3 EXAMINATION TECHNIQUE

If you are studying at college you can start improving your examination technique in the mock/mid term examination which will help you in the coursework assessment during the second half of the course as well as in the final examination. Here are a few tips on improving your presentation.

- *Always do rough workings*. Use essay plans and/or numerical workings to plan your answer, but on a page other than the one on which you start your answer to the question. Cross through your rough working before starting to answer the question.
- Select the questions you intend to answer and *start with the one you think you will find the easiest* to answer. In this way you may gain your highest marks early in the exam which is very important in case you do not complete the examination.
- *Keep an eye on the clock* so that you allow about the same amount of time for answering each question (unless one is a more difficult, compulsory question). Noting the time in order to complete all the questions you are required to answer gives you a better chance of achieving high marks.
- Allow at least a third to half a page for illustrations or diagrams. In this way they look like illustrations rather than scribblings and you have

sufficient space available if you have to return to your illustration to add more detail later in the examination. Always explain what your illustration is supposed to illustrate.

- Unless otherwise instructed, use a complete page of graph paper for presenting graphs and make sure that you provide a title for any entries you have made. Explain what your graph illustrates.
- Do not present workings for numerical subjects such as accounts and statistics without explaining what you are doing and why. If you would like a deeper understanding of study skills and exam techniques a useful book containing a wealth of tips and examples that will help you to succeed in examinations is *How To Pass Exams* by W. G. Leader, published by Stanley Thornes.

4 STUDYING WITH THIS TEXT

Hutchinson's student texts have been specifically designed to act as study aids for students while on a course, as well as present the contents of a subject in a way that is both interesting and informative.

Use this text as part of your study activities, adding your own or your tutor's notes at appropriate points. Study your textbook in great detail, making notes on the chief points in each chapter so that the ideas have gone through your own head and down onto the paper in your own words – though perhaps with key quotations from the text.

Don't get bogged down in any one chapter. If you really can't follow the chapter leave it and go on to the next, returning at a later date. What seems difficult at the start of your course in September will be easier by December and child's play by March! You are going to develop as you do the course – so don't give up too early. Perseverance is everything in acquiring professional status.

Do not just read the specimen answers provided at the end of certain sections. Study their content and structure in the light of what you learned in the particular section and what you learned earlier in this section. In this way your skill in answering questions set by your tutor and/or the examination should improve.

At the end of each section there are examples of past examination questions. Where the answer is to be in essay form jot down beside the question the major points that you think should have been highlighted when answering. Then check back with the appropriate text of the particular section to see if your answer would have been correct. If you are still uncertain, discuss the problem with your tutor.

Talking with the tutor and fellow students is essential for developing the ability to analyse problems.

Always complete the self assessment part of each chapter as they are designed to reinforce what you have learned and improve your recall of the topics. Check your answers with those provided in the manual. As repetition of a process improves one's memory, it is very useful to re-test yourself every few weeks or let someone else read the questions to you and tell you if you got them right.

If the subject covered by the particular manual involves value judgements do not assume that what is mentioned in the manual is the only correct version. Your tutor may have other opinions which are just as valid. What matters is that you have sufficient knowledge of the subject to illustrate a firm understanding of the topic in the examinations.

One of the best ways to study is to buy a lever arch file and make dividing pages from brown paper for each subject or chapter. File your notes, and your essays and any newspaper cuttings, articles, etc. that are relevant in the appropriate topic position. You will then have an easy-to-revise and lively set of notes. If you find it a bit bulky to carry, use a ring binder instead and then at the end of every week or two weeks transfer the notes you have made to the lever arch file, keeping it at home for safety.

Now that you have read these Study and Exam Tips you should feel confident to continue with your studies and succeed in the examinations. It just remains for ourselves and Stanley Thornes to wish you every success on your course.

This book was derived from a text which originally appeared in The Made Simple series, published by Heinemann Professional Publishing Ltd, whose permission is gratefully acknowledged.

PART 1: Introduction to economics

1 Economics and business activity

1 THE NATURE OF ECONOMICS

Those who embark upon business activity need to know what economics is, and what it can tell them about the environment in which their businesses will operate. Everyone knows that business activity is concerned with demand, supply, price, output, profits and losses. What is the economic relationship between businessmen and women and their customers, suppliers, employees, agents, etc? What are the risks of being in business, and how can they be minimised? What are the rewards for enterprise and how can they be maximised? The business world is dynamic and restless; rarely stable or calm. We cannot study it at rest, for it is never at rest. Like a canoe shooting the rapids we have to watch out for snags ahead, pick a clear passage where we can, rest for a moment in an eddy current and then push off again on a new tack. To study economics is to seek a little order in what is a chaotic, frenzied activity.

Economics has been defined by Alfred Marshall, the great Victorian economist, as *'the study of mankind in the everyday business of life'*. The basic problem of life for mankind is to provide the necessary goods and services which make life possible. If hunger and thirst are to be avoided; if the bitter winter is to be survived; if we are not to be washed away by floods – mankind must take steps to provide food, liquid refreshments, shelter, etc. It is this type of activity which the business person undertakes. Unlike the ordinary employee, who merely takes a passive place in the production process, the business person actively promotes the production of goods and services. Stepping out of the common crowd, the sole trader, partner or director of a company assumes responsibility for the planning and organisation of some area of production.

In studying the everyday business of life there are many aspects which must be considered. First it is necessary to understand the general framework of the economy of our own particular nation, and see how it fits into the pattern of economies all over the world. Then we must consider the types of economic organisation which exist to produce the goods and services that we need. How does each achieve success in its particular field? What happens to bring new institutions into existence and why do some fail and cease to exist? What policies and influences are at work on our businesses and how shall we take advantage of them if they are favourable, and avoid them if they are unfavourable? If we cannot eliminate risk, how can we reduce it to manageable proportions? What control devices can we build in to ring the alarm bells before the situation is critical? What key indicators exist to warn of a changing business climate? This is what 'business economics' is all about. It seeks to explain the business environment, to tell us what indicators to watch out for, to help us maximise benefits and minimise costs.

2 THE INTRICATE NATURE OF THE ECONOMY

We must note that a modern economy is an extremely intricate structure, especially if it is a *market (free enterprise) economy*, or a *mixed economy*. With a *controlled economy* such as the economy of a Communist country, the arrangements will appear much less intricate because some sort of planning bureaucracy will be controlling most of the activity, and generating what enterprise is being shown. A free enterprise system will be more diverse than a centrally planned system, but of course it may also be less effective at times, and some enterprises may fail and prove to be a waste of resources. The large number of small business units which are such a feature of market economies will not exist in controlled economies. In the free enterprise economy, and the mixed economy, enterprise will be shown at many levels. Today's tin box with a vacuum-cleaner pipe in it becomes tomorrow's hovercraft; today's new sound is tomorrow's 'top-of-the-pops'; today's drifting spore is tomorrow's antibiotic industry. A business person must be constantly on the look-out for new enterprise. The cast-iron gutter weighing 25 kilograms has been replaced by its plastic competitor weighing 200 grams. The natural gas industry has almost completely replaced the coal gas industry in the UK, and millions of tons of coal which would otherwise have been needed have been left untapped as a stockpile for our descendants' use.

By a constantly shifting process of inter-adjustment the countless firms, institutions and organisations in a modern economy will grow and contract as opportunity expands or shrinks. They will seek to take advantage of new discoveries and trends in the wider world. The intricate nature of our economy forms an *environment* within which the individual firm has to operate. A knowledge of economics can help the businessman to understand this environment, so that he maximises the advantages in any business situation, or minimises the disadvantages. In doing this he will not only benefit himself, but also the rest of the community. We shall see that it is to the national output of goods and services alone that the nation can look for the satisfaction of its needs. However the wealth is shared – from the Sovereign's Civil List at one end to the supplementary benefit of Her most deprived citizen at the other – the standard of living which can be enjoyed is directly related to the total output of wealth in goods and services which we have created.

The businessman will naturally do what he can to ensure that his own rewards are reasonable, but he cannot expect today to enjoy the same share as in the early days of free enterprise. Our tax system smooths out the inequalities of income to some extent, and the monetary satisfactions of business success are correspondingly reduced. They are replaced by the non-monetary satisfactions of status in the community, official recognition in a variety of ways and, ultimately, by an 'Honours' system. Whether these are adequate compensation for the magnificent country houses and estates of former eras is debatable, but at least civil strife is reduced to manageable proportions in today's more egalitarian society.

3   LAW – THE FRAMEWORK OF THE ECONOMY

We frequently talk about the British economy, or the French economy, or the West German economy, which leads us to conclude that the framework of an economy is a framework of national laws. We do not talk about the African economy, for Africa is made up of many nations and each nation has its own economy and its own framework of laws.

Law has been defined as 'a body of rules for the conduct of human behaviour which is *imposed upon*, and *enforced among*, the citizens of a given state'. The phrase 'imposed upon' implies some sovereign power which can make laws. In the UK this sovereign power is vested in 'the Queen in Parliament', a system of sovereignty subject to some extent to democratic control, but with vestigial survivals from more autocratic times – the sovereign and the House of Lords. The phrase 'enforced among' implies the existence of some repressive force which will ensure that laws are obeyed. This is of course the police force and the judicial system. The degree of enforcement is not uniform. One has only to walk along any High Street to notice that the litter laws are poorly enforced, while the frequent complaints about the behaviour of traffic wardens seem to confirm that these officials charged with keeping the streets reasonably clear of parked vehicles are doing their job reasonably well.

The **Rule of Law** ensures that those pursuing legitimate activities will be able to do so undisturbed. Since business activity is largely legitimate the rule of law is a helpful influence in encouraging business activity, though the constraints on business are still massive. If I discover coal in my back garden I shall not be allowed to mine it and market it for coal was nationalised in 1946. If I develop a manufacturing process which emits fumes I shall not be allowed to use it, and even processes which have been carried on for hundreds of years may meet new opposition if new techniques for measuring their harmful effects are developed. The Bedfordshire landscape is pitted with earthworks which are the result of centuries of brick-making, yet opposition to the industry was aroused by complaints of a harmful effect on livestock, and possibly human beings too, caused by a chemical released in the firing process.

Some countries consist of a group of states, each of which has its own laws but also forms part of a larger national unit. Thus the USA has a federal system, with both State laws and Federal laws, and with clearly defined boundaries for each set of laws.

4 THE CYCLE OF PRODUCTION

Given a rule of law within which it can operate, how does an economy develop? We may define an economy as follows:

> An economy is a pattern of organisations and institutions developed in response to the 'wants' of mankind, as a means of providing goods and services to satisfy these 'wants'.

We use the word 'wants' here because wants are more extensive than needs. The things human beings need – the basic wants of mankind – are food, liquid refreshment, clothing, shelter, geographical territory (be it only a *pied-à-terre*) and medical care. Without these essential needs mankind will not survive. When these needs are satisfied we then 'want' more and more things. Our 'needs' are satisfied but our 'wants' continue. We demand more sophisticated goods and services, personal transport, leisure/pleasure facilities, education and domestic paraphernalia of every kind. Appetite grows with feeding, and there is no end to the demands made upon the economy.

Critics of economics often complain that economists talk a lot of 'jargon', employing a specialist vocabulary which the general public does not understand. This is of course true of economics, but no more so than of any other branch of knowledge. A chemist could not manage without his 'oxides' and 'sulphates', the aeronautical engineer needs his 'aerofoils' and 'laminar flows', and the economist must have his jargon too. The basic needs of mankind are called 'wants'; the means of satisfying these wants are called **utilities**. The basic problem of economics is the creation of utilities (goods and services) to satisfy wants. Hunger is a want and food is a utility which can satisfy the want.

How shall we produce this vast mass of goods and services? Every nation state has a certain endowment of natural resources which are of four kinds: animal, vegetable, mineral and human. Of course, humans are only part of the animal kingdom scientifically, but in economic terms we are different. Man is the tool-making animal, and this ability to make tools enables man to operate a capitalistic system of production. All economies are capitalist economies because they depend for their operation on the use of capital goods to create outputs of goods and services. The chief difference between capitalism and communism is in the ownership of the capital assets. Naked capitalism is a free-enterprise system where capital assets are privately owned. Communism is a system where capital assets are socially owned. Between the two we have the *mixed economy*, which until recent privatisations was typified by the UK economy. In a mixed economy some capital assets are socially owned in so-called nationalised industries, while others are privately owned and operated.

The natural endowments of any nation are called the **factors of production**, and are often spoken of as 'factor endowments'. In economics we call these factor endowments land, labour, capital and enterprise.

The term **land** is applied in economics to the resources made available by nature. So the factor land is a general term to describe not only the geographical territory of an economy, but also the crops grown on it, the flocks and herds raised, its timber, minerals, water supplies, fish and even the gases of the atmosphere.

Thus the UK was originally endowed with rich resources of coal, iron, lead, copper, tin, etc. It also has a reasonable area of geographical territory, much of which is fertile and well watered. By contrast, Singapore has very little territory and scarcely any resources, while the Soviet Union and the United States of America have enormous territories rich in almost every type of resource.

The second factor of production is given the name **labour**. Labour is the human resource. We arrive in the world with a pair of hands and a brain to control them. Labour is the factor which takes the products of nature and refashions them to increase their utility. It may merely be a gathering process, like the child picking blackberries at the roadside. It may be agriculture, forestry, fishing or cattle breeding. It may be sophisticated technology, like the cracking of crude oil or the synthesis of complex derivatives from coal gas. It may be the services of the surgeon, the dentist or the communications engineer.

The third factor of production is known as **capital**. Capital is a confusing word. It is usually used in everyday life to mean money: funds which are available to enable a business to be carried on successfully. Of course, economics is concerned with money capital and the part it plays in an economy, but it is more interested in **fixed capital**. The money capital which a businessman contributes to his firm is very soon 'fixed' as physical assets, buildings, plant, machinery, etc. Capital to an economist is not money, but the existing stock of tools and equipment which is used by labour to create utilities.

The things we want are the utilities which give satisfaction when we consume them. They are often called **consumer goods**. However, in order to produce these consumer goods we need premises, plant and equipment, tools and furnaces, catalytic cracking towers, computers and other things. These are called **producer goods** or **capital goods**. We do not want them for consumption, but for production. *It is the stock of capital goods created in the previous period which enables production to take place today, so that we can consume tomorrow.* The British Rail network is a producer good. It took 60 years to build, but when it was finally completed in about 1890 it enabled the nation to enjoy cheaper goods, holidays at the seaside, family convenience travel, etc. The stock of capital we have accumulated in one period raises the consumption level in the following period. However it constantly needs renewing, and since

1890 British Rail's capital assets have been renewed at least three times.

The accumulation of capital is at first a bitter process, and much of the early discontent with capitalism arose from this difficulty – that to create capital goods reduces current consumption in favour of future consumption. 'Jam tomorrow – never jam today' cried the early critics of capitalism. But the experience of other systems is no less bitter; producer goods cannot be created without reducing consumption, but when they are created they increase productivity so that a higher level of consumption is possible. Modern advanced nations are enjoying the fruits of earlier efforts to create a highly-capitalised industrial infrastructure, but even they must be careful to keep consumption down to the level of utilities being created. We must replace the producer goods as they wear out, or we are said to 'live upon our capital' and consume the capital assets so painfully accumulated in earlier periods.

The resources available to create utilities are therefore three: land, labour and capital – three of the factors of production. But these three factors will not create utilities by themselves. They have to be set to work in an appropriate combination. Some industries are capital-intensive, with a few technicians controlling a huge complex of plant. The steelworks, the cement factory and the North Sea oil platform are examples of such complexes. Other industries are labour-intensive, with myriad nimble fingers tying broken threads or assembling complex components.

Who will undertake the work of organising production? Someone has to do so – to step out of the crowd and apply the two factors, labour and capital, to the natural endowments of the country – land. In the early days of capitalism there were certainly some very special individuals who grasped the production nettle and began to raise output to undreamed-of levels. Every generation throws up its handful of such outstanding people. They were given the name **entrepreneurs** – a term still frequently used. Originally it meant 'middleman', a specialist who undertook a particular activity and saw it through to fruition. Later it came to mean one who took the risks of any enterprise. The early entrepreneur conceived an idea, tried it out, denied himself current consumption in order to create capital goods, struggled through the formative years carrying the serious risks of failure, controlling his small workforce and eventually emerged triumphant as a captain of industry. Of course, such men emerge in every generation, the Henry Fords and Frank Whittles of the twentieth century are still true entrepreneurs. The sole traders and partners of many small businesses are performing this function still.

Today, in our major industries, the special functions of the entrepreneur are performed by a number of individuals who cooperate with one another under the general job-description of 'management'. It is difficult to locate any individual who carries out the full functions of an entrepreneur. These were originally as follows:

1 To conceive a product or service that was needed to satisfy a 'want'.
2 To provide the money capital so that it could be 'fixed' into assets. This

'fixing of capital' was carried out by employing skilled workers to make the capital assets, paying them for their labour with the money capital provided. At the end of the programme the entrepreneur had used up most of his money capital, but had a collection of producer goods (capital assets) instead.

3 To control the actual production process and achieve and market the final outputs of goods and services.

4 To run the risks of the business – that the output might eventually not be wanted, or be so expensive that in the end it proved uneconomic or impracticable.

Our modern managers split up these activities between them but the final effect is that utilities are created to satisfy 'wants', in a complex pattern of business organisations. Enterprise in large organisations therefore comes to be performed by a group of managers and administrators who are really just a specialised class of labour.

One final point about production is that to an economist production does not cease until the goods reach the final consumer, possibly halfway across the world. Karl Marx's horny-handed sons of toil, the industrial proletariat, were not very appropriate as a picture of the production force even in his day, for cheap Lancashire cottons were flooding world markets even in 1848. We cannot concede that the actual shop-floor worker is entitled to the full fruits of production, if it means that those who market the product are to starve to death. There is no point in producing goods which cannot reach the consumer. To an economist the salesman is as productive as the turner, the ship's captain is as productive as the mill-hand, the surgeon is as productive as the farm labourer, for man cannot live by bread alone, he needs services too. The soldier who keeps the peace and the police officer who safeguards property are as productive as the computer assembly worker whose product they are protecting.

The rewards to factors

Once production has been organised the fruits of production – a flow of goods and services – begin to be available in our supermarkets, shops, hospitals, schools, etc. Who now owns the fruits of production? The answer is that all who helped must share in the proceeds, but since they cannot each have a piece of a complex product – like a computer – the share-out is arranged by the money system. Each participant receives a sum of money, which reflects his contribution to the total project, and which he is free to spend as he likes. These rewards to factors are called **wages, rent, interest and profit.** The actual money is obtained either from the initial money capital of the business, or later by selling the final product to customers who wish to enjoy that particular class of good. *Wages are the reward to 'labour', rent is the reward to 'land', interest is the reward to capital and profit is the reward to the entrepreneur.* Profit is a little unusual in that it is a residual, i.e. it is what is left over when the others have had their share. Thus if the workers demand more pay, or the owners of nature's gifts demand more rent, the profits must fall unless the price to the final consumer can be increased. Profits may be reduced so much that they become negative, i.e. losses.

Clearly the question of rewards to factors is a highly complex matter and in economics the study of this particular aspect is called **distribution theory**. Distribution theory has nothing to do with transport and warehouses, etc. – it is not that kind of distribution. *It is the theory that seeks to explain how the wealth created by production is distributed among the various people having a claim upon it: the workers, landlords, savers of money capital and the entrepreneurs.* In order to understand this we need to look carefully at each type of reward. This is done in detail in Chapter 7. Decisions about what is a fair reward for each factor bedevil the industrial and political scene. Such decisions are fundamental to the success of the mixed economy and we shall see in Chapter 7 how these rewards fit into the general pattern of economic organisation.

Here we need only stress that each factor employed in production is paid an agreed sum of money as its reward, which it is then free to spend on a balanced 'basket of goods'. The drunkard may spend 90 per cent on alcohol and only 10 per cent on his family's needs. Prudent parents will select their purchases of goods and services more carefully to give a more balanced supply for the family. This process of purchasing a balanced basket of goods is called **exchange**. The owners of the fruits of production (the firms who organised their output) exchange them for the money which they have paid out to the factors of production in the previous period. In this way the money returns to the firms, and the goods and services are enjoyed by the people of the nation. We call the people **consumers** at this point.

Clearly there is much that could be said about this 'exchange' process. At what price will the goods be exchanged? If the price is too high consumers will switch to alternative products. Stocks will accumulate and workers will be laid off in that particular industry and must be switched into production of goods that are in demand. If they refuse to be 'switched' we have a 'work-in' – we may go on making products which no one wants. Not for ever though. The inexorable market forces will exert increasing pressure to stop the process even though the political forces would like it to continue at the taxpayers' expense. This is not the place to discuss such problems. Here we are only concerned to note one further point. We are approaching the end of the cycle of production! Consumption destroys production!

Consumption destroys production

When we consume the goods and service we use them up. Today's dinner will satisfy our bodies for a few hours only. Tomorrow we must eat again. This year's motorcar is next year's old crock; this year's 'new style' is next year's 'has-been'; this year's rough wine is next year's vintage product and 'hangover'. Consumption destroys production and we are back to the beginning of the cycle. We must start up the machinery for a new burst of output, re-employ our factors for a further cycle. We go to work, to get the cash, to buy the food, to get the strength, to go to work, to get the cash, and so on. It is the destiny of economic man to toil on a treadmill to some extent. The real secret – more available to the person who understands economics than most people – is to enjoy it while you are treading it.

The cycle of production therefore moves from 'wants', through 'organisation', 'production, 'distribution' and 'exchange' to 'consumption'. 'Consumption' destroys 'production', and we are back to 'wants' again. This is illustrated in Fig. 1.1.

Fig. 1.1 *The cycle of production*

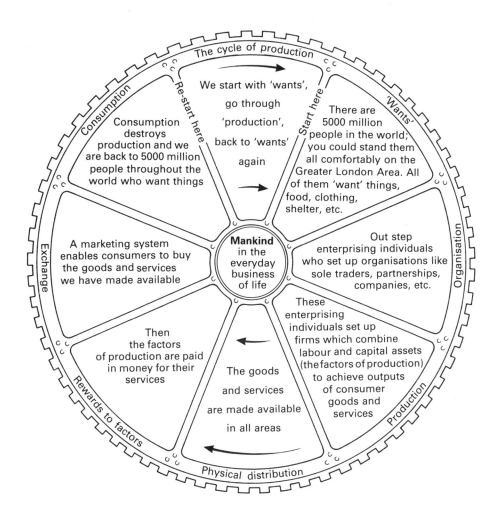

SELF-ASSESSMENT QUESTIONS

(*For answers see page 24*)

1 How did Alfred Marshall define economics?

2 What are the three types of economy?

3 What is the 'rule of law'? Why is it necessary in any advanced economic society?

4 Explain the term 'the factors of production'.

5 What are the rewards to factors?

6 Explain the term 'the cycle of production'.

5   HOW THE MIXED ECONOMY WORKS

In the course of these introductory pages we have learned that the purpose of an economy is to create utilities which will satisfy mankind's wants; that we have certain resources to start with which have been made available by nature; that by working on these raw materials with our human resources (labour) and our stock of tools and equipment (capital) we can produce a wide range of goods and services which will give satisfaction (utilities); and finally that when we do enjoy these utilities and achieve satisfaction it will not be long before we need to start the whole cycle again, because satisfaction only lasts for a limited period and we grow hungry again, or need a fresh supply of clothing, shelter, entertainment, medical care, etc. We may also grow more greedy, and raise the level of our demands.

These basic activities to be found in any economy are problem enough, and for many primitive people they are as much as they can manage. There are still primitive tribes who live for the day only, unable to raise their standard of living above a bare subsistence level. By contrast, with advanced economies millions of people enjoy a standard of everyday living which the rulers of ancient kingdoms or of the Middle Ages would have deemed luxurious. This high standard of living brings its own problems, not the least of which is how to ensure that the raised expectations of the population can continue to be satisfied in the years ahead. The problem of distributing wealth fairly has already been referred to. How shall we reconcile conflicting claims upon the wealth created? What yardsticks should be used to measure the rights of one group against another? Should inequalities be reduced, and if so, how? These are difficult questions, and the answers are not obvious, or easily agreed upon.

It is perhaps enough at this early stage to answer the question, 'How does a mixed economy work?' The answer is that there are two main flows of activity taking place in the mixed economy. One is the flow of factors into production and their remuneration in money terms. The other is the use of that remuneration by the factor owners to buy themselves a suitable basket of goods and services, which will yield satisfaction. This satisfaction does not last long, and a new cycle has to begin. Once again the factor owners offer their factors for employment, and are rewarded with money payments. Once again they use the money received to purchase a basket of goods and services. The cynic who described the capitalist system with the sentence referred to earlier – 'We go to work to get the cash to buy the food to get the strength to go to work' – had some truth in his sneers. That is how the system works; but as one celebrated economist John Stuart Mill said: 'The distribution of wealth is a matter of human institution only. The things once there, mankind, individually or collectively, can do with them as they like.' If mankind chooses to arrange things properly, the basket of 'food' we buy may nourish not only the body for the next round of work, but the mind, and the spirit too.

One thing that the money system does enable us to do is to manipulate the economy to a certain extent. We can, for example, reserve some of our purchasing power for a future period – in other words, we can save. If we do this we usually use one of the financial institutions such as a bank, a building society, etc. By using the funds not required by savers to lend to those who wish to spend more than their current earnings a new direction may be given to industrial investment, or to housing programmes, or to the domestic consumer durable industries through hire purchase transactions. Alternatively, we can use the money system to redistribute wealth more fairly. Since the citizens of a country must between them own all the factors that are available – land (provided by nature), human abilities and skills and the stock of capital (tools and equipment) – they will also receive the total remuneration paid to factor owners. The workers will receive their wages, the landlord his rent, the owners of capital their interest and the entrepreneurs their profits. Of course, we may regard some of these rewards as unjustified anyway. Because a man's ancestors fought with William the Conqueror should he own huge areas of land? Should a monopolist, who is the only producer of a particular commodity, make unfair profits? We might decide to nationalise certain gifts of nature, etc. More simply we can just tax away into a central pool of remuneration all excessive incomes. This requires some sort of government machinery for the collection of the taxes and their redistribution to the needy (as social security benefits of various sorts), or for use in generally recognised worthwhile objects (such as education, defence, etc.).

In manipulating the economy in this way the government is of course the chief institution for influencing the economy and adjusting it to achieve whatever social purposes are currently deemed desirable. As the body responsible for legislation it can enact the laws which are necessary to compel a redistribution of the rewards to factors, and enforce them among the citizens. Other less influential institutions are the charitable organisations, which arrange a certain amount of redistribution, and the criminal classes, who engage in a similar activity with rather less justification.

The two flows in the economy described above – the flow of factors into employment, followed by their remuneration in money terms, and the flow of that money into the firms for the purchase of a basket of goods and services to satisfy wants – are illustrated in Fig. 1.2. The reader is urged to study the diagram and the notes opposite carefully. Some of the ideas in the diagram are amplified later in this book.

Fig. 1.2 *How the mixed economy works*

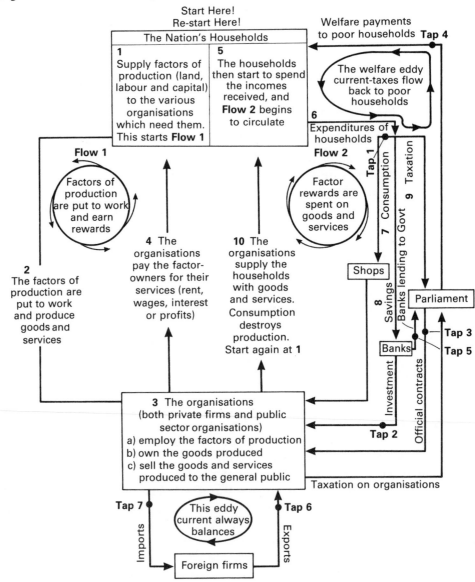

Notes

1 The first flow is of factor services into production and the payment of rewards to the factors, in the form of rent, wages, interest or profits.

2 Almost everything the firms receive in one period is paid out in the next period – either as rent, wages, interest or profits – but there is also a very large flow of taxation to the government which is used to finance the public sector services like defence, education, etc. However, some profits may not be distributed but retained to expand the business by re-investment internally. In the first period any payments to factors must come from the capital provided by those who start the firms up. In later periods the funds come from the sales of goods and services produced in the previous period.

3 The second flow is the expenditure of income on goods and services. The owners of the factors spend the incomes they receive. The incomes flow through a number of taps, which influence the level of activity in the economy. If a tap is closed off for some reason activity in the economy declines (a slump). If taps are opened wide activity in the economy increases (a boom). Two minor taps are not shown; charities re-distribute incomes by using voluntary contributions for charitable purposes, and the criminal classes re-distribute involuntary contributions for their personal satisfactions. Let us look at each tap in turn.

4 Tap 1: Consumption. If the nation's households are spending a great deal on consumer goods and services, business will be booming. If householders are pessimistic about the future and only buying essentials, Tap 1 will be partially closed and the economy will slump.

5 Tap 2: The Savings-Investment Tap. If savings are high consumption will be lower (Tap 1 partially closed). This will not matter if the savings are borrowed by businessmen (or by the government through Tap 5 for the public-sector borrowing requirement – PSBR). An open Tap 2 means strong investment and the economy will keep booming along.

6 Tap 3 and **Tap 4:** These taps are controlled by the government. Tap 4 (welfare payments) allows tax money to flow back to poor families so that they can consume goods and services. This opens up Tap 1 and keeps the economy booming. Tap 3 allows more official contracts for all sorts of things (defence, education, health services, highways, etc.) to be placed. This gives employment to unemployed people and keeps the economy booming. If taxes are not sufficient to pay for these contracts the government borrows through Tap 5 the money that pessimistic householders are saving for a 'rainy day' when they might lose their jobs. The government contracts ensure that the 'rainy day' never comes. Of course the state of these taps is a matter of government policy – not every government believes it is wise to keep the economy booming. A booming economy encourages inflation.

7 Foreign trade always balances (the balance of payments) but sometimes it is a bit more difficult than others. The government does a good deal of manipulating to keep this balance right, and sometimes has to call in the International Monetary Fund to overcome a difficult period. Temporarily, it is possible for Taps 6 and 7 to affect the working of the economy. A wide-open Tap 6 gives an export-led boom (funds flowing in to UK firms). A wide-open Tap 7 gives an import-led slump (funds flowing out to foreign firms, leaving UK firms starved of orders). However, as explained above, neither of these situations can continue indefinitely. A 'balance of payments' has to be achieved. At present we are using floating exchange rates to induce a balance. If we join EMS we shall have to use physical controls to achieve a balance – HP controls, credit controls, etc.

6 THE BUSINESS ENVIRONMENT

We have seen that businessmen operate in an environment which has many different facets. Surrounding all business activity is the shell of laws, which make the nation state. Within this shell is a collection of organisations which create the goods and services which satisfy wants. Exerting a powerful influence on the activities of these wealth-creating organisations is a pattern of institutions, chiefly government inspired, which attempt to ensure the greatest good of the greatest number. They do this by redistributing wealth, monitoring social costs such as pollution and waste disposal, reducing unfair behaviour such as monopolistic pricing policies and unfair trading practices, etc.

Just how much an individual firm is affected by this general environment depends very much upon its size, the demand for its goods and services, the competition it faces, etc. To the extent that it is able to employ clever lawyers or astute accountants it may, perhaps, reduce the adverse effects. Few firms can escape entirely, if only because they must have suppliers of many sorts who will be keen to unload their burdens on to their customers. The incidence of a tax – which means the person on whom the burden finally falls – is rarely the same as the person on whom a tax is levied.

The importance to the businessman of an understanding of the economic environment is particularly great, and it is the purpose of this book to explain most of the important features that affect the businessman in the conduct of his everyday affairs. The entrepreneur is essentially a decision-maker. He puts his money where his mouth is, to use a popular expression. Clearly there may be some occasions when a businessman backs a 'hunch' and carries it off successfully, but they will not be frequent. The more reliable way is to be informed as fully as possible about a firm's affairs and the environment in which it operates. If the 'hunch' is replaced by a reasoned opinion based on sound knowledge the risks are reduced and the prospects of profitability increase. It is in the decision-making areas of product planning, plant investment, marketing, finance and industrial relations that this wide background is most helpful in making wise decisions. An introductory reference to these areas is given below, and they are more fully analysed in later chapters.

Product planning

In planning a particular product some assessment of the likely costs and sales potential is essential and these can be greatly influenced by economic factors. Before an idea can be turned into a product we must know which materials to use; whether they are available; whether shortages or bottlenecks in supply are likely to develop; what technology will be required and how much it will cost to buy or hire the equipment. If there is official discouragement of certain suppliers; if ecological groups are monitoring the use of certain materials; if new technology can only be employed by buying off powerful union voices the whole economics of the project as originally envisaged may be jeopardised. We shall see later that demand for a good or product is related to the price we must charge for it. Demand is not the same thing as 'want'. Everyone *wants* a limousine, but most of us have to be content with *demanding* a car, and some have to make do with a bicycle. Everyone *wants* a holiday in the Bahamas but all most of us actually *demand* is a week at Blackpool or the Costa Brava.

Plant investment

While plant investment is usually regarded as a matter for the accountant, who will evaluate costs and benefits using some sort of **discounted cash flow technique**, the economic implications may be crucial for new investment. Thus at times when the economy is booming plant will be expensive and difficult to obtain. At times of slump it may be possible to pick up items of plant, premises, etc., at a fraction of their cost in boom conditions. There is much to be gained therefore from studying the business cycle of booms and slumps, and acting in the opposite way from other businessmen around you. Like the stock exchange speculator who buys when others are selling and sells when others are buying, it is frequently best to press ahead with the acquisition of plant during slump conditions and hold back on plans to re-equip during booms. If we can use our knowledge of economics to keep ahead of competitors, sailing with the wind that has just veered even though others have not yet noticed the change, we can get an advantage even from a downturn in the economy.

Marketing and the type of market

The concept of the market is very important in economics. There is of course the concept of a **perfect market**, where cut-throat competition is the order of the day, and prices are decided as a direct result of the interaction of supply and demand.

Then we also have the concept of **monopoly**, where a sole supplier has complete control of the supply of a particular commodity, and can presumably hold us all to ransom for it. This would be true, of course, if the monopolist was controlling an essential commodity, such as the air we breathe. The first entrepreneur to lock up the atmosphere and retail it to the public at an exorbitant price will undoubtedly make a fortune if he can prevent the rest of us from making a killing – of him. For non-essentials the monopolist is not in such a favourable position. We shall see that the monopolist is still subject to the authority of the consumer, for he cannot dictate both *output* and *price*. He may say, 'I will make 10 000 of these items' – whereupon the consumer will reply, 'All right, but the most I am prepared to pay is £3.' Alternatively he may say, 'I will make this item and sell it for £10' – whereupon the consumers will reply, 'In that case don't make more than 500.' What he cannot say is, 'I will make 10 000 of these items and you will buy them at £10 each.'

More realistically, somewhere between perfect competition and pure monopoly is the real world of the 'branded product', which economists call **monopolistic competition** or **imperfect competition**. Here the product is unique – like 'Golden Shred' marmalade – but there are also many other brands of marmalade on the market. For some consumers 'other' brands are no substitute for 'Golden Shred', and considerable brand loyalty pertains to a product. This 'unique' nature of the product may be real enough, based on secret recipes, etc., or it may be quite artificial, such as the difference between pink paraffin and blue paraffin. It is in this more realistic situation that the businessman may benefit most from a knowledge of economics. We shall see later that if the 'unique' nature of his product can be indefinitely renewed – by innovations of one sort or another – the supplier can maintain his brand loyalty and continue to enjoy monopoly profits. If competition becomes too fierce, the monopolistic element of competition is eroded, and the profits earned from the branded good are reduced.

Economics is important for marketing in many other ways. It can enable us to count the number of potential customers, and estimate their purchasing power; to compare our own performance with the performance of similar firms; to check distributional channels and locate depots in the optimum position; and to evaluate foreign markets and profit from world trade. These matters are explained in later chapters.

Finance

The study of the money system and the intricate network of financial institutions which exists in the mixed economy is a vital part of economics. Not only do financial institutions spring up as part of the free enterprise sector of the economy wherever they can offer a service to businessmen, but official institutions to implement government policy are also numerous. Thus in the fields of exchange control, finance for industry, regional policy, public finance and local government finance there are institutions for controlling business activity, promoting enterprise, solving industrial problems, lending to those in deficit by those institutions with a temporary surplus and so on. Job-saving and job-creation programmes present businessmen with opportunities to receive financial support while at the same time aiding government programmes for training and retraining. Similarly, in the export field government policies may open lines of credit for less-developed nations which enable foreign importers to purchase our exports on favourable terms, which virtually guarantee that the exporter will receive payment.

Clearly it is important to those in business to be aware of the variety of financial institutions and the part each plays in the mixed economy.

Industrial relations

The relations that exist between managment and staff are a vital element in the success of business activity. A traditional atmosphere of confrontation, with management on one side of the barricades and men on the other has not been helpful. If unions become too powerful they may prevent management from managing, while any return to Dickensian times with management exploiting labour in some sort of 'naked capitalism' is unthinkable. In recent years legislation has restricted the freedom of powerful union leaders to call strikes without a secret ballot of their members, and the whole atmosphere is consequently less frenetic and less disruptive than in former times. A wider understanding of economics is helpful to both sides.

The concepts here for all parties to understand are those of the National Income and the theory of distribution. The national income, as we shall see in Chapter 9, was defined by Alfred Marshall as '*the aggregate net product of, and the sole source of payment for, all the factors of production*'. As we saw in Fig. 1.2, the flow of wealth which we have created has to be distributed by a flow of income to all those who have contributed factors to the pool, and in addition some must go to the young, the aged, and those who for some reason are unable to join in the production process. Arriving at a 'fair' distribution scheme is not easy and involves the bargainers in more considerations than just the exercise of muscle in the negotiations. We may ridicule politicians who find it difficult to stand up to well-muscled protagonists in the wage-bargaining ring, but unless someone stands up to them the final distribution arrived at will cause not only discontent but positive hardship to others.

7 THE USE OF DIAGRAMS IN ECONOMICS

In economics it is often simpler to explain an idea by using a diagram, with explanatory notes. Many of these diagrams are in the form of simple graphs. For those who are not familiar with mathematics a preliminary word of explanation is helpful.

Graph paper is paper ruled with a ready-printed grid of squares. In these days of metrication, we usually use paper ruled with a grid based upon the centimetre and millimetre. Metric graph paper therefore has 100 tiny squares ruled on every square centimetre. In drawing any diagram on such graph paper we can pinpoint any position on the paper by a method introduced by the French philosopher René Descartes (1596–1650). It depends upon the use of two lines of reference, at right angles to one another, called **axes**. One is drawn horizontally, and is called the *x* axis; the other is drawn vertically, and is called the *y* axis. The point where they cross is called the origin **O**. These are illustrated in Fig. 1.3 (below). A full explanation is given in the notes below the figure.

Fig. 1.3 *Using co-ordinates to name any point on a graph*

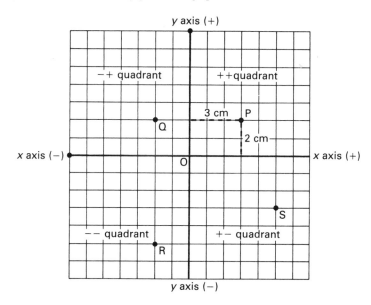

Notes
1 The two lines of reference are called the *x* axis and the *y* axis. They intersect at the origin (O).
2 The point marked **P** has a unique position on the diagram. It is 3 cm to the right of the vertical axis *y* and 2 cm above the horizontal axis *x*.
3 To define its position we need only name these two measurements. As they are both equally important we call them coordinates (both of equal rank). By convention we always write the distance from the vertical axis first, and the distance from the horizontal axis second. So the mathematical expression for the point **P** is written (3,2) which means 3 units of measure to the right of the *y* axis and 2 units of measure above the *x* axis.
4 The two lines divide the paper into four quadrants. If we wish to define the position of any point on the paper we have to be able to say which quadrant the point is in, and we do this by means of positive (+) signs and negative (−) signs. Everything above the *x* axis is positive (+) and everything below the *x* axis is negative (−). Everything on the right-hand side of the *y* axis is positive (+) and everything on the left-hand side is negative (−). This gives us a (++) quadrant, a (−+) quadrant, a (−−) quadrant and a (+−) quadrant.
5 So the true position of the point P is (+3, +2), because it is in the quadrant to the right of the *y* axis and above the *x* axis.
6 The point Q is (−2, +2); the point R is (−2, −5) and the point S is (+5, −3). In introductory economics most of the diagrams we use are in the (++) quadrant (see Fig. 1.4).

Although the system devised by Descartes enables us to pinpoint any position on the 'field' of paper, most of the diagrams used in this book use the (++) quadrant only. For this reason it is unnecessary to waste paper by drawing the other three quadrants, and diagrams are therefore usually drawn with only the (++) quadrant showing. It is usual to indicate the units being used along the appropriate axes. This is illustrated in Fig. 1.4.

Fig. 1.4 *A simple (++) quadrant diagram*

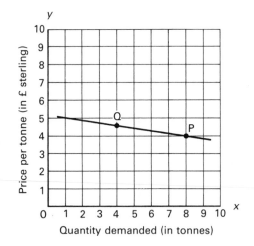

Notes
1 The *x* and *y* axes have been drawn only in the (++) quadrant to enable the diagram to be as large as possible.
2 The coordinates of point P are (+8, +4). At this point 8 tonnes of the product is being demanded at a price of £4 per tonne.
3 The reader is invited to give the coordinates of point Q, and say what they mean about the demand for this product at that point.

SELF-ASSESSMENT QUESTIONS

(*For answers see page 24.*)

7 Explain the flow of factors into production in a mixed economy.

8 Explain what happens to people's incomes when they have earned them.

In your answer explain particularly about:

a) consumption
b) savings
c) charitable donations
d) burglaries and muggings
e) taxation.

9 What is the PSBR?

REVISION TEST

In this book each chapter ends with a test-yourself section, which acts both as a chapter summary and a revision test. Cover the page with a sheet of plain paper and uncover the first question. Try to answer it from your knowledge of the chapter. Lower the paper and read the answer to Question 1. Then read Question 2 and try to answer it.

Answers	Questions
—	**1** How did Alfred Marshall define economics?
1 As 'the study of mankind in the everyday business of life'.	**2** Where do businessmen fit into the everyday business of life?
2 As entrepreneurs, who step out of the crowd and undertake the organisation of some aspect of production.	**3** What are the three types of economies?

3 (a) Market economies (free enterprise economies like the USA); (b) controlled economies (run by central planning, like the USSR); (c) mixed economies (like the UK) with some free enterprises and some nationalised industries.

4 What is the framework for an economy?

4 The system of national laws within which it has developed.

5 What are the basic wants of mankind?

5 Food, liquid refreshment, clothing, shelter, geographical territory and medical care.

6 What is the purpose of an economy?

6 To satisfy the 'wants' of mankind by creating utilities (things that have satisfying power).

7 What forms do 'utilities' take?

7 They may be either 'goods' or 'services'.

8 What are the factors of production?

8 Land, labour, capital and enterprise, (entrepreneurial leadership).

9 What are consumer goods?

9 Goods and services we need for actual 'consumption; food, beverages, clothing, shelter, entertainment.

10 What are producer goods?

10 Capital equipment to help in the process of creating consumer goods; tools, machines, transport, etc.

11 List the stages in the 'cycle of production'.

11 (a) 'Wants'; (b) organisation; (c) production; (d) physical distribution; (e) rewards to factors; (f) exchange; (g) consumption; (h) 'wants' again.

12 What are the three flows around the economy which keep the production of utilities going?

12 a) The flow of factors into employment and their reward with money incomes.
b) The flow of incomes back to the firms as they sell the goods and services produced.
c) The export-import flows of international trade, which – while they balance out in the end – do cause export-led booms and import-led slumps from time-to-time.

13 What is the National Income?

13 It is the total net wealth created by the nation.

14 How was it defined by Alfred Marshall?

14 As 'the aggregate net product of, and the sole source of payment for, all the factors of production'.

15 What does it decide?

15 The total standard of living we can enjoy – we then have to decide how to share it out in some equitable way.

16 What are the rewards to factors?

16 (a) Land earns rent; (b) labour earns wages or salaries; (c) capital earns interest; (d) enterprise earns profits.

17 What are the typical organisations of free-enterprise economies?

17 Sole traders, partnerships, limited companies and public limited companies. The bigger companies may be multi-national companies trading in many countries.

18 What are the typical organisations of centralised economies?

18 (a) State-planning authorities run by centralised bureaucracies; (b) state-run cooperative farms and collectives; (c) a network of enforcement apparatchiks with coercive powers.

19 What are the typical organisations of mixed economies?

19 (a) A wide network of free-entreprise organisations (about 60 per cent of the economy): sole traders, partnerships, limited companies and PLCs; (b) a wide range of nationalised industries run as public corporations and with ultimate control vested in a responsible minister; (c) a large number of quangos – quasi-autonomous non-governmental organisations.

20 How do these different economic systems organise the allocation of resources and the distribution of goods and services?

20 (a) The free enterprise systems rely on market forces – which respond to public demand through the price system; (b) centralised and nationalised industries rely on central planning, with some degree of response to public demand, the development of bottlenecks in supply systems, etc.

Go over this test again until you are sure of all the answers. Now try some of the written work in the questions below.

ANSWERS

(See Self-assessment questions on pages 12 and 21.)

1 Alfred Marshall defined economics as the study of mankind in the everyday business of life.

2 The three types of economy are market economies (free enterprise economies), controlled economies and mixed economies. The USA is the best example of a market economy, the USSR is the typical example of a controlled economy and the UK is the best example of a mixed economy. Actually all markets are mixed to some extent, since some nationalised industries are essential, while even communist countries have found it best to allow some free enterprise.

3 The rule of law is a body of controls promulgated and enforced by the sovereign body in any country to provide a stable environment for social and economic life. Business is a very delicate flower, easily killed off by social and political unrest, and sound laws are essential if it is to grow and prosper.

4 The factors of production are the inputs into a production system which alone can create goods and services (utilities) to satisfy wants. They are land (all the gifts of nature) labour (the human factor) capital (the accumulated store of producer goods – tools and machines, etc.) and enterprise (the entrepreneurial skills displayed by the promoters and managers of business).

5 The rewards to factors are rent (the reward to land), wages (the reward of labour), interest (the reward to capital) and profit (the reward to enterprise). In fact interest and profit are often bound together in many businesses, the entrepreneur contributing both the capital and the enterprise and therefore taking both rewards.

6 The cycle of production starts with 'wants'; to satisfy our wants we begin to organise production. The product then has to be distributed. The factors are now rewarded, and use their money income to buy a basket of goods and services for their families. This is exchange. Consumption now takes place and we are back to 'wants'. The cycle is 'wants' – organisation – production – distribution – rewards to factors – exchange – consumption – 'wants' – and a new cycle begins.

7 Some people own land (gift of nature); some own capital assets of various sorts; some have nothing to supply but their labour power. These factors, land, labour and capital flow into production as they are called for by the entrepreneurs who are offering 'enterprise'. The result is the creation of a variety of goods and services which can be used to satisfy wants.

8 People use their incomes in various ways, but all take part in direct consumption – we eat food, drink beverages, wear clothes, drive cars, etc. We may save some income which is used by those who collect savings (banks and building societies) to loan out to others who need more funds. We give a small proportion of our incomes for charitable purposes and this is used to increase the consumption of special groups who need help. Burglars and muggers help in the redistribution of income but in an unfair way. The rule of law helps restrain them. Taxation is paid by all people, either directly as income tax of various sorts or as indirect sales taxes on expenditures on goods and services. The chief such tax in the UK is Value Added Tax (VAT). This redistribution enables official policies, social security, education, defence, etc., to be carried out.

9 PSBR is the public sector borrowing requirement. It is the difference between taxes collected and expenditures incurred by central government. If expenditures exceed taxes collected the rest of the money needed is borrowed by the Treasury from banks and other institutions. If the Chancellor brings in a balanced budget there is no need to borrow and consequently no PSBR. If the PSBR is negative, because the Chancellor has budgeted for a surplus (taking more in tax than he intends to spend) the result will be a reduction in the National Debt as 'borrowing' changes to 'repayment'.

QUESTIONS ON CHAPTER 1

1 What is a market economy? What is a centralised economy? What is a mixed economy? How do these different types of economic system organise the allocation of goods and the factors of production?

2 Explain the cycle of production. What part does the entrepreneur play in it?

3 What is 'land' in economics? Name three different types of 'land' that might be used by a major company engaged in oil extraction and refining.

4 'Producer goods have a vital part to play in making consumer goods available.' Explain, referring in your answer to the shoe trade or the fashion industry.

5 What is the reward paid to labour? How is it used?

6 Explain the importance of marketing goods in a mixed economy. Give examples from your own experience of what is involved in marketing a sophisticated piece of household equipment.

7 Define economics. What is the importance of economics to the housewife and her family?

8 Compare the standard of living of an average citizen in a developing country with the standard of living of an average citizen of an advanced country. To what extent are the differences between the two a reflection of the economic organisation in their respective countries?

9 'Man cannot live by bread alone, but for countless generations he had to.' Comment on this statement.

10 What is meant by 'the intricate nature of the mixed economy'? In what ways is it intricate? Is it desirable that it should be?

TIPS FOR STUDENTS: A SPECIMEN ANSWER TO QUESTION 6

A mixed economy is one where there is a good deal of free enterprise activity (a market economy) but also a certain amount of nationalised industry and fairly wide provision of services like education, hospital and health services, defence and internal security through official channels. Marketing is more important in the free enterprise side of a mixed economy, but even some centrally provided goods and services may be allowed freedom to select the items purchased, text books, games equipment, etc., within the budget of funds made available to them.

The importance of marketing is that this is the way free choice is exercised in a market economy. The people have certain rewards paid to them for their work in supplying factors into production. Some have earned rent, some have earned wages, some have earned interest and some have earned profit. A few unfortunates have been helped with welfare payments of one sort or another. They all wish to purchase for their families a supply of goods and services appropriate to their needs. The suppliers of goods and services bring their supplies to market in a variety of ways. The goods are displayed in shops or on market stalls for inspection and purchase, or they may be described in mail order catalogues or in advertisements in magazines and the daily press. Those wishing to purchase the goods either go to the shops and markets or telephone or write in for supplies to those who are offering goods in other ways. To obtain personal services we must usually present ourselves at the places where the services are offered; the hairdresser's, the doctor's surgery, the dentist's surgery, the tattoo parlour or whatever establishment is concerned.

Using the example of a television set as a suitable item, the manufacturers of television sets not only make supplies available through wholesalers and retailers but also do a good deal of advertising on television, in magazines and in the press. Customers start to enquire about the product and generally speaking do a good deal of 'shopping around', comparing various styles and makes. We rarely spend £200–£300 after a cursory glance in a shop window. We want to see the product demonstrated; compare it with other items, listen to the sales person's explanations of the features offered, etc. We may need to save up the price, or arrange finance from a bank or finance house, with some sort of consumer credit agreement. It is for the marketing organisation to devise simple ways of displaying the product, helping us to use it and arranging finance if necessary.

PART 2: **How wealth is created and exchanged**

2 Production: how wealth is created

1 WHAT IS WEALTH?

Wealth is an abundance of goods and services which are capable of satisfying the wants of mankind. We know that the economic term for 'things that have satisfying power' is **'utilities'**, so wealth is an abundance of utilities. In all advanced economies the money system is used to make the exchange of goods and services simple. It is very important to understand the term 'exchange of goods and services' clearly. What actually happens in a primitive community is that the best hunters hunt, the best gardeners tend the gardens, clever anglers fish and the best hut-builders build huts. Then they exchange the goods and services they have produced directly; a plump guinea fowl for a sweet potato; a hand of bananas for a fat hen. This type of society is usually referred to as 'primitive communism'.

In an advanced economy the same process happens but it is all obscured by the distances separating those producing various products and the time-lags between production and consumption. The trawler captain fishing around the Falklands Isles has his catch frozen in a factory ship before it sails for Vladivostock. It may be a whole year before a garment worker in Dnepropetrovsk buys that fish, and another year before the trawler operator buys some clothing made in her factory on his next home leave, but they have in fact simply exchanged the fruits of their labour indirectly, through a money system. Economists talk about the 'money-veil' that hides what is really going on. The trawler captain is paid in money for his efforts, and the garment worker is paid in money for her efforts, and they then use the money to buy utilities to satisfy their wants. In effect, through a number of intermediaries in the distribution and marketing fields they have exchanged their outputs to their mutual satisfaction.

The money veil also obscures what is really happening because money can act as a store of wealth. It represents a claim on the output of goods and services. A person who has a large store of money is able to claim goods and services at any time in exchange for surrendering some money in payment.

Such a person is said to be 'wealthy' but of course money is not real wealth. Many a miser in Germany after the two world wars was happy to exchange his entire collection of hoarded notes for a loaf of bread or a bottle of schnaps, and many a marooned pirate died of starvation surrounded by the buried treasure he had recovered and stored in his cave. Money is not wealth – unless production of goods and services is taking place so that they can be obtained in exchange for the money. If the entire nation saved hard and we all retired together we should all starve for lack of current production.

2   THE PROCESS OF WEALTH CREATION

We have already said that wealth is created by entrepreneurs, who step out of the crowd of human beings and proceed to get things organised. These enterprising individuals set about combining the other factors of production, land, labour and capital to create goods and services. The medieval pastry cook, carpenter, stonemason, etc., who started to employ his fellow men and to make arrangements with landowners to use wheat, timber or stone for his trade began, in a small way, the great industries of today. The early factories were places where the factors of production were combined to produce useful goods. It was all rather a slow process, because entrepreneurs had to build their machines and develop their tools by trial and error (often going brankrupt in the process). Even today the world is full of penniless inventors trying to launch new ideas, but in general things are very much easier in the advanced economies. Budding entrepreneurs can usually borrow funds fairly easily to purchase their initial assets, and the accumulation of capital is not quite such a bitter process as it was. Even so, those who try to rebuild after some natural or political catastrophe face a multitude of daunting tasks, as for example the people of Uganda are facing at present. When the rule of law breaks down the resulting destruction requires years of patient recovery work, by dedicated people seeking national recovery. Before considering the fruits of production we must look in more detail at the factors of production.

3   THE FACTORS OF PRODUCTION 1: LAND

Land is the factor provided by nature, which has endowed us with a world in which we have developed and carry out our innumerable activities. From the point of view of the entrepreneur some of these gifts of nature may be used directly, in their natural state, whereas others may need a certain amount of adaptation before use and are therefore called semi-manufactured resources.

Natural resources

Here we may distinguish:

   a) **Geographical land**   The land is a gift of nature, on which we must all live and carry out our everyday activities. No one is more deprived than a person who has no land, no place to lay his/her head at night, no ground to grow food, no forest to cut timber, no lake to fish or meadow to graze cows. Unfair land distribution is a great evil, and free access to the countryside is something all people crave (yet many cannot get). Particularly vulnerable are nomadic people, who move from summer to winter pastures in great migrations, and whose way of life is destroyed if fences are erected at state boundaries. The Kurds of the Middle East, and many nomadic tribes in Africa face such problems today, and even the gypsies in the UK have a far from easy time.

Every productive unit must have a site – whether it is a factory, an office, a shop, a transport depot, etc. We have to buy, or lease, or rent a site from someone who does have land, or has the power to acquire it in some official way – perhaps a local authority or a quango empowered to encourage enterprise by acquiring sites.

Traditionally land was often seized by conquest, or empty land was occupied and title acquired by squatter's rights. In the Australian song *Waltzing Matilda* it is the squatter, riding by the billabong, who resents the swagman (homeless tramp) stopping on his land. In the UK the land originally seized by William the Conqueror in 1066 belonged to the Crown, and to the Crown alone. Under the feudal system it was then infeudated to the important Normans who had helped William. They were called tenants-in-chief, and by them it was sub-infeudated to lesser men. The result was, and still is, that the only rights any Englishman can acquire to land is an 'estate', which refers to his right to hold the land for a period of time.

The rather complex land law which developed in the eight centuries after 1066 was clarified in 1925 by the Law of Property Acts. By these Acts the legal estates which could exist in land were reduced to only two; **freehold estates** and **leasehold estates**.

The full names of these two legal estates in land are:

1 The fee simple absolute in possession, and
2 The term of years absolute.

Without going into detail about the exact meaning of these two legal estates, the 'fee simple absolute in possession' under the 1925 Act is an estate (right to hold land) which is capable of being left in a will (fee), which does not tie the land to any particular heirs (simple), which is not subject to any restrictions (absolute), and takes effect immediately the estate owner occupies the land (in possession). The term 'freehold' implies that the estate lasts for an uncertain length of time; in the case of (**1**) above it lasts until the person to whom it is granted, and all his heirs or those to whom it is left by will, die. When that does happen the land returns to the Crown. By contrast a leasehold right only lasts for a term of years absolute, which may be as long as 999 years but frequently is for much less and in many cases is only one month or even one week. Such a lease, called a tenancy, may be brought to an end by either party giving an appropriate period of notice.

We may therefore say that a person who has acquired the freehold rights to a piece of land (which lasts for an unlimited but indeterminate number of years) may carve out of this indeterminate time any 'term of years absolute' and grant them in a lease to a tenant. He still has the right to enjoy the land in the future when the lease expires and the property reverts to the freeholder.

Clearly the law of landed property is an involved subject and for our purposes it is sufficient if we regard organisations as having the right to occupy property either because they own the freehold to the land they use or have acquired from the freeholder a leasehold right which allows them to occupy it for a certain number of years.

b) **The natural elements**   The economic term 'land' refers to all the gifts of nature, not just geographical land. For example, there are 92 natural elements; we have manufactured several more in our laboratories, but for useful resources we are entirely dependent upon nature's original bounty. The full list of elements is given in a tabulation called the 'periodic table of the elements' in chemistry texts and most encyclopaedias. A careful study of such a table is extremely interesting, because the elements can be grouped into families which are related to one another and have similar chemical properties. These properties are caused by the existence of a certain number of free electrons in the outer shell of the atom. Clearly this is an involved subject. Let us take just one example. The inert gases all have a complete outer shell of electrons and as a result can never under normal conditions combine with any other element – hence their name 'inert'. The members of the family are helium, neon, argon, krypton, xenon and radon. Helium is useful because it is very light and therefore ideal for airships; since it is inert it cannot burn (hydrogen, the other light gas used in early airships, is of course highly inflammable). All these gases glow in electrical discharge tubes – hence the 'neon sign' which glows red. The 92 natural elements include all the metals, most of the gases, including those of the atmosphere, carbon, which is the basic material of living matter, and many other important products – for example, sulphur.

c) **Chemical compounds**   The 92 elements – except the inert gases, which cannot combine with other elements – form an enormous variety of compounds which are sometimes found in huge quantities. The chalk cliffs of Dover, for example, are formed of calcium carbonate, while the waters of the earth are made of hydrogen oxide. Quartz is made of silicon dioxide and amethyst of aluminium oxide. Most of our iron is extracted from haematite, an iron oxide. About 70 000 new organic compounds (compounds including the element carbon) are synthesised every year. Clearly compounds are used in countless ways as resources.

d) **The fossil fuels**   The chief sources of energy are solar radiation, subterranean heat caused by radioactive decay, nuclear power from the fission or fusion of atomic nuclei, and certain inertial forces from gravitational and rotational effects of the earth. Although great attention is being paid at present to the use of all these sources, the major source still is the fossil fuels (oil, coal and gas) which have stored the energy of millions of years of solar radiation. The UK is well supplied with all three fossil fuels for the next decade or two, but its longer-term needs require other energy developments and a wide general appreciation of the importance of energy resources.

e) **Agricultural products** Probably the greatest contribution to solving human 'wants' is made by agriculture. Many agricultural products are directly consumable, like vegetables and fruit. Many products only need simple manufacturing processes: grains have to be milled; tea, cocoa, beer, wine, etc., have to be fermented. Some products require more extensive secondary production, such as cotton, jute, sisal, rubber and many others.

f) **Animal husbandry** Intensive animal husbandry provides another major group of resources for mankind. 'The only part of the pig we don't use is the squeal' is an old slaughterhouse saying, and this applies to all the animal and poultry-keeping industries. Pork, beef, mutton, veal, poultry, fish offal, hides, skins, feathers, bones, bristles, glue, buttons and fertiliser, to name only a few resources, flow from the farms and intensive rearing houses to the supermarkets and factories of the world.

g) **Forestry products** Timber of every kind is used in countless industries. There are hardwoods, used for furniture and durable products, from hundreds of jungle or deciduous forest areas. Softwoods, which can be nailed easily, are used for house timbers, flooring and fencing. Light woods like balsa and heavy woods like jarra have their specialised uses. Near São Paulo in Brazil the world's largest hardboard factory minces a forest of eucalyptus trees endlessly into sawdust. The capacity of the factory was planned to consume the annual growth rate of the forest. The 16 000 000 trees are felled in turn, and grow up again as the felling moves off to other parts of the forest. The product, which tastes strongly of eucalyptus, has one distinct advantage: it is rejected by the white ants which devour other timber in that part of the world.

h) **Fishing** The sea provides a wide variety of products, and in many cases is 'farmed' very much like the land. French fishermen go to West Africa to collect baby lobsters and bring them back to grow to full size in the rocky inlets of the Atlantic seaboard. Oyster and cockle beds are 'managed', and fishing is in many cases restricted to match the annual growth rate. This is an area where a good deal of disagreement still exists, but international arrangements are gradually being hammered out. Pelletised protein (fishmeal) is one important product, and fertiliser is another.

All these natural resources, apart from geographical land, are called **primary products,** or **primary resources** because they are in the state nature supplied them originally. However, many of them go through a partially manufactured stage before they can be of much use to most entrepreneurs. Thus crude oil is of very little use until it has been 'cracked' and turned into usable products such as petrol, paraffin and countless other products. Such resources are called secondary resources – resources which have not only been extracted from their natural situation (primary production) but also turned into an improved product, more convenient for entrepreneurial purposes, by some sort of introductory manufacturing process (secondary production). We often call such products **semi-manufactures**.

Semi-manufactures

Many resources for sophisticated industries are semi-manufactured products or components for assembly into major installations. The range of such resources is enormous, but a few words on some of the major industries follows.

a) Chemicals and refined fuels　One has only to travel a few miles on any motorway to appreciate the huge variety of basic chemicals and refined fuels on the move every day. Many of these are basic building-block chemicals; olefins, aromatics and their polymer derivatives; acids, alkalis, etc. They are raw materials for plastics, fertilisers, fibres, pharmaceuticals and dyestuffs. World-wide production of organic chemicals exceeds 60 million tonnes per annum; 25 million tonnes of plastics and 5 million tonnes of synthetic rubber per year are typical of the scale of production in the chemical industry.

b) Metals　Most metals, like iron, aluminium, copper, nickel, tungsten and molybdenum have to be refined before they can be used and presented in some convenient form to secondary producers who will embody them in actual saleable products. The sheets, bars, rods, etc., represent the basic resource for major industries. World output of refined nickel, for example, is approximately 750 000 tonnes, while world output of steel exceeds 500 million tonnes per annum. World output of aluminium exceeds 10 million tonnes.

c) Fibres　Fibres are extremely important raw material resources for many industries, particularly the clothing and household soft-furnishing industries. The development of synthetic fibres of various sorts over the last 50 years has transformed the pattern of resources, but the following figures give some idea of world outputs. Natural fibres include cotton yarn, with a world output of 7.5 million tonnes; woollen yarn 1.5 million tonnes; other vegetable fibres than cotton, 400 000 tonnes; synthetic fibres include rayon, 3.5 million tonnes; nylon 7.5 million tonnes, etc.

d) Paper products　Paper is an important resource for many industries, particularly journalism and publishing, but its many uses in office practice, in education and in packaging make it of interest to a very wide range of industries. World output of wood pulp in one recent year totalled 120 million tonnes, while output of newsprint reached 22 million tonnes and of other paper and paperboard products 128 million tonnes were produced.

e) Construction materials　Most organisations either engage in constructional activities – building plant, offices, access roads, etc. – or have them built by specialist contractors. World output of cement in one recent year was more than 700 million tonnes; softwood production totalled 1 125 million cubic metres and hardwoods 1400 million cubic metres. UK production in the construction industry involved an expenditure approaching £5000 million in the same year.

f) Components　The production of manufacturing components is so great that no attempt is made to quantify it on a nationwide basis, but in an advanced economy like the UK many small firms specialise in producing components for other industries and thus relieve large firms of some detailed work. Such industries are usually fiercely competitive and a high level of efficiency has to be achieved if customers are to be retained.

4 THE FACTORS OF PRODUCTION 2: LABOUR

Production is impossible without human labour, unless we can develop a fully robotic production line where goods are produced 'untouched by human hand'. Services, as the very name implies, require human labour to provide the service, whether it is hairdressing, dentistry, surgical treatment, nursing or domestic service. Some industries are labour intensive, requiring large numbers of workers. Others are capital intensive, where most of the work is performed by machines which are supervised by only a few operators. Sometimes the invention of a new machine can cause a drastic reduction in the need for labour, as where cotton pickers in the Southern States of America were rendered redundant by a machine which vaccum cleaned the bushes sucking off the ripe cotton. In the UK the Luddite riots of the late eighteenth century were machine-wrecking riots, where the workers made unemployed by the invention of new machines sought to hinder their introduction to new factories.

The first thing organisations must recognise in their pursuit of, and use of, human factors of production is the infinite variety of mankind. People do not only differ in colour, ethnic origin and creed, but also in intelligence, manual dexterity, physical attributes, artistic sensitivity, education, training and basic personality. Few people can assess their own abilities or attainments objectively, so that we have geniuses who are full of self-doubt and ignoramuses who apply for posts beyond their capacities. People who can barely sew a seam aspire to be couturiers, and university graduates who ought to have no problems hesitate about applying for even the simplest posts.

Organisations must therefore be aware of the very wide range of human activities and skills, and select human resources which are appropriate to the work in hand or can be developed so that they are appropriate. In the early days of the capitalist era the technology was of such a low order that almost anyone could be trained to carry out the tasks to be performed. This is less true today, where many jobs require a wide general education, extended in the specific field concerned to include particular skills or techniques.

The recruitment of labour is the chief function of the personnel department in large firms. The Personnel Officer must recruit staff of such types and in such numbers as are required to pursue the firm's objectives. They must have the required qualities, temperaments and skills, or be capable of developing them by training and experience. In a changing world, where at any given time about 30 per cent of people are working with new materials and using new techniques not even dreamed of a quarter of a century earlier, it is essential to be prepared to re-train and adapt to innovations in production.

5   THE FACTORS OF PRODUCTION 3: CAPITAL

We have already seen that capital to an economist is the stock of tools and equipment created in a previous period and available as 'producer goods' to serve labour as it works on the natural resources and semi-manufactured resources selected by the entrepreneur. The chief types of capital resources are premises, industrial plant, machine tools, loose tools, transport equipment and public sector capital resources such as roads, bridges, railway systems, etc. Their essential feature has already been explained – namely that they are created as 'producer goods' for use in production and eventually result in an increased flow of consumer goods and services on to the market.

Organisations need capital before they can start to operate. Even a simple organisation like a tennis club or a football club collects subscriptions from members to provide the initial capital, and fund-raising activities become the treasurer's chief concern. At the other end of the organisational chain, the nationalised industry established by Parliament must take over all the capital of existing firms now to be nationalised, or Parliament must itself provide the funds for a totally new project. In these cases the capital will differ slightly, being largely capital assets in the case of established firms and money capital in the case of a totally new project.

The difficulty which arises because of the use of the same word 'capital' to describe both 'money capital' and 'capital equipment' can best be cleared up by explaining the relationship between the two:

1 In any given period the factors of production are put to work to create a certain volume of goods and services, which will then permit a certain level of consumption in the following period. The factors are rewarded with money incomes.

2 Should some of the factor owners (i.e. the owners of land, labour and capital) decide not to spend all their money incomes in the next period on personal consumption, but instead 'save' money, the savings which they make can be handed over for use by the entrepreneurs. This money becomes **money capital**. Like all money it is a claim upon the goods and services available but these claims have been surrendered by those who saved the money and lent to the entrepreneurs who wish to create producer goods.

3 Because they now control these claims upon goods and services the entrepreneurs can employ land and labour to produce, not consumption goods, but producer goods: **capital equipment**. The workers who create these capital goods will receive in return the money surrendered by the savers. The capital goods will belong to the entrepreneurs. It means that while they are at work producing the capital assets the workers are fed and clothed with the unused consumer goods from the previous period.

4 In the next period the output of consumer goods will rise, because the increased stock of capital equipment enables output to expand. All should thus be better off, if the total output is distributed fairly.

5 The point here is that money capital (savings) is a claim upon the available goods and services. By using these claims to support workers on non-productive capital projects – which cannot become productive until they are completed – the entrepreneurs extend the stock of producer goods. *As a result money capital becomes 'fixed'*. Fixed capital is capital in the form of fixed assets, buildings, plant and machinery, furniture and fittings, etc. The savings are turned into fixed assets – capital goods or producer goods. All savings in any given time period must be lent on to entrepreneurs for investment purposes if incomes in the next time period are to be maintained.

The difference between money capital and fixed capital is that the first is a claim upon resources which are available for consumption, and the second is the result of fixing the money capital, by deciding to use it to support factors while they are creating a producer good. Accountants, with great common sense, refer to money as 'liquid assets', but capital equipment is called 'fixed assets'. Clearly, if the person who saved the money wants it back again he cannot have it – for the entrepreneur has 'fixed' it. The entrepreneur cannot give the saver a length of pipe from the oil refinery built with the money without endangering the plant. What actually happens is that the saver is given a piece of paper called a 'security'. This may be either a share or a debenture. If he wants to recover his money the only way the saver can do so is to sell his share or debenture on the Stock Exchange. *The function of the Stock Exchange is to liquify securities by finding a buyer for any saver who needs to recover the money previously surrendered to the entrepeneur.*

The range of capital goods is very great. Besides plant, machinery, furniture, fittings, tools and equipment which are privately owned, an enormous range of **social capital** such as roads, bridges, hospitals, schools, etc., is created by 'enforced savings'. Enforced savings are taxes of various sorts, local community charges, income tax, VAT, etc. An interesting example was the financing of the Law Courts in London. Under the Judicature Acts of 1873–5, Parliament provided £1 453 000 for the purchase of the site and authorised the use of £700 000 from small balances left in a multitude of bank accounts belonging to intestates whose relatives could not be traced. The resulting liquid capital was promptly 'fixed' into one of London's outstanding Gothic buildings.

Producer goods

When we refer to the factor 'capital' we usually mean the producer goods which enable labour to work more effectively by providing premises, furniture, tools and equipment for the production process. Thus a trawler, with its trawl, ship's gear, freezing equipment, etc., raises the productivity of fishermen. An engineering works, with its presses, drilling machines, milling machines, etc., raises the productivity of its craftsmen. Every trade has its machine tools, patterns, cutting equipment, etc. A full list of producer goods includes the following:

1 Constructional works of every sort, factories, offices, mines, warehouses, depots, aerodromes, railway permanent way, roads, harbours, docks, launching pads, hospitals, schools, etc.
2 Plant, machinery, lifting gear, catalytic cracking towers, heat exchangers, loose tools of every sort, etc.
3 Stocks of raw materials and partly finished goods. Some economists regard stocks of finished goods which are being transported (either geographically or in time) as also being capital. This idea is sensible, since it fits in with the economic viewpoint that a good is not completely 'produced' until it reaches the final consumer. On the other hand, finished goods are available for immediate consumption, and it is confusing to regard them as both consumer goods and producer goods. They are therefore usually left out of calculations of the factor 'capital'.

Capital and the scale of production

An obvious feature of advanced economies is the large size of many firms, and the large-scale methods of production that they use. Many such firms, and many national corporations, have capital budgets far larger than the national capital of many of the developing nations. Large scale is thought by many people to be undesirable, since it tends towards monopoly, and the exploitation of the general public. Unfortunately, the natural tendency must be to greater and greater size now that the computer makes it possible to keep control of bigger and bigger units. Before the advent of the computer large size eventually brought diseconomies as units of production grew more and more remote from the central office seeking to control them. Computerisation has reduced this tendency. It has also been repeatedly proved that monopolies, especially natural monopolies like railway networks, do not necessarily mean expoloitation.

The **economies of large scale** are very great, and most people think it is highly desirable that we should achieve them. There are several principles which lie at the root of the economies of large scale. They are:

1 The principle of bulk transactions.
2 The 'lowest common multiple' principle.
3 The principle of massed reserves.

1 THE PRINCIPLE OF BULK TRANSACTIONS

The principle of bulk transactions holds that in general there are economic advantages in dealing in large quantities. There are many examples in every field. For example, many production plants can only operate at all if they are of a certain critical size, and operate best when they are well above this minimum. Even where the optimum size is not very large, the duplication of a particular unit will permit the ordering of larger quantities so that economies of scale can be achieved in material supply. Most suppliers are prepared to offer discounts on large orders, sometimes very considerable discounts. The transport costs of large movements are generally less, as with VLCCs (very large crude carriers), bulk ore carriers and container ships. The documentation of large orders costs the same as small orders; an invoice for 100 000 tonnes is as cheap to type as an invoice for 10 tonnes. The popular misconception among businessmen that exporting is less profitable than home trade was recently refuted by one firm which announced that part of its export success was explained by the fact that its average order from overseas customers was for £10 000 while for home customers orders rarely exceeded £500.

2 THE LOWEST COMMON MULTIPLE PRINCIPLE

Where there are components entering into a product, the major components often dictate the scale of production. If component A is made on a machine which can produce 15 units per hour, while the other major component B is produced at a rate of 10 units per hour, the lowest common multiple is 30 units per hour. If the management provides two machines for component A and three machines for component B, then all machines will be kept busy at an output of 30 units per hour. Where there are many components it is not possible to arrange that every machine is kept busy all the time. The components which are produced very quickly will be produced by a system known as 'batch production', which provides a suitable batch for the weeks or even months ahead. The batch will be stored and used as required, and a minimum stock level established. When reached, this will signal that a new batch must be manufactured if delays are not to occur.

Even the work of a particular individual may come under the principle of the lowest common multiple. A particularly high-powered mathematician or scientist may be under-utilised unless he is adequately supplied with other resources, both technological and human. University professors should not be starved of junior secretarial help, and plumbers should be adequately supplied with plumbers' mates. The key personnel must be kept fully employed on their specialist activities, and this requires an adequate number of projects whose routine activities are carried on by a suitable team of non-specialists. Sometimes a more economic combination of factors results from the use of this principle. A 44-tonne truck with two drivers is a better combination of factors than a 5-tonne truck with one driver, provided we have enough work to keep it busy all the time.

3 THE PRINCIPLE OF MASSED RESERVES

Every enterprise requires reserves of stocks, money, storage space and staff to overcome the day-to-day problems. Consider a chemist's shop in a busy suburb. Almost any emergency may occur at any minute, from a 'flu epidemic to an individual's need for a particular drug or appliance. To cater for every emergency would require an enormous reserve of stocks, and in fact is quite impossible. By contrast, a multiple-shop organisation could keep at its local depot almost everything required by the 50 or 60 shops served, and could even operate a counter to deal with emergencies day or night. Similarly, it could cater for staff absences by a slight overstaffing. One or two experienced and mobile branch managers can be available at the local depot for secondment at a moment's notice to branches placed in difficulty by staff illness. The principle has very wide applications. Many small firms, given the opportunity to purchase a particular item on favourable terms, may be unable to do so because of storage space. The large firm with many plants and depots can usually find a corner to store such items, and its very ability to take the goods may enable it to demand further discounts from a firm anxious to clear stocks.

The sources of capital

The primary source of all capital is savings; either voluntary savings or compulsory savings. Compulsory saving is imposed by taxation which places funds at the disposal of government departments. Disregarding official saving of this sort, the chief sources of capital for organisations are as follows:

1 **Self-financing**, sometimes called **autonomous saving**.
2 **Private investors.**
3 **Institutional investors**, who have undertaken the collection of funds from a host of small savers, and from firms who happen to have spare cash available for short periods.

In addition to these sources official funds may be available in certain circumstances, if the firm acts in such a way as to assist government policies like job creation schemes, development of 'assisted areas', etc.

  1 Self-financing is in many ways a very desirable method of financing expansion of an organisation. Provided a firm's current projects or products are profitable, funds will be generated which can be reinvested in the firm. This does mean, of course, that the full profit made cannot be returned to the shareholders as reward for their enterprise. The shareholders will be given a reasonable sum, and the rest will be retained as reserves in the business. These reserves still belong to the shareholders, but if they are turned into fixed assets they can no longer be withdrawn in cash form. Sooner or later the profits will be capitalised – in other words, **bonus shares** will be issued to the shareholders so that the investment of the retained profits is recognised.

  2 Private investors In former times, when wealth was unequally shared so that a few rich people controlled a very high proportion of the national income, private investors were a major source of capital. Firms encouraged them to invest by offering a range of shares, each type of which had features that made it attractive to the investor. Some investors wished to obtain a steady income, others wished to have absolute security of capital even though the income was small. Some did not mind running a risk if very high incomes were a distinct possibility. Today there are still about two million people in the UK who have a personal shareholding, so the private investor has not quite died out, though individual shareholdings are probably much smaller than in the past. The more usual source of capital today is the institutional investor.

3 Institutional investors With wealth more equally divided the savings of individuals tend to be smaller than in former times, but savers are more numerous. One insurance company collects £3 million every Friday from its small savers around the UK. There are hundreds of building societies, unit trusts, investment trusts, finance companies, local authorities, and a huge National Savings Movement, as well as thousands of branches of the 'Big Four' banks collecting funds in every corner of the land. These funds are made available as loans, mortgages, hire purchase finance and other forms of credit. In addition, the institutional investors invest in firms by purchasing shares and debentures. This holding of **balanced portfolios** provides funds for the major industrial firms. A 'balanced portfolio' is a mixture of shares and other securities spread across the whole face of British industry, so that the institutional investor is effectively lending capital to both sectors of the economy, but does not have too much invested in any one firm or industry.

All the resources used in production by entrepreneurs as they combine the factors of production into a useful enterprise come into one of the four categories described above, land, improved gifts of nature, labour and capital. They are illustrated in Fig. 2.1.

Fig. 2.1 *The pattern of resources used by organisations*

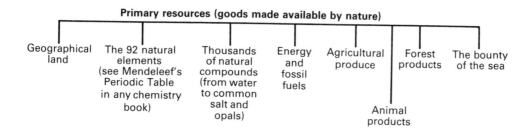

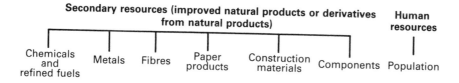

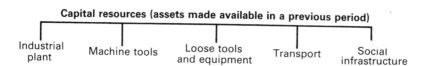

SELF-ASSESSMENT QUESTIONS

1 What is wealth, in economic terms?
2 Explain the exchange of goods and services: (a) in a primitive society; (b) in an advanced sophisticated society.
3 Explain the meaning of 'land' in economics.
4 What is the difference as far as labour is concerned between a labour intensive industry and a capital intensive industry?
5 What is the function of a Personnel Officer?
6 What is 'the principle of massed reserves'?

6   SOME OTHER ASPECTS OF FACTORS

The availability of resources is of great concern to firms, which clearly can only engage in production if they can secure supplies of the resources they need. A particular firm will know exactly what these needs are: certain raw materials, certain machines and tools, certain qualities of labour. Whether they are actually available is another matter, and whether they continue to be available is yet another. Sources of raw material frequently dry up, and alternative sources have to be found. Skilled workers move on, or threaten to move on. The following considerations enter into the calculations of all firms about the availability of factors:

1 The demand for factors.
2 The supply of factors.
3 The mix of factors to be used.
4 The efficiency of factors.
5 The mobility of factors.

One other aspect, the rewards to factors, is dealt with later in this book (see page 192).

Since it is not possible in a book of this type to examine the problems of particular firms, the topics must be treated generally, and for simplicity's sake a chart has been drawn up in Table 2.2 which reviews some of these problems for the various classes of resource. Before considering this table some of the items 1–5 above require short explanations.

The demand for factors

The demand for factors is a derived demand; derived from the demand for consumer goods and services. An entrepreneur who decides to satisfy the demand for teenage fashions will demand land and buildings, machines, cloth, buttons and other accessories and various classes of labour. Because he hopes to make a profit he will demand these factors at economical prices, so that the margin between the cost price (of the input factors) and the selling price (for the sale of the product) is as large as possible.

The supply of factors

The supply of factors which is made available by the factor owners depends upon the rewards that are being offered. The factor owner seeks the **maximum net advantage** to himself from the provision of the factor. The word 'net' means 'clean', and implies that any disbenefits will be deducted in the calculations. Thus a worker who is tempted by a highly paid job in Saudi Arabia, free of income tax, would deduct from the pecuniary advantages the disbenefits of separation from his home.

Inevitably bargaining is a feature of the supply of factors, and the arrangements concluded have a finite duration. A lease of land or a royalty agreement for the extraction of ore or gravel, or for the supply of components or semi-manufactured goods, must be renegotiated from time to time. Wage bargaining is an annual feature of the UK economy at present and the ways of exerting pressure on the negotiations feature daily in news bulletins.

The mix of factors

It is the entrepreneur's function to mix the factors in such a way that the most efficient combination is arrived at. The problem is to relate the price of the factor to its marginal productivity when combined with other factors. The marginal productivity is the extra output produced by taking on another unit of the factor (for example one more employee). The initial 'mix' of the factors is determined by technical considerations at the time, in the light of the machines chosen to carry out the process in hand, the number of operators, layout considerations to give a safe system of work, etc. Later developments may require modifications to the system of work and the use of new machinery. Labour may be made redundant and need retraining or easing out of the system by some kind of compensatory payment.

The mix of factors is closely connected with a famous economic law, the **law of diminishing returns**. This states:

> If the quantity of one factor of production is gradually increased by equal increments from zero, and applied to a fixed quantity of the other factors, the resulting successive increments of output will increase for a period, reach an optimum level where the increments of output remain constant, and then diminish again.

A full explanation of why this must be so hinges around the proportions in which the factors are being combined. There must always be some perfect combination between the factors: so much capital or labour to a certain area of land, etc. As the quantity of the variable factor moves closer to the ideal proportions for combination greater efficiency is achieved and increasing returns to scale result. When the optimum arrangement is reached the increments of output will cease to increase (constant returns) and later – as further units of the variable factor achieve the wrong balance of factors – output will decline (negative returns to scale).

In many cases the law is obvious. For example, if we imagine a smallholding of 10 hectares on which one agricultural labourer is employed, a certain crop will be obtained. If we increase the labour force by one, it is possible that they will, between them, produce more than twice the original output. For example, waste can often be utilised, greater skill can be developed and a more favourable combination of labour and capital achieved. No doubt when the first stone axe maker in neolithic times was joined by a stone axe maker's mate, the two turned out more than two axes in the time previously used to make one. Two farm workers in a 500 acre farm will usually achieve more than twice as much output as one. On the other hand, if we increase the labour force successively by one man there will come a time when diminishing returns set in. Fifty men to a 500 acre farm will be excessive and 50 000 will trample the last blade of young corn to death. Table 2.1 illustrates the problem.

The efficiency of factors

Factors vary in efficiency. Thus some land is highly productive and if efficiently managed will remain so. Other land is less satisfactory and is often called marginal land. This means that it will only be brought into production at times of real necessity and once the emergency is over it will again pass out of use. During the two World Wars the planting of potatoes became a national duty in the UK because of the submarine attacks on ships importing food.

Table 2.1 Eventually diminishing returns from capital applied to land

Area of land (hectares)	Weight of fertiliser used (in 250 kg loads)	Output of potatoes (tonnes)	Increase in output over untreated land	Marginal product, i.e. product of extra load used
1	–	10	–	–
1	1	12	2	2
1	2	15	5	3
1	3	20	10	5
1	4	23	13	3
1	5	25	15	2
1	6	24	14	−1

Notes
1 The area of land in use in each case is the same (1 hectare).
2 Successive increments of the variable factor (capital, in the form of artificial fertiliser) are being added.
3 Output rises with the first load; more than proportionately with the second load; and again with the third load.
4 Diminishing returns begin to set in with the fourth load. Total output is still rising, but the returns from the fourth load are less than those from the third load. The extra capital results in a diminished increment of output.
5 This effect is even greater on the fifth load, and on the sixth load the increment is actually negative. Even total output declines, so that the sixth load of fertiliser was actually harmful.

Much marginal land came under the plough which previously had been just rough pasture, only to be returned to grassland when the wars were over.

Human labour is very variable in quality. The physical ability of individuals ranges from superb manual dexterity on the one hand to complete physical incapacity on the other. Mental ability ranges from the genius at one end to the mentally subnormal at the other. Both intelligence and skill are required for some jobs; for others it is a positive advantage to be less able.

The efficiency of labour is reflected in the qualities of the unemployed. While it would be absurd to suggest that all the unemployed are less able or less intelligent than the employed, it will be partly true. At times of high unemployment there will be many able men and women out of work. Any return to boom conditions will quickly bring these factors back into employment and as the boom gathers pace it is natural that those best able to take employment and those most keen to do so will find work. As we move towards full employment only the less able and the unwilling are left to be recruited. If the handicapped are found work under special schemes and the unskilled are trained to some useful occupation, it leaves the lazy, the unwilling and the downright criminal unemployed. Rather than take on such employees firms will try to poach good labour away from the other firms and inflation begins to creep in as wages rise. This is called **demand-pull inflation**.

Capital assets are usually purchased because they are the best at the time for the job in hand. Over the years they gradually depreciate, and become less efficient. The servicing costs rise, and so does the time lost by breakdowns. At the same time, in a dynamic world, new machines and materials are being developed, which render the old machine obsolete, possibly before it is worn out. It is a fine exercise in judgment as to when an old system of working should be abandoned, with its old equipment and other capital assets, to be replaced by new machinery and a new system of work. There are still some places in the UK where the steam engine is in use, even though it is obsolete and breaks down with montonous regularity.

The mobility of factors

'Mobility' in economics means the ability of a factor to move easily from one employment to another. Thus a petrol tanker may be mobile in the ordinary sense, but rather immobile in the economic sense. It can hardly be changed over to carrying milk on a return journey, and consequently always operates rather wastefully on an empty return leg of a journey. Heavy lorries by contrast can often earn income on return journeys, and some manufacturers (for example, cement works and fertiliser factories) rely for much of their transport on loads carried at cheap rates by road hauliers anxious to take a return load to cover their fuel costs on an otherwise empty leg.

Land is largely immobile – we cannot push a fertile field closer to other fertile fields to make a fertile farm. It can move from one use to another, but usually there is a time lag. A field sown with spring wheat is immobilised until the autumn; a newly planted orchard immobilises the land for the lifetime of the trees, maybe 20 to 30 years. A cement works immobilises the land for a century or two, and a nuclear power station immobilises the land for thousands of years.

Liquid capital (money) is very mobile, and flows from one place to another at electronic speeds. Even in the eighteenth century the savings of the prosperous agricultural community were put to work in a few weeks in the industrial areas. Today funds are available from all over the world to support projects in the UK, while in one recent year the UK spent £8909 million in investments abroad.

Fixed capital assets are much less mobile. The very act of building a specific asset like a catalytic cracking tower presupposes that it will be used in situ for its working lifetime. Buildings tend to be purpose-built, though they may be adapted to other uses at a later date.

The unique feature of labour as a factor is that the factor owner (the worker) must be physically present in the working situation. This is not required of the 'absentee' landlord or the investor of capital. Workers must settle where work is available and develop roots in the locality. Consequently, labour, which is free to move from place to place and job to job, has been called 'the immobile factor'. It is difficult to get labour to move from industry to industry or from place to place, unless special help is given. Family ties and traditional behaviour are not easily abandoned, and the difficulties of finding suitable accommodation, schooling for children, etc., encourage immobility. Skills in one trade are not easily transferred to other trades, and this again encourages immobility.

You should now study Table 2.2 which lists many points about particular factors.

7   SCARCITY – THE CENTRAL PROBLEM WITH RESOURCES

If the purpose of an economy is to create goods and services to satisfy wants the central economic problem is to allocate scarce resources to alternative needs. By 'scarce' we mean something different from a mere shortage. We may have huge supplies of oil, but oil is still scarce. The wants of mankind are limitless but the means to satisfy those wants are limited. Lord Robbins defined economics as: *'The science which studies human behaviour as a relationship between "ends" and scarce "means" which have alternative uses.'* The ends we seek to achieve are the satisfaction of mankind's wants; the means to satisfy those wants are the resources available for production. The problem is to establish an order of priorities for the use of these resources.

Under the free-enterprise system it is left to those who show enterprise to decide the allocation of resources. In 1759 the price of coal in the streets of Manchester was eight pence per hundredweight. The Duke of Bridgwater was

Table 2.2 A review of factors

Type of resource	How may it/they be obtained	The mix of factors to be used (see text)	The mobility of factors (see text)
1a Land: Geographical	a) Outright purchase (freehold) b) Purchase of a lease (leasehold) c) Rental	a) If land is cheap and plentiful it is used 'extensively' b) If land is dear we use it 'intensively' (higher buildings – heavier plant concentration)	Geographical land is immobile, and other factors must move to it. It can move from one use to another over time – the wheatfield can be sold for housing development, but not until harvest-time
1b Land: Other natural resources. Minerals (most of these are the 92 naturally occurring elements (see Mendeleef's Periodic Table in any chemistry book) or compounds built up from these elements over geological time	a) Purchase of ore-bearing land b) Purchase of rights to exploit on a royalty or profit-making basis c) Purchase from a producer or marketing outlet (often from a nationally owned corporation in many countries) d) Purchase from dealers in a highly organised market	a) Such factors are the raw materials for secondary goods. Use is decided by the quality of the product b) Avoidance of waste is a major consideration c) Avoid adverse ecological effects if possible d) Seek efficiency, especially in fuel use e) Keep an eye open for substitutes (in case supplies are interrupted)	Other types of land, ores, crude oil, etc., can be moved, but it is expensive. Hence we frequently move them as concentrates to reduce the bulk. Power sources used to be a problem (industry moved to the coalfields). Today electricity is available almost everywhere in the UK, but at some cost (power losses in cables, etc.)
1c Land: Semi-manufactured goods and components	a) Purchase from the manufacturer b) By manufacture in-plant under licence	a) These are decided by the product and difficult to vary. b) Watch for innovations; new materials, alternative applications, 'better mousetraps'	These factors are essentially mobile and can be moved where they are required

Table 2.2 A review of factors (*Continued*)

Type of resource	How may it/they be obtained	The mix of factors to be used (see text)	The mobility of factors (see text)
2a Labour: Managerial	Management may come initially from the founder of the firm and his/her successors. Later a personnel department will recruit staff of the right quality, or train them. Finding other types of labour is also the function of the personnel department. A variety of methods can be used, such as: a) Advertising b) Use of an agency or specialist recruiting organisation c) Family-recruitment through existing staff d) Grow your own (train semi-skilled and skilled staff by a sound training policy – then bind them to you with bonds of affection. Eventually, there should be opportunities in management at all levels)	a) Too many chiefs and too few Indians is a common fault b) Management should be backed by a sufficient team of supporting staff, including secretarial and clerical grades.	Labour has been called 'the immobile factor'. People do not like to move homes even today, when communications are so good. Many of the unemployment problems in depressed areas could be cured if people would move to more prosperous areas. Hence the 'mobility allowances' given to the unemployed who are prepared to move. Education improves mobility, acquired skills may be specific and discourage movement from industry to industry (but not from job to job in the same industry). Generally speaking, positive assistance is required if mobility is to be encouraged
2b Labour: Skilled		a) Skilled workers must be backed by an appropriate array of tools	
2c Labour: Semi-skilled		b) and c) High productivity of these workers depends upon an adequate array of powered tools, mechanical aids, labour saving systems, noise abatement, etc.	
2d Labour: Unskilled			
3a Capital: Fixed Assets (i) Buildings	a) By construction to order b) By rental from private developers c) By rental from Development Boards, Local Authorities, etc.	a) Plant location, depot location, etc., are studies in themselves b) Review space utilisation at regular intervals	Capital is mobile and flows freely to where it is required but once fixed as 'fixed assets' it is less mobile, and may be specific to a particular industry

	Methods of acquisition	Notes	Mobility
(ii) Industrial plant	a) By new construction to order b) By acquisition of existing assets in a take-over c) By leasing	Idle plant is wasted plant. The lowest common multiple principle may help avoid idle plant, especially for specific assets (see page 41)	Plant tends to be specific and immobile
(iii) Machinery and tools	a) By purchase from a supplier b) By purchase second-hand c) By acquisition of existing assets in a take-over	The aim is to use tools and machines intensively, so that they wear out before they become obsolete. This requires large scale production and a huge marketing effort to utilise the output produced	Machinery and tools may be specific or non-specific
(iv) Motor vehicles	a) By purchase from a supplier b) By purchase second-hand	A correct mix is important – two men to a 44-tonne lorry are better than one man to a 5-tonne lorry	Motor vehicles are reasonably mobile factors, and can move from industry to industry
(v) Office equipment systems	By purchase from a supplier	It is false economy to be mean with the paper clips. Provide an adequate system of work	Once used they tend to be specific, but do have some residual mobility
3b Capital: Working Capital	a) By the issue of permanent share capital (ordinary and preference shares) b) By the issue of debentures (loan bonds secured – usually – on the assets of the firm) c) By borrowing against a mortgage, or other security d) By bank overdraft e) By ploughing back profits	a) It is essential to have adequate working capital so that fixed capital is not wasted for lack of wages to pay hands to use it. b) Suppliers may stop supplies at times of shortage if you are a late payer (due to inadequate working capital)	Capital is very mobile – one bank advertises that it can get funds anywhere in the world in five minutes.

an enterprising man. He conceived the idea of cutting a canal from his coalmines at Worsley to Salford. Later the plans were altered and the canal eventually crossed the River Irwell on an aqueduct directly into Manchester. As soon as the canal was finished, in 1761, the price of coal in Manchester came down below four pence per hundredweight. Was this the best way to spend the energies and efforts of engineers, bricklayers and labourers for three whole years? We shall never know. As Lord Robbins said, the means at our disposal have alternative uses. Instead of using his energies to build a canal, the Duke could have invented hair shampoo, or gone off to discover palm oil in Nigeria. By contrast with the free-enterprise system, in the controlled economies, and in the State-run enterprises of a mixed economy, a committee perhaps sits down to decide what it is best to make, and in what quantities. Even they may make bad choices, and spend time and effort on abortive projects, or wastefully purchase stock that proves to be unnecessary.

Opportunity cost

Because the scarce means at our disposal have alternative uses, or 'opportunities', economists speak of the **opportunity cost**, or **alternative cost**, of a particular good or service. Opportunity cost may be defined as follows:

> The opportunity cost of a particular good or service is the second-best alternative which could have been enjoyed if that particular good or service had not been selected.

Organisations or individuals may use resources in different ways. A man may drive a bus, or manage a restaurant, or write books, or mine coal. Each of these opportunities has its advantages and disadvantages. Driving is a pleasant occupation to many people, but stopping and starting every hundred yards gives many bus drivers gastric ulcers. Running a restaurant is a congenial activity, but you have to work unsocial hours. One cannot drive a bus and mine coal at the same time. *To select one opportunity is to reject all the others.* So we may say that the cost of driving a bus is the lost opportunity to mine coal. If a student skips a lecture to date a girl on the secretarial studies course, the cost of his evening out is the lecture he missed. If he decides to attend the lecture and miss the date the cost of the lecture is his missed opportunity for a pleasant social evening. Once again he will never know whether the choice he made was wise or unwise. We have all attended dull lectures which we could have missed without loss. By contrast a single lecture has sparked off a completely new interest for many students. Many dates prove to be far from enjoyable, but others lead to ecstatic relationships.

In making business decisions we must weigh up the opportunity costs of alternative uses of resources. We should not commit our own efforts and the use of natural and capital resources in one direction if an alternative direction would be more advantageous. The most advantageous opportunity is the one that yields the greatest satisfaction of human wants. Since the resources available to us are scarce, we must employ them advantageously. In one recent hard winter the American President appealed to the nation to conserve fuel oil. The American consumption of fuel oil in that year was 2500 million tons of coal equivalent, yet even this enormous consumption was not enough to satisfy the American wants for domestic heating, etc. Resources are scarce relative to the wants which they have to satisfy; wants are endless. The central economic problem is one of **choice**: *organisations have to choose the best way to allocate scarce resources so as to maximise the satisfactions achieved.*

8   THE PROCESS OF PRODUCTION

Organisations like business firms or public sector corporations and departments take the resources which have been made available and turn them into goods and services which will be of benefit to mankind. This may involve the changing of a natural material into a more useful form, or moving it geographically or in time (by warehousing, storage, refrigeration, etc.). The productive process includes the provision of both goods and services, so that the road haulier is just as much 'a producer' as the farmer whose potatoes he hauls to market; the surgeon is as productive as the instrument maker whose equipment he uses; and the civil servant who collects taxes for redistribution to the underprivileged, or to finance a defence or security system, is guided into that employment because it will play a productive rôle in society.

The provision of a service is in fact a process of changing factor inputs (many of which are material) into services delivered at the time and place required. Thus the dentist uses sophisticated products from secondary production and his own skills acquired over many years to bring relief to patients with exposed nerves and to effect permanent repairs to their teeth. We must now look in a more detailed way at production. It is best to start by classifying it under different headings. The first of these classifications is into **primary**, **secondary** and **tertiary production**. These three words are simply derived from the Latin words for first, second and third.

Primary production

Primary production is the production of goods made available by Nature. It embraces many types of activity. First there is a huge range of extractive industries. Among these there are various types of mining, particularly for coal, iron ore, precious metals, diamonds, non-metals like sulphur and compounds like salt. Other extractive industries involve drilling for crude oil, natural gas, water and geothermal energy. Then there are such activities as forestry, animal husbandry, poultry farming, plantation management in the tea, coffee, cocoa, rubber, sugar cane, banana, palm oil and natural fibre industries and fruit farming in the citrus, peach and temperate-zone orchards. Fishing, whaling and activities such as fish farming, pearl culture, shellfish and crustacea breeding are also primary activities.

Secondary production

Secondary production is production which improves upon nature's gifts and renders them more appropriate for use, enabling them to yield more sophisticated satisfactions. Thus pineapples are a primary product, but tinned, diced pineapple is a secondary good. All such goods require some sort of manufacturing or refining process. The variety of goods is enormous, and includes such things as the complex ranges of chemical derivatives from crude oil – petrol, paraffin, lubricants and waxes; the countless products of our engineering, aeronautical, electronic and nuclear industries; the manufactures of household goods; the provision for our gardens, smallholdings and farms of numerous products and gadgets; the provision by our office equipment industry of a ceaseless flow of new devices to promote efficiency, and so on. All these items are an improvement upon the natural product; wood, copper, aluminium, etc., are transformed into furniture, brassware, aeroplanes and a million other convenient and appropriate articles for everyday use.

Tertiary production

Tertiary production is the production not of goods but of services. Again we notice that production is not just concerned with goods, but also with the means to bring those goods to the consumers (commercial services) and satisfy their other wants, many of them unconnected with goods at all. Education, entertainment, medical care, mental health, religious consolation, security and defence may or may not require goods, but they also involve services of a very personal nature. The provision of these services is 'production' too.

In discussing tertiary production (services) it is usual to distinguish between commercial services and personal services. The group of commercial services is concerned with the eight chief branches of commerce. There are four branches of trade – import trade, export trade, wholesale trade and retail trade – and four activities which are ancillary to trade. These ancillary activities are transport, banking, insurance and communications. The personal services include medical care, education, entertainment and defence. Some of these are provided specifically to individuals, as when a doctor cares for his patient or a lawyer for his client. Others are provided to the community in general, like the services of the police or the government ministries. Even such services have their fullest impact when an individual requires the service which is available to all, as when the British Consul assists a stranded United Kingdom citizen, or the Criminal Investigation Department fingerprints a householder's burgled apartment.

Table 2.3 gives a simple chart which illustrates the classification of production into primary, secondary and tertiary stages.

9 DIRECT AND INDIRECT PRODUCTION

The second method of classifying production is to divide it into **direct production** and **indirect production**. This classification pinpoints the chief

Table 2.3 Types of production

(a) The production of goods		(b) The production of services	
1 Primary production	**2 Secondary production**	**3 Tertiary production**	
(The production of goods made available by nature. Man's inheritance of natural wealth)	(The production of sophisticated products which are derived from the natural primary products)	(The production of services)	
		Commercial services	*Personal services*
Coal miner	Engineer	Wholesaler	Doctor
Gold miner	Electronic Engineer	Retailer	Dentist
Tin miner	Builder	Banker	Nurse
Lead miner	Decorator	Insurance agent	Teacher
Oil driller	Cabinet maker	Stockbroker	Lecturer
Lumberjack	Carpenter	Importer	Policeman
Farmer	Plastics engineer	Exporter	Detective
Fisherman	Refinery technologist	Transport driver	Entertainer
Whaler	Stillman	Merchant-navy	Vocalist
Pearl diver	Potter	captain	TV Personality
Herdsman	Tailor	Ship's crew	Clergyman
Fur trapper etc.	Steelworker	Communications	Undertaker
	Shipbuilder	engineer	Editor
	Aeronautical engineer		Author
			Psychologist

Note: You should consolidate your grasp of these three classes of production by attempting to think of five more occupations in each of the four groups shown.

feature of advanced economies, that man provides the utilities he needs by a system of indirect production. Thus the motor vehicle assembler 'produces' all he needs – food, clothing, shelter, education, entertainment, etc. – by hanging doors in an automobile factory, while the farmers, garment workers, builders, teachers and television producers assemble their cars indirectly by working in the fields, in clothing factories, building sites, schools and television studios respectively. Let us now consider direct and indirect production.

Direct production is production for one's own use, like Robinson Crusoe on his island. The simple life is much commended by those who have never tried it. A primitive existence where one hunts or gathers one's own food, weaves one's own cloth, builds one's own shelter and collects one's own medicinal herbs is vulnerable in the extreme, even when it is only tried as an experiment by first-year students of economics – a not uncommon exercise these days. How much more vulnerable was primitive man; standing inside the door of his grass hut, clutching his wooden spear to repel both wild beasts and enemies. A celebrated film, *Nanook of the North*, recorded faithfully the experiences of a group of Eskimos in about 1927. When the cameramen returned one year later, to shoot the sequel, they could not find the group. A severe winter had wiped them out.

It is not only primitive people who suffer in this way. There have been many cases of people reduced to direct production methods who were quite unable to sustain a satisfactory standard of living. They lost weight, became emaciated and verminous, prone to disease and exposure. One writer describes the gradual physical and moral deterioration of such a party:

> At first they had waited for a comrade who fell behind to die, and had flinched at drawing lots to see who should die to feed the others. They had shrunk from cannibalism even when it meant eating a man already dead. Then they had eaten the food which centuries of civilisation had forbidden them. Then they had plotted to kill men of another race, and the men, and even women, of their own race. They had gone on, leaving comrades behind, and in their frenzy had tried to kill each other in open fight.
>
> *Ordeal by Hunger*, George R. Stewart, Jr.

Finally they murdered two strangers who were themselves too weak to resist. There have been many similar incidents.

What is it about direct production that makes it so disadvantageous as a system? It is the great variety of 'wants' which have to be met which presents the major difficulty to direct production. The skills of agriculture, animal husbandry, forestry, etc., are related but different. The skills of carpentry, joinery, spinning and weaving, and of the smith, the stonemason, the cutler and the cooper, are wide-ranging and to some extent mutually exclusive. We cannot master them all, or even make the tools for every trade. The system of direct production inevitably gives way, in part, if not entirely, to one of indirect production, where the wants we wish to satisfy are catered for by specialist producers who have mastered a particular trade or profession.

Indirect production is production not for our own use, but for the market. It depends upon specialisation in particular trades or professions, so that each individual selects work that is agreeable to him, or within his capabilities, and specialises in it. As a result the output he achieves is much greater than he needs for his own use, and the vast majority of it must be marketed – i.e. exchanged for other goods which he requires. This **exchange** activity is usually carried on through the medium of a money system – every nation having its **legal tender**, a designated currency which by law constitutes a proper medium of exchange having a known value within the country. A tailor may make eight suits in a week, and undoubtedly makes one for himself every now and again. The life of a suit is not short, and he has no need of a new suit every week. He exchanges the fruits of his labour for money, which he uses to buy a balanced range of other goods suitable to his needs.

The process of specialisation is one which involves the **division of labour**. Instead of each person trying to master all trades and skills the work is divided into separate specialist activities. Originally this division gave us the 'trades', such as smiths, potters, bricklayers, glaziers, etc. The mediaeval guilds were organisations of master craftsmen who combined to preserve the secrets of their craft and restrict entry to it. In more advanced economies the trades are broken down into subtrades, and even into individual processes. The mass-production workshop carries this process to its limits, and assigns each activity to a single individual or to groups all performing the same process. Production becomes very indirect indeed, with an individual providing for all the requirements of his family by being an offside rear-wheel bolt-tightener, or something similar.

The first person to describe this sytem of indirect production was the great economist Adam Smith, whose book *The Wealth of Nations* appeared in 1776. The full title of the book was *An Enquiry into the Nature and Causes of the Wealth of Nations* and the enquiries he made led him to conclude that it was specialisation which was the chief cause of any nation's wealth. He studied the methods of production used in many industries. One of his most graphic descriptions reads, in the rather quaint English of his day:

> A man not educated to this business could scarcely perhaps with his utmost industry make one pin a day, and certainly could not make twenty. . . . But in the way this trade is carried on it is divided into a number of branches, of which the greater part are likewise peculiar (distinct) trades. One man draws out the wire, another straights it, a third cuts it, a fourth points it, a fifth grinds it at the top (for receiving of the head). To make the head requires two or three distinct operations. To put it on is a peculiar business, to whiten the pins is another. It is even a trade by itself to put them into the paper, and the important business of making a pin is divided in this way into eighteen different processes, which in some manufactories are all performed by distinct hands.
>
> I have seen a small manufactory of this kind where ten men only were employed, and where some of them consequently performed two or three distinct operations. But although they were very poor, and therefore but indifferently accommodated with the necessary machinery, they could, when they exerted themselves, make among them twelve pounds of pins a day. There are in a pound upwards of 4000 pins of a middling size. Each person, therefore, could make one-tenth of 48 000 pins in a day. But if they had wrought separately, without having been educated to this peculiar business, they certainly could not have each made twenty, and possibly not even one.

The specialisation which Smith so clearly describes has continued to develop since his day. The UK is still a leader in the manufacture of pins, but the processes have been largely mechanised. A modern pin-making machine heads, cuts and points the wire automatically. It makes about 5–600 pins per minute and about 250–300 tonnes are made every year in about 20 different sizes. To market this enormous output of about 2500 million pins the manufacturers need a world-wide market, and pins are exported to many countries, including the USA, which buys about one-fifth of the total.

Smith himself recognised that much of the advantage of the division of labour came from the possibility of equipping labour with simple machinery once processes had been isolated and simplified. Modern machinery merely carries this idea to its logical conclusion, mechanising every process.

Specialisation and the growth of surplus output

Adam Smith held that it was specialisation that was the cause of the wealth of nations, because it enabled output to increase so that it exceeded that necessary to keep the worker alive. Instead of a mere subsistence economy, **specialisation creates a surplus** which is available to support others. The problem of dealing with the surplus output is one that has bedevilled the production scene ever since. Who is to be supported with it? Karl Marx of course held that this surplus, which was plundered from the working classes by the capitalist class, justified their expropriation in the interest of the masses. However true this was in the early days of the capitalist system, it must be conceded that in the modern advanced economy there are millions of ordinary people being supported by this surplus. The creation of wealth in highly specialised primary and secondary production supports those who work in the tertiary services. The extension of education, health services, social services, etc., is only made possible by the surplus wealth produced in primary and secondary industries. These services are paid for by taxation. Taxation is a form of expropriation, but discussions continue about how far it should go, and whether it has gone far enough. Certainly the workers in primary and secondary production cannot receive the 'full fruits of production' Marx claimed for them if fellow workers in tertiary production are to be supported.

Really the discussion of such points is appropriate to a course in economics, but it is important food for thought for all who seek to make organisations work effectively, and helps promote an understanding of the whole system. Let us continue to see how the surplus is created to start with.

The term **mass production** is used to describe any system which aims at producing, with the fewest workers, the greatest possible output of goods. In nearly every industry today techniques have been developed which allow manufacturing processes to be carried on continuously, often day and night. The work flows through the factory in an endless stream, and operators at various stages perform individual operations with specially designed machinery. Henry Ford's definition of mass production was:

> Manufacturing is not buying cheap and selling dear. It is the focusing upon a manufacturing project of the principles of power, accuracy, economy, system, continuity, speed and repetition.

This is an enduring definition, which conveys in a single sentence what engineers have tried to do to achieve the maximum output of utility from the minimum input of resources.

Two other factors have been found to affect greatly the volume of production. They are simplification and standardisation. Together with specialisation they are the source of wealth in our affluent society. These three methods, simplification, standardisation and specialisation, are sometimes called the three S's.

Simplification is the process of making a manufactured article as simple and functional as possible. Our Victorian ancestors took great delight in embellishing their furniture and their homes with decorative knobs and patterns. We have done away with these adornments, and our furniture, kitchen equipment, houses and cars have clean sweeping, functional surfaces – because this is the easy way to make them. When an article is designed to be produced in the simplest possible way, the job for which it is intended is borne in the mind, and quite often the article is not allowed to be more efficient than is really required. Hence a compromise is reached between cheapness and ability to do the job. Like the ballpoint pen which is thrown away once the ink has been used up, many goods are deliberately kept simple and discarded at the first sign of inefficiency. If you simpify an article you make it cheaper and it becomes easy to afford a new one when its working life is over.

Standardisation is the process of making things in standard parts, which can be used in many similar articles. The door handles and window-winders on many makes of car are identical. One or two types of carburettor are found fitted in the various models of cars made by leading manufacturers. Naturally design costs are heavy for these technical products, but the production runs of the finished article are very long and the design costs are spread over the greater volume of output.

Many examples of standardisation can be seen in the motorcar industry. A company or group of companies can economise by using the same standard parts on several different vehicles. By using the same standard parts for all their cars, economies can be achieved which drastically reduce the price of all of them and help the manufacturers secure a larger share of the car market.

10 THE LOCATION OF PRODUCTION

Every enterprise must have its geographical site, but where to locate a new enterprise is often a problem. Every site has its advantages and disadvantages, and the state of development of a country makes a difference. In the Industrial Revolution in the UK (c. 1760–1820) transport was poor, and industry tended to be located near its source of raw materials. The steel industry grew up around Sheffield because of its local iron ore, coal and limestone, the three basic raw materials for steel making. Today Sheffield is still important in the steel industry, but its iron ore was long ago used up and has to be imported from Spain and Scandinavia. The industry stays at Sheffield because of its experienced labour force and its network of specialist subsidiary firms which assist in the high-technology industry of today. It is an example of **industrial inertia**, the industry persisting in the region long after its reasons for locating there originally have ceased to be relevant.

In general we may find firms located in a region because of a variety of reasons including:

1 Closeness to a source of raw materials.
2 Closeness to a source of power.
3 Closeness to a port, airport or other transport facility.
4 Closeness to a sophisticated labour force.
5 Closeness to a market.
6 Because land is cheap there.
7 Because capital assets are available at reasonably economic prices.
8 Because government or local government aid is available.

A word of explanation of each of the above is advisable.

Closeness to a source of raw materials

Materials in their natural state tend to be heavy and difficult to transport. A tree is more unwieldy than a plank and many ores are full of impurities and need to be refined. There is no point in carrying hundreds of tons of waste material long distances – we refine it near the minehead and only ship the refined bars or pellets – for example copper from Zambia or tin from Malaya. Sawmills, refineries, cement works and similar plant are usually situated near the source of their raw materials.

Closeness to power

This is less important than it used to be. In the early days of the industrial revolution machines were driven by water power and industries grew up along the river valleys in the north of England to use the power available as water ran off the Pennine hills. Later the steam engine was invented (stationary steam engines for running factories) and industry moved out of the Pennines and down onto the coalfields. Manchester was the centre of the industrial world, with its coal supplying the power to drive cotton mills and many other industrial plants. Today power is available almost anywhere because it is available as electricity, but even so there are losses in cables as it is transmitted long distances. The economical place to use electricity is close to the power station and all major dams, such as the Aswan dam, have industrial complexes nearby.

Closeness to port, airports, etc.

Generally speaking easy transport is important to all industries, and siting near ports, airports and other transport facilities is common. Ports and airports are the logical places to work on imported raw materials, and also to produce goods which will become export cargoes. If there is an entrepôt trade, where imports arrive, have value added to them and then are re-exported, the port is the logical place to build a factory, processing plant, etc. Some of Glasgow's former prosperity arose from the import of tobacco, its manufacture into various products which were re-exported to Europe from Edinburgh after a short land journey across to the east coast of Britain. A good deal of the UK's entrepôt trade has been lost in the twentieth century to such ports as Antwerp and Rotterdam which do not have to re-export by sea, but can send on the 'value-added' product by road and rail into the heart of Europe – and indeed on the short-sea routes to the UK itself.

Today the development of industrial sites grouped near the access points of motorways is a striking example of location near a means of transport.

Closeness to a sophisticated labour force

Examples of this type of location are not all that common but they do enter into the considerations of many entreprenuers. The Japanese location of car factories in the north-east of England, where an experienced labour force previously used in mining, engineering and ship-building was available and anxious for employment is one example. Similar location of light engineering and electronic factories in Wales, Cornwall and other areas has taken advantage of the availability of well-trained labour. Of course labour can move to the work, so that emigration occurs from an area of high unemployment to more prosperous areas, but labour has been called 'the immobile factor' because it is less mobile than one would expect. Single people are relatively mobile, families are not so easy to move, and it is often easier to bring the factory to them.

Closeness to the market

For many products closeness to the market is important. While it is true that some products travel half a world away to reach their market, others do not travel easily. For example furniture is bulky, awkward to move and has things like hinged doors which are easily strained. Consumer durable goods are not easily moved though they may travel well if properly packaged. Personal services are nearly always provided locally, hairdressing, minor surgery, osteopathy, dentistry, etc. The growth of towns is partly caused by industries moving into the suburbs to supply the market created by the town. This makes advertising, demonstration and delivery simple.

The price of land

Land is expensive and industries which are not forced by other reasons to situate themselves in towns or other sites where prices are high will often locate where land adequate for their purposes is available at reasonable rent, or if purchase is envisaged, at a cheap price. Such land is often 'marginal' land – that is land which is not particularly fruitful for agricultural purposes. As such it is often best used for industry, and planning permission will usually be easy to obtain, while objections on environmental grounds will often be low key because the land itself is neither picturesque nor densely inhabited.

Capital asset availability

Some areas of the country have assets which are in a rather run-down condition but nevertheless can be brought into reasonable condition by a small expenditure. The refurbishment of inner city areas does not always require massive investment (such as the docklands rehabilitation schemes around the Port of London) but can be achieved in a more piecemeal manner by small firms seeking premises and plant that can be obtained relatively cheaply. Where roads, main drainage, power supplies, etc., are already available much of the capital expense of a new site can be avoided and an enterprise can be set up relatively cheaply.

Government and local government aid

There are many areas where official aid of one sort or another is available. For example in the UK there are over 300 Enterprise Agencies in all parts of the country which can assist entrepreneurs to find sites in their areas. Very often there is a 'rent holiday' or 'rates holiday' which allows the entrepreneur to set up an entreprise without paying rent or rates for the first few years. A Freephone Enterprise service puts any caller in touch with the local Small Firms Service which will advise and assist with location problems. Major firms can often get local government help in quite massive projects – for example the construction of roads to give access to a particular site. One local authority agreed to build a reservoir for a major company which had a need for high volumes of water for its activities. Another area which had been asked to build the reservoir but refused lost the proposed industrial complex as a result.

The European Community and location of industry

A concluding thought about the location of industry is that industrial location inevitably reflects the source of a nation's prosperity. In the nineteenth century, when the UK was the centre of a world-wide empire the west coast ports of Bristol, Liverpool, Manchester and Glasgow were thriving prosperous places because the products of the whole world flowed in through them to British factories. Today trans-oceanic trade is much more limited, and much of it arrives and departs by air.

The west coast ports have declined correspondingly. Today the major part of UK trade is with the continent of Europe and much of our world trade comes through Rotterdam and other continental ports because container ships only make one stop in Europe – and the best place to stop is on the continental mainland. The oceanic cargoes largely come on the short-sea routes from Europe. Also the increased air traffic flies from Heathrow, Gatwick and Stanstead rather than from airports in other parts of the country. So the enormous prosperity of the south-east corner of the UK is simply a natural reflection of the fact that industry locates itself in the most sensible, most accessible place to share in the general prosperity.

SELF-ASSESSMENT QUESTIONS

7 State the law of diminishing returns.

8 Explain the concept of 'mobility of factors'.

9 What is 'primitive communism'?

10 What is the importance of specialisation in industry?

REVISION TEST

Answers	Questions
—	**1** What is wealth?
1 It is an abundance of goods and services, available for mankind to enjoy.	**2** How is it produced?
2 By the combination of basic resources, land, labour and capital, to create utilities that can satisfy wants.	**3** What do we call these basic resources in economics?
3 The factors of production land, labour, capital and enterprise (entrepreneurial ability).	**4** List the various types of land.
4 (a) Geographical land; (b) Mineral resources – the elements and compounds found naturally as rocks and gases; (c) Fossil fuels; (d) Agricultural products and the proceeds of animal husbandry; (e) Forest products; (f) The produce of the sea.	**5** What are the two types of legal estate in land?
5 (a) Freehold – the fee simple absolute in possession; (b) Leasehold – the term of years absolute.	**6** What is freehold property?
6 A right to the use of land which lasts for an indefinite period.	**7** What is leasehold property?
7 A right to the use of property which only lasts for a certain number of years (which may include fractions of a year).	**8** Why is geographical land an unusual resource?
8 Because we cannot increase the supply, or move it to a more suitable location.	**9** What is labour?
9 The human resource – every mouth that is born into the world has a pair of hands to help it find food and other necessities of life.	**10** What is its unique feature?

10 Its infinite variety. There is every conceivable kind of skill and aptitude.

11 What is the function of the Personnel Officer in a firm?

11 To recruit staff in such numbers, and with such a range of skills, that the firm is never starved of the human resources it needs to carry out its full range of activities.

12 What is capital?

12 It is the stock of 'producer goods' created in an earlier period, which can be used to increase the output of consumer goods in the present period.

13 What are the main principles behind the economic arguments in favour of large scale production?

13 (a) The principle of bulk transactions; (b) the 'lowest common multiple' principle; (c) the principle of massed reserves (see pages 40 – 42 to revise these principles).

14 What kind of demand is the demand for factors?

14 It is a derived demand. We demand them not because we want them for themselves, but because of the utilities they can create, which will satisfy our wants.

15 What is meant by the 'mix' of factors?

15 It is the way we combine them, so much land, labour and capital. For example if land is scarce we combine more capital with it and build higher buildings on it to make the best use of the space available.

16 What is the law of diminishing returns?

16 A law which says that if we add successive increments of a factor to another factor we shall eventually find diminishing returns set in as the ideal mix of factors (the optimum) is passed and the extra increments are not helpful but hinder production.

17 What is meant by the mobility of factors?

17 Mobility is the ease with which a factor can move over to some other purpose from its present use. Thus a school is not easily converted into a swimming pool. A field of wheat cannot be turned into an orchard until harvest time.

18 What are the central problems of economics?

18 Scarcity and choice. The 'wants' we wish to satisfy are limitless. The resources available are limited. We must choose which is the best, most economical, use of resources.

19 The cost of one opportunity chosen by society is the second-best alternative opportunity which society cannot now enjoy – because it has chosen the first opportunity. To select one opportunity is to reject others.

20 (a) Primary production is the production of goods made available by nature; (b) Secondary production is the production of more sophisticated goods by improving upon primary products in manufacturing industry; (c) Tertiary production is the production of services, either commercial services or personal services.

21 Direct production is production directly for one's own use or to meet the needs of one's immediate family – as in primitive communism. Indirect production is production by specialisation, where goods are produced in return for a monetary reward, which is used to buy a balanced basket of goods and services.

22 (a) Closeness to raw materials; (b) closeness to a source of power; (c) closeness to a means of transport; (d) closeness to a sophisticated labour force; (e) closeness to a market; (f) cheap sites; (g) cheap capital assets; (h) official aid.

19 What is 'opportunity cost', or 'alternative cost'?

20 What are primary, secondary and tertiary production?

21 Distinguish between direct production and indirect production.

22 What factors influence the location of production?

Go over the test again until you are sure of all the answers.

ANSWERS

(See Self-assessment questions on pages 44 and 62.)

1 Wealth is an abundance of utilities; goods and services which are capable of satisfying wants.

2 In a primitive society people specialise in doing the things which they are good at, and then exchange the fruits of their labours directly so that everyone has a balanced basket of goods and services. Thus the best hunters hunt, the best gardeners tend their gardens, the best anglers fish, etc., and exchange of the various outputs takes place directly.

In an advanced society the scale of activities is greater; there is greater division of labour; the end product is greater and needs to be more extensively marketed. Since direct exchanges would be inconvenient the money system prevails. The factor owners who supply land, labour and capital are rewarded with money incomes and then exchange these money incomes for a balanced basket of goods and services, to meet individual or family needs and preferences.

3 In economics 'land' means those resources made available by nature either in the dim and distant past when the elements and compounds found naturally were created in the process of disintegration of some star, or by slow accumulation as a result of natural processes, such as the creation of the chalk cliffs of Dover or of the coal fields, oilfields, sedimentary rocks, etc. 'Land' includes the waters of the seas and lakes and the gases of the atmosphere. Anything provided by nature as a resource endowment which is available for the use of mankind is 'land'.

4 A labour intensive industry is one which requires a lot of labour, whereas a capital intensive industry requires a lot of capital assets which can be supervised by a small labour force. Thus fruit-picking is a labour intensive industry, while oil refining is capital intensive, requiring vast amounts of technological equipment which can be supervised by just a few staff. Generally speaking, as technology improves more and more solutions are found to industrial problems and industry becomes more capital intensive and less labour is required.

5 The function of the Personnel Officer is to find labour in such quantities and of such qualities as are required by the enterprise concerned, so that its activities are never starved of the human resources required. Where a setback in activities calls for a reduction of staff the Personnel Officer has to assist in an orderly divestment of the excess labour through fair redundancy procedures.

6 The principle of massed reserves holds that it is more economical for a large organisation to maintain reserve stocks than a small organisation, since a given reserve will be just as adequate for many outlets as it would be for a few outlets.

7 The law of diminishing returns states 'if the quantity of one factor of production is gradually increased by equal increments from zero and applied to a fixed quantity of the other factors, the resulting successive increments of output will increase for a period (increasing returns), reach an optimum level where the increments of output remain constant, and then diminish again'.

8 The mobility of factors is their ability to move from one opportunity to another. Land is relatively immobile, in that we cannot use it for one purpose without rendering it of little use elsewhere. A corn field is immobilised until harvest time, an orchard is immobilised for between 20 and 50 years, while a quarry immobilises land for a very long time indeed. Some labour is more mobile than others. Young unattached people are mobile, but those with families are less mobile. The more specific skills are the more immobile the person having them is. A deep-sea diver hesitates to take a shore job, etc. Capital assets tend to be specific – a cement kiln is no good to anyone other than a cement manufacturer. A sewing machine is more mobile, and can move from ladies' wear to men's wear to children's wear fairly easily. Liquid capital is very mobile; you can get it anywhere in the world in 30 seconds.

9 Primitive communism is the world of Rousseau's 'noble savage', where the pattern of life is such as to provide only for the genuine needs of natural man, and not for the advanced wants of a sophisticated society. Its chief characteristic is that people work at the things they do best and share the proceeds directly with others in the community.

10 The importance of specialisation is that people choose the work that suits them best, concentrate on acquiring skills and improving work procedures to raise output, and then through the money system draw suitable rewards with which they purchase a balanced basket of goods and services according to their personal needs and preferences.

QUESTIONS ON CHAPTER 2

1 Explain the terms 'primary resources' and 'secondary resources', referring in your answer to any major private sector or public sector industry.

2 Does the existence of economies of scale mean that the market has no place for small firms?

(Courtesy of the Association of Business Executives)

3 What is wealth? How is wealth created? What is the link between money and wealth?

4 Draw up a list of ten primary products and ten secondary products. What is the link between primary goods and secondary goods?.

5 Why is the variety of labour available important to firms in an advanced economy? How do they ensure that labour of the right type is available to the firm at any given time?

6 Discuss the costs and benefits of specialisation and the division of labour from the viewpoints of employers and employees.

7 What sources of capital are available to sole traders wishing to expand their businesses? What are the advantages and disadvantages of each source?

8 Distinguish between fixed capital and money capital, and explain the link between them.

9 What is meant by the term 'the mix of factors'? How may the mix of factors be varied to meet problems in everyday business life?

10 Give ten examples of producer goods likely to be needed in any major industry with which you are familiar. Explain the part played by producer goods in creating wealth.

11 Write short notes (8–10 lines) about each of the following:
  a) Ordinary shares
  b) Self-financing
  c) The principle of massed reserves
  d) Large-scale production

12 What considerations enter into the location of industries? Illustrate your answer as far as possible with examples drawn from the area in which you live.

TIPS FOR STUDENTS: A SPECIMEN ANSWER TO QUESTION 2

The existence of economies of scale does mean that in many industries it will be most worthwhile if the industry is enlarged so that production is achieved at the optimum level and a consequent flood of goods is made available to satisfy consumer demand and raise living standards. However, this does not mean that there is no room for small firms. Small firms have a number of places to fill in the intricate pattern of firms which make up a modern, sophisticated economy. These are:

  a) *Where the total market is small*   There are many markets where total demand is relatively small, and consequently one or two – often very gifted – people are enough to satisfy the demand. Thus the makers of medieval instruments have experienced a boom in recent years and have been very busy, but the mass production of medieval instruments is not likely ever to be required. Many artistic people earn a living with their personal skills, but never become large scale producers. Henry Ford was fascinated by watch mechanisms but turned to motor cars because he couldn't ever envisage a day when everyone would want a watch.

  b) *Where small scale industry acts as the handmaiden of large scale industry*   In sophisticated mass production the main centre of production is fed by many smaller units which may be part of the main organisation. Alternatively it is often more convenient to sub-contract work out to small firms who agree to become suppliers of particular components and may develop specialist skills in particular areas. In this way small firms fill in the gaps in a complex production system, playing their specialist part.

  c) *Where small firms are nodal points in production*   A nodal point is a growth point, where new growth can occur within the production system. Many inventions and experimental techniques would be passed over by large scale industry if it were not for the tenacity and will-power of scientists, inventors and other innovators who insist on pursuing what they believe to be a worthwhile and significant new product. Practically all firms start small and, over a period of years, grow to achieve large scale production using new technologies and expertise.

3 Demand, supply and price

1 'WANTS'

We have already seen, in Chapter 1, that the most basic human condition is 'want'. We all want things from the moment we are born. One of the most fundamental 'wants' is geographical territory, for we are earth-bound creatures and must have somewhere to lay our heads. The immigrant in his doss-house, the migrant worker of the 1930s in his 'Hooverville' (a residence contrived out of a sewer pipe with the side of a packing case at each end to keep out the draught – and sarcastically named after President Hoover), the 'boat-people' stranded on someone else's beach; these are people who have lost, or voluntarily given up, their right to geographical territory. It is of the greatest concern to them that they should achieve the satisfaction of this 'want' above all, and devices such as the 'Nansen Passport', which enables thousands to start new lives, well deserve the Nobel prizes they earn.

After geographical territory we need food, water, clothing, shelter, medical care when we are sick, education if we are ignorant, entertainment when we are bored. There are psychological 'wants' too, such as the need to belong to a 'family' group, the need to be loved, the need for self-fulfilment – but we shall leave these out of the reckoning for the moment. As far as the economy is concerned, it is sufficient at the start to consider only the bare essentials – what psychologists call the 'safety needs' – without which life itself cannot be continued. Even to provide food, clothing, shelter and medical care requires enormous activity.

Having provided these basic needs what happens? Is mankind satisfied? On the contrary: now that he has the strength to lift his head he perceives a more distant horizon. Instead of 'an unrelieved diet of bread and cheese' he becomes an epicure, demanding paté of larks' tongues. In the advanced nations we dine every day on food that has come ten thousand miles to our tables. We abandon home-made beers and 'want' Spanish, Italian and French wines. Our liqueur comes from Curaçao, and our Vodka from Russia. We give up shanks' pony and 'want' motorcycles, private cars, private aeroplanes and – soon – space shuttles. We give up songs round the family fireside for television entertainment in a centrally-heated room. Appetite grows with feeding and there is no end to the things that we 'want'. Eventually even the very biosphere is not sufficient to satisfy our wants. Scientists tell us that if we pursue our present profligate consumption we shall be in grave danger not only of using up the world's resources of many vital minerals, but also of making the earth itself uninhabitable. Fortunately the 'wants' we have are reduced to some extent by our inability to pay for the things we would like to have. We may 'want' a private aeroplane, but most of us cannot – fortunately – 'demand' it. We must move on to consider 'demand'.

2   SOME BASIC IDEAS ABOUT DEMAND

The demand for a particular good or service is the amount of it that will be bought by consumers at a given price in a given period of time. There is no such thing as the demand for motorcars *per se*; we can only discuss the demand for motorcars at a certain price level. If cars are offered for nothing – a free good like air – everyone will demand a Rolls-Royce. If they are offered at a price of £1m each the roads will be much safer for pedestrians, for only a very few people will 'demand' one.

'Choice' and 'demand'

The fact is that each individual has only a certain income available to spend on the 'basket' of resources which his family requires. There are few very rich these days who can afford everything they want, and the vast majority of us have to make choices between the various goods and services. Parents of young families frequently give up even quite necessary things in order that the children shall have some treat which otherwise would be impossible. A number of very important economic ideas spring from the need to make choices. They are listed and explained below.

a) **'Choice' is inevitable in economics**   One celebrated economist, Lord Robbins, defined economics as 'the science which studies human behaviour as a relationship between "ends" and scarce "means" which have alternative uses'. It is an enduring definition, which fits countless situations in real life. We cannot have everything our hearts desire, for the 'ends' we should desire to achieve are countless, while the 'means' to achieve those ends are rather limited. Hitler prescribed 'Guns, not butter' for the German people – but it proved to be a poor choice. Stalin prescribed heavy industrial development rather than consumer-orientated industry for the Soviet state. It was a better choice than 'Guns, not butter', but was it the best choice? That we shall never know. This leads us to (b) below.

b) **'Alternative cost' or 'opportunity cost'**   (see also page 52–3) When we make a choice, we decide to prefer one thing rather than another, or all the others. If I decide to have sardines on toast for tea I reject baked beans on toast (my second choice) and all other possible items I could have chosen. If a nation decides to develop heavy industry it rejects light industry and the products it might have turned out. We cannot have guns *and* butter. The factors of production put to work in armaments factories cannot at the same time work in the dairy industry. If we change our minds after training a host of fitters, turners, sheet metal workers, etc., we cannot switch them over very easily to animal husbandry, or to make butter or any other similar goods.

   c) **Scales of preferences.**   Everyone has an individual scale of preferences, a ladder-like arrangement of things in one's own mind with the most preferred items towards the top of the scale. Some things never climb up the scale higher than the first few rungs, for they are constantly leapfrogged by other unexpected items which must take precedence. Every parent can think of things, often quite essential things, which he or she has been meaning to buy for years, but repeatedly has to reject for other items which the children need if they are to make the progress the parent wishes them to make.

   What is it that decides the position of an item on a consumer's scale of preferences? The answer is that preferences are based upon the consumers' view of the *utility* of a particular good. **Utility is the ability to satisfy wants.** It is a subjective concept, which is to say that each individual must judge it for himself, and each individual's judgment will depend upon his circumstances at the time. Thus a housewife who needs bread for her family will go shopping with bread high on her list of priorities. On the way to the shop suppose she meets a friend who tells her that a bakers' strike is to start the next day. The utility of bread leaps up to the very top of her list and she may decide to buy ten loaves to put in the deep-freeze. On returning home she switches on the radio to hear that the threatened bread strike has been called off – the problem has been solved by a meeting of the master bakers and the union. At this moment the housewife's mother calls in, and is immediately given two loaves – the utility of bread has declined and freezer space has risen in utility.

   d) **Marginal utility and total utility**   Developing our ideas about utility a little more, we must note the term 'marginal utility'. In economics the word 'margin' is important. It refers to the 'edge' of any activity. Thus marginal cost is the cost of one further unit, marginal product is the last unit of product to be turned out, and the marginal firm is the last firm to join an expanding industry, or the next firm to leave a contracting industry. It is always at 'the margin' that decisions are made. Shall we make another one or not? Shall we buy one, or two, or three?

   Marginal utility is the utility of one unit of a good or service. You may say 'How can we value it – for there is no unit of utility?' We do in fact have to value it in imaginary 'units of satisfaction', or 'units of utility' perhaps. Even if this is a little imprecise, it is real enough. Take the housewife buying bread. Her usual daily supply is two loaves, and each of these loaves will have great utility but the first loaf more than the second. Suppose the baker is a good salesman and persuades her to buy a third loaf. This will have less utility than either of the first two. If he presses a fourth loaf upon her she may take it, but all this bread is beginning to be a nuisance. By the time she gets to the fifth loaf she is wondering how she will ever get them home and what is the point anyway.

Diminishing marginal utility sets in as soon as the first loaf is bought; each extra loaf is valued less and less. Another loaf, like the last straw that breaks the camel's back, may have negative utility, and be a cause of dissatisfaction.

We may say then that diminishing marginal utility sets in very soon after we have purchased a normal supply. By contrast, the total utility of all the supply available continues to increase, but the increase is smaller for every loaf until it reaches a maximum at the point where marginal utility reaches zero. This is illustrated graphically in Fig. 3.1.

e) **Choosing between products** Before leaving 'utility' to discuss 'demand', let us note the importance of the concept historically. Early economists had great difficulty in explaining value. At what price things *should* be exchanged seemed very different from the prices at which they *were* exchanged. Bread is cheap, yet it is essential to life. Diamond tiaras are expensive, yet they are manifestly unnecessary, for few of us have one. The 'marginal utility' school of Economics resolved this apparent contradiction by introducing a psychological element into decision-making. Why did people choose the things they did choose? What was the true basis of demand?

The facts are that the housewife has only so much money to spend on her

Fig. 3.1 *Marginal utility and total utility*

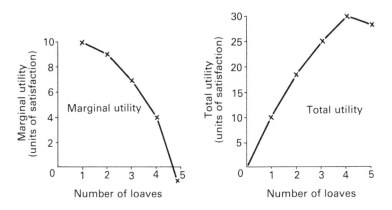

Notes

1 Marginal utility decreases as the quantity purchased increases. The second loaf yields less satisfaction than the first, and the third less than the second. The fifth loaf is too heavy to carry home easily, and would go stale before *this* family could eat it. It has negative marginal utility as far as the period of time under consideration is concerned.

2 Total utility rises each time a loaf is purchased, but the curve begins to flatten out as smaller increases of the total utility are experienced with successive loaves. When marginal utility becomes negative total utility begins to decline.

3 Note that the period of time under consideration is important. If a housewife has a large freezer, and can deep-freeze the bread to arrest deterioration, marginal utility will not decline so rapidly.

family's needs, and must balance the various purchases she makes against the satisfactions to be derived from them. A basic supply of some purchases will be almost obligatory, such as bread, milk, sugar and tea (in the UK). She will be seen pressing into the counters at any crowded supermarket to purchase her needs. Once these basic needs are met a further supply will have less utility.

Other things are a matter of choice from the very beginning. Is it better to buy a jar of strawberry jam or a tin of syrup, a bag of flour or a box of Mr Kipling's cakes. *When she is buying at the margin, the housewife is making considered choices which weigh the marginal utility to her of the various products against their respective prices.*

This process is illustrated in Fig. 3.2 and described in the notes below it. Marginal utility resolved the difficulty in trying to decide what a good was worth. A good was worth what each individual in the circumstances thought it was worth. King Richard III shouted 'A horse, a horse, my kingdom for a horse!' Evidently the marginal utility of the animal to him was high at this point.

Fig. 3.2 *Maximising satisfaction by equating marginal utilities*

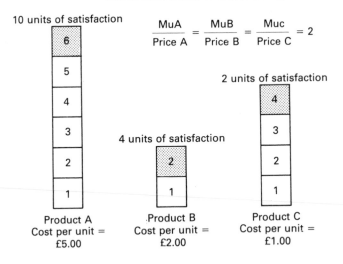

The marginal utility (mu) of the last unit purchased in each case is given (measured in units of satisfaction). Earlier units would of course be higher in value.

$$\frac{MuA}{Price\ A} = \frac{MuB}{Price\ B} = \frac{Muc}{Price\ C} = 2$$

10 units of satisfaction

Product A
Cost per unit =
£5.00

4 units of satisfaction

Product B
Cost per unit =
£2.00

2 units of satisfaction

Product C
Cost per unit =
£1.00

Notes
1   The calculations show that the marginal utilities of the last unit purchased of each commodity are equal. The question is could the housewife have increased her satisfaction by buying a different basket of goods?
2   Imagine that she decided not to have the fourth unit of Product C. This will release £1.00 of money for other goods, and involve the sacrifice of 2 units of satisfaction.
3   The £1.00, if spent on Product B, buys half a unit at £2.00 each.
4   As the marginal unit of Product B is only valued at 4 units of satisfaction, a further unit will have less than 4 units of satisfaction – say 3 units of satisfaction. The housewife will therefore not increase her satisfaction by changing to Product B, since ½ a unit of B will only yield 1½ units of satisfaction.

5   Similarly, if the £1.00 is spent on Product A it will buy one fifth of a unit, but the satisfaction derived from this more marginal purchase will be less than the 2 units of satisfaction to be derived from one fifth of the marginal unit shown in the diagram. She will therefore achieve greater satisfaction by staying with Product C.

6   Of course the busy housewife may not be aware of the complicated calculations she is doing in her head in the split second she is making her decisions. The slightest thing may change the equations – a grimace from the eldest child at the thought of porridge for breakfast may cause her to take cornflakes instead. Even the baby's preference for a red packet instead of a white one may swing the balance. But – and businessmen should note this – the price enters into every calculation. If the price is lower the quantity demanded will be greater, for the marginal utility *relative to price* is the basis of the whole series of calculations.

f)   **The demand for a free good**   If the demand for a good is eventually choked off at the point where its marginal utility becomes negative, what shall we say about the demand for a free good? Some goods are free, like the air, and others are almost free. Water can be used in almost any quantity in the UK for a payment which is so small that it is almost negligible (though that does not stop complaints about the water rates). The point is that where a good is free the consumption of the good will be increased until its marginal utility falls to zero. Since it does not represent any sacrifice of other goods, because extra consumption is free, the marginal utility only falls to zero when further supplies represent a positive embarrassment to the consumer. Such a point may be long delayed. Thus the parent who leaves the garden sprinkler running all day long in the summer so that the children can cool themselves under it is wasting a great deal of water for a very, very small extra satisfaction. If a decision is made to meter the water used by hosepipes and charge for every gallon used they will all be turned off as soon as the flower beds have had

Fig. 3.3 *The marginal utility of a 'free' good*

Quantity of free goods demanded

Notes
1   The first few units of the good give a great deal of satisfaction.
2   The marginal utility quickly falls away to a very low figure, but it only cuts the x axis when any further supply would be a positive embarrassment.
3   Dissatisfaction does not arise so soon, for no sacrifice is involved. This causes a misuse of resources, which would be more economically employed elsewhere.

enough to keep them alive for 24 hours. If the children want to get cool let them lie in the shade. In the early days of the National Health Service in the UK prescriptions were free, and families accumulated whole cupboards full of drugs as a result. The cost of this free service was such that eventually a charge had to be imposed, except for certain types of patient. The result was a considerable reduction in the number of prescriptions issued, and the saving of millions of pounds to the National Health Service. Fig. 3.3 shows the marginal utility of a free good.

g) **Effective demand** It is time to return to our main subject again: demand. What is the demand for any particular product? It is not the quantity which people 'want', for that is infinitely great. It is the quantity that people are prepared to pay for at a particular price. To an economist demand is always **effective demand**; the desire to buy must be reinforced by the ability to pay. We would expect then to find that if the price of a good is high the quantity demanded would be small, while if the price is low the quantity demanded would be large. There is no such thing as the demand for a good divorced from its price. We can only make firm statements about the likely demand once we know how much the supplier is likely to ask for it. Demand therefore is not a quantity, but a schedule of quantities showing how much will be demanded at each price.

3 DEMAND SCHEDULES AND DEMAND CURVES

The total demand for any good or service is based upon the demand of individual consumers for that good or service. If a million housewives every day pick up a tin of beans and say 'I'll have one of these', demand will be great. But those million housewives do not just have a demand for a tin of beans, they have a demand schedule for beans stored away in their heads. If tins of beans are the normal price each may buy a tin. If beans are on 'special offer' a housewife may buy two tins. If she has the storage space she may buy a dozen tins if the offer is especially favourable. That will reduce the marginal utility of an extra tin of beans so low in her mind that for weeks she will not demand any, especially if the price reverts to normal.

Individual demand schedules and curves

We are about to consider the demand schedules of one or two individuals. It is usual to compare the quantity demanded with the price of the good under discussion, and to draw up a schedule showing how the quantity demanded changes. A schedule is simply a list. It is helpful if this schedule is presented also in graphical form. Graphs have certain advantages over lists of figures, in that we can see from the diagram how the demand reacts to changes in price. This is called the 'trend', and we can continue the line in the diagram to predict what the demand will be at higher or lower prices – though of course it does not follow that these predictions will necessarily be true. They may only be more probable than sheer guesswork about what the demand would be.

When attempting to analyse economic situations it is usual to choose a particular aspect and consider it in isolation. Thus we may examine the effect of price on demand, and to do so select different prices from high to low and consider the demand at each level in a given period. During such an examination it is assumed that other influences that are at work do not change. Thus it is assumed that the influence of family tastes and preferences does not alter during the analysis. We have already said that the Latin phrase *ceteris paribus* (other things being equal) is used to describe this sort of situation where it is assumed that only one influence under examination is changing.

Fig. 3.4 shows the individual demand schedule for tomatoes of one consumer, Mrs Bell. It also shows the same information in graphical form. The chief points are explained in the notes below.

Clearly Mrs Bell's demand schedule represents the tastes and preferences of her own family. Had her circumstances been different – for example, if she

Fig. 3.4 *Mrs Bell's demand schedule and demand curve for tomatoes*

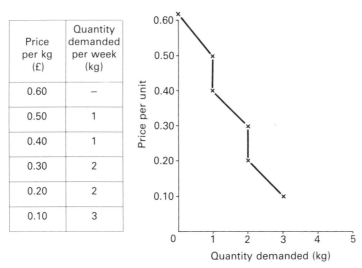

Price per kg (£)	Quantity demanded per week (kg)
0.60	–
0.50	1
0.40	1
0.30	2
0.20	2
0.10	3

Notes

1 When tomatoes are expensive Mrs Bell limits the quantity she demands. She does not buy any if the price is 0.60 since other items are more attractive when tomatoes are this expensive. If the price is 0.50 per kg she buys 1 kg, and does not increase it even when the price falls to 0.40 per kg.

2 As the price falls she increases her family's consumption of tomatoes, as shown in the schedule.

3 When displayed graphically this information gives us a graph which already illustrates the normal property of a demand curve – that it slopes downwards from left to right. When the price of a good is high the quantity demanded is small, and the points plotted on the graph are close to the vertical axis. As the price falls to lower levels the quantity demanded increases and consequently the points plotted are further from the vertical axis.

4 The rather jerky motion of the graph reflects the fact that this diagram illustrates the demand of an individual family, and that tomatoes can only be purchased in kilos. With a large number of families buying the product the graph would be smoother, and the quantities much greater.

had 15 children to feed – the quantities of tomatoes required might have been greatly increased. By contrast, she might have had to do without tomatoes at all and concentrate her resources on a staple diet of bread and margarine. Such goods are known as **inferior goods** and the demand for them behaves in an unusual way. This is explained later in this chapter. Meanwhile let us consider the demand schedules of four more consumers, and draw them on the same graph. Consider Fig. 3.5.

Fig. 3.5 *More individual demand schedules and demand curves*

Price per kg	Quantity demanded per week			
	Mrs Smith	Mrs Gupta	Mrs Hassan	Mrs White
0.60	2	1	–	–
0.50	2	1	–	–
0.40	3	1	–	–
0.30	4	2	1	–
0.20	5	3	1	–
0.10	10	10	2	–

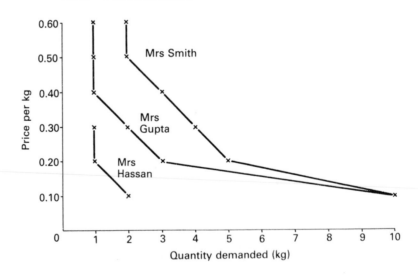

Notes
1   Mrs Smith appears to be quite well-to-do. She is able to afford tomatoes even when they are expensive. She buys a great many when they are cheap. Perhaps she has a freezer, or is an expert on the making of home-made chutney.
2   Mrs Gupta buys less tomatoes when they are expensive, but she also seems to preserve them in some way when they are very cheap.
3   Mrs Hassan may have a low income or perhaps her family does not like tomatoes. She only buys tomatoes in small quantities when they are cheap. Tomatoes do not appear to have much utility for Mrs Hassan.

4 Mrs White never buys tomatoes. Perhaps it is against her religion; or the family is allergic to them; or she is desperately poor. Perhaps she just does not like tomatoes.

5 When presented graphically the three demand curves (Mrs White is not demanding at all) show the usual shape of demand curves; they slope down towards the right, as explained in the notes to Fig. 3.4

Composite demand schedules and curves

Clearly, the entrepreneur who is considering producing a good, and is wondering what the demand for his product will be, is not able to take much notice of individual consumers like Mrs Bell, Mrs Smith, etc. He is interested in the total demand that is likely to arise when the demands of all these individuals are put together into a composite demand schedule. The demand for tomatoes will run into thousands of tonnes if we add together the demands of millions of housewives. When a composite demand schedule is built up and plotted on a graph so that we can see the demand picture clearly, we have something like the state of affairs shown in Fig. 3.6.

We still find, as explained in the notes to Fig. 3.6, that the quantity demanded increases as the price falls and that the demand curve slopes downwards from high on the left to low on the right. This general rule is

Fig. 3.6 *A composite demand schedule for tomatoes, and its demand curve*

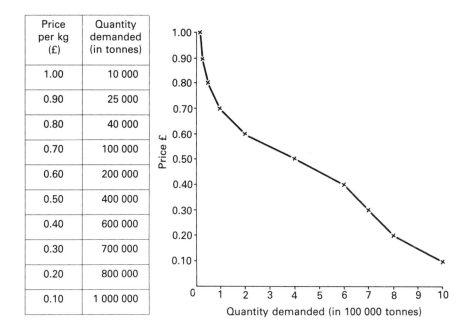

Price per kg (£)	Quantity demanded (in tonnes)
1.00	10 000
0.90	25 000
0.80	40 000
0.70	100 000
0.60	200 000
0.50	400 000
0.40	600 000
0.30	700 000
0.20	800 000
0.10	1 000 000

Notes

1 As the price of tomatoes falls the quantity demanded increases.

2 The quantity demanded is relatively low when the price is very high, but as it falls it brings the price of tomatoes within reach of most consumers' pockets, and the quantity demanded grows very rapidly.

3 The full importance of this diagram is made clear later in this chapter (see Fig. 3.17).

recognised in economics as the First Law of Demand and Supply. The laws of demand and supply are of great importance, because they are part of that section of economics known as **price theory**.

> The first law of demand and supply states that when the price of a commodity falls the quantity that is demanded will be increased.

The general demand curve

In economic theory we often wish to discuss demand in general terms, without relation to any particular commodity or service. What we are usually interested in doing is establishing in our own minds a clear general theory of demand, as part of a general theory of demand, supply and price.

We find it helpful in this type of general discussion to use a general demand curve, which conforms roughly to the First Law of Demand and Supply. Such a general demand curve is shown in Fig. 3.7. The vertical axis is labelled 'price' and the horizontal axis is labelled 'quantity', but it is not usual to put in details of the units being used. Prices must obviously be in some sort of money units, and quantity must be measured somehow, in kilograms, tonnes, units of electricity perhaps, or any other measuring unit.

Fig. 3.7 *The general demand curve*

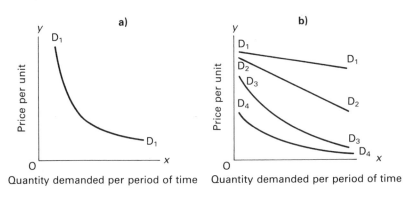

Notes

1 In Fig. 3.7 (a) we have the shape of a general demand curve, obeying the First Law of Demand and Supply.

2 In Fig. 3.7 (b) we have a number of different general demand curves such as economists might use to discuss particular aspects of a demand situation. There are millions of possible demand curves, but they must all (except for a few special cases – see Fig. 3.10) obey the First Law of Demand and Supply.

The reader must form a really clear idea of what the general demand curve looks like and what it means. It is usually labelled DD at each end of the curve. We might draw it in all sorts of ways to illustrate the argument we are developing, and a few examples are given in Fig. 3.7 just to illustrate some of the millions of possibilities. One point to note here is that even a straight line is spoken of as a curve, and in many of our discussions we do use straight lines because we are imagining a very short section of an actual demand curve, which we have magnified to show more clearly what is happening over that range of the curve.

The demand curve is really an endless series of points. It has no real meaning at all until we actually select a point and relate it to the reference lines Ox and Oy. For example the point R on the general demand curve shown in Fig. 3.8 means that when the price of this particular good is P_1 units of money, the amount demanded will be Q_1 units of the good. As with all graphs, the point R has no meaning except when it is referred to the two axes by dropping perpendiculars on to them. The point S means that at the price of P_2 units of money, the quantity demanded will be Q_2 units, and so on. Clearly Q_2 is a greater quantity of the good than Q_1, being further from the origin O, while the price P_2 is less than the price P_1, being closer to the origin O. The reader should now answer the following questions:

1 What can I say about the quantity demanded for this commodity at the point T on the demand curve – in relation to what price?
2 What can I say about the quantity demanded for this commodity at the point U on the demand curve and in relation to what price?

Fig. 3.8 *Extensions and contractions of the quantity demanded with changes in price*

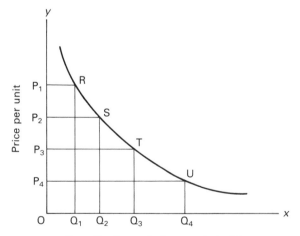

Quantity demanded per period of time

Notes
1 At R on the demand curve the price is P_1 and a quantity Q_1 will be demanded.
2 At S the price has fallen to P_2 and the quantity demanded *extends* to Q_2.
3 As the price falls further to P_3 and then P_4 the quantity demanded extends further, to Q_3 and Q_4.
4 If the price then rose from P_4 to P_3 the demand would *contract* again, to Q_3.
5 These alterations in demand are called **extensions** and **contractions** of the quantity demanded, not *changes* (i.e. increases or decreases) in demand. For a change in demand it is necessary to move to a completely different demand curve (see Fig. 3.9).

A further important point about demand curves is that they represent the state of demand at a given time relative to a range of prices. If the price is P_1 the quantity demanded will be Q_1, but if the price falls to P_2 the quantity demanded will be Q_2. So if the quantity demanded moves from Q_1 to Q_2 because the price has fallen, this is not a *change* of demand. We know already that a reduction in price to P_2 would alter the demand, causing it to *extend* to Q_2. Similarly, we know that if the price rises to P_1 again the demand will *contract* back to Q_1.

We therefore talk about **extensions** and **contractions** of demand as we move from one point on a demand curve to another point on the same curve. A **change, or shift, of demand** is something quite different, and involves moving to a completely new demand curve. This might be caused by a change in one of the other **conditions of demand**.

The conditions of demand

The word 'conditions' is used here in its legal form, to mean the things that decide or determine what demand will be. The chief conditions of demand are as follows:

1 The price of the good under discussion.
2 The price of other goods.
3 The income of households.
4 The tastes of the household.

THE PRICE OF THE GOOD OR SERVICE

The most important influence on the quantity of any good or service which is demanded is the price of the article or service. Since the money payable represents all other goods, the price to be paid enables the consumer to compare the utility of the good in question with the utility of all other goods. The severity of the decisions to be made is reduced in real life by the existence of a wide range of 'products' in some fields. For example, while cheese is rarely bought second-hand, this is not true of caravans. Many people purchase durable consumer goods at second-hand, and by a series of trade-ins over many years eventually reach the point where they can buy the new article. One gipsy reported by the police to be living in a luxury mobile home pointed out to the Court that it had been a lifetime's work to reach his present position, and did not really represent affluence. His demand for the new article had been postponed many times by the high price. The influence of price on the demand for a good or service is rather different from the other conditions of demand, and is referred to again at the end of this section.

THE PRICE OF OTHER GOODS OR SERVICES

One feature of the mixed economy is the rich variety of goods and services available to consumers. Most of these products are in competition with one another. The poor musician may postpone his consumption of bread to save up for a new clarinet although at first sight one would not imagine them to be competing goods. Where goods are a close **substitute** for one another, like oranges and tangerines, the competitive nature of the goods is more obvious, and the low price of the tangerines will seriously affect the demand for oranges, while cheap oranges will dispose the housewife to reject tangerines.

Some goods are linked together, like bread and butter or lettuces, tomatoes and radishes. These are called **complementary goods**. The housewife who is proposing to make a salad but finds tomatoes very expensive may decide against the idea and consequently reject lettuces and radishes as well, even though they are cheap. Similarly, a motorcycle is useless without petrol. They are said to be in **joint demand** and the motorcyclist is unlikely to refuse to buy petrol even if the price has risen. These non-price influences run counter to the general conclusion of this section, which is that if other goods and services are cheap they may reduce the demand for a highly-priced good, while if other goods and services are expensive they will lead consumers to increase their demands for a cheap good or service.

INCOME OF THE HOUSEHOLD

Family income plays a large part in determining the demand for goods. Its chief effect perhaps is to predetermine the priceband within which the housewife usually buys. The system of price-lining adopted by many fashion houses reflects this feature although other considerations also enter into it. Under the price-lining system the shop selects three ranges of prices – say, £12.99, £15.99 and £19.99. The poor housewife will come into the shop to look only at the £12.99 range, though for a special occasion such as birthdays or at Christmas time, or on a rare impulse, she may buy in the next range up. A more prosperous housewife will visit the shop for the £15.99 range, but will occasionally buy in the lower range and on special occasions will move up into the top range. The prosperous woman will sweep into the section of the shop where the top-range goods are displayed but on special occasions will phone her couturier.

Household income rules out many items for normal families, but the various sytems of budgeting for large capital items, such as mortgages, rolling credit systems, hire purchase, etc., have raised the demand for housing and durable consumer goods to levels undreamed of by our ancestors.

The affluence of an economy is a crucial factor affecting household income. If the total purchasing power of a nation is great the demand for goods and services will be strong. It will be even stronger if the spread of income throughout the population is even. Thus a paternalistic economy, where a few rich families own a large proportion of the total wealth, will not demand nearly as many staple products of a manufacturing economy as a neighbouring economy where a more egalitarian society spreads the wealth down to all the strata of society.

Lower-income groups display a very high **propensity to consume**; high-income groups have a higher **propensity to save**. This does not mean of course that their standard of living is lower than that of the lower income group. A man earning £4000 per year may spend it all – a 100 per cent propensity to consume. Another man earning £10 000 per year may spend £8000 of it. His consumption of £8000 is twice as great as the poor man's consumption, but his propensity to consume is only 80 per cent. It follows that where a broad system of equality exists within a society household incomes will be evenly distributed and demand for many goods and services will tend to be strong. Where the social system is one of a privileged few and an under-privileged majority the demand for many products will be reduced, but the demand for luxuries may be increased to serve the privileged in their pursuit of sumptuous living.

THE TASTES OF THE HOUSEHOLD

Households vary in size and each member of the family has his or her own tastes and preferences. These may be based on very ancient origins, which are quite insusceptible to explanation. The average citizen of the UK is of mixed descent, with the blood of Romans, British, Saxons, Norsemen, etc., mingled in his veins. More recent immigration is producing Afro-Asian strains in the cultural heritage. When time has passed all that is left of originally distinct races is a preference of individuals for one type of food or another, or preference for a particular form of recreation, entertainment, type of employment, etc.

Fig. 3.9 *A change in demand (to a new demand curve)*

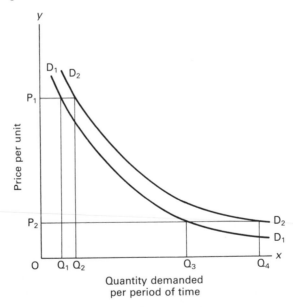

Notes

1   A change in demand, caused perhaps by a change of taste or fashion, has led to a completely new demand curve for the product. More of the product is being demanded at *every* price in the range. The curve D_2D_2 is further from the origin at every price than the D_1D_1 curve.

2   At the price P_1 the quantity demanded has changed from Q_1 to Q_2 and at the price P_2 the quantity demanded has changed from Q_3 to Q_4.

Superimposed upon these ancient traits other patterns of behaviour and choice may be observed influencing our selection of goods and services. The structure of a population affects household tastes. Thus the demand for perambulators is stronger when there is a bulge in the birthrate, which then leads in due course to a demand for nursery furniture, primary readers, etc., until 70 years later the demand for crematorium services increases. Religious, moral, ethical and psychological influences are at work, while the commercial and social pressures exerted upon us in everyday life may similarly modify the things that we demand. So we may select goods because they are fashionable, or acceptable to our peers, while other goods which are unfashionable, or less well promoted by advertising, will not be demanded. The tastes of the household are a prime consideration in determining the utility of goods.

To return to the point made earlier, a change in any of the last three of these conditions of demand will produce a shift in the demand curve. A change or shift of demand cannot be caused by a change in price of the commodity which is under discussion; such a change only produces an extension, or contraction, of demand. A change to a new demand curve is illustrated in Fig. 3.9.

4 REGRESSIVE DEMAND CURVES

Sometimes demand reacts differently from what one would expect if the first law of demand and supply were always true. The law, which says that the demand for a good usually extends as the price falls, is not always obeyed. We expect demand to *contract* as price rises, but in some cases we find that it *extends*. We expect demand to extend as price falls and the good gets cheaper but instead demand *contracts*. This means that we get *regressive* demand curves; demand curves which turn back upon themselves. Regression may take place at either end of the curve; at the top, where prices are high, or at the bottom, where prices are low. Explanations for these two types of regression are as follows:

1 Regression at the top of the curve

If a demand curve is regressive when prices are high, it means that instead of the high price choking off the demand it causes an extension of the quantity demanded. The actual situation is explained in the notes below Fig. 3.10.

There are several possible explanations. One is the behaviour associated with fashionable articles such as costume jewellery. Every retailer of these goods knows that they sell best when they are highly priced and not when they are cheap. A young man buying his sweetheart a piece of costume jewellery will not look at something with a low price. A brooch costing £0.25 to make will yield a good profit if sold at £0.50, but the young man will not buy it. He would lose face if the girl found out how cheap it was. The same brooch priced at £5.00 makes a 'worth-while' gift, and sales rise. So much for 'value'. No wonder early economists found 'value' a difficult concept to explain! Such goods are called **goods of ostentation**.

A second example of regressive demand at the top of the demand curve is the demand for goods which are expected to become scarce. If expectations lead that special type of entrepreneur called a **middleman** to anticipate that goods will become scarce, he will be keen to buy them even though the price is high. The rising price leads to even fiercer competition to obtain the good, and on occasions a mad scramble develops for the product. Similar behaviour is seen by consumers: in a tanker drivers' strike motorists rush to fill their tanks even though forecourt prices have been raised.

2   Regression at the bottom of the curve

If a demand curve is regressive at the bottom, where prices are low, it means that instead of a further reduction in price leading to an increased demand, as one would expect, it leads instead to a reduced demand for the good. Again there are several explanations. As we might expect, they are the reverse of those referred to above. If a good is an 'inferior good', one that is rejected because of its cheapness, then the demand as price falls will be regressive. Very often such a rejection of cheap goods is illogical. The French housewife, at a time when cabbages are in prime condition and very cheap, buys cabbage as

Fig. 3.10 *Regressive demand curves:* (a) *at the top of the curve where prices are high;* (b) *at the bottom of the curve where prices are low.*

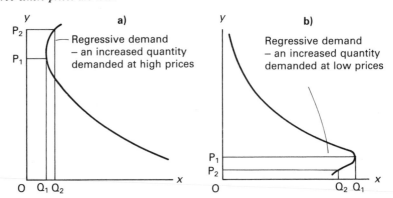

Notes
1   In Fig. 3.10(a) at a price P_1 the quantity of goods demanded is low, Q_1.
2   When prices rise further, to P_2, we would expect the quantity demanded to fall, and Q_2 would be even closer to the origin than Q_1. Instead the quantity demanded increases, giving a regressive demand curve.
3   Examples of this type of regressive demand, which are explained in the text, are 'goods of ostentation' and goods which are expected to become scarce.
4   In Fig. 3.10(b) the regression is at the bottom end of the curve. Here, at a price of P_1 the quantity demanded is very large, Q_1. We would expect that as price falls even lower, to P_2, that the quantity demanded would extend still further. Instead the quantity demanded falls away, and Q_2 is closer to the origin than Q_1.
5   Examples of this type of regressive demand, which are explained in the text, are the demand for inferior goods and the demand for goods expected to become cheaper.

the obvious vegetable to accompany her roast. The British housewife frequently acts illogically. When cabbages are cheap and plentiful she will buy cauliflower, frozen Brussels sprouts or exotic green peppers. She tends to buy cabbages when they are dear and in poor condition.

Expectations can cause regression at the lower end of a demand curve. For example, if goods are expected to become cheaper, middlemen will often hold off from buying in expectation of being able to buy them even cheaper. Thus 'bears' on the Stock Exchange are speculators who expect prices to fall, and therefore sell shares even when prices are low, because they hope to buy back again even lower, and thus make a profit. The quantity demanded is reduced when price is low, causing prices to fall even lower, and 'the bottom falls out of the market' as the amount demanded slumps.

A third example of regressive demand is the special case of 'Giffen goods'. Sir Robert Giffen (1837–1910), a celebrated Victorian economist and statistician, published a study of the incomes of working people in the mid-nineteenth century. He was the first to draw attention to the behaviour of the demand for a special type of 'inferior goods', now often called 'Giffen goods' in his memory. Giffen goods were such goods as potatoes and bread, which formed the staple diet of the very poor in the mid-nineteenth century, as they do today. He described a paradox about the demand for these goods: when they were expensive the quantity demanded was large, but when they were cheap the quantity demanded was smaller. Thus the Irish peasant, when potatoes were expensive, was forced by their high price to live on a diet of potatoes only, but when potatoes were cheap their falling price enabled him to buy other things and thus improve the variety of his diet. In hard times when corn was dear the English labourer was reduced to a 'bare diet of bread and cheese'. When corn was cheap, he reduced his consumption of bread and ate more meat and fish, because the reduction in the price of corn gave him a larger real income, which he could spend on something other than inferior goods. The explanation lies in the 'income-effect' of changing prices. When goods change in price they effectively change the income of consumers. This change in real incomes may lead to a shift in demand from inferior goods to other goods.

SELF-ASSESSMENT QUESTIONS

1 Define demand.

2 Explain the link between 'demand' and 'utility'.

3 Explain the 'general demand curve'.

4 Distinguish between an extension of demand and a change in demand.

5 What is a regressive demand curve?

5   SATISFYING DEMAND BY SUPPLY

Just because a thing is 'wanted' does not mean it will actually be supplied by any entrepreneur, but if 'want' becomes 'effective demand' then almost certainly some enterprising individual will step out of the crowd and start to supply it.

When Henry Ford was a child he was fascinated by clock mechanisms and chains of gears. He used to 'play hookey' from school, to repair clocks and watches. He seriously thought of manufacturing watches but felt that the mass of the population would never buy them. What they needed, especially in the 'big country' of the prairies, was a cheap and efficient form of personal transport. For this, thought Ford, there really would be a large effective demand: people would put their hands deep into their pockets for personal transport. At his death Ford's fortune was $748m, so it seems that he was right.

To be effective, demand must be such that at the market price the entrepreneur can make a reasonable level of profit. Just how market price is decided is explained later in this chapter. Here we must note that just as utility is the basis of demand, the **prospect of profitability** is the basis of supply.

Supply may be defined as the quantity of a good or service which entrepreneurs are prepared to make available at a given price in a given period of time. Clearly an entrepreneur will not be prepared to supply if the price of the final product is so low that he cannot even recover his expenses. Production requires that the factors of production – land, labour and capital – are combined. If the factors of production are to be used they must be rewarded: land will earn its rent, labour its wages and capital must earn its interest. The final price must be such that these rewards to factors can be earned, and a little extra for profit. Unless he has these prospects of profitability the entrepreneur will not proceed.

As with demand, price is crucial to the discussion of supply. There is no such thing as the supply of motorcars *per se*. It is the supply at a price, e.g. £10 000 or £15 000, which can be estimated and considered.

In a competitive market some suppliers may have highly efficient systems of work and unit costs will consequently be low. Such low-cost suppliers will be able to bring in supplies of goods at lower prices than other suppliers. Other firms may be high-cost firms. Perhaps they are small-scale firms, or are less well situated than their rivals so that they have to meet extra transport costs. Perhaps they are less competitive because they are using out-of-date machinery. Such firms will only bring in supplies when demand is so strong that price rises. When the price goes up they are attracted into the market because they can now cover their costs and make a profit.

It should be noted that many large-scale manufacturers are not producing in a competitive market at all, but have some degree of monopoly in their activities. Such firms are influenced rather differently by the demand in the market, which they can manipulate to some extent. A discussion of such firms must be left until later.

When studying demand we noticed that there were certain influences at work which affected the demand for a particular 'good' or 'service', and we called these the *conditions of demand*. In the same way there are certain factors at work which condition the supply that comes on to the market. The chief **conditions of supply** are the costs of production and the price which consumers are prepared to pay; but supply is also influenced by natural events, by political factors and by technological advances which influence systems of work.

6   THE CONDITIONS OF SUPPLY

The costs of production

A full study of the costs of production takes account of the fixed costs and the variable costs, and requires some knowledge of accountancy. Briefly we can say:

1   *Fixed costs* are the costs of building and equipping a factory or an industrial plant. They can be enormous; millions of pounds. To prevent the figures being too large, let us imagine a small concern whose **fixed costs** (often called the capital costs because we are creating fixed assets with the capital provided by the entrepreneur) are £50 000.
2   Suppose we now produce one garden spade and the materials used and labour involved cost £4. These are the **variable costs** because they vary with output – if we only make one spade we only need one handle and one metal spade. The cost of this spade is £50 004.
3   Suppose we now produce another spade. The variable costs are now £8 and each spade costs half of £50 008 = £25 004. Note that as we increase output the capital cost element in each spade is reduced. The fixed costs are shared out equally over the output, but the variable costs are the same for each unit of output.
4   If we increase ouptut to 50 000 spades we shall incur variable costs of £4 per spade – £200 000. Total costs are now:

$$\text{Fixed costs} \quad + \quad \text{Variable costs} \quad = \quad \text{Total costs}$$
$$\text{£50 000} \quad + \quad \text{£200 000} \quad = \quad \text{£250 000}$$

$$\text{The cost per spade is now} \quad \frac{\text{£250 000}}{50\ 000} \quad = \quad \text{£5}$$

The cost per spade is now made up of £4 materials and labour and only £1 fixed costs.

So much for the accounting aspect of costs. From the economic viewpoint when we say that the costs of production are one of the conditions of supply we mean that if the costs rise the entrepreneur's profit margins will be reduced and he/she will cut back on production and reduce supply – unless of course the price to the consumer can be raised to keep the profit margin at an appropriate level.

Developing the idea of fixed costs just a little further than in **1** (on page 89), we must say that apart from the actual building and plant there are the administrative costs of running the building and plant, which make a further element of fixed costs which have to be shared out over the units of product and recovered in the sale price to the consumer.

Finally, since a reasonable profit margin is essential if production is to continue economists regard **normal profit** as a cost of production. If we do not recover a normal profit the enterprise will close down, for there is no incentive to the entrepreneur to show enterprise. In diagrammatic form we could therefore show costs as shown in Fig. 3.11.

Fig. 3.11 *The costs of production*

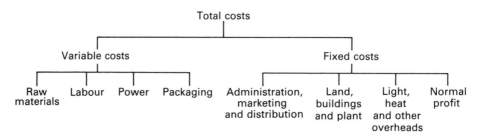

The level of technology

The level of technology greatly affects the ability of entrepreneurs to supply. If the level of technology is primitive, with producers equipped with hand-held tools production will be at a bare subsistence level, and there will be little or no surplus production to go to market and form a 'supply' in the economic sense of that word. If technology is advanced and sophisticated a flood of output will be available and the problem will be to distribute it and market it before it deteriorates or is pilfered. We have to overcome the time gaps and the geographical gaps that separate consumers and producers in a sophisticated market economy. Between the primitive society and the advanced society we have the world of 'intermediate technology' where a reasonably developed, but not excessively advanced, economy provides for the needs of the population without raising expectations too high. Many economists, faced with ecological nightmares of 'holes in the ozone layer' and the 'green-house effect' of rising carbon-dioxide levels in the biosphere, argue that a return to intermediate technology is the best hope for mankind.

Natural influences and political influences

Much production is subject to the whims of nature. Carribean sugar crops can be ruined by hurricanes; salad crops and grain output can be destroyed by locusts; frost kills off coffee and citrus plantations. When supply is affected in these ways shortages develop and prices rise. High prices encourage new producers to come in, and just as they bring their extra product to market the old areas recover and a glut of output reduces prices to an inadequate level. Political influences are also at work to affect sources and volumes of supplies. Wars may disrupt production, or the transportation of supplies. Governments may interfere to impose quotas both by volume and value. Once the quota has been purchased further supplies are shut out either because of shortages of foreign exchange or to protect home producers, and the resulting shortages influence prices on the market.

These are some of the conditions liable to affect supply.

7 SUPPLY SCHEDULES AND SUPPLY CURVES

When studying 'demand' earlier in this chapter we looked at the demand schedules and demand curves of certain housewives for tomatoes. There are millions of consumers demanding a very small quantity of tomatoes each for their particular families, but when put together into a composite demand schedule the quantities do become very great.

When we come to examine the 'supply' side of any good or service we find that the numbers of suppliers are much smaller and in some cases there is only one supplier – called in economics a **monopolist**. Sometimes there are a few suppliers, who share the total output between them. They are called **oligopolists** (from the Greek word *oligoi* meaning 'few'). Thus in the cement industry there are about ten major producers in the UK, while in the detergent industry two firms supply 94 per cent of the total output. In market gardening there are many firms, which vary in size from smallholders with a few greenhouses to large firms with acres of tomato plants under glass. Even so, the number of firms supplying tomatoes is very small compared with the number of consumers demanding them. Just as consumers vary in their demands for goods, suppliers vary in their ability to supply. Some, because they are better situated, or more skilful, are low-cost producers, while others are high-cost producers. In Fig. 3.12 we have two such producers: A. Smallholder, who is a high-cost producer, and Tom Glomerate (Guernsey) Ltd, a low-cost large-scale supplier. The notes below Fig. 3.12 explain their supply positions.

A composite supply schedule and curve

When the supplies which individual suppliers are bringing to market are added together we can draw up a composite supply schedule which shows what the whole industry is prepared to supply at given prices, in a given period of time. Fig. 3.13 shows such a composite supply schedule and also a graph of the total supply by the industry. It illustrates a very important aspect of supply, known as the Second Law of Demand and Supply.

> The Second Law of Demand and Supply states that when the price of a commodity rises the quantity that will be supplied is increased.

Fig. 3.12 *Two supply schedules and supply curves for tomatoes*

Price per kg	Quantity supplied per week (tonnes)	
	A. Smallholder	Tom Glomerate (Guernsey) Ltd
0.60	25	500
0.50	20	250
0.40	10	200
0.30	–	100
0.20	–	50
0.10	–	–

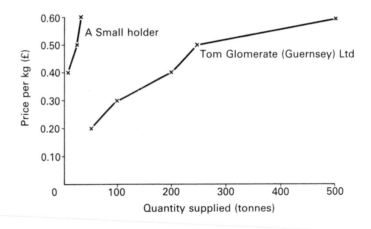

Notes
1 A. Smallholder is a high-cost producer. It will not pay him to supply tomatoes when the price is below 40 pence per kilogram.
2 Tom Glomerate (Guernsey) Ltd are low-cost producers. They can supply tomatoes as cheaply as 20 pence per kilogram.
3 Unlike the demand schedule shown earlier where consumers demand more as the price falls, suppliers reduce the supply they are willing to bring to market as price falls. When prices rise, they pick and dispatch more fruit to market, so that the amount supplied rises.
4 One point not shown either in the schedule or on the graphs is the difficulty suppliers face in extending supplies suddenly. If tomatoes are fetching a good price they can pick and dispatch more fruit from plants which are fully grown and bearing fruit. They cannot plant more tomatoes and obtain a yield immediately. It takes time to extend supply. Economists say that in the short run the supply of tomatoes is **inelastic**. This means that when you have too little you cannot easily expand supply, and, equally, when you have too much (a glut of tomatoes) you cannot contract it. All you can do then is to throw away the surplus output.

Fig. 3.13 *A composite supply schedule and a composite supply curve*

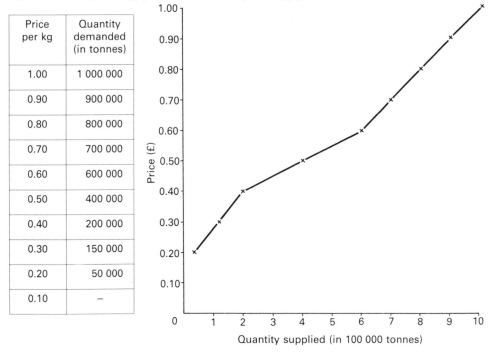

Price per kg	Quantity demanded (in tonnes)
1.00	1 000 000
0.90	900 000
0.80	800 000
0.70	700 000
0.60	600 000
0.50	400 000
0.40	200 000
0.30	150 000
0.20	50 000
0.10	–

Notes
1   At a price of 20 pence only the most efficient firms in the industry are able to bring in any supplies. One of them is Tom Glomerate (Guernsey) Ltd.
2   As price rises other firms are able to bring in supplies, and the quantity supplied extends.
3   As prices rise, more and more supplies join the industry and bring in their outputs to market. As price falls the least efficient producers leave the industry and the quantity supplied contracts.
4   Note that the graph rises higher and higher on the right-hand as price increases, because the quantity supplied is extending. This is the opposite effect to that shown in the demand curve in Fig. 3.6. The demand curve is high on the left and low on the right.

This is the opposite effect noted in the First Law of Demand and Supply given earlier, which said that when the price of a commodity falls the quantity that will be demanded is increased.

The general supply curve

As with demand, it is useful in Economics if we can discuss supply in general terms, without referring to the supply of any particular commodity or service. For this purpose we usually use a general supply curve like the one shown in Fig. 3.14. This conforms roughly to the Second Law of Demand and Supply. The axes are labelled 'price' and 'quantity' but the units are not given – they will be given by the economist who wishes to make a point in the discussion. It is usual to label the supply curve SS. It will start low down on the left, where suppliers are only prepared to supply a small quantity because price is low,

Fig. 3.14 (a) *A general supply curve.* (b) *Extensions and contractions (but not changes) of supply with changes of price*

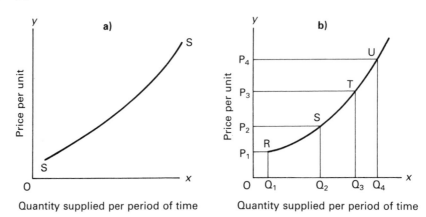

Quantity supplied per period of time   Quantity supplied per period of time

Notes
1 The general supply curve follows the Second Law of Demand and Supply: the higher the price the greater the quantity that is supplied.
2 The points, R, S, T, U may be understood by reference to the *x* and *y* axes. At point R price is low (P_1) and the quantity supplied is also low (Q_1). At point S price is higher (P_2) and supply extends to Q_2 as more suppliers are prepared to join the industry.
3 When price falls (say, from P_4 to P_3) supply contracts as the less efficient suppliers find they cannot make a profit at the lower price, and leave the industry.

and it will finish high up on the right where prices are high and the quantity suppliers are prepared to supply is large. Once again, such a curve really represents a succession of points, which are fixed relative to the two axes. We can follow the way in which supply extends as price rises, and contracts as price falls. Suppliers either join the industry as prospects of profitability improve, or leave the industry as prospects of profitability decline.

The extensions and contractions of supply with changes in price illustrated in Fig. 3.14(b) depend on price alone. They are not changes in supply. A change in supply is a change to a new supply curve altogether. This must be caused by a change in the conditions of supply – an advance in technology perhaps, or some natural disaster, or some form of interference by government activities like legislation or the imposition of taxes. When there is a change to a new supply curve so that a different supply is available at *every* price, we have the situation illustrated in Fig. 3.15 and described in the notes below it.

Regressive supply curves

The regressive type of curve discussed in the section on demand is also met with in supply. While a supplier will usually bring in larger supplies if the price rises he may not do so if he is in a special privileged position. For example, a wholesaler who has the only supply of a particular commodity may still withhold it so that he can force up prices still higher. This is much rarer than is popularly thought, because most wholesale trades are highly competitive and

Fig. 3.15 *A change of supply*

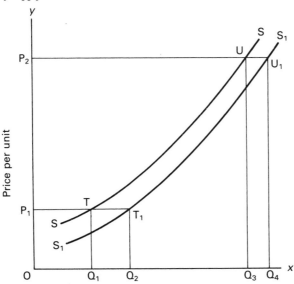

Notes
1   Some change in the conditions of supply has altered the whole supply position. The new curve S_1S_1 is to the right of the original supply curve SS.
2   This means that at every price suppliers are willing to supply a larger quantity than before. At P_1 they will supply Q_2 instead of Q_1 and at P_2 they will supply Q_4 of the product instead of Q_3.

involve investing a great deal of capital in stocks. When the opportunity comes to sell those stocks at good prices and thus realise his profits a wholesaler is unlikely to hold them back. The chief idea of the 'middleman' system is for the middleman to buy goods when they are cheap and store them until they are scarce and price rises. He thus removes surpluses as they arise and relieves shortages which would otherwise occur, earning a profit in the process. These are wholly meritorious activities, and abuse of the middleman is usually unjustified.

One interesting case of regressive supply is the supply of labour. If wages are low the supply of labour is usually good as workers anxious to secure a living wage seek to do as much overtime as possible or even take on two jobs. As wages rise the supply of labour reduces. The utility of marginal income falls and extra leisure becomes more attractive. Naturally the effect is most noticeable in industries where the work is unpleasant, boring or difficult. Thus higher wages in coalmining usually result in a decrease in the amount of labour supplied. Absenteeism grows since the miner's family now has a reasonable standard of living and any extra goods and services are not worth the risks and unpleasantness of extra hours in the mine. The same sort of absenteeism can be seen in repetitive work on motor vehicle assembly lines, and in the number of migrant workers prepared to stay on a job once they have achieved their original 'target income'. The supply curve for such types of labour is illustrated in Fig. 3.16.

Fig. 3.16 *The regressive supply curve for labour*

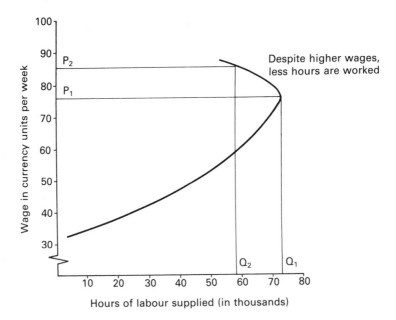

Notes
1 As wages rise the supply of labour extends as workers offer themselves for employment.
2 When wages reach a high level further increases cease to attract a larger supply of labour. The utility of marginal income declines, and extra leisure becomes more attractive. The supply curve for labour becomes regressive.

8 HOW PRICES ARE FIXED IN A FREE MARKET

A market is a place where exchanges are made; suppliers are in contact with buyers with a view to selling them goods or services, at prices to be determined by market forces. The typical market force is competition; there are many sellers wishing to sell and even more buyers wishing to buy. From the consumer's point of view competition is desirable in a market, for it usually results in lower prices and greater satisfaction for the consumer. Economists therefore call a situation where there is plenty of competition a **perfect market**. All other market structures display some degree of imperfection.

Perfect markets

A perfect market is one which displays the following characteristics:

a) A large number of buyers and sellers, none of whom dominates the market.
b) A homogeneous commodity, so that buyers are indifferent from whom they buy. (For example, all sacks of potatoes are very similar.)
c) An absence of friction in the market.

d)   Perfect knowledge in the market.

e)   No one receiving preferential treatment.

f)   Free access to the market exists for both producers and consumers, who may enter or leave the market as they choose.

A few words of explanation are needed about these characteristics.

a)   A seller or buyer may be said to dominate the market if they can influence prices by withholding their supplies or not placing their orders. Thus if the oil producing countries of the Middle East withheld their supplies they might be able to force up the price of oil on the world markets. If all that happened if they did this was that other oil producers simply increased production to take the Middle East's share of the market, oil prices would stay the same, but there would be a shift in the pattern of oil supplies.

b)   Homogeneous products are found most easily in the commodity markets where one sack of wheat or barrel of oil is very much like another. It is not quite so easy to compare a Ford car with a Toyota, or an Italian washing machine with a British one. So the car market is less perfect than the copper market, or the cocoa market.

c)   Friction in a market is any factor which prevents supplies moving from a place where prices are low to one where prices are higher, or which prevents buyers from moving from places where prices are high to places where prices are lower. Thus Christmas shoppers moving across the English Channel to buy supplies of wine, liqueurs, etc., in France is a common feature of the Christmas trade. For such buyers a ferry strike is a form of friction in the market place; it stops them moving to the place where they can get the 'best buy'.

d)   Perfect knowledge in the market enables buyers to know where prices are cheapest, and enables sellers to know where demand is strongest and prices are highest. Sometimes housewives buy an item in one shop only to find later in their shopping expedition that another has the same item as a 'special offer' at a bargain price. In the USA local radio stations announce 'best buys' at breakfast time so that housewives have a better knowledge of the market place. This is not yet a common feature of local radio in the UK. Perhaps it should be.

e)   Preferential treatment to a particular group reduces the perfection of a market. For example, a wholesaler buying in bulk gets a better price, for a perfectly good reason, than a consumer buying a single item from the same supplier. It is less satisfactory, for example in war time, if Mrs Moneybags gets a larger share of food in short supply while Mrs Quiverful, who has many children, cannot obtain supplies because she is too poor. That is why rationing is a common feature of war-time arrangements.

f)   Free access to the market is important if it is to be a perfectly competitive market. In the Soviet Union it is well-known that certain privileged people can buy in special shops where the ordinary public cannot buy. This makes the market very imperfect and robs the market of any chance of fixing prices by the laws of supply and demand. Instead the price is fixed by officials, without regard to the economic principles which should act to fix prices.

The importance of price in the mixed economy

The mixed economy has two sectors, the public and the private. The public sector consists of nationalised industries, public corporations and central or local government institutions. The private sector is the free enterprise sector, consisting of firms which are sole traders, partnerships and limited companies of one sort or another. The firms and institutions in both of these sectors are ultimately producing goods and services for the use of consumers, and exchanging these utilities with the consumers for a money payment called the 'price'.

'Price' has always presented great difficulty to those seeking to understand how an economy works, and treatises about 'price', 'value' and 'profit' have always commanded a ready market. In the controlled economies prices are frequently fixed by decree. In some cases Soviet prices have remained unchanged for a quarter of a century. In the public sector of a mixed economy such as the UK prices may be dictated by the necessity to abide by the original rules of the Act of Parliament which nationalised the industry. A requirement 'to avoid losses, taking one year with another' decides what prices must be charged to consumers. While this will often be a perfectly satisfactory system it does leave the door open for some unwise decisions. Thus any decision to allow wages to rise in the industry must inevitably raise prices to consumers in the absence of any gains in productivity. A decision to extend the service offered or maintain a full service when demand is declining requires that the extra expense shall be covered by allowing prices to rise, again financing the extra service at the consumer's expense, whether or not this is popular.

With the private sector very few prices can be fixed by decree or by the authority of Parliament. The free enterprise nature of much of the private sector ensures that goods and services will be sold by the producers to the consumers at prices which reflect market forces – in other words, the interaction of supply and demand. Since producers and consumers are free to choose whether or not they will trade, exchange will only take place if the prices agreed are mutually acceptable. Even a monopolist cannot say, 'I will make this product available for £100, and you will buy 20 000 of them.' He/she is still subject to the authority of the consumers, who will refuse to buy if the price is not right. Only where the monopolist's product is absolutely essential can an unfair price be exacted. If there is no demand for the product even the monopolist must lower the price, while the firm in a competitive industry is exposed all the time to market forces which seek to decide price by the interaction of demand and supply.

The interaction of demand and supply

In the first part of this chapter we considered the nature of demand in Economics and examined demand schedules and demand curves. Then we considered the nature of supply, and examined supply schedules and supply curves. In order to understand how demand and supply interact to fix prices it is necessary to present the demand schedules and supply schedules side by side.

In Fig. 3.17 the composite demand schedule for tomatoes given in Fig. 3.6 is reproduced alongside the composite supply schedule for tomatoes given in Fig. 3.13. The forces at work in the market reflect the aim of producers (to secure the highest price possible for their supplies so that profits will be maximised) and the opposite aims of consumers (to achieve the maximum satisfaction from their outlays by paying as little as possible). During the course of trading supply and demand will act upon one another and this will result in an equilibrium price. Suppose that early in the day there are more goods available than are demanded by consumers. This will cause the price to fall because consumers have to be coaxed into buying. The effect of a lower price will be twofold. First, some producers will decide not to sell at the prevailing low price and will withdraw from the market temporarily. Second, the prevailing low price will encourage consumers to demand, and they will increase their purchases. The result will be that the fall in prices apparent at the start of the day will be arrested; prices will steady, and may even rise. If

Fig. 3.17 *Composite demand and supply schedules*

Price per kg (£)	Quantity demanded (in tonnes)	Quantity supplied (in tonnes)
1.00	10 000	1 000 000
0.90	25 000	900 000
0.80	40 000	800 000
0.70	100 000	700 000
0.60	200 000	600 000
0.50	400 000	400 000
0.40	600 000	200 000
0.30	700 000	150 000
0.20	800 000	50 000
0.10	1 000 000	–

Notes
1 The quantity demanded falls as price rises, because consumers increasingly prefer other goods and services.
2 The quantity supplied rises as price rises, because producers' prospects of profitability improve.
3 At a price of 50 pence per kilogram the quantity demanded, 400 000 tones, is exactly the same as the quantity supplied by the producers. This is called the **equilibrium price** and the market is said to be in equilibrium. Equilibrium exists where the quantity of goods being supplied to the market exactly equals the quantity of goods being demanded.

the price-rise continues hesitant sellers will return to the market to offer their supplies, while consumer demand will fall away. This increase in the quantity supplied and decrease in the quantity demanded will halt the rise in prices and once again establish price at the point which equates demand and supply.

This illustrates the Third Law of Demand and Supply.

> The Third Law of Demand and Supply states 'Price will adjust to the level which equates demand and supply'.

The important point about the resulting price, which is called the equilibrium price, is that at this price there is no surplus; buyers wish to buy the same quantity as suppliers wish to sell. This equality of demand and supply is brought out clearly in Fig. 3.17. The same information is conveyed graphically in Fig. 3.18.

Fig. 3.18 *Composite demand and supply curves*

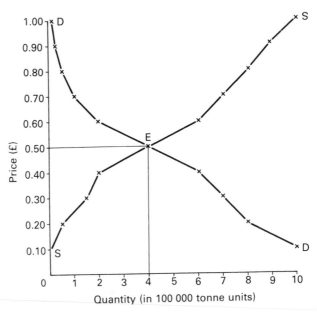

Notes
1 The quantity demanded increases as price falls (curve DD).
2 The quantity supplied increases as price rises (curve SS).
3 At the point where the two curves intersect, at a price of 50 pence, the quantity demanded and the quantity supplied are the same. This is called the equilibrium price, or market price.

A general diagram of price determination

Just as it is convenient to discuss demand and supply in terms of a general demand curve and a general supply curve, it is convenient to discuss price determination in general terms. The general diagram is shown in Fig. 3.19. The demand curve, of course, slopes down from left to right, with quantity demanded increasing as price falls. The supply curve slopes upwards from left to right, with quantity supplied to the market increasing as price rises. Where the two curves intersect is the equilibrium point E, *where at the equilibrium price P₁ the quantities supplied to the market by producers exactly equal the quantities demanded by consumers Q₁.*

Fig. 3.19 *The general 'equilibrium price' diagram*

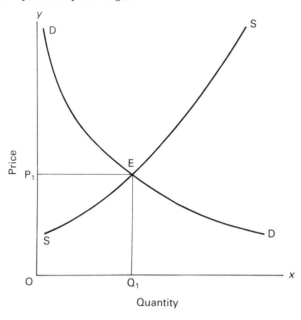

Notes
1 The quantity demanded is small when the price is high, and great when the price is low (DD).
2 The quantity supplied is great when the price is high, and small when the price is low (SS).
3 At E (equilibrium) the demand curve and supply curve intersect.
4 At this point E, demand and supply are in equilibrium: as much is being brought into the market as is being taken away by consumers (Q₁).
5 The price P₁ is called equilibrium price or market price. It is that price which equates supply and demand.
6 At this price there is no shortage, for every consumer who is demanding the product is able to obtain the supplies which he wishes to purchase.
7 Similarly, at the equilibrium price there is no surplus, for every unit that is being brought to market by the suppliers is able to find a consumer who wishes to purchase it.

SELF-ASSESSMENT QUESTIONS

6 What are 'the conditions of supply'?

7 What is the general appearance of a supply curve?

8 What is a regressive supply curve?

9 Explain how prices are fixed in a competitive market?

9   CHANGES IN MARKET PRICES

When markets are free, so that prices are decided by the interaction of demand and supply, any change in the conditions of demand, or any change in the conditions of supply, will mean a change in price. Thus if there is a major change of fashion, so that effective demand shifts from one product to another, there will be a decrease in demand for the former and an increase in demand for the latter. The whole demand curve of both products will shift. For the product in decreased demand the demand curve will shift to the left (see Fig. 3.20) and at every price a lower quantity will be demanded. By contrast, the demand curve for the alternative product will shift to the right, further from the origin of the diagram (see Fig. 3.21), and at every price an increased quantity will be demanded. Study these two diagrams carefully, and the notes below them.

Fig. 3.20 *Effect on price of a decrease in demand*

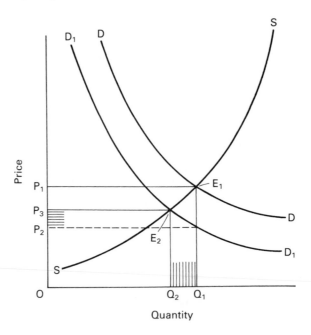

Notes
1   Due to some change, perhaps of taste or fashion, demand has decreased from DD to D_1D_1.
2   Entrepreneurs supplying the commodity cannot immediately cease production of it, and as a result there is too great a supply for the demand. Price falls drastically to P_2. Some entrepreneurs at this price are making losses.
3   Under the influence of these losses, entrepreneurs reduce production, and the quantity supplied gradually falls from Q_1 to Q_2.
4   As the quantity supplied decreases price begins to recover and creeps up from P_2 to P_3.
5   The new equilibrium price P_3 is decided where the old supply curve (supply having contracted) cuts the new demand curve D_1D_1.
6   Conclusion: a decrease in demand lowers the price and leads to a contraction of supply from the industry.

Fig. 3.21 *Effect on price of an increase in demand*

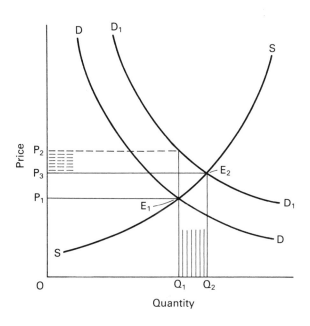

Notes

1 Due to some change in the conditions of demand – perhaps a change of taste or fashion, or a change of income – demand has increased from DD to D_1D_1.

2 Supply cannot react at once because entrepreneurs have to modify plans. There is therefore a shortage and price rises steeply to P_2, the point where a supply of Q_1 cuts the new demand curve. Entrepreneurs supplying the goods are now making excellent profits.

3 Under the influence of these profits, firms expand output and the quantity supplied begins to creep up from Q_1 to Q_2.

4 As the quantity supplied increases the price falls from P_2 to P_3.

5 The new equilibrium price of P_3 is established at E_2, where the old supply curve (which has extended to E_2) cuts the new demand curve, which has changed to D_1D_1.

6 Conclusion: an increase in demand raises price and extends the quantity supplied by the industry.

Similarly, a change in the conditions of supply will lead to new supply curves. Imagine a situation where a serious failure of crops in a particular year leads to high prices for cattle feed. Farmers who have been particularly hard hit and have grown insufficient food to carry their cattle over the winter months may decide to slaughter cattle in the autumn before their condition deteriorates. The supply of beef to market will increase and the supply curve will move to the right (see Fig. 3.22). In the following years, now that herds have been reduced, the supply of beef will decrease and the supply curve will move in towards the origin, as shown in Fig. 3.23. Study these figures now, and the notes below them.

Fig. 3.22 *Effect on price of an increase in supply*

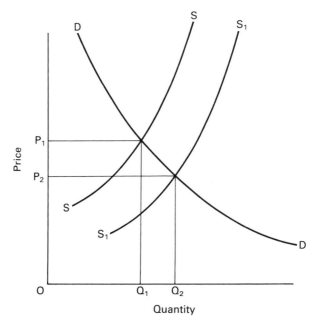

Notes

1 For some reason, perhaps a need to slaughter cattle due to crop failures, supply has changed from SS to S_1S_1.

2 The increased supply causes a surplus on the market, and price falls.

3 Due to the swift reactions of consumers, demand extends to take up the new supply at the price P_2.

4 Conclusion: an increased supply causes a fall in price and an extension in the quantity demanded.

Fig. 3.23 *Effect on price of a decrease in supply*

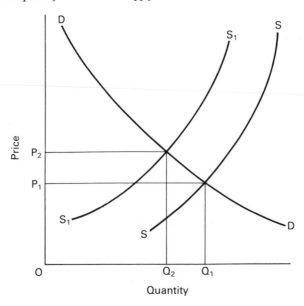

Notes
1 For some reason, decreased supplies are available: perhaps cattle slaughtered earlier have reduced the herds available for culling.
2 The decreased supply causes a shortage, and price rises.
3 Consumers react quickly and the demand contracts to Q_2, achieving equilibrium at the new price P_2.
4 Conclusion: a decreased supply causes an increased price and a contraction of the quantity demanded.

It is worthwhile looking at these four diagrams (Figs. 3.20–3) again to notice two further points. The first concerns the way in which consumers and suppliers react to changes in price.

The responsiveness of demand and supply to changes in price

The reactions of consumers and suppliers to changes in price are very different. The consumers react very quickly to price changes, because demand is based upon an appraisal of the marginal utility to be derived from the purchase of a particular good and service. The housewife who is doing her shopping only takes seconds to weigh up the price change and either presses in to make her purchase of the now cheaper article, or reduces the amount she demands, perhaps even rejecting the item under consideration as outside her price range now that its price has risen. In Figs. 3.22 and 3.23 the changes in supply bring about an immediate reaction from the consumers, who at once extend or contract their demand to take account of the change that has occurred.

By contrast, suppliers cannot always react so quickly. To meet an increased demand requires a certain amount of effort on their part, not just a mental calculation. At the least they must ask employees to work overtime to step up production. Possibly it may be necessary to lay down new production lines; buy sophisticated machine tools; even build new factories and warehouses or arrange mass-distribution networks. To react to reduced demand the supplier has to lower production – perhaps by dismissing staff, closing down plant, etc. This again cannot be done at a moment's notice. There will be a tendency to delay a decision until the pattern of demand is clearer; to stockpile product meanwhile and retain key workers who otherwise may be lost to the employer. In Figs. 3.20 and 3.21 the gradual adjustments of supply to the changes in price caused by a change in demand are illustrated graphically.

The second point is that the reader must remember that a *change* in demand means a shift to a completely new demand curve, and a *change* in supply means a shift to a completely new supply curve. As was seen in Figs. 3.20–1, a change in demand (to a new demand curve) causes an extension (or contraction) of supply along the supply curve, which of course has not changed. Similarly, a change in supply (to a new supply curve) causes an extension (or contraction) of demand along the demand curve, which again has not changed.

The reader should now study Figs. 3.20–3 again, together with their explanatory notes, noticing these two points in the four diagrams.

10   THE PRICE MECHANISM AND PRICE CONTROLS

The price mechanism described above and illustrated in Fig. 3.19 is a self-regulating mechanism which equates demand and supply by the economic forces operating in the market. It therefore has the effect of deciding what shall be produced, and to whom the goods and services produced shall be supplied. This last decision is based upon economic factors and ignores non-economic considerations like 'justice' and 'fair play'. For example, at a time of great shortage when supplies are practically non-existent the little that does reach the market will go to the rich who can afford the high market prices. Others will be starved of the product.

It follows that attempts to control prices are frequently made, and with varying degrees of success. The economist is in difficulties over such matters, which are aspects of situations requiring value-judgments. Whenever politicians attempt to manipulate the economy to achieve some 'desirable' end the economy adapts to the manipulation as individuals within it adjust their patterns of behaviour to avoid (or perhaps take advantage of) the political decisions made. The economist can perhaps advise and assist the politician in devising a scheme which will have the minimum adverse effect, and achieve the ends with the least possible disturbance to the economy. There have been some spectacular examples of how far out they have been in their calculations.

Other sources of complaint against the price mechanism include the anti-social overtones of a system which is incapable of responding to anything but demand and supply. The Colombian cocaine baron justifies his output of cocaine by claiming that he is merely meeting an effective demand. The fact that it involves not only peasant expropriation in his own area, but a worldwide network of corruption to bring the addict the drug he/she demands is immaterial. It is universally recognised that society has a right to object and to take action against such activities as the drugs trades. Clearly the price mechanism cannot answer all problems.

In real life, governments and legislative bodies interfere a good deal in the free play of the price mechanism, and manipulate the market to achieve what they feel to be desirable social ends. The weapons used include taxation, which raises effective prices; subsidies which lower effective prices; and price controls, which dictate maximum and minimum prices. The first two are discussed elsewhere in this book.

Price controls, sometimes called physical controls, have interesting side effects, and are illustrated in Figs. 3.24 and 3.25.

Maximum price controls

When a maximum price is imposed on a product the supplier cannot expect more for his product than the maximum price which has been announced. He knows therefore exactly what the prospects of profitability are, and he also knows that they are vulnerable to uncontrolled influences such as weather, disease, etc. A farmer who knows the controlled price for a tonne of wheat can estimate his profits exactly provided he achieves his anticipated yields, since he knows his costs of production. He also knows that if the price of labour (wages), or fertiliser, or the rent of land rises he will not be able to raise the price of his product wheat to match these increase in costs. He will therefore hesitate to plant too much wheat, for the profit he is likely to make may disappear if costs rise. At the same time, the low price of the product encourages demand, which will exceed the supply. Where demand exceeds supply, shortages must develop. This shortage would be overcome by the price mechanism, which would raise price to encourage supply and reduce demand. With a maximum price control the price mechanism cannot operate, and the shortage will lead to abuses where privileged customers are sold 'under the counter' supplies, or goods may have to be rationed in some official way. The situation is illustrated in Fig. 3.24.

Fig. 3.24 *Maximum price controlled: rationing*

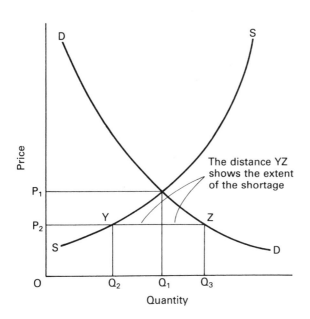

Notes
1   Market price is P_1 and the quantity supplied is Q_1.
2   For some reason – perhaps because the commodity is a basic food in wartime and the market mechanism is enabling the rich to eat while the poor starve – the government fixes a maximum price of P_2.
3   At this price quantity Q_2 is distributed by the suppliers, but the people would like to buy quantity Q_3. This means that there is a serious shortage. Unscrupulous shopkeepers will keep supplies under the counter for favoured customers prepared to pay higher prices.
4   The only fair way to solve the problem is to introduce a rationing system.

Minimum price controls

It frequently happens that where an industry faces competition from more efficient producers overseas an entire industry might cease to exist if some sort of 'fair' reward is not arranged for suppliers. This usually means that the minimum price is controlled, the minimum being set at that level which gives the home producer a reasonable income for his efforts.

There have been numerous examples of this type of interference with the price mechanism but perhaps the best known is the Common Agricultural Policy. This seeks to ensure that European farmers achieve a reasonable reward for their farming activities. A series of prices called **target prices** is established at which goods will change hands in the markets. These target prices are not the same in all areas, because they take account of transport costs, etc., in different regions. Imported agricultural products come into the Community at **threshold prices** which are so arranged that by the time they have had transport costs added the imported goods will sell at 'target prices' only. Cheap imports must therefore pay a tariff as they cross the threshold to

Fig. 3.25 *Minimum price controlled: State stockpiling*

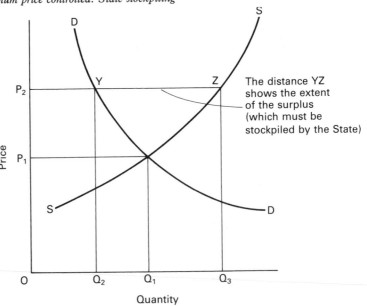

The distance YZ shows the extent of the surplus (which must be stockpiled by the State)

Notes

1   Market price is P_1 and quantity supplied is Q_1.

2   For some reason, e.g. to guarantee farm incomes, the government decrees that prices cannot fall below P_2.

3   At this price people wish to buy only Q_2 of the commodity, but suppliers insist on producing Q_3.

4   Since the public will not buy the commodity, the government has to do so, and vast stockpiles of food and raw materials are built up which have been purchased with taxpayers' money. Sometimes quite ridiculous situations develop, with hungry people unfed while granaries are bursting. The Common Market countries have huge reserves of farm products which they cannot sell within the Community without lowering prices.

bring them up to the threshold price. A Community farmer who cannot sell his produce in the market at the 'target price' because of insufficient demand, is able to sell it to the Intervention Board, which intervenes to buy it at slightly lower **intervention prices** (about 8 per cent below target prices).

The result is that the ordinary price mechanism cannot operate to equate supply with demand. The suppliers can always sell their produce to the Intervention Board. Theoretically the Board stores it for use in times of shortage, but in practice a shortage never develops. The result is a 'butter mountain', or a 'beef mountain', or a 'wine lake'. The storage costs rise year by year. Attempts to reduce the mountain by selling it cheaply to countries which are genuinely short of food – usually countries with controlled economies – naturally raise howls of protest from less-well-paid Community citizens who cannot afford butter, beef or wine at the high target prices. The situation is illustrated in Fig. 3.25.

11 SUMMARY OF THE LAWS OF DEMAND AND SUPPLY

The Laws of Demand and Supply may be summarised as follows:

First Law: When the price of a commodity falls the quantity that is demanded will be increased.

Second Law: When the price of a commodity rises the quantity that is supplied will be increased.

Third Law: Prices will adjust to that level which equates demand and supply.

Fourth Law: An increased supply lowers market price and causes an extension of demand.

Fifth Law: A decreased supply raises market price and causes a contraction of demand.

Sixth Law: A decreased demand lowers price and also brings about a contraction of supply.

Seventh Law: An increased demand raises price and also brings about an extension of supply.

SELF-ASSESSMENT QUESTIONS

10 What are the characteristics of a perfect market?

11 Explain why maximum prices imposed on goods lead to 'under the counter' sales and calls for rationing.

12 Explain why minimum prices for wine, imposed to provide grape growers with a good income, mean 'wine lakes' of state-purchased wine.

REVISION TEST

Answers	Questions
	1 Define demand.
1 The demand for a particular good or service is the quantity of it that consumers are prepared to pay for at a given price, in a given period of time.	**2** How did Lord Robbins define economics?
2 As 'the science which studies human behaviour as a relationship between "ends" and scarce "means" which have alternative uses'.	**3** What is 'opportunity cost'?
3 It is the cost of a chosen good or service, measured in terms of the satisfaction which could have been enjoyed if the money had been spent on the next most favourable opportunity.	**4** What is a 'scale of preferences'?
4 An individual ladder-like arrangement of preferences for goods and services with the most preferred items towards the top of the scale.	**5** What is the basis of a 'scale of preferences'?
5 It is the concept of 'utility', a subjective estimate of the satisfaction to be derived from various goods and service.	**6** How does the housewife choose a balanced basket of goods and services?
6 By comparing in her mind the marginal utilities of a further unit of the various goods and services, one with another, and choosing the ones which will maximise her family's satisfaction.	**7** What is the supply of a particular good or service?
7 It is the quantity entrepreneurs are prepared to make available at a given price in a given period of time.	**8** How are prices decided in the market place?

8 Price is decided by the interaction of demand and supply. The price will be the equilibrium price, at which the quantity demanded by consumers exactly matches the quantity suppliers are prepared to bring to market.

9 Why can consumers react more quickly to market changes than producers?

9 Because all consumers have to do is to re-assess the marginal utilities of the goods or services to them, and either press in for a purchase or withdraw from the market for that particular item. The producer has to reweigh the advantages and disadvantages of supplying and either employ more factors to raise production or put plant into mothballs to wait for better times. Both these processes take time.

10 What are the seven laws of demand and supply?

10 The answers to this question are to be found in Self-assessment question 11 above.

Go over the test again until you are quite sure of all the answers. Then try some of the written questions on page 113.

ANSWERS

(See Self-assessment questions on pages 87, 101 and 109.)

1 The demand for a good or service is the quantity of it that consumers are prepared to pay for at a given price, in a given period of time.

2 The link between demand and utility is that utility is the measure of a good's (or service's) ability to yield satisfaction. If this ability is high, demand will be strong, while if the good's ability to yield satisfaction is low, demand will be weak. As this measure of utility is a subjective estimate made in the minds of every consumer, which places a good or service high or low on his/her scale of preference, it varies considerably from person to person, but the overall effect is a demand for the product which reflects the preferences of consumers.

3 The general demand curve is a succession of points recording the demand for a good or service at a succession of prices. Since little is demanded at high prices and more is demanded at low prices the curve slopes downwards towards the right of the diagram.

4 An extension of demand is an increase in the quantity demanded due to falling prices. It is a movement along the demand curve caused by a change in price, and not a change in the conditions of demand. A change in demand is an increase (or decrease) in demand due to a change in one of the conditions of demand (for example, a change in taste or fashion) which has led to a completely new demand curve, with an increase in demand (or a decrease in demand) at every price (see Figs. 3.8 and 3.9).

5 A regressive demand curve is one which turns back upon itself and does the opposite of what we would have expected. It can occur at either the top of the graph or the bottom. At the top of the graph, instead of a further rise in price choking off demand, it increases demand. This happens with 'goods of ostentation' and goods likely to become scarce. At the bottom of the scale instead of a fall in price increasing demand it lowers demand. This is because the goods are inferior goods, and at the lowest prices consumers experience an increase in income (in real terms) and hence reduce the demand for the inferior good, and buy something else instead. It also happens with goods likely to become even cheaper.

6 The conditions of supply are the influences at work to encourage an entrepreneur to produce goods and services (or to discourage him/her from doing so). The chief condition of supply is the cost of production, but other influences are the level of technology required, and the natural and political influences at work. A fruitful soil will encourage agriculture, a poor soil will discourage it, etc.

7 The general appearance of a supply curve is that it starts off low near the origin of the graph (at low prices supplies are small) and rises towards the right hand side as prices rise, supply extending as higher prices make production more profitable.

8 A regressive supply curve is one that turns back upon itself and does the opposite of what we expect. Thus increased prices encourage increased supplies normally, but in the case of the supply of labour higher wages (especially for unpleasant work) simply encourage absenteeism as the worker can support an adequate life style with fewer hours of work (see Fig. 3.16).

9 Prices are fixed in a competitive market by the interaction of supply and demand. Demand slopes downwards towards the right and supply rises towards the right. Where they intersect (the equilibrium price) the demand for the good is equal to the supply of it, and the market is cleared. At any other price this will not be so. At a higher price the supply will be greater than demand, causing prices to fall and at a lower price demand will be greater than supply, causing prices to rise.

10 The characteristics of a perfect market are: (a) a large number of buyers and sellers; (b) no buyer is so large a buyer that he/she can affect the market by refusing to buy; (c) no seller is so large a seller that he/she can affect the market by refusing to sell; (d) a homogeneous commodity, so that buyers are indifferent from whom they buy; (e) perfect knowledge of the market; (f) free access to the market for all buyers and sellers; (g) no preferential treatment of any sort; (h) an absence of friction in the market.

11 If a maximum price is fixed for a commodity it means that price cannot rise above a certain point. If demand is strong it will force prices up but this is not allowed

to happen because of the controlled maximum price. Therefore demand will not be choked off by the rising price, and will exceed supply. As a result what supplies are available will be kept under the counter and sold illegally at high prices to privileged customers. To ensure 'fair' treatment people will demand some sort of rationing arrangement (see Fig. 3.24).

12 If a minimum price is fixed to help farmers the result will be that if supplies exceed demand the price can only fall to the minimum. At this price supply will exceed demand, since price cannot fall enough to bring in the increased demand necessary to clear the market. The state will have to step in and buy the surplus, creating a wine lake of state-purchased wine (see Fig. 3.25).

QUESTIONS ON CHAPTER 3

1 Distinguish between 'wants' and 'effective demand', illustrating your answer with examples.

2 Explain how a housewife selects a basket of goods when visiting her local supermarket. What influence might (a) special offers, (b) product positioning, (c) special family events, (d) the presence of her children and (e) the presence of her husband have on the selection?

3 Explain the influence of equi-marginal returns of utility upon the selection of goods.

4 Define demand. Define supply. In a free market what is the link between demand, supply and price?

5 Fill in the missing words in the sentences below:
a) The price of a commodity rises when . . . . is supplied.
b) The price of a commodity rises when . . . . is demanded.
c) The price of a commodity falls either because . . . . is supplied or because . . . . is demanded.
d) In a competitive market, price is established where demand and supply are in . . . .
e) A change in supply is caused by a change in the . . . . of supply.
f) An extension of supply results from an . . . . in price.
g) A change in demand is caused by a change in the . . . . of demand.
h) A contraction of demand results from an . . . . in price.

6 How is price determined in a freely competitive market? Explain with the aid of a labelled diagram which refers to an important commodity in everyday use.

7 What impact have home-freezers had on the prices of green vegetables?

8 What is equilibrium price? Consider in your answer the example of tomatoes on sale at New Covent Garden Market in London (a) in August and (b) in December. Account for any difference in the prices observed.

9 Why does the price of lettuces fluctuate more than the price of tinned soup?

10 Discuss the likely effect of: (a) a good harvest on the price of wheat, (b) a sudden frost on the price of autumn flowers, (c) a change to automation in the electronics industry on the price of television sets; (d) rising family income on the price of cars. Illustrate your answers with diagrams.

11 What will be the effect of a decision to fix a low price of milk so that the farmer finds milk production barely possible?

12 Why do 'butter mountains' occur in the EEC under the Common Agricultural Policy?

TIPS FOR STUDENTS: A SPECIMEN ANSWER TO QUESTION 7

It is a little difficult to answer this question because a number of possibilities might be envisaged. For example:

a) It is so easy to buy pre-frozen green vegetables such as peas, beans, cauliflower and broccoli, frozen within a few hours of being cut or collected in the fields, that many families have given up buying greengroceries from a greengrocer with all the preparatory work that is necessary before they can be eaten. Therefore many greengrocers have gone out of business and this can only be because it is less profitable to operate a greengrocery than formerly.

b) On the farming side, the farmer probably gets as good a price as before, though he/she may be subject to more rigid control about quality, variety grown, etc., than formerly. Harvesting is more intensively carried out, and this has probably cut costs.

c) From the greengrocer's point of view the supply available has almost certainly fallen, with many farmers supplying their entire crop to the freezing plant, so that although demand at the ordinary greengrocer's has fallen, supply has also fallen. This would offset the fall in price following a reduced demand, to restore prices to a reasonable level.

d) Greengroceries have in the past, like many agricultural products, been subject to wide fluctuations in price. At times there are huge quantities of produce available (a glut) resulting in rock-bottom prices which make it hardly worth-while sending the produce to market. Many crops used to be ploughed back – a process known as green-manuring. Today the seasonal availability of green vegetables has been changed to continuous availability of the frozen product. Year-round availability has steadied prices, the glut being carried over time throughout the year, and at a uniform price instead of the former fluctuations between a very low (glut) price and a very high (scarcity) price. This has also been accompanied with increased convenience to the consumer and less business for the greengrocery trade, now by-passed by the retailing of green vegetables from frozen food cabinets.

4 Elasticity of demand and supply

1 THE CONCEPT OF ELASTICITY

The demand for a particular good is the amount of it that will be purchased by consumers in a given time at a given price. If price falls it is likely that demand will extend, and if price rises it is likely that demand will contract. This reaction of demand to changes in price is called the **price elasticity of demand**. Similarly, the responsiveness of supply to changes in price is called the **price elasticity of supply**.

The property of elasticity in everyday life is the ability to extend and contract. Elastic stretches when forces are applied to it, but returns to its original length when the forces are released. A rubber ball is compressed when it strikes the ground, but rebounds as it resumes its original shape. In Economics there are many forces at work to influence supply and demand. Sometimes the response is large and demand, or supply, extends greatly. We then speak of **elastic demand** or **elastic supply**. Sometimes the response is smaller, and we speak of demand, or supply, as **inelastic**. We usually link descriptions of elasticity to the force which is at work to change the existing situation. The commonest of these influences is price, so we speak of **price elasticity of demand, or price elasticity of supply**. Income is another influence. A change in the distribution of income within a State may affect the demand for particular products, and we speak of **income elasticity of demand**.

It is often of great importance, in the launching of a new product or the introduction of a new policy, to assess the elasticities of demand and supply. Thus a Chancellor proposing to raise government revenues by increasing taxation on a particular product must assess the price elasticity of demand for the product. If the tax is to be doubled, but as a result of the new tax the sales of the product are halved, the Chancellor will only raise the same income as before. If the demand for that product is very elastic with respect to price, so that the increase in price caused by the tax leads to a more than proportional reduction in sales to, say, one quarter of the original total, the revenue raised by doubling the tax will be half the original revenue. The figures in this case might be as follows:

	Before increase	After increase
Unit price	£100	£100
Rate of tax	10%	20%
Selling price	£110	£120
Sales	100 000 units	25 000 units
Tax collected	£1m	£500 000

If the Chancellor's proposals are designed to raise revenue from the product the elasticities are clearly unfavourable. If his desire is to suppress that particular industry, which his party regards as antisocial, the price elasticities clearly indicate that he will largely achieve his aim.

In defining elasticity we must include in our definition the force we are considering, so that we may define as follows:

> The **price elasticity of demand** is the responsiveness of the amount demanded of a particular product to changes in the price of that product.

> The **income elasticity of demand** for a particular product is the responsiveness of the demand for that product to changes in the income levels of consumers.

Absolute and relative changes

Changes are measured first of all in 'absolute' terms. This means that the actual, or real, changes are noted. For example, a price-cutting campaign may lead to an increase in sales of 10 000 units. This may seem at first glance to be a large increase. The importance of this absolute change can only be assessed when we compare it with the total sales previously being achieved. Thus if sales before the campaign started were 10 000 units the increase in sales is very satisfactory relative to the original sales. Expressed as a percentage the relative change is 100 per cent.

If sales before the campaign were 40 000 000 units the change is relatively insignificant:

$$\frac{10\ 000}{40\ 000\ 000} \times 100 = 0.025\%$$

Clearly the campaign was a dismal failure.

It follows that in measuring elasticity of demand and elasticity of supply we are not really interested in the absolute changes but in the relative changes of both amount and price. We note, or try to estimate, the absolute changes, but they must be related to the previously existing situation before we can decide their significance.

2 THE PRICE ELASTICITY OF DEMAND

Suppose the price of a good is reduced by 10 per cent, and as a result the quantity demanded extends by 10 per cent. The amount demanded has responded proportionately to the change in price, and this is described as unitary elasticity. In order to have a numerical measure of elasticity (a coefficient of elasticity) we use the formula

$$\text{Coefficient of elasticity} = \frac{\text{Percentage change in quantity of } x}{\text{Percentage change in price of } x}$$

In the example quoted above the coefficient of elasticity (e) is found as follows:

$$E = \frac{10\%}{-10\%} = \frac{10}{-10} = -1$$

Suppose the price of beef rises by 10 per cent. Will housewives cut back on their purchases of beef? Probably they will, for there are several good substitutes, such as lamb and pork. The demand for beef is therefore price elastic (responsive to changes in the price of beef) and we may expect a more than proportional response. If the quantity demanded contracts by 25 per cent what is the elasticity of demand?

$$E = \frac{-25\%}{+10\%} = -2.5$$

Housewives demand potatoes every day, and regard them as a staple diet for the family. Suppose potato prices rise by 10 per cent. Will this cut back demand for potatoes? It is unlikely, for they form a major part of the chief meal of the day, and may even feature in minor meals too. This means that potatoes are in inelastic demand – a less than proportional response to a change in price. If the quantity demanded falls by only 1 per cent, what is the elasticity of demand?

$$E = \frac{-1\%}{+10\%} = -0.1$$

There are two points to make here. First of all notice that as the amount demanded falls away when price rises and vice versa, the result of the calculation is always a negative quantity. This means that the elasticity of demand is always negative (except where demand is regressive and actually increases as price rises). Since regressive demand is very rare the elasticity will usually be negative but by convention we disregard the minus sign. The three elasticities given above would therefore by convention be described as 1, 2.5 and 0.1.

   The second point to note is that where a response is exactly proportional to the change in price the answer comes out exactly to 1, which has already been described as **unitary elasticity**. If response is elastic (more than proportional to the change in price) the elasticity will be a number greater than 1. In the second case above it was 2.5, which is clearly greater than 1. If response is inelastic the answer comes out to a fraction, such as 0.1 in the third example.

Elasticity varies therefore from elastic demand (elasticity greater than 1), through unitary elasticity ($E = 1$), to inelastic demand (elasticity less than 1). The five typical cases are described below. Unitary elasticity may be described as a watershed separating elastic demand from inelastic demand.

The spectrum of cases of price elasticity of demand

It is difficult to be more precise about elasticity without using mathematical terms which are beyond the scope of this book. It is perhaps sufficient to describe the five typical cases of price elasticity. These are:

a) infinitely elastic demand with respect to price;
b) fairly elastic demand with respect to price;
c) unitary elasticity of demand with respect to price;
d) fairly inelastic demand with respect to price;
e) zero elasticity of demand with respect to price.

Consider each of these cases in turn.

CASES A) AND E): THE LIMITS OF ELASTICITY
The limits of elasticity at either end of the above group are **infinitely elastic demand** and **zero elasticity of demand**. The first implies that as price falls demand extends to infinity. The second implies that no matter how much price changes demand never alters. Clearly both of these cases are a little theoretical. They are illustrated and described in Fig 4.1.

Fig. 4.1 (a) *Infinite elasticity of demand, i.e. $E = \infty$*; (b) *Zero elasticity of demand, i.e. $E = 0$*

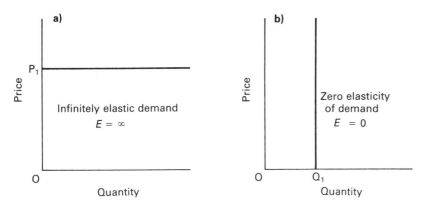

Notes
1 At prices above P_1, in Fig 4.1(a), no quantity at all is demanded.
2 As the price falls to P_1, quantity increases to infinite demand.
3 This seems to be a highly theoretical situation, and it is chiefly to be regarded as a mathematical limit; elasticity can go no further than infinity. It is, however, highly realstic *if we think of the demand in perfectly competitive markets for the supplies of a single producer*. If the market price is P_1 for 'Hoover' shares and I offer them for a little less than P_1 I shall immediately dispose of my entire supply.

4 By contrast, in Fig 4.1 (b) the quantity demanded does not change at all; there is absolutely zero response to any change in price, however great. The demand curve is a vertical line.

5 Again this is a highly theoretical situation, for it is difficult to imagine such a commodity. The demand for some things – for example, habit-forming drugs – is very inelastic. Addicts have been known to beg, borrow, steal, and even murder for the price of a shot of heroin. Demand continues to be strong even when price increases, though it may be argued that eventually some price will be so high that 'effective demand' will cease.

CASE C: UNITARY ELASTICITY

The middle item in the list above is *unitary elasticity of demand*, which implies that demand extends or contracts in exact proportion to the change in price. In the special case illustrated in Fig. 4.2 (the rectangular hyperbola) elasticity is 1 all the way along the curve. In other curves unitary elasticity will occur somewhere along the curve, and it will be the 'watershed' point which separates off elastic demand from inelastic demand.

Fig. 4.2 *Unitary elasticity, i.e. E = 1*

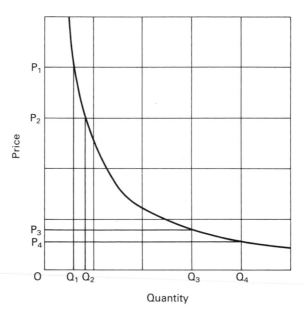

Notes

1 At every point along this curve the change in the quantity demanded is proportional to the change in price. We must remember that it is the relative changes that are important. From P_1 to P_2 is a 33⅓ per cent reduction in price; from Q_1 to Q_2 is a 33⅓ per cent extension of the quantity demanded. So, by our formula

$$E = \frac{\text{Percentage change in quantity of } x}{\text{Percentage change in price of } x} = \frac{33\frac{1}{3}}{-33\frac{1}{3}\%} = -1$$

From P_3 to P_4 is also a 33⅓ per cent reduction in price, while at this point a 33⅓ per cent extension in the quantity demanded requires demand to shift from Q_3 to Q_4, which is a much bigger absolute movement. The formula still gives $E = 1$.

2 It is often said that the slope of a demand curve gives an indication of the elasticity. But in this diagram elasticity is unitary everywhere (i.e. the amount demanded is changing proportionately to price all the way along the curve), even though the gradient of the graph varies from almost vertical to almost horizontal. This shows that slope is no indication of elasticity, though where two curves are being compared with each other on the same scale, their slopes may give a relative indication of elasticity (the more vertical curve being more inelastic than the more horizontal curve).

CASES B) AND D): FAIRLY ELASTIC DEMAND AND FAIRLY INELASTIC DEMAND

One common difficulty in understanding elasticity arises from the tendency of students to link elasticity with 'the slope of demand curves'. There is really no such thing as the elasticity of demand curves, for almost always elasticity varies with price. There are only three demand curves with uniform elasticity all the way along the curve. These are the demand curves which have infinite elasticity, unitary elasticity and zero elasticity as illustrated in Figs. 4.1 and 4.2. One of these is horizontal, one is vertical and the curve displaying unitary elasticity throughout its length is a rectangular hyperbola which slopes from practically vertical to practically horizontal. Apart from these three cases, demand curves have differing elasticities over every range along the curve, so that the really significant thing is the price elasticity over a particular arc on a curve (i.e. around a particular price).

Some difficulty arises because we have to distinguish between **arc elasticity** and **point elasticity**. A movement from one point on a demand curve to another point is a movement along an arc of the demand curve, and the changes in price and quantity observed enable us to find the arc elasticity of demand. This arc elasticity of demand is really an average elasticity over the range of the price change. A more mathematical measurement of elasticity, point elasticity, measures elasticity over a minute range of price change. For the present we are only considering arc elasticity.

If our product is being sold currently at a price of £0.40 is the demand for the product elastic or inelastic over the range of the proposed price change?

If we raise the price will our customers desert us and turn to some alternative product (thus demonstrating that demand over the range of the price change is elastic) or will they stay with us and keep buying the product even though the price has risen? If they do continue to purchase the product it is clear that demand at prices just above £0.40 is inelastic.

Elasticity and inelasticity work both ways of course. Thus if demand is very elastic over a particular arc on the demand curve a rise in price will greatly reduce the quantity demanded, and a reduction in price will greatly increase the quantity demanded. If demand is inelastic over a particular arc on the demand curve a rise in price will not affect the quantity demanded very much (thus producing extra revenue since the price has been raised), while a reduction in price will not increase sales more than proportionately (thus reducing revenue because each unit is now being sold for less).

It is clearly possible to demonstrate fairly elastic demand and fairly inelastic demand on the same demand curve. This is illustrated in Fig. 4.3, and the calculations are given in the notes below the diagram.

Fig. 4.3 *Fairly elastic demand and fairly inelastic demand*

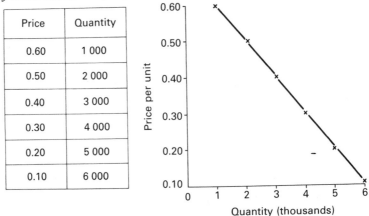

Price	Quantity
0.60	1 000
0.50	2 000
0.40	3 000
0.30	4 000
0.20	5 000
0.10	6 000

Notes

1 What is the elasticity of demand at price £0.50? Imagining a price reduction of £0.10 the figures are

$$\text{Elasticity} = \frac{\text{Percentage change in quantity demanded of } x}{\text{Percentage change in price of } x} = \frac{\frac{1000}{2000} \times 100}{\frac{£0.10}{£0.50} \times 100} = \frac{50}{20} = 2\frac{1}{2}$$

which represents a fairly elastic demand.

2 What is the elasticity of demand at a price of £0.20? Again, imagining a price change of £0.10

$$E = \frac{\frac{1000}{5000} \times 100}{\frac{£0.10}{£0.20} \times 100} = \frac{20}{50} = 0.4$$

which represents a fairly inelastic demand.

At this point it is helpful to introduce the idea of a **spectrum of elasticity**, which may be described as follows:

1 The two ends of the spectrum are zero elasticity (total lack of response to changes in price) and infinite elasticity (an infinitely great response to a change in price).

2 The 'watershed' between these two ends of the spectrum is unitary elasticity, where responses to changes in price are exactly proportional.

3 On the 'zero' side of the 'watershed' we have a range of inelastic responses to changes in price, ranging between 0 and up to (but not including) 1.

4 On the 'infinity' side of the 'watershed' we have a range of elastic responses to changes in price, ranging above 1 and up to ∞.

Diagrammatically this may be illustrated as shown in Fig. 4.4.

Fig. 4.4 *The spectrum of elasticity*

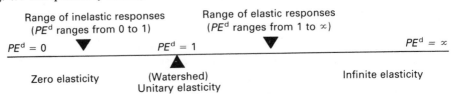

Point elasticity

Where a straight line demand curve extends from the price axis on the left to the quantity axis on the right, as in Fig. 4.5, it can be demonstrated mathematically that the elasticity ranges from infinity at the price axis to zero at the quantity axis, while halfway along the line it is 1. This is explained in the notes below Fig. 4.5.

Fig. 4.5 *Elasticity of demand along a straight line demand curve*

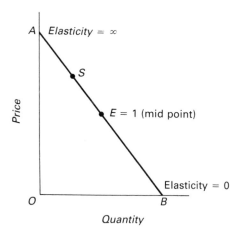

Notes

1 It can be shown mathematically that the elasticity of demand varies from infinity at the price axis to zero at the quantity axis.

2 The explanation is as follows. Our formula for elasticity of demand is

$$E = \frac{\text{Percentage change in quantity demanded of X}}{\text{Percentage change in price of X}}$$

$$= \left(\frac{\text{change in quantity demanded of X}}{\text{original quantity demanded of X}} \times 100\right) \div \left(\frac{\text{change in price of X}}{\text{original price of X}} \times 100\right)$$

$$= \left(\frac{\text{change in quantity demanded of X}}{\text{original quantity demanded of X}}\right) \times \left(\frac{\text{original price of X}}{\text{change in price of X}}\right)$$

We can rearrange this to read

$$E = \frac{\text{change in quantity demanded of X}}{\text{change in price of X}} \times \frac{\text{original price of X}}{\text{original quantity demanded of X}}$$

Now the first of these fractions is the reciprocal of the slope of the curve. The slope of any curve has the general formula $\frac{\text{change in } y \text{ axis}}{\text{change in } x \text{ axis}}$; in other words, $\frac{\text{change in price of X}}{\text{change in quantity demanded of X}}$. Our first term is the reciprocal of the slope, i.e. $\frac{\text{change in quantity demanded of X}}{\text{change in price of X}}$. Since, with a straight line, the slope is constant, the reciprocal of the slope must be constant too. Let us disregard this constant for the present and consider elasticity by just taking account of the other term in the equation. This may now be written

$$E = \text{Constant} \times \frac{\text{original price of X}}{\text{original quantity of X}}$$

$$= \text{Constant} \times \frac{P}{Q}$$

At the price axis $Q = 0$ so that $\dfrac{P}{Q} = \dfrac{P}{0}$ which can only be described as ∞ (infinitely elastic demand). At the quantity axis $P = 0$, so that $\dfrac{P}{Q} = \dfrac{0}{Q} = 0$ (zero elasticity of demand.) Neither of these, ∞ or 0, will be affected by the constant factor related to the slope of the curve.

3 It can further be shown mathematically that the elasticity at any point on the curve can be found by using the formula

$$E = \frac{\text{Distance from point to the quantity axis}}{\text{Distance from point to the price axis}}$$

Thus the elasticity at point $S = \dfrac{SB}{SA} = \dfrac{3}{1} = 3$ and the elasticity at the midpoint will always be 1. (The proof of the formula mentioned above is given in the notes to Fig. 4.6.)

Where the demand curve is not a straight line, the slope of the demand curve at any point is the tangent to the curve at that point. If we then extend this tangent as a straight line to the x and y axes the elasticity is found by taking the fraction

$$\frac{\text{Distance from point to } x \text{ axis,}}{\text{Distance from point to } y \text{ axis}}$$

This is illustrated in Fig. 4.6.

Fig. 4.6 *The elasticity of demand at points on a demand curve*

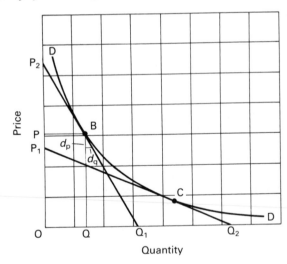

Notes

1 The formula for point elasticity is

$$E = \frac{\text{Distance of the point from the quantity axis}}{\text{Distance of the point from the price axis}}$$

Thus at point B

$$E = \frac{Q_1B}{P_2B} = \frac{3.6 \text{ cm}}{2.8 \text{ cm}} = 1.285$$

While at point C

$$E = \frac{Q_2C}{P_1C} = \frac{2.2 \text{ cm}}{4.8 \text{ cm}} = 0.458$$

Thus the price elasticity at point B is fairly elastic (a number greater than 1) but at point C price elasticity is **fairly inelastic** (a number between 1 and zero).

2   The proof of the formula is as follows. Taking point B as the point on the curve for which we wish to determine the elasticity of demand, imagine a very tiny change in price (d_p) producing a very tiny quantity change, (d_q). With such a tiny change the slope of the curve is the slope of the tangent to the curve drawn at the point B, which in the diagram is the line P_2BQ_1. As given in the notes to Fig. 4.5

$$E = \frac{\text{Change in quantity demanded of X}}{\text{Change in price of X}} \times \frac{\text{Original price of X}}{\text{Original quantity demanded of X}}$$

$$= \frac{d_q}{d_p} \times \frac{P}{Q}$$

$\frac{d_q}{d_p}$ is the reciprocal of the slope of the tangent, and since the tangent is a straight line it must be a constant. Since the slope is $\frac{BQ}{QQ_1}$ the reciprocal is $\frac{QQ_1}{BQ}$. Thus

$$\frac{d_q}{d_p} = \frac{QQ_1}{BQ}$$

The other half of the formula is

$$\frac{P}{Q} = \frac{PO}{OQ} = \frac{BQ}{OQ}$$

So

$$E = \frac{QQ_1}{BQ} \times \frac{BQ}{OQ} = \frac{QQ_1}{OQ}$$

However, the line BQ is parallel to the line OP_2, so that it divides the lines OQ_1 and P_2Q_1 in similar proportions.

So

$$\frac{QQ_1}{OQ} = \frac{BQ_1}{P_2B} = \frac{\text{Distance of point B from the quantity axis}}{\text{Distance of point B from the price axis}}$$

So

$$E = \frac{\text{Distance of the point from the quantity axis}}{\text{Distance of point from the price axis}}$$

3   WHAT DETERMINES THE PRICE ELASTICITY OF DEMAND?

The price elasticity of demand depends upon several factors. The chief ones are listed below.

The existence of close substitutes

Some products can easily be replaced by alternative goods if their price rises. If there are no close substitutes for a commodity, demand for it will be inelastic, since customers will be forced to buy it if they want that particular class of satisfaction. Thus while the demand for cabbage is elastic, since there are many other vegetables, the demand for tobacco is relatively inelastic, since there are no close substitutes for tobacco. A shortage of close substitutes is a particular feature of goods that are habit-forming, like tobacco and alcohol, the demand for which tends therefore to be inelastic.

Although it is sometimes said that the demand for luxuries is elastic and the demand for necessities is inelastic, this statement is not necessarily valid. Thus luxuries having no near substitutes, like diamond engagement rings, are usually in inelastic demand, while necessities like brown bread are in elastic demand, for there are dozens of similar products available on the shelves of supermarkets as substitutes.

Where products can be varied by the addition of special features it is essential to define clearly the goods under consideration. Thus if the Chancellor increases the tax on tobacco, demand for different brands will vary, reflecting the comparative brand loyalties. Almost any form of branding reduces elasticity of demand, by developing a brand loyalty in which the customer believes that similar products are not substitutes for the favoured brand.

The relative insignificance of the cost of an item

Where a commodity represents a very tiny fraction of total income, demand for it will be inelastic, so that demand will be unresponsive to price changes. On occasions the old adage that 'there is no point in spoiling a ship for a ha'porth of tar' tends to encourage inelasticity. Thus a rise in the price of Christmas crackers is unlikely to affect the amount demanded, for the appearance of the festive table is enhanced by their use, and the occasion enlivened out all of proportion to their cost.

Advertising and brand loyalty

Any activity which ties customers to a product by developing brand loyalty will make demand for the product inelastic because it makes substitution more difficult. Advertising seeks to induce the customer to adopt the brand, and then stay with it for the future, so that he/she becomes insensitive to changes in price.

The range of possible uses

Where a product has several possible uses, e.g. flour, demand is likely to be more elastic with respect to price than a good which can only be put to one use, for the less essential uses will be discontinued as price rises.

4   THE IMPORTANCE OF PRICE ELASTICITY

There are many business situations where the elasticity of demand with respect to price may be of crucial importance. A few of the chief cases are described below.

Decisions to raise or lower prices

However well a firm may be placed with respect to competition, all situations change over a period of time. New products and new variations on old themes may erode markets previously considered safe. Even a firm which believes demand for its products to be inelastic may find to its chagrin that a rise in price proves to be the last straw as far as its customers are concerned. If every demand curve varies from infinite elasticity at the price axis to zero elasticity at the quantity axis successive price increases *ceteris paribus* must eventually arrive at the point where the demand becomes elastic.

Before considering the effects of elasticity on income of the firm (see Fig. 4.8) note that the revenue received for any particular quantity sold is represented on a diagram by the price-quantity rectangle. Thus in Fig. 4.7 the rectangle OQ_1DP_1 represents the revenue from selling Q_1 items at a price of P_1. If the price is raised above P_1 will this bring in extra revenue or not? It depends upon the elasticity of demand. If demand is inelastic the revenue received will increase. If demand is elastic and many customers turn to some alternative product the revenue received will decline. This is illustrated in Fig. 4.8, and explained in the notes below it.

Every decision to raise prices or lower prices will therefore be affected by the entrepreneur's estimate of the price elasticity of demand. If his intention is to lower prices and thus attract increased sales in the belief that this will raise total revenue he will achieve the desired effect if demand is elastic. Sales will increase more than proportionately, and total revenue will rise. There will be no point in lowering prices if demand is inelastic, for sales will not increase much. Total revenue would then fall because he would receive less for each unit sold. Of course, an entrepreneur who is seeking to maximise profits will have to bear the cost side of his operations in mind when making decisions to

Fig. 4.7 *The total revenue (price × quantity) of a firm or an industry*

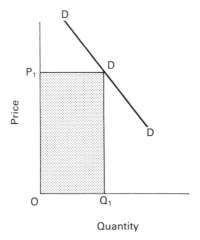

Fig. 4.8 *Price elasticity and changes of revenue*

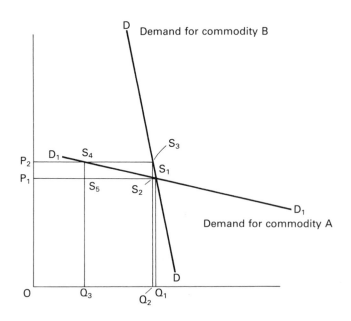

Notes
1   The demand curves for Commodity A and Commodity B intersect at S_1. At a price of P_1 sales of Q_1 of both commodities are made (the commodities are quite unrelated to one another). The revenues that result are shown by the rectangle $OQ_1S_1P_1$, each firm making the same revenue from the sale of its product.
2   It can be shown mathematically that where two demand curves intersect at a point, as in this case, the demand for the product which has the steeper curve is more inelastic than the demand for the product which has a gradually sloping demand curve.
3   A decision is made in each case to raise the price by 10 per cent.
4   In the case of Commodity A, the demand is elastic and quantity falls to Q_3. Revenue is now represented by the rectangle $OQ_3S_4P_2$. The decision to raise prices brought in extra revenue of $P_1S_5S_4P_2$, but involved losses of revenue of $Q_3Q_1S_1S_5$. Clearly it was an unfortunate decision, resulting in a fall in total revenue and excess capacity in the firm (over half its output is no longer needed).
5   In the case of Commodity B the demand is inelastic. Revenue rises to the area shown by the rectangle $OQ_2S_3P_2$. The decision to raise prices brought in an extra revenue of $P_1S_2S_3P_2$ and only caused losses of $Q_2Q_1S_1S_2$. Total revenue rose and the plant is still working at almost full capacity.

raise or lower prices. Even if demand is elastic and lower prices mean higher sales and therefore higher total revenue it will not necessarily be worthwhile if the costs of producing the extra units rise and devour the extra revenue.

Conversely, an entrepreneur who is thinking of raising prices to raise total revenue will only be successful in achieving his aim if demand is inelastic. Then the higher price will not choke off demand, and increased revenue will result. If demand is elastic the increased prices only result in reduced total revenue as customers are frightened away by the price rise, and he will lose not only income but also his share of the market. The reader should draw diagrams like Fig. 4.8, but only with one demand curve, and examine the effects of raising and lowering prices.

Decisions to impose taxation

If the Chancellor proposes to introduce a tax on a particular product the success of the tax as a method of raising revenue will depend upon the elasticity of demand for that product. If the consumer is not particularly interested in enjoying that class of satisfaction he will avoid the tax by giving up the satisfaction. If the consumer is unable to give up the satisfaction, because he is addicted to it perhaps, he will continue to purchase the product and pay the tax as he does so.

It follows that the most successful taxes are imposed on products for which the demand is inelastic because generally the public prefer not to surrender that particular type of satisfaction. Traditionally taxes on the 'poor man's luxuries' – tea, beer and tobacco – have been the easiest to impose when revenue had to be raised. In recent years the taxes on petrol and on motor vehicles have been extremely lucrative, for in times of poor public transport even the poor person must afford a car or van to get to work. Once the capital cost of a vehicle has been accepted the utilisation of the vehicle for other simple pleasures – outings and holidays – becomes economic and the tax represents only a marginal addition to total costs. The motorcar is the new 'poor man's luxury' and chancellors have seized on petrol as a vital revenue raiser. Indeed in 1973, when the oil producers raised prices by as much as four times, they justified the increase on the grounds that they were entitled to share in the enormous incomes governments in advanced nations were collecting from taxes on oil products.

If taxation on goods and services for which the demand is inelastic ensures that the government raises large revenues from the taxes imposed, it is equally true that taxation on goods for which demand is elastic results in changes in the pattern of demand. Consumers prefer to do without the taxed item, and sales fall away to the discomfiture of entrepreneurs who have invested capital in its production. Thus a government may decide to discourage demand for a particular product which it considers socially undesirable.

Many taxes are small relative to the price of the taxed article. A change in taxation from, say, 5 to 10 per cent is unlikely to affect demand greatly and demand has to be very elastic indeed to lower total tax revenue when taxation is increased.

Elasticities in overseas trade

The elasticities of imports and exports are vital in any decision to raise or lower currency values, either by devaluation or 'floating' upwards or downwards in the modern manner. If demand for UK exports is elastic it will pay to depreciate the pound and make UK goods effectively cheaper to foreigners, provided the extra supplies can be produced. The increased sales will raise total revenues and thus improve the balance of payments position. If demand for UK goods is inelastic there will be little point in depreciating sterling, for not only will demand increase only a little, but the total revenue from foreigners will actually decline, making the balance of payments position more difficult.

Viewed from a different angle, it is often suggested that West Germany, with a strong currency, should raise its prices by revaluing the Deutschmark. This will, it is said, reduce demand for German goods and enable other countries to sell their products more easily. Is this true?

Once again it depends upon the elasticity of demand for the goods. If the quality, design, etc., of West German goods is such that demand is inelastic, so that foreigners still prefer to buy them to French, Italian or UK goods, the revaluation of the Deutschmark will only make things worse. The total revenue from the sale of slightly fewer German goods will increase because of the price rise, and the West German balance of payments will improve still further, while foreigners buying German goods will have even less foreign exchange to spare for the products of other nations.

SELF-ASSESSMENT QUESTIONS

1 Define elasticity.

2 Define price elasticity of demand and explain how we calculate it.

3 Explain 'the spectrum of elasticities'.

4 Can we talk about the elasticity of a demand curve?

5   THE PRICE ELASTICITY OF SUPPLY

Price elasticity of supply is the responsiveness of supply to changes in price. Once again it is found by the formula.

$$\text{Price elasticity of supply} = \frac{\text{Percentage change in quantity of } x \text{ supplied}}{\text{Percentage change in price of } x}$$

Supply curves with constant elasticity

As with demand, certain supply curves have constant elasticity all the way along the curve. They are illustrated in Fig. 4.9. This shows that perfectly elastic supply is a straight line, parallel to the quantity axis, while zero elasticity (supply completely unresponsive to price) is a straight line parallel to the price axis.

Perfectly elastic supply is rather improbable in real life: it indicates that at

Fig. 4.9 *Supply curves with constant elasticity*

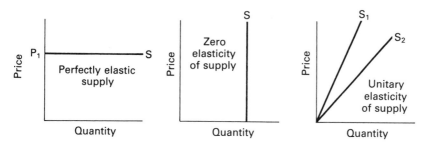

prices below P_1 suppliers are not prepared to supply at all, but at the price of P_1 they are prepared to supply any quantity required. A supplier motivated by non-economic motives might behave in this way. For example, if as a matter of principle he/she would not supply below the 'fair' price, nor charge more than the item was 'worth' even when demand was strong, it means that at prices below P_1 nothing would be supplied and at a price of P_1 the entire output of his/her plant would be available.

Supply with zero elasticity is quite common in real life; the paintings of Rembrandt have zero elasticity of supply and the price they fetch is entirely dependent upon demand. Since supply cannot change the only changing influence which can find the 'fair' price is demand, and equilibrium price reflects the change in demand since the last time that particular work was offered for sale.

Unitary elasticity of supply is a special case. Every straight line supply curve passing through the origin must have unitary elasticity. Quantity supplied must change proportionately to price if the 'curve' is to be both straight and through the origin.

Elasticity of supply and business decision-making

The elasticity of supply depends upon decisions made by entrepreneurs and expansion or contraction can rarely be put into effect at a moment's notice. At the very least stocks have to be released from storage if extra supplies are to come on to the market. More frequently output must be raised by working overtime, increasing machine loading, etc. Supply will therefore tend to be elastic in the following circumstances:

1 Where supplies have been stockpiled in anticipation of a change in demand, and are available to come on to the market at short notice.
2 Where an entrepreneur produces for several different markets and can divert supplies to the market offering the best rewards.
3 Where an entrepreneur produces a variety of products and can turn production over easily from less profitable lines to more profitable ones.
4 Where the costs of entering the industry, or the losses suffered by leaving

it, are small. A stall-holder whose overhead costs consist of a £2 stall rent is unlikely to hesitate about leaving the field of activity if the produce on offer proves unremunerative. A manufacturer with specific capital assets is less mobile (see page 157).

5   Avoidance of contractual commitments encourages elasticity of supply. Contractual commitments may prevent an entrepreneur changing over from one activity to another more profitable alternative use which has arisen subsequently. The shipowner who has chartered his vessel on a long-term basis may see profitable opportunities slip away – indeed, this is the chief advantage to the charterer of a long-term arrangement. Landed proprietors who grant long leases in inflationary times are similarly disadvantaged.

In each of the cases 1 – 5 above an increase in price will quickly attract supplies into the market, while a decrease in price will drive supplies away, or discourage the supplier so that he/she reduces output, or stockpiles, or diverts goods to more lucrative markets.

6   PRICE FLUCTUATIONS AND THE ELASTICITY OF SUPPLY AND DEMAND

Fluctuations in price are a source of much inconvenience both to producers and to consumers. In the market economies (as distinct from the planned economies) of the world the development of highly organised markets is an attempt to smooth out fluctuations in price.

Generally speaking, the prices of primary products fluctuate more than the prices of secondary products. Not only are the agricultural products susceptible to interruptions of supply due to bad weather, crop diseases, etc., but all primary products tend to be carried long distances to the market, so that they are peculiarly susceptible to delays due to strikes, wars or rumours of wars.

Fluctuations in price are difficult to illustrate because of the ease with which wrong ideas about elasticity can be conveyed. Readers are apt to forget that elasticity refers only to a particular price: it is not constant all the way along a demand curve, except in the special cases of infinite elasticity, zero elasticity and unitary elasticity.

To avoid confusion, Fig. 4.10 has been drawn showing two demand curves and two supply curves meeting at a point. The diagram has then been split into four parts, to illustrate the effect of four possible cases which will cause prices to fluctuate. These are:

1   A change in demand, supply being elastic – Fig. 4.11(*a*).
2   A change in demand, supply being inelastic – Fig 4.11(*b*).
3   A change in supply, demand being elastic – Fig. 4.12(*a*).
4   A change in supply, demand being inelastic – Fig. 4.12(*b*).

Fig. 4.10 *Demand and supply curves with different elasticities*

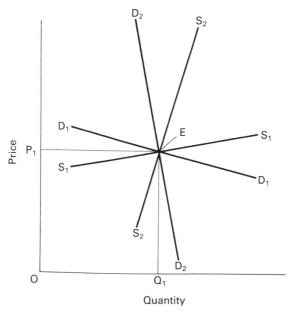

Notes

At the price of P_1 the demand curve D_1 is more elastic than the demand curve D_2, and the supply curve S_1 is more elastic than the supply curve S_2. The diagram is now split into four parts and discussed in Figs. 4.11 and 4.12.

Fig. 4.11 *Elasticity of supply and change of demand:* (a) *supply elastic;* (b) *supply inelastic*

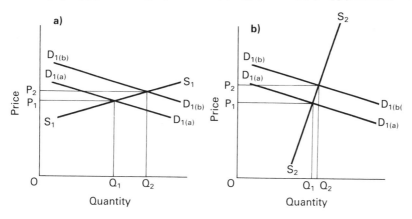

Notes

1 Demand is elastic like D_1 in Fig. 4.10.

2 The result of an increase in demand in Fig. 4.11(*a*) is that supply adjusts easily to the changed demand, turning out the increased quantity required with only a small increase in price.

3 The result of an increase in demand in Fig. 4.11(*b*) is that supply adjusts with difficulty to the changed demand. To call the extra supplies on to the market at all, large increases in price are needed, because supply is inelastic.

4 The reader should work out for himself on a piece of scrap paper what would have happened in each case if: (*a*) demand had decreased, instead of increased; (*b*) demand, instead of being like D_1 in Fig. 4.10, had been like D_2 in Fig. 4.10, i.e. less elastic.

Fig. 4.12 *Elasticity of demand and change in supply: (a) demand elastic; (b) demand inelastic*

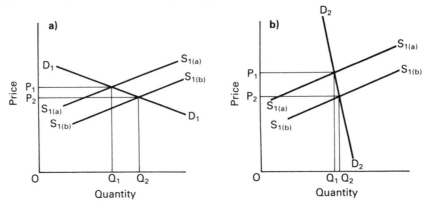

Notes

1   Supply is elastic, like S_1 in Fig. 4.10.

2   The result of an increased willingness to supply is that demand in Fig. 4.12(*a*) extends rapidly to consume the increased supply offered. Price falls only slightly and the increase in goods supplied is large.

3   The result of an increased willingness to supply in Fig. 4.12(*b*) is that demand extends only slightly, price falls a good deal, and the extra quantity supplied is small.

4   The reader should again work out for himself the effects of: (*a*) a decrease in supplies offered by producers: (*b*) the changes that would have resulted had the supply curve, instead of being elastic as in S_1 been inelastic like S_2 in Fig. 4.10.

7   INTER-RELATED DEMANDS AND SUPPLIES

It frequently happens that two commodities are closely related either with respect to the demand for them or with respect to their supply. Thus the process of cracking crude oil to derive petrol from it inevitably produces a host of other derivatives which are inseparable from the process. As the motorcar age developed the quantity of petrol required rose accordingly. In 1946 there were 1.8 million motor vehicles on the roads of the UK; by 1987 the number had risen to 22.2 million. The production of vast quantities of petrol (gasoline) meant the production of vast quantities of products which were in joint supply, such as domestic heating oil. If this vast output was to be used and not just wasted it was necessary to devise boilers which would use it, domestic heating appliances which would make an economic package of equipment for householders, etc.

The research and technical problems arising from the need to deal with waste products and discover some useful utilisation of them are, of course, extremely interesting, but in this chapter we are concerned with elasticity. What kinds of inter-related demands and supplies are met with, and how do price elasticities affect the prices of the goods concerned?

We must consider the following types of inter-related demand and supply:

1 **Joint demand** – of which we may distinguish two types, complementary demand and derived demand.

2 **Joint supply.**
3 **Competitive demand of substitutes.**
4 **Composite demand.**
We must now examine each of these more closely.

Joint demand

Sometimes two products are required together. They may be of equal importance in the situation, each complementing (or completing) the other. Thus knives and forks, gin and tonic, strawberries and cream, and bread and butter are complementary goods, said to be in **complementary demand**. Where one product is paramount and the other subsidiary, as with motorcars and petrol, we speak of **derived demand**. The need for petrol is derived from the posession of the motorcar. If you sell your motorcar you cease to concern yourself about petrol.

Complementary and derived demands are similar, in that an increase in the demand for one product leads to an increase in the demand for the other. What effects such a change in demand has on the price of commodities depends on the conditions of supply. In Fig. 4.13 the supply curves have been drawn at different slopes to indicate different elasticities, but readers are reminded that slope is not always the same as elasticity.

Fig. 4.13 *Joint demand: motorcars and petrol*

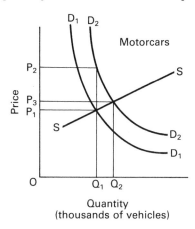
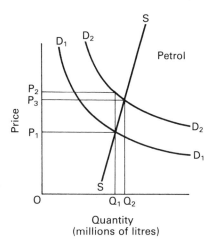

Notes
1   The change from D_1 to D_2 represents a similar proportional increase over D_1.
2   For the purpose of this example, vehicles are imagined to be in elastic supply but the supply of petrol is inelastic. Consequently, the change in demand affects the price of the two goods differently.
3   Both products eventually settle at a price of P_3 and a quantity of Q_2. Because of the different elasticities of supply the price of vehicles rises by one ninth, but the price of petrol increases by about half.

The reader is now invited to consider what would be the effect on the price of petrol of a change in the conditions of supply of motor vehicles. Imagine that a major vehicle manufacturer has restructured plant to lower prices, i.e.

to give a new supply curve for cars. What will be the effect of this on the demand for vehicles and on the demand for, and price of, petrol? No similar change in the conditions of supply of petrol has occurred.

DERIVED DEMAND – A SPECIAL CASE

A special case of derived demand is the demand for the factors of production, which is derived from the demand for 'utilities' to satisfy 'wants'. If entrepreneurs are to produce, they must have land, labour and capital. The demand of the motorcar manufacturers for land, premises, plant and machinery, raw materials, labour and power is derived from the need to produce motor vehicles to satisfy the demand for them.

Joint supply

Some products are in joint supply – that is, one cannot be produced without the other. We cannot increase the supply of hides without producing beef. In the extraction of petrol from crude oil profitable disposal of the many by-products is essential if costs of the main process are to be reduced. By skilful use of petrochemical technology, the oil industry uses the majority of its derivatives, but not without affecting the price of any commodities with which they compete.

Simple cases of joint supply, like hides and beef, may be illustrated as shown in Fig. 4.14.

Fig. 4.14 *Joint supply: hides and beef*

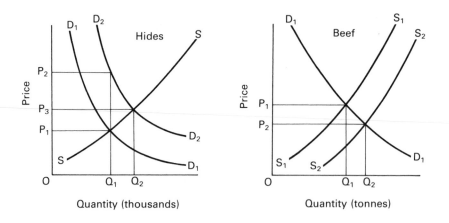

Quantity (thousands) Quantity (tonnes)

Notes
1 A change in demand for leather goods increases the demand for hides. Demand moves from D_1D_1 to D_2D_2 and supply extends to Q_2. Price settles at P_3.
2 The increased output of hides throws more beef on the market. The supply of beef therefore changes from S_1S_1 to S_2S_2 but there has been no increase in demand. This means that the price of beef must fall to P_2. As it does so, demand extends to consume the extra output.

Competitive demand of substitutes

Sometimes one commodity is a substitute for another, and an increased demand for one will lead to a reduction in demand for the other. An obvious example is margarine, which is a substitute for butter. Similarly, modern artificial fibres are excellent substitutes for natural fibres. An increased use of fluffy synthetic fibres will lead to a decline in the demand for wool. Fig. 4.15 illustrates the situation when an increased demand for butter leads to a reduced demand for margarine.

Fig. 4.15 *Competitive demand: butter and margarine*

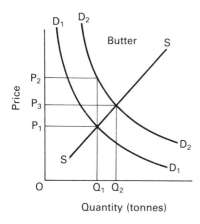 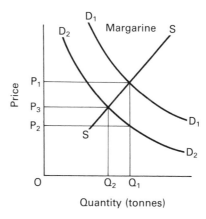

Notes

1   The elasticity of supply of both butter and margarine have been deemed to be similar.

2   Owing to some change in the condition of demand, butter is more strongly demanded. The price of butter rises from P_1 to P_2 settling at P_3 as the quantity supplied extends from Q_1 to Q_2.

3   Margarine is now not demanded so strongly, since butter has been substituted for it. Price falls from P_1 to P_2 but recovers to P_3 as supply contracts from Q_1 to Q_2.

COMPETITIVE DEMAND – THE NEED TO CHOOSE

Substitution takes place not only when the qualities of the substitute are almost identical with those of the goods it replaces but also when the purchase of one commodity prevents the purchase of the other. To this extent all goods are in competitive demand, especially where a particular product is expensive. The family buying its first motorcar finds it must give up many other items it previously enjoyed, and a young couple with a large mortgage may postpone having a family.

This type of competitive demand affects the total demand for any particular class of goods, and explains why prosperity in particular industries is often accompanied by a decline in business elsewhere. It illustrates again the idea of 'opportunity cost': that having selected one opportunity, the other opportunities which we might have chosen are lost to us. This leads to an effect called **cross elasticity** (see Section 8 overleaf).

Composite demand

Many commodities are non-specific – that is, they may be used for a variety of purposes. Steel may be used to build ships, lay railways, store fuel oil, make consumer durables like washing machines and refrigerators, or form the framework of hospitals, hotels and office blocks. The demand for steel is the sum of all these varied demands. Such a demand is said to be a composite demand.

8 CROSS ELASTICITY OF DEMAND

Sometimes it is helpful to know the change in demand for a commodity that is likely to follow a change in the price of some other commodity. This is particularly true where the goods are substitutes for one another, or are complementary goods. For example, a change in the price of butter might cause a large change in the demand for margarine, while a change in the price of petrol might influence the demand for new motor vehicles.

The responsiveness of demand for one commodity to changes in the price of another commodity is called the cross elasticity of demand. The formula is

Cross elasticity of demand =

$$\frac{\text{Percentage change in quantity demanded of commodity X}}{\text{Percentage change in the price of commodity Y}}$$

Cross elasticity varies from minus infinity to plus infinity and is greatly affected by the degree of complementarity or substitutability. Thus with items in complementary demand, such as fish and chips, a rise in the price of potatoes may lead to a large reduction in the consumption of both goods. With butter and margarine, by contrast, which are substitutes for one another, a rise in the price of butter will lead to a rise in the demand for margarine. Typical figures might be as follows with respect to fish and chips: suppose a 20 per cent rise in potato prices causes a 40 per cent drop in sales of fish:

$$\text{Cross elasticity of demand for fish} = \frac{-40\%}{+20\%}$$
$$= -2$$

(Complementary goods have negative cross elasticities.)

With respect to butter and margarine, if a 20 per cent rise in the price of butter causes a 50 per cent increase in the quantity demanded of margarine

$$\text{Cross elasticity of demand for margarine} = \frac{50\%}{20\%}$$
$$= 2\frac{1}{2}$$

(Substitute goods have positive cross elasticities.)

9   INCOME ELASTICITY OF DEMAND

Income elasticity of demand is the responsiveness of demand to changes in income, and is found by the formula

Income elasticity of demand =

$$\frac{\text{Percentage change in quantity of a good or service demanded}}{\text{Percentage change in income}}$$

Income elasticity of demand is of crucial importance in planning many aspects of production, and the more advanced a nation is the more influence income has on the pattern of demand. The standard of living of the 7 million inhabitants of the UK in 1750 was very similar to that of their ancestors in Norman times. By 1850 it had changed considerably and by 1950 it had changed out of all recognition as the pattern of demand altered. A product may be in great demand at a time when incomes are low, but when incomes rise the demand may fall away considerably as other products become attainable. This is especially true of inferior goods. A smaller and smaller fraction of total income has to be spent each year on basic necessities like food and clothing. The demand for durable, sophisticated consumer goods rises enormously as we enter an affluent era, and later still the demand for services increases too. The leisure/pleasure industries experience boom times when general affluence prevails. Table 4.1 illustrates the range of income elasticities.

Table 4.1 The range of income elasticities of demand (see notes overleaf)

Effect on demand of a 25% increase in real incomes	Type of commodity				
	(a) Inferior good	(b)	(c)	(d)	Sophisticated good or service
Change in demand	Fall of 20%	No change	Rise of 1%	Rise of 25%	Rise of 60%
% Change in quantity / % Change in income	$\frac{-20}{+25}$	$\frac{0}{25}$	$\frac{1}{25}$	$\frac{25}{25}$	$\frac{+60}{+25}$
Value of income elasticity	−0.8	0	0.04	1	+2.4
Type of income elasticity of demand	Negative income elasticity	Zero income elasticity	Inelastic demand with respect to income	Unitary elasticity of demand	Elastic demand with respect to income

Notes
1 For most goods demand increases as income rises so that the income elasticity of demand is positive. The demand for inferior goods declines, however, since the standard of living of consumers is raised above bare necessities. Inferior goods therefore display negative income elasticity.
2 For some goods demand does not increase, but is maintained at the same level. This probably becomes true of many goods and services once the level of income reaches a point where families enjoy a steady sufficiency of the product. The demand for such goods then has zero income elasticity.
3 With other goods demand continues to rise to a certain degree. This may be only to a limited degree (inelastic demand with respect to income) or proportional to the rise in income (unitary income elasticity of demand), or it may be more than proportional, a larger share of the increase in income being spent on the good or service. Sophisticated goods (such as motorcars) are demanded in this way. The man who climbs into an income bracket where he can afford his first car buys a small family saloon. Five years later he has a more expensive model and fifteen years later his Bentley or Mercedes is the pride of the district.

The most important aspects of changing incomes are as follows:

a) **The growth of egalitarianism** In most countries, but particularly in the UK from 1945–1979, the trend has been towards greater equality of incomes. When incomes are spread more equally consumption rises dramatically as the poorer section of the population is able to afford a better standard of living. Demand for luxury goods declines with the incomes of the formerly rich people. Demand for mass-produced consumer durables rises more than proportionately, as does the demand for prepared foods, labour-saving devices, popular entertainment and leisure/pleasure facilities. This trend has important implications for the consumer goods industries. Since 1979, despite the return to a more market-orientated economy, this trend is still continuing.

b) **Reduced investment** When incomes rise the level of consumption of a broader spectrum of the population is increased. This means that overall savings do not grow quickly enough to finance the necessary retooling and investment. This has implications for the machine tool industries, the construction industries and the whole range of industries making producer goods.

c) **Increased tertiary activity** Increasing incomes lead inevitably to increased demand for personal services. While the demand for basic needs like food, clothing, shelter, etc., continues to be strong, the relatively large increases are in the demand for education, entertainment, medical and dental treatment, vacational pleasures, etc. Consultancy services in fashions, interior decoration, landscaping and gardening, etc., are also affected.

d) **Income elasticity and the balance of payments** Income elasticity of demand and supply has important implications for the balance of payments. This is explained more fully later, but basically it refers to the general demand for imports and exports. Home demand, as UK affluence rises (or is more equally spread), sucks in imports and consumes home-produced goods which would otherwise be available for export. Foreign changes in affluence affect the demand for UK exports and the availability of raw materials and basic foods we wish to import.

e) **Variability in the economy** The most important side-effect of increasing affluence is the general unrest that prevails in all aspects of the economy. A primitive economy may persist for centuries with little alteration in its general conduct. Fat and lean years will occur, but the broad framework of production will alter little. With increasing affluence the income elasticity of demand for particular products has its effect upon the investment opportunities available. Some industries will grow only slowly. Others will be expanded as demand for their products increases more than proportionately. These changes affect the demand for skills: declining industries and expanding industries compete for the best grades of labour to the disadvantage of the declining industry. The demand for 'growth' – greater and greater levels of affluence – leads to the aggressive exploitation of the earth's resources, and political results follow which change even the patterns of societies themselves.

SELF-ASSESSMENT QUESTIONS

5 Why are the responses to market changes of those who demand goods or services more rapid than the responses of suppliers?

6 What is the relationship between wool and mutton as far as demand and supply are concerned?

7 Give an example of two items that are in competitive demand. What would be the effect on one of them of a fall in price of the other?

8 Incomes are expected to rise in a third world country where many people live at a subsistence level. What would you expect to change in the pattern of demand in such a country?

REVISION TEST

Answers	Questions
	1 What is meant by 'the price elasticity of demand'?
1 The price elasticity of demand is the responsiveness of the quantity demanded to changes in price. The formula is $$E = \frac{\% \text{ change in quantity demanded of X}}{\% \text{ change in price of X}}$$	**2** What are the limits of elasticity?

2 Infinite elasticity at one end of the spectrum and zero elasticity at the other.

3 Where is the dividing line between elasticity and inelasticity?

---

3 At unitary elasticity, i.e. $E = 1$.

4 Which demand curves have constant elasticity?

---

4 The infinitely elastic curve, the curve with zero elasticity and the curve with unitary elasticity.

5 What determines the price elasticity of demand for a good?

---

5 *(a)* Whether close substitutes exist for the good; *(b)* whether the cost is insignificant relative to the good's utility; *(c)* whether the good is well promoted and the subject of brand loyalty.

6 What is meant by 'price elasticity of supply'?

---

6 Price elasticity of supply is the responsiveness of supply to changes in price.

7 When does supply tend to be elastic with respect to price?

---

7 Supply tends to be elastic where the conditions of supply permit rapid response to business decisions, and inelastic where response can only be slow because plant has to be designed and built, etc.

8 What is meant by cross elasticity?

---

8 It is the relation between the changes in demand for one product with respect to changes in the price of another. Example: a rise in the price of butter causes an increase in the demand for margarine.

9 Why might a change in the distribution of income be of interest to the businessman?

---

9 Because it might produce a more than proportional change in the demand for his product.

Go over the test until you are quite sure of the answers.

ANSWERS

(See Self-assessment questions on pages 130 and 141.)

1 Elasticity is the tendency of some things to extend when forces are exerted upon them, and then to return to their former positions when the force is removed.

2 Price elasticity of demand is the responsiveness of the quantity demanded to changes in the price of a good or service. It may be found by using the formula:

$$E = \frac{\% \text{ change in the quantity demanded of X}}{\% \text{ change in price of X}}$$

Thus if price decreases by 5 per cent and the quantity demanded rises by 20 per cent we have:

$$E = \frac{20\%}{-5\%} = -4$$

Demand is said to be elastic because the rise in the quantity demanded is more than proportional to the change in price. Although strictly speaking the answer is −4 by convention we disregard the − sign and just speak of the elasticity of demand as 4.

Similarly if the price rose by 10 per cent and the quantity demanded fell by 2 per cent we should have:

$$E = \frac{-2\%}{10\%} = -0.2$$

Demand is said to be inelastic, and if we disregard the − sign again we would say the elasticity of demand is 0.2 (a less than proportional response to the change in price).

3 The spectrum of elasticities means the complete range of elasticities, from infinite elasticity at one end to zero elasticity at the other. The 'midpoint' of the spectrum is at unitary elasticity, where $E = 1$. Below 1, with values from 0 up to 0.99999 etc., we have varying degrees of inelasticity. At 1 we have the percentage responses of demand to changes in price exactly proportional to the price change. At values above 1, up to infinity, we have more than proportional responses of demand to changes in price.

4 We can only talk about the elasticity of a demand *curve* to changes in price in three special cases, infinitely elastic demand, unitary elasticity of demand and zero elasticity of demand. In all other cases the elasticity of demand will vary from infinite elasticity at the price axis to zero elasticity at the quantity axis. (Re-read Fig. 4.5 if you find this difficult.)

5 When market changes occur those who demand goods or services have only to make a quick, subjective re-appraisal of the changed situation, before either pressing in to snap up the bargains available (obviously prices have fallen) or to withdraw from the market and exercise their choices in some other direction (obviously the goods are less attractive now – probably because they are dearer). By contrast suppliers who elect to supply more have to overcome a number of problems before they can increase the supplies available. At the very least they must transport supplies in from other areas – possibly they have to set up new production facilities, take on more staff, order up raw materials, etc. Equally suppliers who elect to reduce production have to close down production lines, give out redundancy notices, etc. Supply cannot react immediately to a changed situation, but demand is almost instantaneous in its reactions.

6 Wool grows on mature sheep, and mutton is the meat from mature sheep. If we wish to keep wool production going we must not slaughter sheep and if we wish to increase our sales of mutton we must give up the wool crop. Wool and mutton are therefore in competitive supply; the supply of one prevents the supply of the other.

7 Butter and margarine are an example of items which are in competitive demand. If one of them falls in price it will become relatively more attractive than the other, and some consumers will switch demand to the item that is now more attractive than it was before. Similarly a fall in the price of tea may reduce the demand for coffee, since some of those who are indifferent to which they drink will increase their purchases of the item that is now cheaper.

8 In the third world country where many consumers are living at a subsistence level an increase in incomes will be a welcome development. Those whose prosperity rises will seek to vary the products previously purchased (which may be largely inferior goods) and purchase a more interesting basket of goods. This would not necessarily mean that they switched to luxury items, but to a marginally improved diet, marginally better clothing, household utensils, housing, etc. To the extent that some of the increase transfers to the better-off sections of society there could be a switch by these groups into improved secondary goods, and increased demand for tertiary services such as education, entertainment, health care, etc.

QUESTIONS ON CHAPTER 4

1 What is meant by the term 'elasticity of demand?' Illustrate ways in which this concept can be applied in marketing.

(Courtesy of the Institute of Marketing)

2 What is meant by 'the concept of elasticity'? How may this concept affect (a) a businessman seeking to expand his share of the market for a particular consumer durable; (b) a Chancellor seeking to raise revenue?

3 Define 'price elasticity of demand'. A motor vehicle priced at £7600 is selling 2000 models per week. The price is reduced to £6710 and the sales increase to 2050 models per week. What was the price elasticity of demand at £7600?

4 Define and discuss the concept of elasticity of demand and show by examples how it is related to total revenue.

(Courtesy of the Institute of Commercial Management)

5 What are the determinants of the value of elasticity for any particular product of your choice?

(Courtesy of the Institute of Marketing)

6 Explain the concepts of price elasticity of demand and income elasticity of demand and discuss their importance in marketing.

(Courtesy of the Institute of Marketing)

7 a) What is price elasticity of demand?
b) What are its implications for the pricing strategies of a firm and for tax revenue?

(Courtesy of the Association of Business Executives)

8 a) What is meant by the term elasticity and, giving examples, explain the importance of elasticity in relation to demand and supply.
b) From the small table of figures calculate the price elasticity of demand for wine and explain the meaning of your answer:

	Period 1	Period 2
Price of wine	100	90
Quantity of wine demanded	100	120

(Courtesy of the Association of Business Executives)

9 Distinguish between price elasticity of demand and income elasticity of demand. Illustrate by reference to particular commodities.

(Courtesy of the Institute of Commercial Management)

10 Explain how (a) price elasticity of demand and, (b) income elasticity of demand may influence the Chancellor of the Exchequer in taxing or subsidising a good.

(Courtesy of the Institute of Commercial Management)

11 'Natural rubber is in inelastic supply'. Do you agree with this statement? Justify your answer. What effect will a war affecting a major rubber growing area have on the incomes of rubber planters in areas unaffected by the hostilities?

12 The demand for tobacco is inelastic! The demand for tomatoes is elastic! Comment on these statements.

13 'It is no good cutting the price of our rail tickets,' said the accountant. 'The elasticities are against us in these affluent times.' What elasticities was he referring to? How were they operating against the railway company?

14 Draw and label fully: (a) an infinitely elastic demand curve; (b) a supply curve of zero elasticity; (c) a curve of unitary elastic demand.

15 A motorcar retailing at £10 000 is bringing in a total revenue of £15 000 000 per month. When the price is lowered to £9000 the total revenue increases to £18 000 000. What is the elasticity of demand at £10 000?

16 Why are percentage changes more useful than absolute changes when measuring elasticities? Illustrate your answer by reference to the elasticity of demand for two products, **A** and **B**, whose prices are cut by 10 per cent. Each improves its sales by five units per week. **A** had previous average weekly sales of 20 units, **B** had previously been selling 2000 units per week on average.

17 Explain how total revenue is affected by the elasticity of demand for a product. What is the impact on total revenue of raising the price of (a) a product in elastic demand and (b) a product in highly inelastic demand?

TIPS FOR STUDENTS: A SPECIMEN ANSWER TO QUESTION 6

Price elasticity is the responsiveness of demand to changes in the price of a good or service. The price elasticity of demand E_p is found by the formula:

$$E_p = \frac{\% \text{ change in the quantity demanded of X}}{\% \text{ change in price of X}}$$

Thus if an article falls in price by 10 per cent and as a result sales increase by 60 per cent:

$$E_p = \frac{+60\%}{-10\%}$$

$$= -6$$

By convention the − sign is disregarded and we say the elasticity is 6. The − sign simply means that the change in volume demanded is in the reverse direction to the price movement, i.e. a fall in price brings an increase in demand. 6 is an elasticity greater than 1, and therefore we can say the demand for that particular good is elastic at that price.

Income elasticity is the responsiveness of demand to change in income. Income elasticity of demand, for example, is found by the formula (where y = income):

$$E_y = \frac{\% \text{ change in quantity demanded of X}}{\% \text{ change in income}}$$

For example if incomes rise by 10 per cent and the quantity demanded rises by 2 per cent:

$$E_y = \frac{2\%}{10\%} = 0.2$$

This is a figure less than 1, and indicates that the demand for the good concerned is inelastic. It may be a basic requirement, which need not be demanded so strongly when incomes rise and a greater variety of goods may be enjoyed. It may be an inferior good which is positively spurned by those with higher incomes.

In marketing elasticities have great importance because they influence sales volume, market share and total income. For example, the price of our products is an aspect of our marketing policies. If we raise prices we would expect sales to decline, and if we cut prices we would expect sales to increase. Whether these expected results do in fact occur will depend upon the elasticity of demand for our products at the time. For example, if we are selling festive items (such as Christmas gifts in December) demand for our products will be strong and an increase in price would not necessarily cause a fall in demand – demand is inelastic just before the festival. It becomes much more elastic after the festival and we tend to cut prices to keep sales reasonably buoyant.

Changes in income are longer-term developments than price changes, but marketing staff should be aware of trends in incomes, particularly in the main markets for their particular products. For example, if incomes are rising it will be more sensible to aim at a quality line than an inferior line. The system of price lining, where firms market three lines, a cheap range, a better range and a top range, give some chance of capitalising on income changes. When incomes are rising we produce more of the middle and top ranges; when incomes are falling the middle and cheaper ranges are pushed more strongly.

5 | The theory of the firm

1 THE MARKET PLACE AND THE FIRM

Before studying the theory of the firm it is helpful to remind ourselves about the various market places in which firms operate, since the climate of activity in which firms operate influences their structure and their modes of operation.

A market is a place where exchanges are made; suppliers are in contact with buyers with a view to selling them goods or services, at prices to be determined by market forces. The typical market force is competition; there are many sellers wishing to sell and even more buyers wishing to buy. From the consumer's point of view competition is desirable in a market, for it usually results in lower prices and greater satisfaction for the consumer. Economists therefore call a situation where there is plenty of competition a **perfect market**. All other market structures display some degree of imperfection.

Perfect markets

A perfect market is one which displays the following characteristics:

1 A large number of buyers and sellers, none of whom dominates the market.
2 A homogeneous commodity, so that buyers are indifferent from whom they buy. (For example, all sacks of potatoes are very similar.)
3 An absence of friction in the market.
4 Perfect knowledge in the market.
5 No one receiving preferential treatment.
6 Free access to the market exists for both producers and consumers, who may enter or leave the market as they choose.

In this type of market price is decided by the free competition between suppliers and those who are demanding the product, and will be fixed by market forces at an equilibrium level called **market price** (see Chapter 3).

Imperfect markets

Where a good or service is marketed in such a way that free competition does not take place the degree of imperfection decides the type of market structure. The most imperfect market is one where a single individual supplies the product or service. This is known as **monopoly**. Clearly a monopoly rules out any possibility of competition. In the UK the statutory definition of a monopoly is a situation where one firm has at least 25 per cent of the market. Such a 'monopoly' may be referred to the Monopolies Commission for investigation. Economists use the term **duopoly** for situations where there are only two firms in an industry and **oligopoly** for situations where a few firms form the industry. For practical purposes these terms should all be called 'monopolies' under the statutory definition given above. The chief feature of duopolies and oligopolies is that each firm is limited in its pricing policy by the thought of the likely repercussions of any changes in price upon its competitors. We shall see that a degree of rigidity and inflexibility in price structures results, and in the absence of controls they tend to form 'rings' and 'cartels' for the fixing of prices. Such arrangements are usually against the public interest.

The most widespread form of imperfection in markets today is the 'branding' of goods. This confers upon the branded good a 'brand image' which becomes a focus of consumer interest. Branded goods are differentiated from competitors in such a way that they are not complete substitutes for one another. A particular brand of tea is preferred to other brands which in fact are equally good. A certain amount of 'brain-washing' advertising material is directed to preserving the brand image, to the irritation of many consumers.

This type of marketing is a major feature of the modern commercial scene, and the most usual type of imperfection in markets. It is often called **imperfect competition,** or **monopolistic competition.** To the extent that the brand image can be created and sustained, a degree of monopoly can be built into a situation which is basically competitive.

2 THE CONVENTIONAL THEORY OF THE FIRM

The theory of the firm seeks to explain why firms are formed; what motivates those who control the firm; what level of output will be reached; what limitations are placed upon the size of firms; and why in the end they go out of existence and cease to trade.

The conventional theory which developed in the rough, free enterprise world of the nineteenth century is that firms come into existence to create goods and services; that the founders of firms are rugged entrepreneurs with a burning desire to create a particular good or offer a particular service; that in harnessing the other factors of production they are in fact *motivated by the desire to maximise profits*, and that if profits are reduced below a certain level they will cease to trade. Profit is therefore not only the force that brings firms into existence but also *the force that allocates resources*. The entrepreneur whose profits fall below a minimum acceptable level will cease to produce the goods or services – which manifestly are in such poor demand that market prices are at rock-bottom level. At these prices production is not worthwhile for this entrepreneur, and he/she will withdraw and move into some more popular field where prospects of profitability are better. Thus some industries gradually lose firms (the least efficient ones) and the industry contracts, while other industries expand as resources are reallocated to them.

Whether this is a good description of firms today is discussed later in this chapter, but anyone who knows the small firm sector will agree that much of this is still true. For the small firm the entrepreneur is still in sole charge. He/she is still chiefly motivated by profit maximisation. While we cannot dismiss workers quite as easily as in the nineteenth century it is still possible (at some sacrifice perhaps in the form of redundancy payments) to reduce the workforce. The need to make some financial sacrifice only sharpens the decision-making. The need to make redundancy payments may force an entrepreneur to lay off workers even more quickly, and often postpones re-engagement indefinitely. In the late 1970s the refusal of many small firms to take on new employees, even when they needed them, because of the obligations that had to be assumed, dismayed the government. We must begin our studies of the firm by considering this conventional theory.

3   THE DECISION TO SUPPLY – INTRODUCTION

Just as consumers make decisions to demand goods or services, entrepreneurs make decisions to supply them. The decision to demand is based on the marginal utility of the good to the consumer, as already explained (see page 73). The decision to supply is based on the prospects of profitability. This is closely connected with the price that can be obtained for the product, and the level of output that should be produced. Decisions to supply are therefore price-output decisions, and depend upon the relationship between the marginal cost and the marginal revenue. We must now define these terms, and note a number of interesting points about costs and revenues.

Types of cost

Every enterprise involves certain costs, which may be listed and defined as follows:

a) **Fixed costs**   Fixed costs are costs which do not vary with output. They include costs of setting up the enterprise in the first place; of purchasing premises, plant and machinery, fixtures and fittings, etc. These are the **assets** of the business, often called **capital assets**, and they are purchased for use in the business over a long period of time – although, of course, they do gradually depreciate with use. If we borrow capital at a certain rate of interest that is a fixed cost, and economists also find it useful to include 'normal profit' as a fixed cost. Thus the entrepreneur who puts money into a business looking for a 10 per cent return on capital invested will expect to get this rate of return each year. If the rate of return drops to 7 per cent he will withdraw from the firm if he can. So the need to meet a 10 per cent 'normal' profit requirement is a considerable constraint on the firm. Administration costs are a fixed cost, since the business cannot operate without an adequate management structure, but some of these costs might be reduced by adroit management at slack times so they are not quite as fixed as some other costs.

b) **Variable costs** These are costs which do vary with output. Thus if we double the number of kitchen units we make we must double the quantity of wood, hinges, brackets etc., that we use in them. We shall also need more labour (though perhaps not double the labour as *economies of scale* might be achieved). Extra power would be needed to run the machines longer, etc.

c)**Average cost** Clearly average cost means the average cost per unit of a given output and may be found by the fraction:

$$\frac{\text{Total cost}}{\text{Number of units produced}}$$

d)**Marginal cost** Marginal cost is the addition to total costs incurred by producing one further unit, so it may be considered as the variable cost of the last unit produced.

Increasing and decreasing returns to scale

One feature of production that must be mentioned here is that of **returns to scale**. Scale means size. From the very earliest days it was noted that larger enterprises could usually achieve greater efficiency than smaller enterprises. Generally speaking, big is beautiful, but some of our modern industries have carried the process too far, and have demonstrated quite clearly the dis-economies of very large scale.

The relationship between marginal cost and average cost

Returning to average cost and marginal cost, Table 5.1 shows the relationship between the two. It is a very important relationship for it is marginal cost which decides the shape of the average cost curve, and marginal cost is always equal to average cost at the lowest point of the average cost curve. The notes below Table 5.1 explain why, and Fig. 5.1 illustrates the point graphically.

Table 5.1 Marginal cost and average cost

Output	Fixed costs	Variable costs	Total costs	Average cost per unit	Marginal cost of the extra unit
0	100	–	100	–	–
1	100	50	150	150	50
2	100	90	190	95	40
3	100	120	220	73.3	30
4	100	160	260	65	40
5	100	210	310	62	50
6	100	270	370	61.7	60
7	100	340	440	62.9	70
8	100	420	520	65	80
9	100	510	610	67.8	90

Notes
1   Fixed costs, as their name implies, are constant.
2   Variable costs – the costs of raw materials, direct labour, power, etc. – increase as output rises, but not in a constant way, because of increasing returns to scale and then decreasing returns to scale.
3   The alterations to variable costs are the marginal costs of successive extra units. Note that they decrease from 50 to 30 under the influence of the economies of scale, but then begin to rise as diminishing returns set in.
4   Average costs per unit fall from 150 to 61.7 but then begin to rise. Note that marginal costs begin to rise first, but as long as marginal costs are below average costs average costs continue to fall. Each extra unit, since it costs less than average, lowers the average cost. When marginal cost rises above average cost, each extra unit, since it costs more than average, raises the average cost. This happens in Table 5.1 at 7 units of output, and from that point average cost begins to rise. (Now see Fig. 5.1.)

Fig. 5.1 *Average and marginal cost curves*

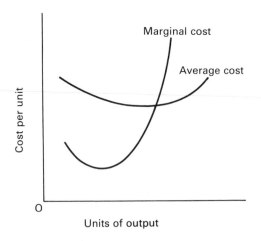

Notes
1   As long as marginal cost is lower than average cost, average cost is falling.
2   As soon as marginal cost rises above average cost it drags the average cost up with it.
3   Therefore the marginal cost curve always cuts the average cost curve at its lowest point.

4   THE DECISION TO SUPPLY IN COMPETITIVE SITUATIONS

Average revenue and marginal revenue

In the decision to supply, the revenue that is to be received is of crucial importance. Entrepreneurs supply goods and services for a money consideration called 'the price'. In deciding to supply, the entrepreneur will be influenced by the price. If price falls he may decide to hold back his supplies from the market (in hopes of a better price later). If prices continue for a period to be so low that he cannot make a profit at the reigning prices he may leave the industry. Other considerations enter into the calculations where the entrepreneur is a monopolist or an oligopolist. Since it is necessary to discuss these different situations separately, let us consider first a situation where there is a state of **perfect competition**, or what economists often refer to as a **perfect market.**

The supplier who comes to a perfectly competitive market with a supply of goods will receive the market price for each unit he sells. Since the market is very large relative to the supplies offered by any one supplier the supplier cannot affect market price by withholding his supplies. Each unit he offers will be paid for at market price (the marginal revenue) and all units will fetch the same price. So, in perfect competition:

Average revenue = Marginal revenue = Market price

However, although price in the market is steady, costs are not steady, but falling or rising per unit according to whether we are experiencing increasing or decreasing returns to scale. The situation is best explained diagrammatically. This is shown in Fig. 5.2 and explained in the notes below it.

Fig. 5.2 *Deciding what quantity to supply in perfect competition*

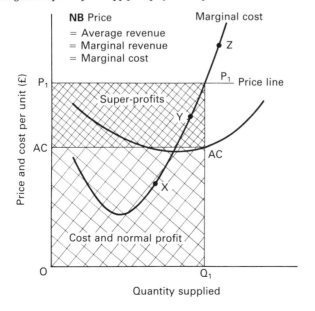

Notes
1 We are considering one supplier only in this diagram.
2 For this supplier, price is fixed at market price.
3 This supplier is a low-cost firm, because his average costs are well below market price. He is therefore going to make some very useful temporary profits.
4 Consider the point X on his marginal cost curve. At this point the marginal cost is £X, but he will receive £P_1 for the sale of this unit. This will be a profitable unit.
5 At point Y the marginal unit is costing him £Y, but he will receive £P_1 for its sale, so that this will again be profitable, but not as profitable as the unit costing £X.
6 At point Z the marginal unit costs £Z, but he receives only £P_1. He will therefore lose money on it.
7 It follows that an entrepreneur will not increase production beyond the point where his marginal cost becomes equal to marginal revenue. The next unit will cause him to lose money. Thus at an output of Q_1 the entrepreneur's income from the marginal unit will be P_1, exactly the same as he pays to produce it. Any output greater than Q_1 will cost more than P_1 but he will only receive P_1 for it. Profits are maximised at an output of Q_1.
8 We can therefore say that for every producer in perfect competition at the point where he ought to cease expansion

$$\text{Price} = \text{Average revenue} = \text{Marginal revenue} = \text{Marginal cost}$$

9 This producer is receiving $OQ_1P_1P_1$ of income. His average costs at this output are found where the quantity line cuts the average cost curve, i.e. at AC.
10 The area shaded in single hatching, OQ_1AC, AC is the income received to cover costs + normal profit, so that this income includes a reasonable return on his invested capital. Remember that economists usually include 'normal profit' in the costs of production, since an entrepreneur who cannot recover this 'cost' will leave the industry and cease to trade.
11 The area shaded in double hatching, i.e. AC, P_1, P_1, AC, is the income he receives over and above normal costs and profits; we will call this 'super-profit' for the moment. We can thus see that this entrepreneur is doing very nicely.
12 However, the entrepreneur cannot hope to enjoy these super-profits for long. Freedom of entry will mean that competitors will join the industry, supplying goods which will lead to price reductions, and his super-profits will be competed away from him as price is reduced to AC and possibly even lower. This situation is explained more fully in Fig. 5.3.

Conclusion about the decision to supply in competitive situations

The conclusion to be drawn from Fig. 5.2 is that in competitive conditions the entrepreneur *will cease to produce at that point where marginal costs rise to equal marginal revenue.* Of course, it can be argued that in fact the entrepreneur cannot measure marginal costs in the accurate way that is implied in Fig. 5.2. He cannot tell when marginal costs become greater than market price. While this is true, it is also true that he has a very good idea what the marginal costs are. He knows that if he goes into overtime and has to pay workers time and a half, for example, this is going to eat drastically into his profit margins and make the game much less worth the candle.

Since the very term perfect competition implies that anyone is free to enter or leave the market the industry will be in a state of flux with firms which cannot make normal profits leaving the industry and new firms with the latest equipment and ideas entering. In some industries it is easier to leave than others. Firms which have **specific assets** (assets which can only be used in that particular industry) find it difficult to leave. In an industry where assets are non-specific it is easier to turn over to produce other things. Thus a cement

Fig. 5.3 *Five firms in the same industry*

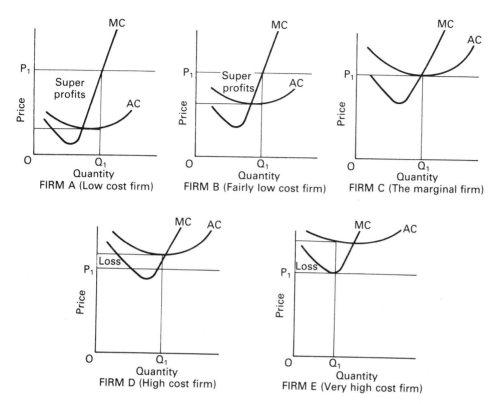

FIRM A (Low cost firm)   FIRM B (Fairly low cost firm)   FIRM C (The marginal firm)

FIRM D (High cost firm)   FIRM E (Very high cost firm)

Notes

1   These five firms are all supplying in the same market. They range from a very low-cost firm (Firm A) to a very high-cost firm (Firm E). In each case the firm raises output only as far as the point where the marginal cost curve cuts the price line. At this point marginal cost = marginal revenue. Any further increase in output would make marginal costs greater than marginal revenue and would reduce the profits earned.

2   Firm A is like the firm already discussed in Fig. 5.2 above, making super-profits because it is a low-cost firm – presumably with modern, highly productive plant.

3   Firm B is not as efficient as Firm A, but it is still making more than normal profit. It is operating closer to optimum production (i.e. minimum average cost).

4   Firm C would be the marginal firm in an ordinary competitive industry, but, as will be seen below, this industry is unusual because it has 'specific assets' which are of no use in other industries. Firm C is making normal profit and is operating at the optimum, i.e. minimum average cost.

5   Firm D is a firm that is looking for a way out of the industry. It looks as if it is making losses, but this might not actually be true – it might just be making less than normal profits. In other words, its capital could be better used elsewhere. Why doesn't it get out? It would like to leave, but it cannot, because its assets are no use in any other industry.

6   Firm E is really making losses, and it would go if it possibly could. It looks as if this industry must have very specific assets.

7   In the short run even a competitive industry can have high-cost firms and low-cost firms. In the imaginary case of perfect competition, especially in the long run, all firms like D and E will leave the industry. Firms like A and B will have their super-profits competed away from them. All firms will be like Firm C, the marginal firm. For the marginal firm in perfect competition

Price = Average revenue = Marginal revenue = Marginal cost = Average cost

The firm will be producing at the optimum level with average cost at the minimum.

Fig. 5.4 *The equilibrium output of a competitive industry*

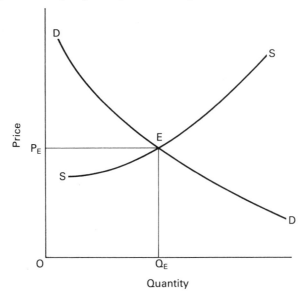

Notes
1   With a whole industry the supply curve of the industry is the sum of the supplies brought in to the market by the individual firms in the industry.
2   In Fig. 5.3 the demand curve is the same as the price line and is drawn horizontal for each firm in the industry (since in a perfect market we assume that each firm has only a trivial share of the total market and cannot itself influence price, which is therefore constant as far as any particular firm is concerned). For the whole industry the demand curve is of course a downward-sloping demand curve.
3   Price is decided at the equilibrium point, where demand and supply are equal.
4   At this point the industry is in equilibrium and each firm in the industry is producing that output where its marginal cost equals its marginal revenue. Firms whose marginal costs exceed market price will contract output, and firms whose marginal costs are less than market price will extend output to maximise their profits.
5   Any change in the conditions of demand, or in the conditions of supply, which brings about a change of price will result in an adjustment by all the firms in the industry, and may result in firms leaving the industry (if price falls) or in firms joining the industry (if price rises).

works can only make cement, but a bespoke tailor who is having his profit margins squeezed can easily change over to make off-the-peg garments. The position of firms in a typical industry is illustrated in Fig. 5.3, while Fig. 5.4 illustrates the situation of a whole industry.

One final point about firms with specific assets, such as Firm E in Fig. 5.3. Because of the difficulties of putting specific assets into 'mothballs', it will be the tendency for such firms to remain in the industry even where they are achieving less than normal profits. Once the assets have been purchased, or built, they are 'sunk' costs, which cannot be retrieved by resale. In that situation, so long as all the working expenses can be recovered the firm might as well continue. If it proves impossible to cover even working expenses (variable costs) then it would be madness to continue for it would be throwing good money after bad. This is explained in Fig. 5.5.

Fig. 5.5 *Leaving the industry: firms with specific assets*

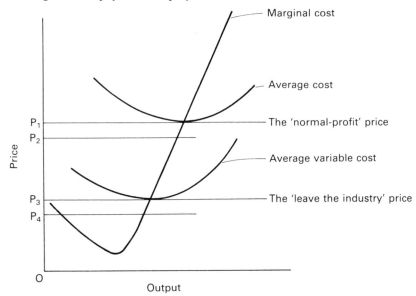

Notes

1   At P_1 the firm is making normal profits: it is the marginal firm.

2   At prices below P_1 the firm is making less than normal profits. Suppose it receives a price of P_2 when it is paying costs of P_1. It is definitely now earning a less-than-normal return on capital invested, and ought to leave the industry.

3   If we examine the costs at P_1 we find that these costs are made up of Fixed costs + Variable costs + Profit. The fixed costs have already been suffered (the entrepreneur has already built the factory, installed the plant, etc.); indeed, some accountants describe these costs as 'sunk costs' because they have already been sunk into the business. The variable costs are payments for wages, raw materials, etc. incurred with each unit of output. These are shown in the diagram by the Average variable cost curve. As long as price is above average variable cost, it will pay the entrepreneur to keep production going. At the price P_2 for each unit of production sold he receives: (*a*) everything he spends on variable costs plus (*b*) something towards his 'sunk' costs or 'fixed' costs. It is still worth while producing.

4   At price P_3 he is receiving back his variable costs, but nothing more.

5   Suppose price drops below P_3 – say to P_4. The entrepreneur will now be paying for wages and raw materials a price of P_3, but will receive back less than P_3 for the goods produced. Clearly this is ridiculous: it would be throwing good money after bad. The only thing to do here is to put the plant into mothballs and shut down. P_3 is therefore the 'leave-the-industry' price, even for an entrepreneur with very specific assets. He must then wait for better times to return.

The merits of the market economy

Politicians frequently recommend a return to the merits of the free-market economy, and blame bureaucratic interference with the market for many of our modern ills. What are the supposed merits of the free market system? Really they are two:

a) An ideal allocation of resources.
b) An optimum efficiency in industry.

These two satisfactory situations are achieved in the following ways. First, since output is always increased to the point where marginal cost equals market price, it means that the value to the marginal consumer of the product is exactly the same as the cost of producing it. If price was above marginal cost it would mean that the marginal consumer valued the unit at more than it cost to produce, and there would be a strong case for increasing output to squeeze extra satisfaction from the industrial set-up we have established. If price was below marginal cost it would mean that the extra units of output cost more to produce than the consumers believe they are worth, and an in-put of factors is therefore being wasted. The ideal employment of resources is therefore at that point where

Marginal cost = Marginal revenue = Price. (See Fig. 5.2)

As to (b) above, this is achieved where

Marginal cost = Marginal revenue = Average cost = Average revenue = Price.

This is case Firm C in Fig. 5.3 above, where the assets are not specific and firms leave the industry at once when they cannot make normal profits. At this point Marginal cost = Average cost, which is the same as saying average cost is at a minimum. This means all firms in the industry (in theory) are producing goods at minimum cost for the bare amount of profit that will keep their entrepreneurs in the industry, and this is usually the most economical production position possible.

So in perfect competition we have both an efficient allocation of resources and an industry of exactly the right size to meet the demands of consumers.

In modern conditions it is probably true to say that no market is entirely free. We live in a world where controls of one sort or another abound, and the pressures on business are enormous from all points of the compass. There is little point in advocating a return to the free market if trade unions, employers' organisations or international trading partners will not permit it. It is a theoretical situation which applies to a considerable extent to some industries where 'cut-throat' competition is still a feature. In most of the major industries of an advanced nation it no longer applies, and a return to fully free competition is almost impossible.

SELF-ASSESSMENT QUESTIONS

1 What are the characteristics of a perfect market?

2 What are the two chief types of cost in any business?

3 List five costs which a cement manufacturer might have to meet, in each type of cost mentioned in your answer to Question **2**.

4 Define marginal cost. Define average cost. Now explain the link between the two.

5 Continue this sentence: The marginal cost curve always cuts the average cost curve . . .
Explain why the sentence must be true.

6 What is the position of a marginal firm in the clothing industry?

5   THE DECISION TO SUPPLY IN A MONOPOLY SITUATION

In theory, the term monopoly means 'only one supplier', and consequently rules out any possibility of competition. We have already seen that in actual practice in the UK a monopoly is defined as a situation where one firm has at least a 25 per cent share of the market. However we choose to define a monopoly, the decision to supply in a monopoly is in some ways similar to the decision in a free market. It is still based upon the relationship between marginal cost and marginal revenue. Before making this clear there are two points to notice:

1 We have already noted (see page 98) that even a monopolist is subject to the authority of the consumer. He cannot say, 'I will make 50 000 of these and you will buy them at £25 each.' He can decide the output, leaving consumers to decide the price; or he can decide the price, leaving consumers to decide how many units they will buy. This is the same as saying that he faces a downward-sloping demand curve. If he doubles output he will only be able to dispose of the extra units by lowering the price. In perfect competition the price line for an individual firm was parallel to the x axis (in Fig. 5.2, for example). This is because the small supply brought on to the market by an individual supplier is negligible compared with total demand. In perfect competition demand is infinitely large as far as any one supplier is concerned. The monopolist is less well placed. As the only supplier any extra quantity he brings into the market will tend to reduce the price.

2 This downward-sloping demand curve has an important impact on the marginal revenue. Imagine a monopolist selling 100 items at £100 each – total revenue £10 000. He decides to produce an extra unit, but is forced to lower the price to £99.50 in order to sell it. This means that the revenue received from the sale of *every* item will drop by £0.50. The total revenue from 101 items will be 101 × £99.50 = £10 049.50. The marginal revenue from the sale of the extra item is thus only £49.50. The effect of this on the monopolist's decision to supply is shown in Fig. 5.6.

Fig. 5.6 *The decision to supply under monopoly conditions*

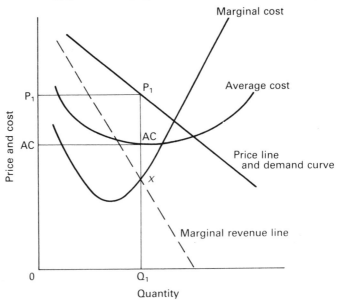

Notes

1 The downward-sloping demand curve, which is also the price line and the average revenue curve, reflects the monopolist's subjection to the authority of the consumer: he/she can only sell a bigger output if the price is reduced.

2 As the price is reduced average revenue falls for every unit, but the marginal revenue falls much more quickly. This is because the revenue received for the extra unit is reduced by the lower price received on all the other units.

3 So the production of further units ceases where the marginal cost curve cuts the marginal revenue curve, at point x, and an output of Q_1. This is well before the marginal cost curve cuts the price line.

4 Price will be decided by the point where a line from Q_1 parallel to the price axis cuts the price line, at price P_1P_1.

5 The entrepreneur will earn revenue of $OQ_1P_1P_1$ at a cost (including normal profit) of OQ_1, AC, AC. He/she is therefore earning super-profits of AC, P_1, P_1, AC. But these super-profits will not be competed away, as they would in competitive conditions, because the entrepreneur is a monopolist. Other firms are not able to enter the industry.

6 Production has ceased before the marginal cost curve cuts the average cost curve (at minimum average cost). This means that the industry is not operating at the optimum level of output, and there is **excess capacity** in the industry. Some capital resources are therefore being wasted.

7 To conclude, in monopoly conditions price tends to be higher and output less than in competitive circumstances.

6 THE DECISION TO SUPPLY 'BRANDED GOODS'

Modern supply tends to be of 'branded goods' which have been manufactured or treated in some way by the supplier so as to confer upon them some degree of 'uniqueness'. Thus Ford cars and Toyota cars have their own 'unique' qualities, as do Robertson's Golden Shred marmalade and Hartley's marmalade. In some cases the uniqueness simply refers to the fact that the goods have been washed and pre-packed. No longer does the grocer weigh up ½ kg of currants from a sackful of the product – we select a prepacked carton from the display rack.

To such suppliers their own product is unique, but it has several close substitutes in rival brands. Therefore while each will have its own downward-sloping demand curve, like any monopolist, it will also be in competition with other brands whose demand curves are very similar. The name '**monopolistic competition**' has therefore been given to this type of supply. The supplier will be most sensitive to, and most influenced by, the behaviour of firms with very similar products to his own, though a much wider range of products also represents at least some competitive threat.

If we take a firm which has a relatively new product protected by patent rights (which last for 20 years in the UK) and is therefore able to preserve a reasonably 'unique' product in the short run, the situation will be rather similar to that of the monopolist and super-profits will be enjoyed. As the competitiveness builds up, the demand curve for the product will be moved to the left in successive periods. The increasing competitiveness of rivals amounts to a change in the conditions of demand – an alternative source of substitute goods is now available. This causes a shift of the demand curve, the public being prepared to buy less of the product at every price. This reduces the super-profits being earned, the demand curve eventually becoming tangential to the average cost curve, where all super-profits have been eroded away. This is shown in Figs. 5.7 and 5.8.

Fig. 5.7 *The short-term position of a supplier in monopolistic competition*

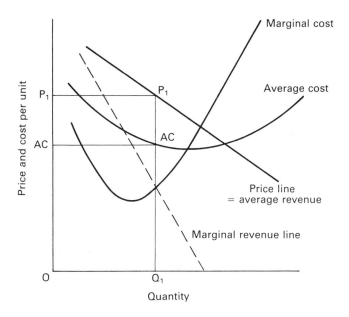

Notes
1 The supplier in Fig. 5.7 is like a monopolist, making super-profits with brand equal to AC, P_1, P_1, AC.
2 New firms will be attracted into the industry, selling the same goods in a differentiated form. The new supplier or suppliers will have to be aggressive in advertising and pricing policies if they are to make inroads on the market of the established brand, and to the extent that they are successful there will be a change in the conditions of demand.
3 The demand curve for the supplier of the established brand will therefore move to the left, a decrease in demand.
4 The marginal revenue line will also move to the left, so that it cuts the marginal cost curve even earlier than before. Output will be reduced, price will be reduced, and some of the entrepreneur's super-profits will be competed away. The long-term position is shown in Fig.5.8.

Fig. 5.8 *The long-term position of a supplier in monopolistic competition*

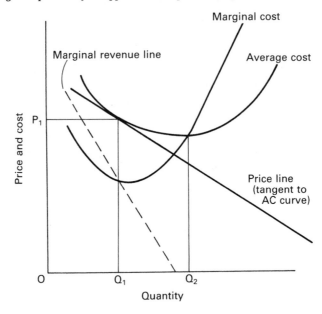

Notes
1 The demand curve has moved, owing to the changed conditions of demand, so far to the left that it has become tangential to (only just touching) the average cost curve.
2 At this point all super-profits are competed away and the firm is making normal profits only.
3 There is excess capacity in the industry; the supplier could increase output to the optimum level of minimum average cost at OQ_2 and decrease unit costs by doing so, but the marginal revenue would decrease even more, leaving him worse off. It is therefore a feature of monopolistic competition that excess capacity exists in the industry in the long term.
4 If the super-profits are to be maintained, the competitive thrust of rivals must be countered by equally aggressive marketing techniques. This may take a positive form, as with the endless re-vamping of an old product (the motorcar industry facelift) or a more negative form (the tedious readvertising of detergents to reiterate their whiter-than-white whiteness). Either way it involves costs which are borne ultimately by the consumer.

7 THE DECISION TO SUPPLY BY AN OLIGOPOLY

Oligopoly occurs where there are only a few firms forming an industry. Typical examples in the UK are the cement industry, the oil industry and the detergent industry. The chief features of oligopoly (competition among the few) are:

1 Each firm produces a significant proportion of total output. In the report by the Monopolies Commission on the detergent industry it was found that two firms shared between them 94 per cent of the total market and a third firm had almost all the remaining 6 per cent. There is thus a strong possibility that an individual firm can influence the price of products by changing its output.

2 Because there are so few firms in the industry, factor inputs are greatly influenced by them. This applies particularly to suppliers of raw materials and to skilled labour, which is less able to seek employment elsewhere.

3 In making price-output decisions it is necessary to bear in mind what the competition will do, and there is a strong tendency for 'cartels' to form – groups of firms acting in cooperation with one another to maintain prices, restrict output, keep out competition, etc. It does not follow that this is always against the public interest, but it is a useful assumption.

It is not possible to draw up demand and supply curves for individual firms in oligopoly because any assumptions we make about the slope of the demand curve and the supply curve (marginal cost curve) depend upon the reactions of other firms in the industry. Generally speaking, the demand curve will be 'kinked', with the kink occurring at the 'agreed' price decided by the overt or covert arrangement between the firms. This is explained in Fig. 5.9.

The general conclusion we can draw about oligopoly is that the result of having a few firms only in an industry is very similar to the effect of pure

Fig. 5.9 *A 'kinked' demand curve in oligopoly*

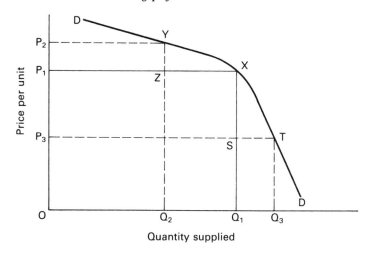

Notes

1 At price P_1 (the 'agreed' price) an output of Q_1 is being supplied by this firm and its profits will depend upon its own cost structure. A high-cost firm will be making a less than fair share of the industry's profits and a low-cost firm will be doing rather better, but both will be making more than normal profit anyway.

2 If this firm tries to raise prices and other firms do not it will lose market share to them. In other words, demand is price-elastic above the kink in demand, for the individual firm trying to raise prices. The extra revenue earned by raising prices to P_2 (P_1P_2YZ) will be less than the revenue lost in smaller market share (Q_2Q_1XZ), and the firm will be worse off.

3 If this firm tries to lower prices to P_3 ('There is always one fool who cuts' – sad comment by an oligopolist) the other firms will follow him down to preserve their market share. In this case the extra revenue gained by selling the small extra quantity (Q_1Q_3TS) will be less than the revenue lost by reducing the price (P_1P_3SX). In other words, demand is inelastic with respect to price below the kink in the demand curve.

4 There is therefore no incentive to change prices in oligopoly, and they tend to be rigid unless an overt or covert agreement to change them is made, perhaps to meet some new situation in the international market.

monopoly. Prices will be higher than in perfect competition; super-profits will be made; and there will be excess capacity in the industry. At the same time, super-profits cannot be allowed to go too high or new firms will jump over the barriers to entry (requiring rearrangements to be made in the agreement between firms). Worse still, the manifest exploitation of the public that is taking place may invite nationalisation or expropriation by the State in the public interest, or it may invite fines for anti-competitive activities which infringe competition laws in either the nation state or larger bodies, such as the European Community.

8 CONCLUSIONS ABOUT MARKET STRUCTURE

We have considered four types of market structure: perfect competition, monopoly, monopolistic competition and oligopoly. Of these four we have seen that in theory the system of perfect competition is the only one that achieves both the output of goods and services at minimum average cost (with the output decided at the price where Marginal cost = Average cost = Price) and the optimum allocation of resources, firms investing in new industries in such a way as to eliminate super-profits and avoid less-than-normal profits. The other market structures are less satisfactory in that they all result in prices being charged for goods and services which are more than the marginal cost, while a series of institutional devices prevents the free movement of investment into and out of the industry. In practical terms, however, we find that the whole tendency in advanced economies is for the perfectly competitive structure to be abandoned in more and more industries, to be replaced by one or other of the alternative structures. Why is this so?

First, it appears that the perfectly competitive system is too precarious for the full exploitation of the economies of large scale, especially where the assets to be created with it are specific, so that if forced out of use with competition there will be a serious capital loss. Some type of restriction has to be placed upon competition. In the early days of capitalism it was common for Parliament or the Crown to grant a monopoly for a minimum period to encourage investment in capital-intensive industries. Much of the transport infrastructure of the UK was created in this way by an enormous number of Canal Acts, Harbour Acts, Turnpike Acts and Railway Acts. Even today bridges and tunnels are constructed using the same device. The fact that these temporary immunities from competition often lengthened into permanent immunities is explained more by the pace of change than the machinations of early capitalists. Renewal became as expensive as the original capital cost when it took account of changes in technology. In many modern industries, oil, detergents, petrochemicals, cement, etc., the huge capital cost of specific assets is a barrier to new entrants to the industry, especially since high taxation makes it so difficult to accumulate capital with which to enter, but is not a barrier to expansion from within because all such expenditure is tax deductible.

Second, a major influence in the achievement of the economies of large scale is the work of research and development departments. While an outsider may occasionally make an inspired contribution to the technology of an industry, the vast majority of advances are made within the industry itself. There is an enormous incentive to create new products and services in such areas as the utilisation of waste materials, the utilisation of machines not fully employed by the main product and the use of spare capacity in computers, distribution networks, storage space, etc.

Third, the multinational nature of many large-scale industries enables them to evade the constraints of particular governments by an amoeba-like ability to divert activities to areas where they are not under pressure. The very threat of doing so may be sufficient to reduce the pressures upon them. To a degree the multinational corporation can insist upon 'laissez-faire' and can often demonstrate that if left to pursue its own best interests it will incidentally achieve the best interests of the nation it deigns to honour with its presence.

The close link that appears to exist between an advanced economy offering its nationals a high standard of living and a prevalence of market structures displaying oligopoly and monopolistic competition seems to lead us to conclude that this is probably the best way for production to be organised. The worst abuses of monopoly can be controlled without killing the goose that lays the golden eggs, and this appears to offer the best chance of achieving the economic aims of mankind. The modern firm, in contriving to adapt itself to its economic environment, is not purely bent on the maximisation of profit. It must attempt to meet all the constraints upon it from customers, employees, shareholders and those imposed by governments pursuing their macro-economic policies.

SELF-ASSESSMENT QUESTIONS

7 What is the dictionary definition of a monopolist? What is the statutory definition in the UK of a monopolist?

8 Explain the statement 'Even a monopolist is subject to the authority of the consumer.'

9 Explain why the price line for a supplier in a perfectly free market is horizontal, but for a monopolist it slopes downwards towards the right. (Re-read the notes to Figs. 5.2 and 5.6 if you are not sure.)

10 Why must a seller of branded goods expect the demand curve for his product to shift to the left. How can he resist this, and move it to the right?

11 Explain why the demand curve for an oligopolist is kinked at the agreed price.

12 Justify the 'branding' of goods, even though branding is 'anti-competitive'.

REVISION TEST

Answers	Questions
—	**1** What are the chief types of market situation?
1 (a) Perfect competition; (b) monopolistic competition; (c) oligopoly; (d) monopoly.	**2** What are the chief features of perfect competition?
2 (a) A large number of buyers and sellers; (b) a homogeneous commodity – all units are exactly alike; (c) no friction in the market; (d) perfect knowledge exists of prices in the market; (e) no one receives any preferential treatment) (f) free access to the market for both producers and consumers.	**3** What is monopolistic competition?
3 Competition between firms selling 'branded' goods, which therefore command a degree of brand loyalty and are not perfect substitutes for one another.	**4** What is oligopoly?
4 Competition among the few – who therefore make price-output decisions bearing in mind the effect upon competitors of any changes.	**5** Why is the demand curve in oligopoly kinked?
5 Because demand is price elastic above the kinked point (the agreed 'fair price') and price inelastic below it.	**6** What is meant by the phrase 'the monopolist is subject to the authority of the consumer'?

6 The monopolist can decide price or output, but not both. Consumers are still free to reject the goods if they wish to.

7 Why is free competition the exceptional, rather than the usual market form?

---

7 (a) Because it is too precarious for large-scale enterprises, especially with specific assets.
(b) Because growth from within is easier than entry from outside – for taxation reasons.
(c) Because research and development has a great impact on growth and cannot be afforded by small new entrants to an industry.
(d) Because multinational firms which can 'vote with their feet' are able to escape the constraints of rigid controls imposed by an anti-capitalist nation state.

8 At what point is output restricted?

---

8 At the point where marginal cost equals marginal revenue. At this price there will be no point in increasing production because marginal costs will go above marginal revenue and make the extra output unprofitable.

9 What firms reach a position where marginal cost = marginal revenue = average cost = average revenue = price?

---

9 Marginal firms in a freely competitive industry, because they are at the point where the price line coincides with the point where the marginal cost curve cuts the average cost curve at its lowest point. Any further fall in price will leave them making less than normal profits and ready to leave the industry.

Go over this test until you are sure of all the answers. Then try the exercises below.

ANSWERS

(See Self-assessment questions on pages 158–9 and 165–6.)

1 The characteristics of a perfect market are (a) a large number of buyers and sellers; (b) a homogeneous commodity (so that buyers are indifferent to whom they buy from); (c) an absence of friction in the market; (d) perfect knowledge in the market; (e) no preferential treatment; (f) free access to the market for all.

2 The two chief types of cost are fixed costs (costs which do not vary with output) and variable costs, which do vary with output.

3 A cement manufacturer might have to meet the following fixed costs (a) construction of the works; (b) installation of kilns to roast the cement; (c) bagging machines (to pack the cement into paper sacks); (d) bulk cement vehicles for transporting bulk supplies; (e) word processors to type the invoices. Similarly, as far as variable costs are concerned, we could list clay and limestone (the raw materials), paper sacks, labour and power supplies.

4 Marginal cost is the cost of producing one extra unit of a product. Average cost is the cost of producing each unit when total cost is divided by the number of units produced. The link between the two is that at times of increasing returns to scale the marginal cost is falling, and hence reduces average cost, but when diminishing returns set in marginal cost begins to rise and starts to drag up average cost once it cuts the average cost line (see Fig. 5.1).

5 The sentence continues: 'at its lowest point'. The sentence must be true because it is the marginal cost which dictates the shape of the average cost curve. So long as marginal cost is less than average cost it will cause average cost to fall, but as soon as marginal cost exceeds average cost it causes average cost to rise.

6 A marginal firm in the clothing industry is one that is just about to leave the industry (if the industry is becoming less prosperous) or has just joined the industry (if the industry is expanding). It is making normal profits only.

7 A dictionary definition of a monopolist would be something like 'one who has the exclusive trade in a particular product or commodity'. The statutory definition of a monopolist in the UK is one who controls 25 per cent of the market in a particular class of product or commodity.

8 The statement draws attention to the fact that even a monopolist cannot dictate both the supply side and the demand side of any transaction. The monopolist cannot say, 'I will charge £5000 for this article and you will buy 100 000 of them. He/she can say, 'The price of these articles of which I am the sole supplier is £5000! The consumer will then decide how many to buy. Alternatively the monopolist can set output at 100 000 items, whereupon the price will reflect what sort of level price must settle at to sell that number.

9 For any supplier in a perfectly free market the quantity he/she can supply is negligible compared with the total supply of all suppliers. Hence the price cannot be influenced by the supplier, who will sell all items at the market price. The monopolist has the whole supply under his/her control, and the price line is the same thing as the market demand curve, which always slopes down to the right – price falling as a larger supply has to be disposed of.

10 A seller of branded goods is in the position of 'competitive monopoly'. This means that while he/she has a monopoly of the brand, and consequently a downward sloping demand curve, other brands may compete with it on price or quality. Any increase in a rival's share of the market will reduce the demand for the seller's brand, shifting the demand curve to the left. To resist this the seller of branded goods must maintain advertising and constantly revive interest by cosmetic, or real, improvements in the product.

11 The demand curve for an oligopolist is kinked at the 'agreed' price because demand is elastic above the kink (a flattened curve) and inelastic below the kink (a more steep curve). Above the kink prices for the oligopolist's product cannot be raised without losing market share (competitors will keep their own prices steady) while below the kink any attempt to cut prices will be followed down by rivals to resist the competition, so that greater sales will not be achieved.

12 Branding of goods is justified even though it is anti-competitive for the following reasons: (a) it encourages enterprise because it makes it more certain that a reasonable return on capital invested will be earned before other brands can be developed to compete with it; (b) it does lead to improvements in the product and new approaches to that type of product, both from the original entrepreneur seeking to find cosmetic or real improvements in the original product and from outsiders seeking to develop a rival brand. Henry Ford said of his original cars 'The customer can have any colour car he likes so long as it is black'. He had to change his ideas when his competitors proved that coloured cars could eat into the Ford market.

QUESTIONS ON CHAPTER 5

1 How is price determined in (a) pure competition and (b) monopoly conditions? Illustrate your answers by diagrams where possible.

2 'Output will not be allowed to increase when marginal cost equals marginal revenue.' Explain.

3 With the help of diagrams, explain the difference between the pricing and output policy of a firm producing under conditions of perfect competition and one which is a monopoly producer.

(Courtesy of the Institute of Commercial Management)

4 The theories of perfect competition and monopoly are based upon assumptions which do not prevail in the real world. What, then, is the purpose of building such models?

(Courtesy of the Association of Business Executives)

5 What can economic theory tell us of the advantages to a firm of product branding and why might a firm develop a brand name for an individual product?

(Courtesy of the Institute of Marketing)

6 What are the theoretical assumptions and predictions in the model of monopolistic competition?

(Courtesy of the Institute of Marketing)

7 Explain why a firm will eventually go out of business if it cannot cover its costs.

(Courtesy of the Institute of Marketing)

8 What is the distinction between fixed costs and variable costs in both the short run and the long run, and why is the distinction important?

(Courtesy of the Association of Business Executives)

9 Generally speaking, a firm with specific assets will be reluctant to leave an industry which is experiencing a recession. Why is this? At what point will the arguments for leaving the industry be overwhelming?

10 Using economic theory, discuss the contention that product differentiation is wasteful.

(Courtesy of the Institute of Marketing)

11 'It is a feature of oligopoly that prices tend to be inflexible.' Explain why this is so, if possible illustrating your answer by reference to a particular industry with which you are familiar.

12 Despite the theoretical advantages of competition, modern industry tends to be increasingly monopolistic or oligopolistic. Why is this so?

TIPS FOR STUDENTS: A SPECIMEN ANSWER TO QUESTION 4

We may regard the question as being 'Why bother with theory, why not go to the real world and get the facts?'

There are two major problems with facts. One is that it is not always easy to say just what the facts are – anyone who has visited at length a court of law will be aware of this! The second problem with economic facts is that there are far too many of them – millions rather than thousands. Millions of families in the UK, all producing and consuming tens of millions of items per day. In the wider world there are billions of families. It is therefore impossible to go to the real world and 'get all the facts'.

Theory is a systematic description of reality which selects the essential features and shows the relationships between them. Theory consists of a set of generalisations and casual relationships.

Economic theory consists of the building and using of economic models which are sets of interconnected economic relationships. A model contains only the essential and relevant relationships that can explain an aspect of the economy towards which it is directed, e.g. the price of agricultural output. Model builders recognise that they have left out many hundreds, perhaps thousands of facts, and this leads them to exercise caution when using their models. In a particular application one of the omitted things might turn out to be crucial. A model in which businesses always act so as to maximise profit has to be modified when it is applied in circumstances where businesses don't attempt to do this.

The great advantages of models such as those of perfect competition and monopoly are:

a) The basic relationships are clarified and stated.
b) Order develops from what would be an unmanageable tangle of millions of facts.
c) Time is saved — the relationships don't have to be proved over and over again.
d) Exceptions can be accommodated; they usually require a more involved model — they are usually not contradictions, but just complications. In seeking to simplify things we develop a clear picture of basic relations. The real world is more intricate, and our theory may need to be treated with caution, because it is certain that variations from it exist.

6 | The firm and its markets

1 MARKET-ORIENTATED FIRMS

A market-orientated firm is one which is chiefly preoccupied by its markets, and carries out a substantial amount of market analysis in order to continue to achieve its share of the market. Other firms may be production-orientated, being in the happy position that the market will look after itself. Thus a cement manufacturer will be part of a tight ring of heavy-capitalised companies where entry by outsiders is extremely difficult because of the large-scale works required and the specific nature of the assets. Such a firm does not need to pursue its market share aggressively; it is restrained by an explicit agreement (or perhaps a tacit understanding) to a certain level of production. It will be preoccupied with achieving that level of output in the most economical way. The market-orientated firm, by contrast, is usually in a state of competition, or at least monopolistic competition, with rival firms. Its goods will be sold in a buyer's market, where the consumer to some extent is king; where choice is available not only between home produced goods but also imported products, which the manufacturer cannot exclude.

The market-orientated organisation sees its function as one of satisfying particular human 'wants' by providing products or services which are appropriate to the needs of consumers. Such an organisation will be sensitive to changing markets and to the increased competitiveness of rival firms. It will foster product research and development, creating innovations in old products to renew their appeal to the consumer. It will take the market's pulse at intervals to detect changes in taste or fashion. It will watch for changes in the distribution of the national income so that it continues to address itself to the sections of the population which are affluent, and it may largely ignore other sections of the community.

To the market-orientated firm the whole world is available as a potential market, and it is essential to engage in forward planning. The marketing plan will take account of the firm's present achievements and present production, but it must look ahead to assess the market opportunities available. The consideration of new customers in existing areas, new areas at home and abroad, new products to develop the range currently being offered, changes in quality, style, material, etc., may lead to quite different company objectives from the existing ones. This in turn will require a reappraisal of company assets, consideration of new methods and techniques, the need to find or develop staff with appropriate skills, etc. The marketing plan must be subdivided into time periods so that attainable aims can be set and compared with actual results as the months pass. Forward planning is designed to take an objective view of the firm, from the point of view of an outsider. What are its strengths and weaknesses? How can we take advantage of the strengths and reinforce the weak points? The aim may be profitable growth from increased turnover, an increased market share or the creation of new markets previously untapped.

2 DEMAND ANALYSIS

Demand analysis is a systematic investigation of the pattern of demand for the products of a firm in its traditional trading areas, or in new areas which it is proposed to enter. The problem is to set marketing objectives and develop marketing strategies in the various markets that are available. This also involves choosing the best opportunities available, since to develop all markets simultaneously is not possible. The problem is made more difficult in the international field because different languages and vocabularies make the information available somewhat suspect and often not strictly comparable.

The framework for comparing markets is a **market structure profile**, which attempts to discover all the information about the market in a practical way – i.e. related to actual products that the firm is marketing or is about to market. The information required is in two parts:

a) The product market potential. This is the total possible sales in the market for that type of product. The product market potential is the number of relevant consumers for a durable product such as electric shavers. For a consumable product it is the number of relevant consumers multiplied by the number of use occasions which arise per consumer per period (usually taken as per annum).

b) The second available piece of information is the current sales figures for the area – provided the firm is already selling in the market. The extent to which the firm's current sales fall short of the product market potential is the measure of the growth that is possible to bridge the gap between present sales and total market penetration. However, this gap really consists of a number of separate 'gap problems'. For example, sales may be missed because the firm does not offer the full range of products available in the market. Thus the domestic heating market includes many types of installation. A firm which offers a gas heater but no oil-fired or electrical appliances will experience a 'product gap' which partly explains its failure to dominate the market. Other gaps are the 'competition gap' which is filled by its competitors' sales in the market, and a 'distribution gap' which is caused by the firm's failure to establish a network of agents and depots throughout the entire market. Finally, there is a 'usage gap' which reflects the failure of the potential customers to use the product, a gap which might be bridged by informative or persuasive advertising.

The marketing strategy needed to achieve full control of the market requires the bridging of all these gaps, though in practice total domination of the market will never be achieved. Viewed diagrammatically the situation might be as shown in Fig. 6.1.

Fig. 6.1 *Market structure and strategies*

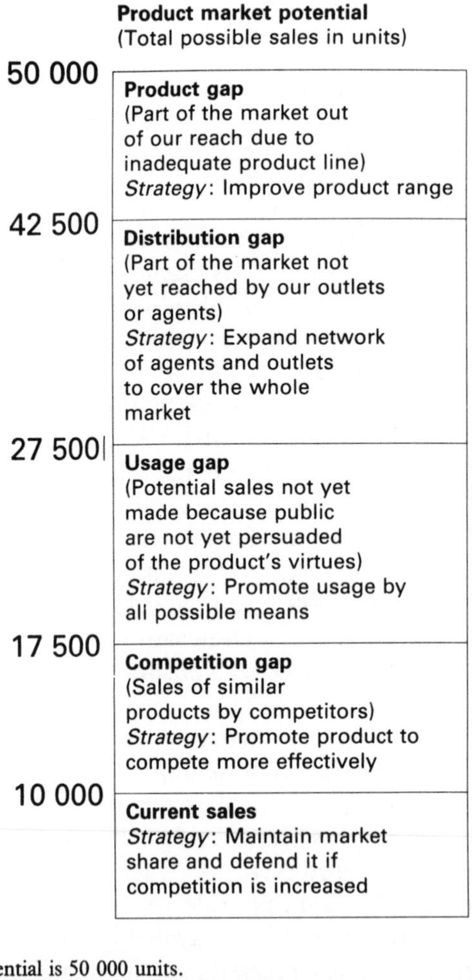

Product market potential
(Total possible sales in units)

50 000	**Product gap** (Part of the market out of our reach due to inadequate product line) *Strategy*: Improve product range
42 500	**Distribution gap** (Part of the market not yet reached by our outlets or agents) *Strategy*: Expand network of agents and outlets to cover the whole market
27 500	**Usage gap** (Potential sales not yet made because public are not yet persuaded of the product's virtues) *Strategy*: Promote usage by all possible means
17 500	**Competition gap** (Sales of similar products by competitors) *Strategy*: Promote product to compete more effectively
10 000	**Current sales** *Strategy*: Maintain market share and defend it if competition is increased

Notes
1 The total market potential is 50 000 units.
2 7500 units cannot be obtained because of the inadequacy of our product range.
3 This leaves a potential 42 500 units, but our distribution is inadequate in some areas and for this reason a further 15 000 units cannot be reached.
4 Of the remaining 27 500 units 10 000 are not being achieved because the public who might purchase them are not convinced of the usefulness of the product, relative to its price.
5 Of the 17 500 units which can be supplied our competitors at present supply 7500. We must devise a method of penetrating the positions of these competitors.

Market structure profiles

A market structure profile is appropriate to all markets and all products, while at the same time being practical and down-to-earth, providing we know which market we are involved in and which range of products. For example, 'what is the market for petrochemical products in Tanzania?' is a precise question even if the answer is going to need a lot of research. We know the range of products and we can obtain fairly precise estimates of the population and the national income. Some sectors of this population will be outside the main economic stream and unlikely to demand any of the product range. Some products may only be of interest to official purchasers and the income available to these nationalised industries will be the effective income for this particular range of products. Product line managers and other planning executives will argue about the estimates but they should at least be arguing about the same thing.

Once the market potential has been agreed the reasons why current sales fall below the potential can be analysed. In this connection the existence of different types of gaps illustrated in Fig. 6.1 points to the need for a series of strategies to bridge the gaps. The order of the gaps is important. For example, increased usage and better distribution cannot be effective if we simply do not have certain products in our product range. The sales team will justifiably cry 'Give us the products and we will raise sales.' Similarly, improved usage is of little help if our distribution system is unable to reach the new customers.

The result of analysing the gap between present sales and potential sales is a series of marketing strategies arranged in the order of possible effectiveness. This list of alternative strategies for expansion then converts fairly directly into a series of marketing programmes, where objectives can be set, targets proposed and **management by exceptions** applied. This means that actual results are compared with anticipated results and the exceptional results are analysed. Those areas who fail to meet their targets will be investigated. Is it the target or the marketing effort that is at fault? Similarly, those who surpass their targets superlatively well will also be investigated. Is there anything they are doing that could be helpful to other groups – or was the target unrealistically low for some reason? The latter will at least help future planning.

Seasonal and cyclical changes

Even where a market profile has been analysed and the market widely penetrated, it is dynamic not static. It must be constantly monitored if the future of the firm is to be secure. Demand analysis gives an objective view of the pattern of demand from area to area, range to range and product to product. The marketing pattern must be sufficiently adaptable to change in response to demand trends. Sales per foot of counter-run may reveal that lines that were selling well last week have little appeal this week. The sweep of the seasons affects demand in countless ways. There are man-made seasons like the educational year, Mother's Day, Father's Day and Guy Fawkes' Day. Comparative shopping may reveal that rival products are making headway while our own products are losing ground. In what ways have their products outstripped ours so that last season's brilliant success is this season's relative failure?

Seasonal monitoring helps management to anticipate changes in demand and prepare for them. An observed seasonal trend in one year should repeat itself the following year and preparations should be made to take advantage of the pattern of trade. Dull seasons can be utilised more effectively, for training purposes perhaps, for redesigning and renewing premises, for streamlining systems of work, etc. Staffing may be varied to suit the pattern of work – the fortuituous departure of staff at a slack period may enable their replacement to be delayed to reduce wage bills. Even outright slumps can be turned to advantage.

The astute manager uses the alternation of booms and slumps to the firm's advantage, consolidating in slump periods ready for a great leap forward when business picks up again. In slump times it is often possible to acquire assets – from firms which are contracting their activities – for a fraction of their cost in boom times. Installation can be a routine activity of maintenance staff not under pressure because of slack times. Layout can be rearranged without disruption. If demand analysis pinpoints a slump ahead we can quietly cut back on orders at times when other firms are buying stock, which they will never need, at high prices.

Demand analysis has many aspects. It seeks to assist the producer to discover what the customer requires, and which form of product or service will attract customers best and please them most. It therefore analyses contemporary human 'wants'. The basic wants of mankind, land, food, clothing, shelter, etc., do not change, but the means of satisfying those wants change constantly. The firm which has just built several estates of detached houses in outlying villages may be badly hit by a petrol shortage that causes customers to seek their 'shelter' in terraced town houses. Materials, styles, accessories, colours and prices of ladies' fashions change from month to month. The bandwagon only passes once; demand analysis ensures that the firm is ready to jump on as it makes its profitable and successful way to the head of the parade.

3 SOURCES OF INFORMATION FOR DEMAND ANALYSIS

Official sources

There are many official sources of statistics which can play a valuable part in any demand analysis exercise. Statistical methods are penetrating more and more into industrial and commercial life. A short description of some of these is helpful at this point. Although government statistical publications are rising in price they are still relatively inexpensive. At a time when the cheapest clerical help costs about £100 per week a few pounds for an annual statistical review is almost negligible. Remember, though, that it is essential to approach any set of official statistics with caution. The tendency is to turn to the statistics before turning to the definitions which tell you what the statistics are about. Population figures which exclude children under 16 are not much use to a manufacturer of school-age footwear, and so on. Always read the small print, the introductory notes and definitions on any set of statistics you are consulting for the first time. A short review of available publications is **Profit from Facts** from the Government Statistical Service, which is available from the Central Statistical Office, Great George St, London SW1P 3AQ. It describes:

1 **Business monitors**, which assess market share trends in a large number of product fields, and analyse the growth of existing and potential markets.
2 **Census publications**, which analyse the number of persons in particular industries, walks of life and regions. Examples are the *Agricultural Census*, *the Census of Population*, the *Census of Production*, *Education Statistics*, the *Census of Distribution, Social Surveys*, etc.
3 **Expenditure surveys**, which enquire how people spend their money. The *Family Expenditure Survey* and the *National Food Survey* are two examples.
4 **Regional statistics**, which help fix quotas for salesmen, plan distribution depots, etc.

Trade sources

Most trade associations and trade journals give helpful information about the industry in general, its market potential, product ranges, etc. Comparative studies are often carried out, and most associations have a research department which collects and publishes statistics about the industry. The trade journals carry informative articles about marketing aspects written by leading personalities, while the reports of company failures and bankruptcies by other firms make salutary reading at any time.

Similar publications are the free journals made available to most industries by publishers offering advertising space. This growing field of journalism combines a regular review of a particular industry with detailed appraisals of particular areas of interest. Thus *Business Equipment Digest* reviews developments in reprography, word-processing, flexible hours, etc., which include much of interest to potential customers but also to marketing managers seeking to analyse demand.

An organisation called the British Business Press at 15–19 Kingsway, London WC2B 6UN, is the trade association for publishers of such journals and has done some interesting research in this field.

In-house data

Part of any market analysis is the consideration of the current sales and the degree of market penetration achieved to date. A great deal of sales data should be accumulated 'in-house' and these should be analysed closely. This is called **desk research**.

In inflationary times it is essential to take inflation into account when examining the trend in figures. To do this we need to use the inflation rate, which is recalculated each month and published in various handbooks (for example, *Croner's Reference Book for Employers*).

Inflation rate

The inflation rate can be calculated by dividing the change in the index of retail prices over the last year by the starting index, and multiplying the result by 100. The Index of Retail Prices is reproduced in Table 6.1, by courtesy of Croner Publications Ltd.

The calculation of the inflation rate for the year to November 1988 is

$$\frac{110.0 - 103.4}{103.4} \times \frac{100}{1} = 6.4\%$$

The impact of inflation when evaluating sales data may be seen from the following example.

Suppose sales one year ago totalled £585 730 but now total £619 540. The increase of £33 810 is 5.8 per cent which appears *prima facie* quite good. With inflation running at 6.4 per cent we should have achieved an increase of £37 487 just to remain stationary – we actually lost market share during the year.

Clearly, if our desk-research reveals that sales, despite an apparently rising trend in current-price sales, have actually fallen when inflation is taken into account, the reaction of management must be sharp. Perhaps a complacent sales force, instead of being congratulated, must be sharply criticised and their poor performance penalised. Perhaps sales volumes have risen but our prices have not been raised to take account of inflation and criticism should be directed at pricing policies.

4   ASSESSING THE MARKET

Market assessment is a continuing activity for the market-orientated firm with a brand image to establish and maintain. Even if demand analysis leads us to conclude that we have a viable project that can command a reasonable share of a proven market, we can still fail if we lose track of the dynamic pace of events. Every market expands or contracts under the influence of changes in population, income, competitive forces, etc. Some of these dynamic influences may be listed as follows:

1 Has the total population interested in our product changed in the last six

Table 6.1 General Index of Retail Prices
(prices at January 1974=100)

Year	Jan.	Feb.	Mar.	Apr.	May	June	July	Aug.	Sept.	Oct.	Nov.	Dec.
1974	100.0	101.7	102.6	106.1	107.6	108.7	109.7	109.8	111.0	113.2	115.2	116.9
1975	119.9	121.9	124.3	129.1	134.5	137.1	138.5	139.3	140.5	142.5	144.2	146.0
1976	147.9	149.8	150.6	153.5	155.2	156.0	156.3	158.5	160.6	163.5	165.8	168.0
1977	172.4	174.1	175.8	180.3	181.7	183.6	183.8	184.7	185.7	186.5	187.4	188.4
1978	189.5	190.6	191.8	194.6	195.7	197.2	198.1	199.4	200.2	201.1	202.5	202.4
1979	207.2	208.9	210.6	214.2	215.9	219.6	229.1	230.9	233.2	235.6	237.7	239.4
1980	245.3	248.8	252.2	260.8	263.2	265.7	267.9	268.5	270.2	271.9	274.1	275.6
1981	277.3	279.8	284.0	292.2	294.1	295.8	297.1	299.3	301.0	303.7	306.9	308.8
1982	310.6	310.7	313.4	319.7	322.0	322.9	323.0	323.1	322.9	324.5	326.1	325.5
1983	325.9	327.3	327.9	332.5	333.9	334.7	336.5	338.0	339.5	340.7	341.9	342.8
1984	342.6	344.0	345.1	349.7	351.0	351.9	351.5	354.8	355.5	357.7	358.8	358.5
1985	359.8	362.7	366.1	373.9	375.6	376.4	375.7	376.7	376.5	377.1	378.4	378.9
1986	379.7	381.1	381.6	385.3	386.0	385.8	384.7	385.9	387.8	388.4	391.7	393.0
1987	394.5	396.1	396.9	401.6	402.0	402.0	401.6	402.8	404.0	405.9	407.9	407.5

(Prices at January 1987=100)

Year	Jan.	Feb.	Mar.	Apr.	May	June	July	Aug.	Sept.	Oct.	Nov.	Dec.
1987	100.0	100.4	100.6	101.8	101.9	101.9	101.8	102.1	102.4	102.9	103.4	103.3
1988	103.3	103.7	104.1	105.8	106.2	106.6	106.7	107.9	108.4	109.5	110.0	

(Reproduced from *Croner's Reference Book for Employers*)

Notes

1 One of the major drawbacks of any index is the selection of items to be included. Obviously items have to be representative, but the Index of Retail Prices can in no way be regarded as exhaustive.

2 Problems do not cease once the 'basket' of goods and services to be included in the Index have been selected. There remains the thorny problem that a weight (or stress) needs to be given to each item, since items are unlikely to be of equal importance to purchasers.

3 The effect of **1** and **2** above is generally that the Retail Price Index represents some non-existent average consumer. A vast number of consumers will not have purchasing patterns sufficiently close to the 'average' for the Index to reflect their purchases accurately.

4 From time to time a complete revision of the items included is necessary – the last time this was done is shown in the heading to the Index, i.e. 1987 in this case.

months? There may be 'bulge' effects in the population which will increase or decrease demand significantly.

2 Has the affluence of the population changed in recent months? If so will it mean more income available to purchase our product, or less? If the product we sell is a basic requirement hard times will mean we sell more, but prosperity for the population means less business for us. We are selling 'inferior goods'. Can anything be done to predict changes in affluence and estimate the income elasticity of demand for our product?

3 What motivates customers to demand our product? Has the product manager any innovations in mind to raise demand? Has he an adequate advertising budget for the consolidation of our brand image?

4 What seasonal variations affect this product? Have we prepared stocks to meet these variations and reminded customers that they should order in anticipation of increased demand?

5 What political and economic influences are at work? Is the prospect of profitability good or bad? Should we press ahead or hold back?

6 Have we taken account of changes in the end-user market? For example, ecological objections reduce the demand for particular products; educational syllabuses change and render textbooks and other educational aids obsolete; cross-elasticities affect demand for products – a rise in petrol prices cuts the demand for tyres and a petrol shortage damages the tourist trade in remoter regions.

7 Are we monitoring the trade literature to keep an eye on competition? Who are our rivals and what are they up to? Have they changed styles, materials used, packaging or prices? Should we be doing any test purchasing? Are they forcing the demand curve for our brands in towards the left to reduce our super-profits and threaten our brand's image (see pages 161–2)?

8 Have we evaluated the application, commitment and perseverance of sales staff? Who has done better than expected and who has done worse? Was it the plans that were wrong, or their respective performances? What can the successful representative teach us, and what lessons can we learn from the failures? Who needs help, and who needs a reprimand?

SELF-ASSESSMENT QUESTIONS

1 What is a market-orientated firm?

2 What is a market structure profile?

3 A sales manager draws up an estimate of the market potential. It shows a number of 'gaps'. What would these gaps be, and how could they be closed?

4 What is 'the business press'? How could it be of use to a Sales Manager?

5 SUPPLYING THE MARKET – PHYSICAL DISTRIBUTION MANAGEMENT

Commerce has been defined as follows:

> Commerce is the distribution and exchange of all the surplus goods produced in the fields, mines, seas, forests, and factories of the earth so that they reach the final consumer in the right place and the right condition, at the right time, in the right quantity, and at the right place.

If we are to ensure that our customers receive the goods we have produced in sound condition where they want them and when they want them at prices they can afford we obviously have a large physical distribution problem. For example, everyone knows that production problems are analysed very carefully to discover ways of making goods at minimum cost. Since the final price to the consumer must cover both the production costs and the distribution costs, we should give just as rigorous attention to the cost of distribution, warehousing, transport, handling, etc., as we do to production costs. In other words we must engage in **physical distribution management**.

'Physical distribution' is a term that has gained general currency in the last decade as a convient description of a wide range of activities which take place after goods have been produced and before they reach the consumer, or the next stage of production if they are part of a continuing process. These activities include materials handling, storage and warehousing, packaging and unitisation and freight transportation by all modes of transport. Related activities such as vehicle routeing and scheduling and vehicle maintenance are also included. The purpose of these activities is the bridging of gaps between the producer and consumer. They ensure the safe passage of goods from the point of production to the point of consumption, so that they arrive in perfect condition where they are wanted when they are wanted.

In performing such a wide range of activities in a world where specialisation is a major feature of the method of production, long geographical journeys will be inevitable. Vast quantities of raw materials and finished products move restlessly along the major trade routes, subject to attack by climatic changes, insect pests, desiccation, humidity, pilfering and large-scale theft. To counter such influences strategies must be developed and plans prepared. At the same time these plans must be economically viable, because safe arrival over the geographical time barriers will be fruitless if the final cost to the consumer is greater than he/she can afford. Goods must reach the consumer not only in the right quantity, the right condition, the right place and the right time, but also at the right price. A chief function of physical distribution management therefore is to ensure economic operations.

Physical distribution is a full-scale study in its own right. Readers who are engaged in this branch of activity and would like to study it in depth should read *Transport and Distribution* by Don Benson and Geoffrey Whitehead (Pitman Publishing).

An outline of the physical distribution process

There are a number of functions in the distribution process, not all of which will appear in every distribution system. As management moves into fully sophisticated control of physical distribution it embraces activities previously thought to be separate functions from physical distribution so that a full list now includes the following:

1 A purchasing function.
2 An 'assembly' activity.
3 A packaging and unitisation activity.
4 A storage function (warehousing).
5 Inventory management.
6 A transport function.
7 A depot activity.
8 A marketing function.

While the particular circumstances of a firm may be such that some of these functions will not be necessary, most of them will be necessary in all firms. A brief description of each is given here.

THE PURCHASING FUNCTION

This function procures for the business those items that it requires for the successful prosecution of its activities. For manufacturing concerns it will be raw materials, components and capital items like machinery. For wholesale business the purchase of stock for resale will be the major requirement. Haphazard and intuitive purchasing has probably led to more failures in business than any other weakness, and the purchasing function must be fully reviewed at regular intervals.

AN 'ASSEMBLY' ACTIVITY

This will be less apparent in a factory manufacturing situation than in a farming or market gardening system. With many types of produce – fruit, vegetables, milk, poultry, etc. – there will be a process of collection to take place. Fruit does not all ripen on the same day, and a succession of collections will be necessary during the season. The assembly function leads into a packaging and unitisation function.

PACKAGING AND UNITISATION

This is a major feature of modern distribution. More than anything else the selling of prepacked, often perishable, products has transformed the retail trade in recent years, breaking down barriers between retailers that have existed for centuries. The skilled tradesman who understood his merchandise and how to market it has been replaced by the self-service trader, whose sole function is to display and sell. The prepackaging function is of great importance, and greatly simplifies distribution. Its compact units lend themselves to palletisation and modern mechanised handling, while bulk haulage by containerisation makes for economic transport over long distances.

STORAGE AND WAREHOUSING

Storage is inseparable from distribution for a variety of reasons. Goods are often produced seasonally but consumed continuously. A notable example is wheat, and the bread we make from it. Others are consumed seasonally, but produced throughout the year, like Christmas decorations and fireworks. Others may be produced in batches – because the demand for a period can be produced in a few days. Almost any product may require storage at a particular time for reasons quite external to the product itself – a strike, or a dislocation of transport, or a minor depression reducing demand temporarily. The storage function may involve many types of expertise, often referred to as 'merchandising' knowledge. Every product has its peculiar properties, its own **inherent vice** which must be controlled by appropriate treatment.

INVENTORY MANAGEMENT

Related to the purchasing function, but most obvious in warehousing, is the question of inventory management. Stocks which are not turned over represent capital tied up without return. It must be a management function to control stock levels and in the interests of shareholders to ensure a good return on capital invested. It involves decisions about 'assortments', optimum ordering, maximum and minimum stock levels, etc. 'Assortment' is a term which refers to the variety of stock available. It is a matter of policy how wide a variety of stock shall be handled and what limitations shall be placed on the range of sizes, colours and qualities available.

THE TRANSPORT FUNCTION

Transport alters the geographical position of the goods from the production point to the point of consumption. They can rarely go the entire journey in a single trip, because the economic load for the major part of the journey is usually greater than any single customer can use. In rare cases they might do so: for example, a road tanker might leave an oil refinery with a full load of petroleum for a single customer's garage. More usually some sort of depot network will be used as a buffer where the uneven nature of supply and demand can be accommodated. Sometimes a wholesaler will perform this function as an intermediary at whose premises bulk can be broken. A large organisation will use its depots as bulk-breaking centres.

DEPOT ACTIVITY

The depot constitutes a local warehouse for temporary storage where merchandise is secure and properly cared for by staff who understand its characteristics. The depot acts as a buffer to accommodate excess of supply over demand, and a source of reserve for emergency requirements. It often provides an area stock of slow-moving items to reduce stocks held in branches, the slow-moving item being ordered up when required.

THE MARKETING FUNCTION

Marketing is the final link in the distribution chain. It puts the product into the hands of the consumer, or perhaps the retailer who serves the consumer. It is of enormous importance, bringing to fruition the activity commenced long ago when the production process started.

Each of these functions is a lifetime of activity for someone. There are drivers who do nothing but load and haul bulk cargoes and order-pickers who spend all day in the alleyways of storage depots picking out slow-moving stock ordered up by branches. If they are all working efficiently customers will receive the goods in the right condition and in the right quantities at the right time at a price they can afford.

6   MARKET POWER

In the modern mixed economy the tendency is for private sector firms to be few in number and large in size, while public sector corporations are invariably monopolies. 'Seller concentration' is a pronounced feature of the characteristic structure of markets. One investigator found that the 100 largest firms produce 50 per cent of total net output. Current legislation permits reference to be made to the Monopolies Commission either by Ministers or by the Director General of Fair Trading if a firm appears to have more than 25 per cent of the total market in a particular product. Of the 100 largest firms more than half have two or more monopolies, and some as many as five. Such concentration gives firms considerable market power.

'Market power' means that a firm or corporation is in a position to exploit its position as the sole supplier, or one of the few suppliers of a range of products. Because it is in a position to exploit its position does not always mean that a firm will actually do so, but generally speaking if we assume profit maximisation as an important objective there is a *prima facie* case for assuming that the firm will exploit its natural advantage. The manipulation of prices is an obvious example. Harsh treatment of suppliers, often smaller firms unable to sell their product to anyone but the dominant firm, is another. Failure to pay on time is another. One freight forwarder who 'landed' an enormous contract for the export of the entire output of a major motor vehicle manufacturer had to perform £9 million worth of services before he received his first cheque. By that time he had been taken over by a merchant bank to find the finance needed, and the proprietor was not sure who had 'landed' whom.

'The consumer is no longer king'

In the real world 'market power' changes some of the basic economic concepts. Some criticisms of monopoly are given below, but it has to be recognised as a fact of life that alongside the market economy, which holds that the consumer is sovereign, there is a second economy run by mature corporations, where the producer is king.

As huge corporations become more and more the typical business unit, there is less and less feedback from the consumer to the producer. Every outsize and undersize lady these days knows how difficult it is to get garments to fit her. The producers are producing what it is convenient, economical and profitable to produce. The outsized and the undersized must take care of themselves. Many consumers experience a take-it-or-leave-it attitude to their complaints about a commodity which all the bureaucratic bumbledom in the Consumer Advice Centres is powerless to change. The mature corporations are able to control both the prices at which they buy, and the prices at which they sell. They can persuade the consumer to want what is available and they can evade criticism by a variety of delays, both administrative and legal.

The framework of the organisation is such that those who most studiously support market power rise highest in the hierarchy, and reinforce their own positions. They may incidentally change its motivations to fit more closely to their own, so that society and corporation are more closely identified with one another. When this is extended to include trade union organisations within the hierarchy we have a very monolithic structure indeed, pursuing its own identity in the community at the expense of the general public as a whole. This is referred to again below.

'Monopoly power' in the market

Monopoly practices may be criticised from the economic viewpoint for the following reasons:

a) Since marginal cost is lower than monopoly price, output is cut off earlier than in competitive circumstances, with consequent misallocation of resources and a reduction in consumer satisfactions.

b) The super-profits made result in a redistribution to the producers of income which properly belongs to consumers.

c) The excess profits available may lead to waste, because economies of operation are not so urgently pursued. Even though the general climate is one of profit maximisation, the urgency to pursue an absolute maximum is reduced.

d) Excess profits also foster such abuses as price discrimination in favour of particular customers and price cutting to starve out smaller competitors by loss-making operations subsidised by profits achieved elsewhere.

e) Monopoly profits also make it easier to satisfy shareholders by giving them a reasonable rate of return on capital invested, while leaving management to satisfy its own aims at the expense of consumers. These include high salaries, generous 'perks', a quiet life (without industrial unrest), empire-building, status satisfactions, etc. If a truly corporate image can be established which extends from the highest to the lowest level of employees the whole corporate structure can be a very powerful, self-perpetuating body. Often the basic requirement is to keep the shareholders happy by achieving an agreed level of profits which permits a reasonable return to them of capital invested. The gap between that declared level of profit and the actual profit made by selling the goods produced can be filled by a wide variety of 'business expenses' which would never be incurred in non-corporate enterprises. How many managers would concede the pay demands, reduced working weeks, longer holiday periods, hospital schemes, pension schemes, etc., if the money had to come out of their own pockets? A powerful trade union or staff union lobby which has to be bought off by such rewards can have an inflationary impact on the whole economy. When it has nibbled away the gap between the true profits and the level of 'satisfying' profits which will keep shareholders happy it can only be satisfied by raising prices to consumers or eating into the shareholders' share of profits.

While a domestic market can be managed to a considerable extent export markets are vulnerable to world-wide competition. Higher prices to the consumer will therefore lead to loss of markets and the domestic markets may also suck in imports of competitive products. At some point prices cannot be raised any more and the shareholders' margin may therefore be eaten into, to their considerable dissatisfaction. Further investment will not be forthcoming and the industry is vulnerable to technological change. Even the bluest of blue-chip companies may go out of business in such circumstances.

Against these criticisms we must reiterate that monopoly is not necessarily bad. If the exploitation of the advantages of large scale leads naturally to a monopoly or oligopoly it is absurd not to allow it to take place by a series of mergers, take-overs, etc. In the long run we are left with pursuing that policy which will bring the greatest economy, i.e. the largest output, from the smallest input of resources. If it leads to inequalities of wealth these should be sorted out in other ways.

Nationalisation is one solution to the problem of natural monopolies – and this need not imply inefficiency. Progressive taxation has some part to play in restoring the balance between consumers and producers. Watchdog bodies like the consumer protection departments have a considerable part to play in advising the public. It is possible to point to such bodies and argue that they serve no useful purpose and act so slowly that they are often accused of only closing stable doors after the horse has bolted. It is much more difficult to prove that such bodies serve no useful purpose. It is often not necessary for a watchdog actually to bark. The mere fact that it is there, with its teeth bared, may lead a monopolist to seek other solutions to his/her financial problems. The threat of a full investigation into possible economies in operation may be sufficient to turn the industry into seeking economies itself.

It is certainly a fact that in inflationary times the tendency is for firms with market power to fuel the inflation by keeping not only abreast of, but ahead of, the inflationary spiral. Society will need some sort of control on market power until firms themselves actually begin to consider consumption as the real end purpose of their production, and price cuts as one form of maximising consumer satisfaction. Cuts are anti-inflation measures that seem unlikely to be realised speedily.

SELF-ASSESSMENT QUESTIONS

5 What is physical distribution management?
6 Explain the function of transport.
7 Explain the function of a depot.
8 What is meant by 'market power'? How can we control firms who have it?

REVISION TEST

Answers	Questions
—	**1** What is a market-orientated firm?
1 One which is chiefly preoccupied with its markets, and carries out market analysis, consumer research and heavy advertising expenditure.	**2** What factors chiefly affect the market for goods and services?
2 (a) The 'population' interest in a particular item. (b) The affluence of that population.	**3** What is 'demand analysis'?
3 A systematic investigation of the pattern of demand for a firm's products.	**4** What is a 'market structure profile'?
4 An attempt to describe a market, by collecting all the relevant information about it in a practical way, relevant to the firm's existing products.	**5** What is 'product market potential'?

5 It is the potential market for a product, drawn up as a vertical bar chart with five sections. From top to bottom these are:
   e) Product gap;
   d) Distribution gap;
   c) Usage gap;
   b) Competition gap;
   a) Current sales.

6 Explain each of these gaps in terms of lost potential sales.

---

6 (b) Competition gap: the sales we can't make because our competitors are succeeding instead. (c) Usage gap: the sales we cannot make because consumers are not persuaded to use the product yet. (d) Distribution gap: the sales we cannot make because we have no distribution network in certain areas. (e) Product gap: the sales we cannot make because our range of products is not extensive enough.

7 What market strategy is necessary to bridge each of these gaps?

---

7 (b) Promote the product to compete more effectively. (c) Promote usage by informative and persuasive advertising. (d) Expand the network of agents and outlets. (e) Improve the product range.

8 What is physical distribution management?

---

8 It is that part of managerial science which bridges the gaps between the product and the consumer.

9 What 'gaps' are these?

---

9 The geographical gap, which has to be bridged by transport, depot location, etc. The time gap, which has to be bridged by warehousing and merchandising skills.

10 What is 'market power'?

---

10 It is the power exercised by a large corporation in a commanding position in a given market.

11 How may this power be exercised?

11 (a) To dominate its suppliers. (b) To persuade consumers into preferring what it offers at the prices it wishes to charge. (c) To 'satisfy' shareholders without returning to them the full fruits of their investment. (d) To pursue managerial (including trade union) objectives rather than profit.

Go over the test again to ensure that you are familiar with these matters.

ANSWERS

(See Self-assessment questions on pages 180 and 187.)

1 A market-orientated firm is a firm which is chiefly concerned about its markets, and its share of the market. Such firms are usually operating in a situation of monopolistic competition, i.e. they sell branded goods which are to some extent unique, but are in competition with other brands of a similar product.

2 A market structure profile is an analysis of the market for a particular good or service, which shows what share of the market a producer's brand is capturing, and seeks to discover why it is not achieving 100 per cent of the market.

3 The gaps might be: (a) a product gap; (b) a distribution gap; (c) a usage gap; (d) a competition gap. We can only close the product gap by extending the range of our products so that we are able to supply products that meet the situations of all potential consumers. We can only close the distribution gap if we set up depots or find agents in all areas of the country. We can only close the usage gap by informative or persuasive advertising to bring our product to the attention of all potential users. We can only close the competition gap by finding ways of eating into our competitors' markets – perhaps by improving our product, competitive advertising, etc.

4 The business press is a collection of magazines, often 'free circulation' magazines, which deal with the needs of a particular industry and draw the attention of those interested to the 'state of the art' innovations as they appear.

5 Physical distribution management is management of the procedures needed in moving goods from the point of production to the point of consumption, across the geographical gaps and time gaps. It involves knowledge of packaging, packing, unitisation of cargoes, transport, warehousing and merchandising skills (knowing how to carry merchandise over time gaps without deterioration, dessication and other losses).

6 Transport bridges geographical gaps, bringing goods and services to the consumer and consumers to goods and services. It also brings raw materials and labour to the production point, ready to create goods or give services.

7 A depot is a place where stocks can be held pending requisition by producers or demand by consumers. It must be appropriate to the product concerned, convenient for deliveries inwards and outwards, well organised so that different goods can be located when required and properly equipped with mechanical handling equipment.

8 Market power is the power exercised by a large corporation with a controlling influence either as a supplier or a customer in a major market. Essentially if the company is a big enough buyer to be able to influence prices by refusing to buy, or a big enough seller to influence prices by refusing to sell, it can exercise market power. We can control such firms by administrative measures such as referring them to the Monopolies Commission.

QUESTIONS ON CHAPTER 6

1 What is the importance of the market to a firm making consumer durables? How may it assess the market and what strategies might it use to improve market share?

2 Explain the terms 'market structure profile' and 'product market potential' by reference to some range of products with which you are familiar.

3 Forty per cent of all the costs to be recovered by the sales of UK goods are distribution costs. How may such costs be reduced?

4 'Physical distribution is the activity of moving goods safely from the point of production to the point of consumption, despite the variety of hazards that are presented at every stage.' Explain these hazards, and the techniques used to surmount physical distribution problems.

5 'The consumer is no longer sovereign. The arm of the corporate producer reaches forward to control its markets, and to manage market behaviour and shape the social attitudes of those, ostensibly, that it serves.' – JK Galbraith. Explain.

6 What are the characteristics of a market-orientated organisation?

7 List some of the dynamic forces influencing markets. Mention in your answer the market for crude oil and the market for washing machines.

8 What is involved with the concept of 'consumer being king'?

9 Why are monopoly practices often criticised?

TIPS FOR STUDENTS: A SPECIMEN
ANSWER TO QUESTION 8

The idea that the consumer is king is associated with economic theorists of the nineteenth century but still influences many people today. It is argued that consumers, through the purchasing power they command, are in a position to dictate what producers provide to the market. If the consumer does not get what he/she requires purchases cease, starving the supplier of orders and funds, and forcing him/her to change the product to one which the consumer does want. There is much truth in this argument, but it is not quite as influential a doctrine as it was. The huge size of many businesses today means that they wield considerable power themselves and if they have a monopoly of a product people need orders will flow in anyway. They can influence demand by informative and persuasive advertising, and very often the consumer is treated with a 'take it or leave it' attitude.

7 | The rewards to factors

1 DISTRIBUTION THEORY

The early economists found it difficult to explain why, with production being so well organised and wealth pouring off the production lines in a steady stream, there were still poor people about. They talked about production being a bitter process, subject to harsh laws of competition. In an age when there was no public schooling, and children were free to enter factories at the age of five, or even earlier, it seemed clear that child labour would replace adult labour and they could see no way in which adult unemployment could be avoided. It was John Stuart Mill (1806–73) who pointed out the better way, by developing a theory of distribution of wealth. Distribution theory is not about transport or the movement of goods, it is about the distribution of wealth that has been created.

John Stuart Mill was a boy genius, who had already learned Latin and Greek by the age of six and by the age of 12 was studying philosophy, logic and political economy. His distribution theory said that while the creation of goods and services might be subject to the harsh laws of competition, the distribution of wealth was not. It was a matter of human arrangement only. Having created wealth we could use it in any way we liked, and spread it around evenly if we wished. This simple idea became the foundation of socialist, and probably communist, thought, though much time was to pass before doctrines like 'From each according to his ability, to each according to his need' were to be widely adopted. If you look carefully at such a doctrine it is really only a suggested method for achieving what some regard as fair results when dealing with the subject matter of this chapter – rewards to factors. How do we create wealth? By employing factors (land, labour and capital) to create goods and services. How shall we share out the wealth we have created? By whatever distribution method we choose to use – of which 'to each according to his need' is the most humane – if never quite realisable – method.

Firms employ factors to create wealth in the form of goods and services. In return for the use of the factor, the factor owned is paid a reward. The landlord receives his rent, the person who provides capital is paid interest, the worker receives his wages. Having paid out all these rewards there is a residue left called the profit. In earlier days we would have said that this profit was the reward for showing enterprise, and it belonged to the entrepreneur who stepped out of the crowd to organise production. Today it is much less easy to pinpoint the entrepreneur, who does not tower above his contemporaries like some Richard Arkwright or George Stephenson of earlier eras. Who does show enterprise is discussed below.

Before looking at these rewards in more detail there is one other aspect of rewards which explains some of the anomalies about rewards to factors which puzzled the early economists. Because it was first noticed with regard to land, it was called **'economic rent'**. Later the same idea was found to apply to the other factors too, and 'economic rent' is today used as a term which can be applied to any factor.

> Economic rent has been defined as a payment to a factor over and above what is necessary to keep it in its present employment.

For example, if a skilled worker is paid £180 per week there is usually some element of economic rent in that wage. Would he leave the job if his wages were cut to £175? Probably not, but if wages were lowered progressively to £170, £165, etc., there must come a point where he would go. This point is called the **'transfer earnings'**, and the sum paid above that figure is 'economic rent'. The difference is really due to a difference between the supply price (for which the factor is prepared to be employed) and the demand price, a higher price which the entrepreneur is prepared to pay.

Entrepreneurs are prepared to pay higher prices for certain business sites than for others – in London's Oxford Street, for example. The bidding-up of rents in Oxford Street is the result of the strong demand and the 'economic rent' thus paid is called 'rent of situation'. The pop-star who moves from one-night shows at £50 a night to a booking at the London Palladium at £50 000 per week is earning economic rents called 'rent of ability'. The entrepreneur who is making more-than-the normal profits because he has a monopoly or a branded-good that is differentiated from its rivals in monopolistic competition earns economic rent which is called 'monopoly rent'. Only capital, which is very easily moved about to places where it is required, does not earn economic rents sufficiently regularly to deserve a special name for them.

A general name for economic rents is **'scarcity rents'**. It is appropriate because the demand price for a factor is most likely to be above the supply price when the factor is scarce. This illustrates a common criticism of those earning economic rents. Suppose a speculator lays in stocks of produce when it is cheap, and releases it when prices have risen due to some natural event like frost or bad weather. The speculator is often accused of profiteering out of the shortage. To this he will reply that he has not caused the shortage – in fact, he is the only one relieving it. The high prices are not the result of his activities – in fact, prices would go even higher if he were not there to supply the goods. In short, 'scarcity rents' are not the *cause* of high prices, but only the *result* of high prices. We may list the rewards to factors as follows:

Factor	Reward	Excess payments
Land	Commercial rent	Rent of situation
Labour	Wages	Rent of ability
Capital	Interest	—
—	Profit	Monopoly rents

We must now look at each of these rewards in more detail.

2   THE REWARD TO THE FACTOR LAND: RENT

The word 'land' in economics means the resources made available by nature, including the geographical territory and the other natural resources. Rent is the payment made by one person – the tenant or user of the resource – to another person, the landlord, for the use of the resource. The term 'landlord' reflects the original ownership of land in the UK by the King, who infeudated it to the lords and nobles, who infeudated it to lesser men. Gradually the release of land to freeholders and leaseholders spread the ownership of land. Where 'land' is a resource, such as iron ore, coal, salt, etc., the rent charged is payable as a royalty on the tonnage extracted.

The price of land is fixed by the inter-action of supply and demand. The supplier of the land (the landlord) seeks to maximise the net advantage to be gained from making it available. He/she will therefore take the best price obtainable for it, bearing in mind the expenses that will be incurred, which must be deducted from the yield obtained. An entrepreneur, by contrast, will not pay more for a site, or a resource, than the marginal productivity to be obtained from it. The word 'marginal' implies that the next unit taken into production will be less productive than the last (for example entrepreneurs – who are always deemed to behave rationally – will already have taken the good land into production, so that the next unit of land is bound to be marginally inferior). Similarly with a resource. Although the next ton of coal may be just as good quality as the last, the extra supply will tend to reduce the price. So the entrepreneur will not pay more for land than the earnings from the best crop that can be grown on it, or more for a ton of a resource than can be obtained for it.

Where the price of land is high the entrepreneur may combine it with other factors to make its use profitable. Thus a highly priced site may be made viable by increasing the amount of capital to be applied, for example building high-rise buildings, or skyscrapers, upon it. Prime sites are allocated by the pricing mechanism to industries which are highly profitable, and can afford the high rents, while less viable projects are forced to accept less convenient property more remotely situated or less attractive.

Commercial rent is the agreed contractual sum of money payable for the use of land. Whether landlords have any 'right' to own land, which was originally a free gift of nature, is a debatable point. We have seen that all land tenure in the UK, for example, derives ultimately from the Norman Conquest when the land was seized by right of conquest in the king's name. Our present 'freehold' tenures derive from the sale of parts of this seized property over the course of nine centuries, while leasehold tenures only permit the use of the land for a period of years (ranging from 999 years at the longest to one week at the shortest tenancy). Probably if there is one act of nationalisation that ought to take place it is the nationalisation of land. It is part of the methodology of economics to avoid discussion of such controversial matters, which are called 'value judgments'. A value judgment is one that cannot be verified by reference to the facts, but is based upon opinions. Sticking to the facts, rent paid to landlords amounts to some 7½ per cent of the national income.

Economic rent and land

We have already seen that land in certain specialised situations (such as Fifth Avenue in New York or Oxford Street in London's West End) commands higher prices due to the scarcity of good sites in the area. This extra price is called 'economic rent' or 'rent of situation'.

3   THE REWARD TO THE FACTOR LABOUR: WAGES

Labour is the human factor; we are all possessed of minds and bodies which can be employed in the production process, and for the vast majority of us these human qualities are all we do have to offer to the production scene. Marx's lament that the proletariat 'has nothing to sell but its labour power' is still very true. If you have been dispossessed of your land, like the eighteenth century peasants driven off the land by the Enclosure Acts, you are reduced to selling your human skills in the labour market or living off your accumulated savings. For most people savings are small relative to their needs, and consequently soon exhausted, reducing them to a penniless, landless proletariat. This is why unemployment is such a disastrous condition for ordinary people, especially in the absence of a welfare state. If unemployment is eased by reasonably adequate unemployment benefits most people can survive it, but it is still a demoralising condition. However, while this explains why a mixed economy should always feature an adequate social security system, it is not the point at issue here. We are considering the rewards to those who offer their labour power in the services of production. Such rewards are called **wages**. The wages payable to any particular type of labour are decided in a free-enterprise society in the market place.

We have already defined a market as a place where buyers and sellers are in contact with one another to fix prices. The labour market is a market where employers can buy human resources and where workers can sell their labour power. The employers are demanding labour and the workers are selling it. What motivates the two sides, and how is the price of labour decided? There is no simple answer to these questions but some of the main points are as follows:

(a) The demand for labour – the marginal productivity theory

The **marginal productivity theory** holds that entrepreneurs will demand factors as long as the marginal unit of a factor which they purchase – in this case labour – yields the entrepreneur in increased output more than it costs him in the market place. Thus if the wage of a labourer is £100 per week and the result of the labourer's efforts is £110 per week it will be worthwhile employing him/her. If the labourer demands a £10 per week rise and it is not possible to raise the price of the contract the worker is to be employed on, then it will not be worth while taking on the extra employee. The reader will easily see how difficult it is to simplify such examples, for it will be at once apparent that if all the other labourers are also to receive a £10-per-week increase the contract is going to make a loss anyway, and bankruptcy stares the contractor in the face. Even great firms who make fixed price contracts can become insolvent, as the shareholders of the original Rolls-Royce aero-engine firm found to their cost a few years ago. Encouraged by the Government at the time to make a long-term contract for the supply of aero engines at a fixed price a steep rise in wages during a bout of inflation resulted in the whole company collapsing.

From the employer's viewpoint, therefore, the cheaper labour is the better, since it makes it more likely that the marginal revenue produced will exceed the cost of the marginal unit of labour. It also enables him/her to keep down the cost of the product on the market and thus keep the product competitive.

The marginal productivity theory is illustrated in Table 7.1 and Fig. 7.1 while the notes below the figure explain it fully.

(b) The supply of labour – maximum net advantage

From the worker's viewpoint, the price of labour is the reward for his/her services which will enable him/her to buy the basket of goods and services required to support him/her. Naturally, the higher the reward the higher the employee's standard of living. The employee therefore hopes to sell his/her labour power at the price which yields the **maximum net advantage**. The term 'net' advantage implies that we must deduct from the wages we receive any losses to be suffered if we take that particular employment. These may be monetary losses or non-monetary losses. Many a worker offered employment

Table 7.1 Marginal physical product and marginal revenue product (Units valued at £25 each)

Number of employees	Units of output	Marginal physical product (i.e. output of extra employee)	Marginal revenue product, i.e. extra employee's output valued in money (£)	Wage paid (£)
1	5	5	125	100
2	12	7	175	100
3	22	10	250	100
4	33	11	275	100
5	43	10	250	100
6	50	7	175	100
7	55	5	125	100
8	59	4	100	100
9	62	3	75	100
10	64	2	50	100

Fig. 7.1 *Deciding how many people to employ*

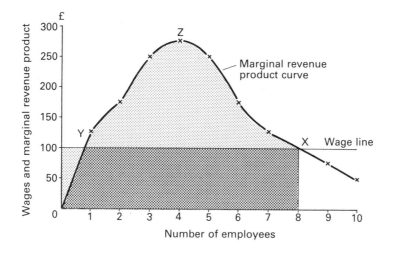

Notes
1 Marginal revenue produced increases at first, and reaches a maximum at the point Z when four employees are engaged.
2 The fifth worker produces an increase of £250 which is less than the fourth worker's marginal product but it is still worth while employing him/her for the wage is only £100.
3 When the marginal revenue product falls below the wage line at the point X (eight workers employed) it is not profitable to employ any more.
4 The total wage is shown by the area 08X 100 = £800
5 The total revenue is the shaded area under the curve 0YZX8, and is equal to £1475 (the sum of the marginal-revenue products).
6 The reader should note that the rewards to the other factors land and capital can also be seen from the diagram. They are the area under the curve YZX minus the area of the triangle 0Y100.

at higher wages elsewhere does not take it because it will take the family away from relatives or the children will need to change schools. If the advantages of the bargain outweigh the disadvantages, labour will move between firms and industries. We would therefore expect to see workers in industries where wages are low moving off into other industries where wages are higher. In a freely competitive labour market this certainly does take place.

We may therefore say that in a freely competitive market wages will be fixed by the interaction of supply and demand in the same way that other prices are fixed. Supply will be governed by the workers' estimate of the maximum net advantage. Demand will be governed by the marginal productivity theory. Where there are restrictions on entry – for example, in professional occupations where a certain agreed level of educational attainment is required – salaries will be decided in a climate of shortage of labour, which will tend to force salaries up. Similarly, if craft unions are able to insist on apprenticeship schemes which make entry to a trade difficult they can prevent the dilution of their labour. The entry of less well trained persons can be avoided and although individuals are unlikely to be free to bargain with employers the collective bargaining conducted on their behalf by unions will take place in a climate of negotiation which is favourable to workers. Similar restrictions are achieved by closed shop arrangements.

While such restrictive practices are understandable in view of the historical development of the capitalist system, which caused working people to unionise in order to achieve fair wages, they have had an unfair effect at times of severe unemployment. Unemployed labour is prevented from moving across into industries where there is a shortage of labour and retraining schemes to relieve shortages can only take place in industries where trade unionism is weak. Long-term unemployment must be endured by valuable human factors, while industries which are prosperous are forced to pay higher wages than necessary and consequently are less competitive not only in the export market but in the home market, where imports from countries which do not have restrictive practices can undercut home-produced goods.

Recent legislation on trade unionism, as part of a broader band of legislation known as supply-side measures, has redressed these unfairnesses to a considerable extent. We may characterise supply-side measures as measures designed to make the markets work better, and in this case the markets referred to are the markets for factors, including the labour market.

Economic rent and labour

We have already seen that where labour is especially gifted, it can command extra wages called 'rent of ability'. Thus the opera soprano, the concert violinist and even the skilled golfer or snooker player command salaries well above the rewards necessary to keep the people concerned in their present employment (see the definition of economic rent on page 193). For those who would argue that such payments are really unnecessary, or even undesirable, we can only say that they can best be recovered through the tax net, and it is for Parliament to decide such re-distributions of wealth.

Wages and the national income

We have seen that wages is the reward paid to the factor labour. The word 'salaries', which is often used for payments to office and administrative staff, comes from the Latin *salarium*, which originally meant 'salt-money'. It was an extra payment of salt to soldiers on the African campaigns for their sweated labour. In economics no difference is made between wages and salaries. The share labour receives of the national income is given in the National Blue Book on Income and Expenditure and in 1987 amounted to 63 per cent. This is a reduction from the 1970s, when labour was receiving over 70 per cent of the national income. The change represents the results of government efforts to restore investment in UK industry by shifting the balance marginally in favour of increased profits for industry.

4   THE REWARD TO THE FACTOR CAPITAL: INTEREST

Interest is the reward paid to capital. It is difficult to define interest clearly, since the rate of interest tends to reflect government policy which seeks to manipulate it. There are many rates of interest. Most vital is the rate of interest the Bank of England deems to be desirable in the current market situation. These days the desirable rate is not announced formally, as it once was, though the Bank of England still reserves the right to announce a Minimum Lending Rate (MLR) if it considers it essential to do so. This may be defined as the minimum rate at which the Bank will discount first-class bills of exchange. For most of the time the Bank of England, as part of its prudential supervision of the banks, is content to indicate covertly, to banks that look likely to get into difficulties, that it deems it desirable for them to raise their rates to customers. It also indicates covertly to all banks what rate of interest it deems desirable at any particular time. Whatever this covert rate may be all other rates as far as the general borrowing public are concerned are above the covert rate. For example the mortgage rate will be several percentage points higher, and such things as credit card annual percentage rates will be at least 10 per cent per annum above the basic rates, and often much more. Some credit card companies at the time of writing, when interest basic rates are about 15 per cent are charging 34 per cent – which is surely extortionate. Even the more respectable cards are charging about 24 per cent.

Why do such rates vary so widely? The answer is that capital employed in risky circumstances (such as hire purchase, where defaulting on debts is common) requires extra rewards to keep funds available in that particular sector of the market. Similarly if the method of accounting imposes burdens on the lender (Barclaycard alone sends out 8 million statements every month, and issues new cards every two years) the costs have to be recouped from somewhere. Part of the 'interest' charged is for the service provided, and is not 'interest' in the true sense of the word at all.

Economic rent and capital

It is said that money, being liquid, can flow fairly easily from one sector of the market to another and therefore it does not really command 'economic rent'. If one area of the market is offering high rates of interest other money will rush into it and bring the interest rates down, while if another area is offering low interest rates money will cease to be employed there as soon as it can get away (for example as loans are repaid) and will seek a better rewarded use. This will cause interest rates to rise in that sector.

Money can certainly flow more quickly than other factors to areas where it will earn a better reward, but it is still a fact that there are many rates of interest. 'Hot' flows of money do not entirely eliminate rate differences. Some credit card issuers must be earning economic rents, but there is no special word for economic rents earned by capital. Where capital does appear to be earning a more than normal reward we therefore use the term 'scarcity rent' to indicate that there is an element of economic rent in the high interest rate being earned.

5   THE REWARD TO ENTERPRISE: PROFIT

Profit is the residue of the wealth created which has not been paid to one of the factors for services in the production process. In former times we could have said without hesitation that it was *the reward to the entrepreneur for showing enterprise and risking his capital in the production process*. This is still true today for small-scale businesses, but although they are still very numerous they are relatively insignificant. The Bolton Report, which was published in 1972, as a result of an enquiry into the influence and activities of small firms, found that there were 1¼ million of them in the UK, of which about ½ million were private companies. In manufacturing 94 per cent of firms were small (with an average of 25 employees) and in retailing 96 per cent of firms were small, with turnover of less than £1000 per week. In manufacturing the 94 per cent of small firms only did 16 per cent of the work carried out by the industry. In retailing 96 per cent of the firms were small but they had between them only 32 per cent of the turnover. Large firms did 84 per cent of manufacturing, 68 per cent of retail trade, 73 per cent of building and construction, 71 per cent of motor vehicle production and repair work, 89 per cent of wholesaling and 80 per cent of mining and quarrying. There are now (1990) about 1½ million small firms.

A 1979 investigation found that eight UK firms accounted for 25 per cent of the total turnover of all UK companies quoted on the Stock Exchange; they had a total turnover of £50 000 million.

The typical organisation today is the public limited company (PLC). In this type of organisation, as its name implies, the shareholder's liability is limited to the capital that is actually contributed to the company. It is rare to commit much money to a particular company (the wise private investor spreads his/her investment across a range of companies). More important, most savers invest their money with financial institutions like banks, building societies, life assurance companies, unit trusts and similar institutions which invest it across a huge balanced portfolio of shares. The relevant point here is that in fact no one is running any real risk. Of course, major firms do go bankrupt and rescue operations do have to be launched, but it is rare for any individual to suffer seriously and where this does occur it is due to imprudent behaviour in putting too many eggs into one basket.

If the shareholders do not run any real risk, do they show any enterprise? Here again the answer is 'No!' By law a shareholder may not take part in the day-to-day activities of the firm, unless he/she happens to be a director. The Board of Directors is the group entitled to manage the company. So we cannot regard profit in the *typical* organisation of the private sector of the mixed economy as being a reward either for enterprise or for running risks. It becomes a residual reward to provide the shareholders with a nominal sum to reflect their capital-providing role, **and for the protection, preservation and enlargement of the corporation itself**. Since the directors control the distribution of the profits made they can ensure that the amount distributed is limited to that sum which will keep the shareholders quiet, and the rest is ploughed back as reserves. Its function is to perpetuate the company. In whose interest is the company to be perpetuated? This is explained later (see page 203).

First let us see how the profit is ploughed back – in other words, how firms grow. The unsatisfactory aspect of this growth is that it may not be the optimum place for reinvestment to take place. The firm continues to grow even after it has reached its optimum size. Where shall it go now? The economy is to some extent littered with stranded leviathans seeking to diversify into little-known or misunderstood sideline activities, while real inventiveness in the open market is denied the capital it requires.

We must note that the profits retained in this way remain the property of the ordinary shareholders (to whom all reserves of the company belong) and consequently result in an increased value of the shares, but the shareholder can only realise this capital gain by selling his shares on the open market. An example will illustrate the situation.

Example The XYZ Co. PLC is set up on 1 January with capital as follows: Ordinary Shares, £50 000; 8 per cent Preference Shares, £30 000. It also borrows money by issuing 8 per cent Debentures for £20 000. After trading for a year it makes a profit of £20 000. It pays the interest on the Debentures, the Preference Share dividend and 12 per cent to the Ordinary Shareholders.

To understand what has happened to the profits it is necessary to draw up two Balance Sheets, one at 1 January and one at 31 December.

Balance Sheet as at 1 January

Assets	£	Liabilities	£
Cash in hand	100 000	Ordinary Shareholders' interest in the company	50 000
		8% Preference Shareholders' interest in the company	30 000
		8% Debentures	20 000
	£100 000		£100 000

Of the £20 000 profits at the end of the year, £1600 will be paid to the Debenture Holders, £2400 to the Preference Shareholders, and £6000 to the Ordinary Shareholders. There is thus £10 000 to be 'ploughed back' into reserves. The result is that the assets will have risen in value to £110 000. The new Balance Sheet reads:

Balance Sheet (as at 31 December)

Assets	£	Liabilities	£
Sundry assets	110 000	Ordinary Shares	50 000
		Reserves ploughed back	10 000
		Ordinary Shareholders' interest in the company	60 000
		8% Preference Shareholders' interest in the company	30 000
		8% Debentures	20 000
	£110 000		£110 000

The 50 000 Ordinary Shares are now worth £60 000, so that each £1 share is now worth £1.20, but the only way a shareholder can realise this extra value is to sell his shares in the market. Note that no part of this increase belongs to the Preference Shareholders. Their contract with the company is for a dividend in preference to the Ordinary Shareholders should the company have a bad year – they cannot also have a share of the reserves unless they are Participating Preference Shareholders.

So the figment of the law which holds that the limited company is run in the interests of the shareholders to whom all the profits belong is really a delusion. They do not really have these profits available to reinvest elsewhere in an alternative investment opportunity. It is tied up in company growth which they are powerless to control. It is true that they may dismiss the Board at the Annual General Meeting, but in practice it is not very easy for them to get together and do so. Each investor usually has such a miniscule share of the total holding. Where in fact then does the power lie?

The answer is that it lies with the Board of the company, and to a lesser extent today with the organised trade unions. In the 1970s the trade unions were a particularly powerful force, who, because of a succession of Labour governments and a climate of opinion in the nation about the need for representation for all working people, had perhaps become too powerful. The situation can be understood most easily if we consider what happens to profits when trade unions engage in fierce wage-bargaining.

Economic rent and profit

Where a particular enterprise earns a higher than normal profit it is usually because it is marketing a popular product which is in strong demand but which other firms cannot produce yet – usually because some legal prevention (such as a patent right) excludes them. The lucky producer has a monopoly, and can exclude competitors. The extra profit is economic rent, and is called **monopoly rent**.

SELF-ASSESSMENT QUESTIONS

1 What is distribution theory in economics?

2 What is economic rent, and how can it be applied to each of the factors, land, labour, capital and enterprise?

3 How does the marginal productivity theory explain the decisions of employers about whether to take on staff?

4 What principle underlies the decision of an employed person to give in his/her notice and take up an alternative job elsewhere?

5 What is minimum lending rate? Why is a minimum lending rate only announced on rare occasions these days?

6 Why is it said that profit is a residue?

6 WAGE BARGAINING AND THE PROFITS RESIDUE

Wage bargaining takes place between management and men. Both management and men are part of the factor 'labour'. At one time management was held to be a special class of factor with entrepreneurial expertise. Today almost anyone can become a manager. We live in the century of the common man, and there is very little uncommon about management. The increasing sophistication and expertise of trade unions was a major feature of the mid-twentieth century, and management and workers were indistinguishable. Attending any major business function you found them both present, both making very similar speeches, and – dare it be said – with some union leaders accepting Board Room places with alacrity when the opportunity arose, in the name of 'ensuring good industrial relations'.

If profit is a residual reward it can be eaten into by the rewards paid to the other factors. However, landlords and owners of capital are not too well placed for bargaining about rewards. Their contracts for the supply of land and capital tend to be long-term and difficult to renegotiate. By contrast, the two sections of employees (management and workers) were in strong bargaining positions.

Since management alone has the right to manage (Table A, Section 70, SI [1984] No. 1717) and workers were in a position to harm the company by industrial action, both groups were well placed to gain advances at the expense of the profit. Of course, too extreme a position might lead to the bankruptcy of the company, a situation which both parties could view with a certain amount of equanimity since the only loss they would both suffer was a loss of employment.

The so-called confrontation between management and workers was largely a mirage, mere shadow-boxing to distract attention from what was really happening, which was a joint attack upon the wealth created by the company's activities that largely went unnoticed because it simply reduced the residue of profit available. In many cases the division of the spoils did not go so far as to reduce the distributions to shareholders, but only reduced that part of the profit going to reserves. The result was a reduction in new investment, which eventually reduced competitiveness in world markets and job security. A side-effect was inflation which resulted from the conspicuous consumption that was taking place at all levels from the Working Men's Clubs upwards.

Some managements became positively frightened to manage and some major company failures occurred.

Perhaps the worst feature of this phase of industrial 'co-operation' between management and workers was the helpless situation of the unrepresented majority. The pensioners, the unemployed and the weaker non-unionised labour (particularly immigrants) suffered not only from low wages but also from inflation. If the government tried to hold the balance on their behalf it was largely powerless in the face of strike action from powerful unions. The result was, after the Conservative election of 1979, a sustained effort began to reform trade union law and to remove some of the trade union and management privileges which had become an abuse of power.

7   REWARDS TO FACTORS IN THE 1990s

As we enter the 1990s, after a decade of policies characterised by the popular press as 'Thatcherite', what is the position with regard to distribution theory and the rewards to factors? We can say that the proportion of the national income going to 'labour' has fallen from 69 per cent in 1975 to 63 per cent in 1987. Much of the reduction has been borne by those former employees of feather-bedded, strongly unionised, industries, who are now unemployed. The huge subsidies enjoyed by the coal miners, the steel industry, British Rail and other sections of industry have largely disappeared. Those still left in the leaner industries are better off in many cases than before, but they have to work harder for their pay today. The proportion of national income going to 'rent' has risen from 7.5 per cent in 1975 to 7.8 per cent in 1987, so that the rewards to the factor 'land' have changed very little in those years. The other 29.2 per cent of national income in 1987 went to either capital or profit. the figures are inseparable, and as the two are closely linked together we need not try to separate them. This extra profit has resulted in a considerable expansion in investment and a return of confidence to management no longer committed to sharing the spoils with the powerful unions. The increase from about 24.2 per cent to 29.2 per cent has meant considerable sums being made available for UK (and overseas) investment. The adverse effect of this is that the new machinery etc., being installed is to a considerable extent imported, and large sections of UK industry need re-building, as do the skills of its labour force. Readers will debate whether this change in the rewards to factors has been desirable or not. In the debate due emphasis should be given to the question whether a prosperous economy can be sustained indefinitely if some sections of the economy are overmanned and over-rewarded at the expense of others who happen to be old, or weak, or under-represented in the discussions about how rewards should be shared.

There is one further aspect of the rewards to factors. How in fact do these rewards take place? The answer is by the general money system, which is illustrated in Fig. 1.2 (see page 14). The various factors are rewarded as their human representatives, landlords, workers, savers of capital and entrepreneurs take their monetary rewards from the various institutions, sole traders, partnerships, limited companies, public limited companies, local and central government institutions. If we take the accounts of each of these types of institutions and study them we see the various payments going out. Let us consider each of them briefly to see what happens.

8   THE WEALTH CREATED AND THE DISTRIBUTION OF WEALTH

The wealth created is the total value of the goods and services produced. We shall see later that in calculating the national income one of the ways of doing it is by counting up the national output of goods and services. This is explained later (see Chapter 9). Here we are trying to follow the distribution of wealth. We can see the actual process of wealth creation in Fig. 1.2. It is the households of the nation who have control of all the factors of production, the resources which can create wealth. Some own land and can make it available for use in agriculture, industry, housing, etc. Some own capital assets, or liquid capital (money) which can be used to purchase raw materials, the use of capital assets and to pay workers. Some have nothing to contribute but their labour and must take employment if they are to share in the wealth creation process. These factors of production move into action and create wealth as part of some organisation. The end result is that goods and services are created, and belong to the organisations concerned, while those who supplied the factors of production are rewarded with money payments called rent, wages and interest. There is a residue of value left over (in most cases) called the profit. This is also returned, in this case to the families who showed enterprise in setting up the organisations.

Every part of the wealth created in any given trading period is given as a reward to the factors which produced it, though it may occasionally be held over into the next period. There is nothing at all left unowned at the end of any given period. A few illustrations will make this clear. Let us take the entire range of institutions to be found in the mixed economy, and see where the wealth that has been created goes. There are five cases:

1 Sole trader and partnership businesses.
2 Limited companies and public limited companies.
3 Public corporations like nationalised industries.
4 Clubs and societies (like cooperative societies).
5 Local and Central Government institutions.

Taking these in turn, where does the wealth they create go?

Sole traders and partnerships

Workers in these firms receive their wages; landlords (if any) are paid their rent; any borrowed capital is rewarded by paying the agreed interest to the bank, finance company, etc. The rest of the wealth created is profit, which is enjoyed by the sole trader, or shared between, or among, the partners. In fact, some of this profit figure could be regarded as wages to the trader(s) for working in the business; some of it as interest on the capital they have personally invested in the business; the rest is true profit – the reward for running risks and showing enterprise.

Limited companies

The workers will have received their wages and salaries as a reward for working in the firm; the landlord (if any) will have been paid his rent – but of course the company may actually own the freehold; any capital borrowed either from banks and other institutions, or from debenture holders, will have received its reward in the form of interest. The residue is profit to be shared among the shareholders. This profit may be regarded partly as interest on the capital subscribed and partly as 'true' profit – the reward for bearing the risks of the enterprise. Equity capital (ordinary shares) is often spoken of as 'risk capital'.

However, this view of limited companies dividing the profit among the shareholders is in fact too naive – although it may still be true of many small private companies. For public companies it is only what happens to the profit in theory; we find that in practice the profit is largely used to expand the company and only a very small proportion of the profit actually goes to the shareholders; enough to keep them quiet (bearing in mind that many of them are portfolio investors and can exert some pressure to see that the dividend is reasonable).

Public corporations

The workers are paid their wages. There is generally no rent to pay, but if the corporation has hired premises for any reason the rent will of course be paid. Capital may have been raised by issuing securities, or it may have been borrowed from official bodies. The interest on all such sums will be paid. Finally the residue of profit, whatever it is, will be paid over to the Consolidated Fund to be used for the Nation's purposes. Here it simply cancels out some deficit on the government's many loss-making services.

Clubs and societies

These bodies vary from very tiny organisations like the local tennis club to huge organisations like the Automobile Association. Any employees will receive their wages and salaries, interest will be paid on any capital borrowed, rent will be paid to any landlord. Strictly speaking – since these are non-profit-making organisations – there is no profit. Any surplus is an overpayment by members for the services they receive, and will be carried forward to the next period and used for capital assets or working capital in that period.

Local and central government institutions

The reader may feel that these institutions are not creating wealth at all, but this would be a mistake. Man cannot live by bread alone; he also needs service. The creation of a system of education, a health service, a public transport system or a sewage system are just as much wealth-creating activities as the rearing of cattle or the manufacture of motor vehicles. An affluent society usually has many more of these services provided than an underdeveloped society. Many public sector activities even make a profit, though many others are run from the proceeds of taxation. The workers will be paid their wages; the landlords (if any) will be paid their rents for land used; any capital borrowed will be paid the agreed rate of interest (chiefly the servicing of the National Debt); and any profits will be returned to the Consolidated Fund, or retained in the local authority's balances for use in the next financial period.

We see, therefore, that all the wealth created in any financial period is made available to the factors who created it. Whether the distribution is 'fair' is a matter for politicians to decide, though economists may perhaps advise them about it. We are back to that supreme genius, John Stuart Mill. The distribution of wealth is a matter of human ingenuity only. Only the people can decide what is a 'fair' share for everyone. Their chosen representatives are in Parliament, and in the last analysis it is the procedures of Parliament which decide what are 'fair' rewards to factors.

SELF-ASSESSMENT QUESTIONS

7 In what ways is a 'closed shop' fair?

8 In what ways is a 'closed shop' unfair?

9 Explain how a local shopkeeper rewards the factors he/she employs in creating wealth.

REVISION TEST

Answers	Questions
	1 What is wealth to an economist?
1 An abundance of goods and services.	**2** What resources are available to produce wealth?
2 (a) Geographical land; (b) Primary (natural) resources; (c) improved, incomplete, natural goods, i.e. semi-manufactured secondary products; (d) capital – liquid capital and assets created in a previous period; (e) human resources.	**3** The demand for factors is said to be a derived demand. What is it derived from?

3 From the basic demand for goods and services to satisfy mankind's wants.

4 What decides the demand for a particular factor?

---

4 The revenue which it will produce; to be precise, the marginal revenue product of the factor.

5 What decides the supply of any factor?

---

5 The net advantage that it will bring to the factor owner. Workers, for example, seek to maximise the net advantage to them from the work they agree to do.

6 What are the rewards to factors?

---

6 (a) The reward to land is rent.
(b) The reward to labour is wages.
(c) The reward to capital is interest.
(d) The reward to enterprise is profit.

7 What is economic rent?

---

7 A payment to a factor over and above what is necessary to keep it in its present employment.

8 What types of economic rent are payable?

---

8 (a) Land may earn 'rent of situation'; (b) labour may earn 'rent of ability'; (c) those entitled to the profit may earn 'monopoly rents'; (d) on occasions even capital may earn a 'scarcity rent'.

9 What is minimum lending rate (MLR)?

---

9 It is the minimum rate at which the Bank of England will discount first class bills of exchange. When a bank gets into difficulties and has to replenish its cash reserves it does so by cashing in first class bills of exchange which the Bank of England takes as 'lender of last resort', giving cash in exchange.

10 When is MLR announced?

---

10 Today it is only announced publicly on very rare occasions when the Bank feels the market needs a clear idea of what it considers to be a desirable rate of interest. Most of the time it signals its wishes covertly.

11 Why is profit called 'a residual reward'?

11 Because it is what is left after land, labour and capital have been rewarded.

12 What happens to profits?

---

12 Tecnically they belong to the owners of the business, but as far as limited companies are concerned the shareholders only get a reasonable dividend – the rest are held in reserves for future use in the company.

Go over the test again until you are sure of the answers. Then try some of the questions below.

ANSWERS

(See Self-assessment questions on pages 203 and 208.)

1 Distribution theory is that part of economic theory which seeks to explain how the wealth that is created in capitalist society is shared out among the population; how wealth is distributed. John Stuart Mill was the first economist to draw attention to the fact that whatever the rules might be about producing wealth the distribution of wealth was entirely up to the people concerned – we can distribute it in any way we decide upon. The actual procedure is to pay the factors of production a money reward which they can then spend on a balanced basket of goods and services.

2 Economic rent is a payment to a factor over and above what is necessary to keep it in its present employment. If land is earning an amount over what would be normal for that type of property it is said to be earning 'economic rent'. If labour is earning an excess amount (as opera stars, pop stars, actors and computer programmers do at times) this is called 'rent of ability'. Capital only rarely earns economic rents, but where risks are high rates of interest may include a premium – scarcity rents – because capital prepared to take that sort of risk is scarce. Where entrepreneurs earn excess profits these are called 'monopoly rents' because other entrepreneurs are unable to work their way in and compete away the profits.

3 The marginal productivity theory says that an entrepreneur will never demand a factor if its price is higher than the extra reward the entrepreneur will get from employing the factor. In other words the entrepreneur will never pay more in wages than the marginal product to be earned by the use of the labour.

4 The principle underlying the employee's decision to move is 'maximum net advantage'. The rule says that a factor owner will only make a factor (in this case labour) available to the entrepreneur which offers the highest net advantage to the factor owner. If the reward earned (minus any expenses or losses resulting from the move) is greater in the new occupation the employee will move.

5 Minimum lending rate is the lowest rate at which the Bank of England will discount first class bills of exchange. It sets a basic rate below which the Discount Houses will hesitate to lend, because if they do lend more cheaply than that and as a result get into financial difficulties (because every institution will rush to borrow from them) they will have to pay the minimum rate, or even more, to borrow from the Bank of England in its capacity as 'lender of last resort'. Consequently they will be making losses on all the contracts they made at lower rates. Today the Bank of England rarely announces a minimum lending rate, because it detects adverse trends in the economy at an early stage, and signals the need to raise rates to the Discount Houses.

6 Profit is a residue because it is what is left when all other factors have had their rewards. It is even possible for profit to be negative (i.e. the firm or company makes losses) because the other factors – land, labour and capital – have eaten up all the available funds.

7 A 'closed shop' is fair if it enables workers who were previously disadvantaged to negotiate fair wages free from under-cutting by unemployed people outside the industry. The employer is forced to concede reasonable rates of pay since otherwise the organisation will be brought to a standstill.

8 A 'closed shop' is unfair if it enables workers who are already well-paid by most standards to secure economic rents in the form of unjustified pay increases, when without the 'closed-shop' unemployed workers would move into the industry and perform the work for the fair rates of pay already prevailing. It is in these circumstances an abuse of power which secures those privileged to be in the industry monopoly rents because they can exclude competition from other workers. We certainly can't call these economic rents 'rents of ability'.

9 A local shopkeeper rewards the factors employed as follows: (a) rent is paid to the landlord (if there is one); (b) wages are paid to labour; (c) interest is paid on any loans, hire purchase or other borrowings of capital; (d) the residue left over is the profit which is the shopkeeper's reward for showing enterprise.

QUESTIONS ON CHAPTER 7

1 What is meant by 'distribution theory' in economics? How is a fair distribution achieved?

2 'Economic rent is payment to a factor over and above what is necessary to keep it in its present employment.' Explain.

3 Explain how wealth created by a limited company is distributed.

4 Explain how the wealth created by a public enterprise such as British Coal is distributed. Imagine that this industry is subsidised to the extent of £200 million per annum.

5 (a) What motivates employers to offer work to labour? (b) What motivates labour to take employment? (c) How does the free enterprise system work to ensure that employers have labour in the numbers they need, with the right qualities and skills?

6 Why do barristers earn more than their clerks? Why might some earn less?

(Institute of Commercial Managment)

7 a) Explain the traditional economic theory of wage determination.
b) What factors can prevent wages being determined in this way?

(Association of Business Executives)

8 a) What economic functions does the entrepreneur perform in a capitalist economy?
b) In the large organisations where no individual dominates who performs these functions?

(Association of Business Executives)

9 A quality jeweller is looking for a site for premises in New Bond Street. How will the rent payable be decided upon, and what elements might be discovered in the rent payable in this fashionable part of the West End of London?

10 Consider the following statements about labour:
a) The market for labour is very competitive.
b) Skilled money market operators can command enormous salaries in the City of London.
c) It is difficult for drama students to break into the theatrical world, where the labour market is very imperfect.

TIPS FOR STUDENTS: A SPECIMEN ANSWER TO QUESTION 10

The three statements need to be considered against the following background to the employment situation the UK. There are about 28 million people of working age in the UK of whom about 3 million at the most are unemployed. With 25 million people at work there must be a huge range of different situations; people with different skills, different experience, different qualifications and different family circumstances. Almost any statements made would be true for someone.

With so many people seeking employment the first statement that the labour market is very competitive is certainly true. But a labour market is not really just one market, it breaks down into many different markets – the market for word processor operators, the market for engineers, the market for teachers, etc. Many of these sub-markets will be highly competitive.

When we come to deal with a specialised market like the market for skilled money market operators we could have a situation where there were only a few hundred people in that category. With about 60 or 70 firms at least operating in the money markets it would not be surprising if there was a shortage and this would bid up prices. It is quite likely that some of them could command economic rents of ability.

When it comes to drama students trying to break into theatrical employment not only do we have a lot of students trying to get work where there are only a few positions, but there is also a powerful trade union restricting entry to the profession. However justifiable this may be, and many actors and actresses spend more time 'resting' than they do working, it is a fact that the trade union does restrict entry to a considerable extent.

It follows that all the statements are true and they are not conflicting with one another in any way. The economic world is an intricate one, and we must expect every variety of situation to arise. The problem is to extract general statements from a complex mass of statements, all of which may be true, but some are more significant than others.

PART 3: International aspects of business activity

8 Overseas trade

1 THE NATURE OF EXPORT TRADE

Export trade is trade with other countries, in which we sell them produce made at home. The 'ex' part of the word means 'going out of' the ports, so when we export goods we are selling our goods to foreigners and the goods go out of our country and into theirs. The opposite to exports is of course imports and we shall see that exports and imports must be equal in value, taken one year with another. We can have an occasional imbalance, one year's exports being less than imports, for example, but if this happens year after year we shall run out of foreign exchange to pay for our imports, and trade will cease.

Why do we engage in international trade? The answer is that it enables us to lead more varied and interesting lives. We can enjoy a greater variety of foods, beverages, goods and services because we have the produce of the whole world coming into our ports, which we pay for by selling them some of our goods and services. This is what export trade is all about; enriching the variety and choice available to us not only of foods and basic materials, but even more of manufactured goods and luxuries. The staples of trade for countless centuries were luxury goods – wine, furs, fine china and pottery, jewels, gold and silver ware, ivory, exotic animals, silk, etc. These were the imports which Britain paid for with its wool trade in the Elizabethan era. Later the export of woollen goods, cotton cloth, ironware and cheap tin trays brought the produce of the entire world to London, Liverpool, Bristol and Glasgow.

Today imports flood in with every tide. We pay for them not only with our goods (mostly highly technological finished goods) but also with our services – banking, construction, insurance, shipping, tourism, etc. The resulting transactions are complex; the market operators are sophisticated and knowledgeable; there are specialists who handle the financial aspects, others who handle the physical goods; 'barter and swap' merchants who find safe havens for everything from 'dumped' Polish footware to surplus French toupées – yet in the end we finish up with a 'balance of payments'. The balance of payments must always balance. Any deficit must be covered, which explains the consternation at No. 11 Downing Street if loans cannot be arranged. The final resort in such circumstances is to the International Monetary Fund.

Clearly we need to know why we trade with foreign countries.

2   WHY TRADE WITH FOREIGN COUNTRIES?

There are several reasons why we trade with foreign countries, some obvious and some less obvious. We may list them as follows:

1 Because nature has been haphazard in bestowing her bounties.
2 Because climates vary around the world.
3 Because population density varies around the world.
4 For strategic reasons.
5 Because of comparative advantage, and the optimisation of the output of world wealth.

The haphazard distribution of natural resources

It is obvious that nature has produced resources haphazardly over the surface of the globe. Dover has plenty of chalk, but no iron ore; Yorkshire has coal but no opals; Sweden is rich in iron ore but short of oil. Clearly, the sensible solution to these surpluses and shortages is trade. If different districts within a nation trade with one another the products of each district will be available to the whole country. If different nations trade with one another every country in the international community will be able to share in nature's worldwide bounty.

Climatic influences of trade

Jungle hardwoods will not grow in the tundra, and conifers do not do well in deserts. Tobacco will grow in the UK, but cannot be properly cured; as the enthusiast said to his gardening society, 'What can't be cured must be endured'. Citrus fruit requires a Mediterranean climate, and coffee bushes are killed by frosts. Clearly, if we are to have tea, coffee, cocoa and drinking chocolate we must trade with countries which can grow these products. In exchange we will supply them with technical products and cover their ships against losses on the high seas and their aircraft against accidents in flight.

Population and trade

Singapore has 3577 people per square kilometre, on a total land area of 580 square kilometres. Canada has 2.2 people per square kilometre, on a total land area of 9 976 185 square kilometres. Clearly, Singapore finds it hard to grow enough food to feed her population, however productive her agriculture, while Canada has an enormous surplus of food for export.

Where population is dense and natural resources are limited the skills of the population must be harnessed to pay for imports. For centuries the Netherlands and Belgium supported their dense populations by the skill of their craftsmen in the cloth trades, in lace-making, in the working of precious stones, etc. Today the dense populations of Hong Kong and Singapore are supported in the same way.

Strategic reasons for trading

It frequently happens that a nation may trade for strategic reasons even to the detriment of home produce. Thus the Texan oil producers complain that government restrictions prevent them raising output, at the same time as imports of foreign oil to the USA are weakening the value of the dollar. It is domestic nonsense, but strategic sense for America to use Middle Eastern crude, Soviet-refrigerated gas and Venezuelan oil products to conserve domestic output for the use of posterity.

The doctrine of comparative advantage

When we examine how wealth (in goods and services) is created we find that certain people have an advantage over other people, due to physical, mental and other characteristics. Similarly, some nations have a comparative advantage over other nations in the production of particular goods. As the immigrants flooded across the plains of the Middle West of the USA, breaking with their ploughs land with the stored fertility of a thousand million years, they had a comparative advantage over the heavily worked soils of Europe. A flood of cheap American corn poured across the Atlantic to strike a severe blow at British agriculture, which was forced to reduce its output of wheat and other cereals, and turn to dairy farming, beef production and poultry, where it still had some advantage.

Consider two people, Sally Couture, a fashion designer and Mr Scrubbit, a cleaner. Mr Scrubbit is an excellent cleaner and earns £3 an hour cleaning offices and private houses. Sally Couture is also an excellent cleaner, having a Diploma in Fashion, Design and Institutional Management. In fact she is twice as good a cleaner as Mr Scrubbit, but she prefers to work as a fashion designer because she can earn £18 an hour. We therefore have the following situation:

	Sally Couture	Mr Scrubbit
Normal hourly wages	£18	£3
Earnings as a cleaner	£ 6	£3

We can see that if Sally Couture worked in her own home to clean the house she could have twice as much effect as Mr Scrubbit and improve the house by the equivalent of £6 of work per hour. She therefore has an **absolute advantage** over the cleaner whether she works as a cleaner or as a fashion designer, but at which job has she the **comparative advantage**? Clearly it is as a fashion designer, because in that way she earns £18.

Suppose Sally works in her own home cleaning the place for one hour. The house looks as clean as if Mr Scrubbit has worked for two hours. But if Sally works in fashion design for one hour and earns £18 she can employ Mr Scrubbit for six hours, and the house will then look three times as good as if she had done the work herself.

$$\text{The ratios of earnings above are } £18:£3 = 6:1$$
$$\text{and } £6:£3 = 2:1$$

and the comparative advantage lies with 6:1. (It is three times better than 2:1.)

> The **law of comparative advantage** say that generally speaking it will be advantageous for mankind if people specialise in those occupations at which they have the greatest comparative advantage, or the least comparative disadvantage, leaving others to produce the goods and services for which they have little aptitude.

This principle of comparative advantage is the basis of specialisation into trades and occupations, and it is of great importance in the theory of international trade.

It is now time to look at this theory more closely.

3   THE THEORY OF INTERNATIONAL TRADE

The theory of international trade is known in economics as the **law of comparative costs**. Before stating the law, and learning it by heart, we need to remind ourselves of the economic attitude to costs. All costs in economics are regarded as **alternative costs** or **opportunity costs** because when we decide to produce a particular good or service we have to use factors; land, labour and capital, which consequently cannot be employed on any other alternative product or opportunity (see page 52).

Suppose we take a country, Prairieland, which uses a basic set of factors, say one entrepreneur, five workers, £10 000 of capital and 100 acres of land. Suppose these factors can together grow 500 tonnes of barley. Had these factors been employed differently, say in making steel, they might have made ten tonnes of steel. Under the concept of opportunity costs, or alternative costs we may regard these two outputs as being alternative costs for one another. This means that if we decide to grow barley we cannot have steel, so the cost of the barley is ten tonnes of steel, and if we decide to have the steel, we cannot grow the barley, so the cost of the steel is 500 tonnes of barley.

The alternative costs of barley and steel in Prairieland are:

$$500 \text{ tonnes of barley} : 10 \text{ tonnes of steel}$$
so   barley : steel : :   500 : 10
or   barley : steel : :   50 : 1

Now in another country, Europeana, the factors they employ, using the same combination of factors, produce quite different outputs. A set of factors can produce 600 tonnes of barley and 40 tonnes of steel, because Europeana is very experienced at steel making. So in Europeana the alternative costs are:

600 tonnes of barley : 40 tonnes of steel

so   barley : steel : : 600 : 40

or   barley : steel : :   15 : 1

We see that the alternative costs of barley and steel are different in the two countries. In Prarieland barley and steel are produced in the ratio of 50:1 and in Europeana they are produced in the ratio 15:1. Exactly what this means for trading between the two nations we shall see in a minute. First let us learn the law of comparative costs.

The law of comparative costs states that nations will find it profitable to trade with other nations when (a) they have different alternative-cost ratios and (b) the international terms of trade lie within the limits set by their domestic alternative-cost ratios.

This is not an easy law to understand and the reader is urged to study the next page or two very carefully.

An example of specialisation in international trade

We are considering two countries, Prairieland and Europeana, both of which can produce both barley and steel. First notice that Europeana has an absolute advantage over Prairieland in both products, because with similar sets of factors Europeana can produce 600 tonnes of barley (against Prairieland's 500 tonnes) and 40 tonnes of steel (against Prairieland's 10 tonnes).

However, we are not interested in absolute advantage, but in comparative advantage. Which country has the comparative advantage in producing each of these products? We can best compare them by comparing their alternative costs. Taking steel first, we have to ask 'What is the cost of steel in terms of barley?' We have seen that the figures are:

Prairieland   1 tonne of steel costs 50 tonnes of barley
Europeana   1 tonne of steel costs 15 tonnes of barley

Clearly the advantage in steel production lies with Europeana, for 1 tonne of steel only costs 15 tonnes of barley whereas in Prairieland it costs 50 tonnes of barley.

Now, which country has the advantage in barley production?

Prairieland   1 tonne of barley costs 0.02 tonnes of steel
Europeana   1 tonne of barley costs 0.067 tonnes of steel

Clearly the cost to Europeana of giving up steel production to grow barley is far higher than in Prairieland, so Prairieland has the natural advantage in growing barley.

It looks as though Prarieland should concentrate on growing barley and Europeana should concentrate on making steel. Before we try to see what happens if they do this we must first look at the present 'world' output (although this is imagined to be a two country world). This is shown in Table 8.1.

Table 8.1 World output before specialisation (units of 1000 tonnes)

Country	Barley	Steel
Prairieland	1200	60
Europeana	1800	84
World output	3000	144

The first thing to note about the outputs shown in Table 8.1 is that the outputs of the two countries are totally unrelated. They simply show what these countries are producing at the moment with the various sets of factors they have devoted to barley production and steel production.

What we now want to do is to see what happens to world output if Prarieland gives up steel production and specialises in growing barley, while Europeana gives up barley production and concentrates on making steel. To do this we must look at their **production possibility schedules**. A production possibility schedule is a list which shows the outputs possible if factors move out of an industry where the nation does not have a comparative advantage and into an industry where it does. We can see this in Table 8.2 opposite.

Note that as Prairieland gives up steel production every unit of steel not made releases factors which can produce 50 units of barley. As steel output falls barley output rises until Prairieland is producing no steel and 4200 units of barley.

Similarly, note that as Europeana gives up barley production every 15 units of barley not grown releases factors which can produce one unit of steel. As barley output falls steel output rises, until Europeana is producing no barley at all and 204 units of steel.

What is the new 'World' output of barley and steel now? The figures are shown in Table 8.3.

Table 8.3 'World' output after specialisation (units of 1000 tonnes)

Country	Barley	Steel
Prairieland	4200	–
Europeana	–	204
World output	4200	204

Clearly world output has risen because of the specialisation. Barley output has risen from 3000 units (3 000 000 tonnes) to 4200 units (4 200 000 tonnes) while steel output has risen from 144 units (144 000 tonnes) to 204 units (204 000 tonnes). The only trouble is that Prairieland now has all the barley

Table 8.2 Moving factors over into specialised production

(a) Production possibility schedule: Prairieland

Present output

Units of Barley	4200	4000	3800	3600	3400	3200	3000	2800	2600	2400	2200	2000	1800	1600	1400	**1200**	1000	800	600	400	200	0
Units of Steel	0	4	8	12	16	20	24	28	32	36	40	44	48	52	56	**60**	64	68	72	76	80	84

Prairieland moves into specialisation in barley (it gains 200 units of barley for every 4 units of steel given up, i.e. 50:1)

(b) Production possibility schedule: Europeana

Present output

Units of Barley	3000	2800	2600	2400	2200	2000	**1800**	1600	1400	1200	1000	800	600	400	200	0
Units of Steel	4	17.33	30.67	44	57.33	70.67	**84**	97.33	110.67	124	137.33	150.67	164	177.33	190.67	204

Europeana moves into specialisation in steel. (It gains 13⅓ units of steel for every 200 units of barley given up (i.e. 1:15).

Note
When specialisation is complete world output of barley is 4200 units (all produced by Prairieland) and 204 units of steel (all produced by Europeana).

and Europeana has all the steel. To share it out they must trade; *but on what terms will they trade?*

THE TERMS OF TRADE

The law of comparative costs says that nations will find it profitable to trade: (a) if they have different alternative cost ratios; and (b) if the terms of trade lie between the limits set by their domestic alternative cost ratios. We have seen that these two nations do have different alternative cost ratios. Barley is to steel in Prairieland as 50:1, while in Europeana it is 15:1. What exactly does part (b) above mean?

At present Prairieland has all the barley and needs steel. Suppose it says to Europeana, 'I will sell you 32½ units of barley for 1 unit of steel' – 32½ is exactly halfway between 50 and 15 – the domestic cost ratios for steel. Europeana might accept. But supposing Prairieland drives a hard bargain, offering 30, or 25 or 20 barley units for 1 of steel. This is getting to be a very bad buy for Europeana. Suppose the bargaining got worse and fell to 19, 18, 17, 16, 15, 14 units only of barley for 1 unit of steel. At 15 units Europeana could say, 'Well, no thank you. I can take factors out of steel production and put them into barley production and get 15 to 1 so there is no point in trading. I'll produce steel myself.' Trading is – as the law of comparative costs says – only profitable when the terms of trade lie within the limits set by the domestic cost ratios.

Now suppose the demand for barley falls away, and the terms of trade shift in favour of steel. It is Europeana that can now drive a hard bargain. It demands not 32½ units of barley for a unit of steel but 35, 40 or even 45 units of barley. But if it gets too greedy and demands 50 units of barley for each unit of steel Prairieland will say, 'No thank you. We can take factors out of barley production and make steel ourselves, so there is no point in trading. We'll produce our own steel.'

WHO GETS THE LION'S SHARE OF THE EXTRA WEALTH CREATED?

The answer depends entirely on where the terms of trade settle. Let us take two examples.

Example 1 The terms of trade favour Europeana and the price of steel is set at 42½ units of barley = 1 unit of steel. At this price Europeana decides to buy 2805 units of barley. This will cost them 2805 ÷ 42½ = 66 units of steel.

The share of the world's wealth is then:

Country	Barley (units)	Steel (units)
Prairieland	1395	66
Europeana	2805	138
World output	4200	204

Prairieland has 195 extra units of barley and 6 extra units of steel. Europeana has 1005 extra units of barley and 54 extra units of steel. Clearly Europeana has the lion's share of the extra wealth.

Example 2 Suppose the terms of trade favour Prairieland and the price of steel is 20 units of barley. Instead of Prairieland giving up 42½ units of barley for 1 unit of steel it only has to give up 20 units of barley for one unit of steel. At this price Europeana decides to buy 2200 units of barley. This will cost them 110 units of steel.

The share of the world's wealth is now:

Country	Barley (units)	Steel (units)
Prairieland	2000	110
Europeana	2200	94
World output	4200	204

Prairieland has 800 extra units of barley and 50 extra units of steel. Europeana has 400 extra units of barley and 10 extra units of steel. This time Prairieland has the lion's share of the extra wealth.

4 CONCLUSIONS ABOUT THE THEORY OF INTERNATIONAL TRADE

It is clear that in a perfectly rational world nations would specialise in those things at which they had the greatest comparative advantage, or the least comparative disadvantage, and if they did specialise in this way world wealth would increase. There are however a number of reasons why they do not completely specialise in the way described. A few words about these may be helpful.

Strategic reasons for incomplete specialisation

In a world which is composed of nation states there are often strategic reasons for not abandoning completely things that we can do, even if we don't do them very well. At the start of the Second World War the UK found it could not really start fighting because it had abandoned the manufacture of many things that it desperately needed to fight a war. One example was the insulators used in many electrical components. These were made of pottery, and we had been importing them from Germany and Poland. We had to have a crash programme to rebuild our ceramics industry in this field, before we could make many of the electrical devices we needed. Even if a thing makes economic sense we don't do it if it makes strategic nonsense.

The assumption that all units of factors are equally efficient

In Table 8.2 the production possibility schedules used assumed all factors to be equally efficient, and as the nations moved out of one production area into another each step was exactly the same size. In fact this would not be so. The first group of Prairieland steel workers to move out of steel production to go into farming would be those who disliked making steel and longed for the fresh country air. As we moved successive groups out of steel we could find them less and less willing to go, and before long we would be trying to turn those who really liked making steel out of their factories to grow barley – a job they disliked. Similarly there would come a time in Europeana where the very best farmers actually hated going into steelworks. There would be no point in forcing them to do so either, because their output as top class steel workers would be high, whereas their output as third rate barley growers would be low. So in fact complete specialisation would not take place in real life. The crucial point where specialisation ceases is where native production (the very best Europeana farmers) are better than the Prairieland farmers and similarly the very best Prairieland steel makers might be just as productive as those of Europeana.

The specific nature of some assets

Many non-human resources are specific, and cannot be re-deployed elsewhere. Thus we cannot take Prairieland steel furnaces and rolling mills out of steel production and into barley growing – at least not without scrapping them and turning them into agricultural machinery. Prairieland would hesitate to scrap its steel works until the plant was worn out, or obsolete.

Transport costs

Although specialisation produces increased wealth it brings extra costs as well. Even if the barley and steel are now of excellent quality they do have to be carried half-way round the world to reach the consumers who need them and transport costs enter all the decisions. They effectively narrow the band between the domestic alternative costs and make complete specialisation less worthwhile.

Can the market justify complete specialisation?

If the world cannot absorb the product created by having one super-producer of a particular good there comes a point when any further specialisation is pointless. Thus if in the Table 8.3 world demand for steel is only 180 units there is little point in producing 204 units.

Protection of home industries

In the real world where there are many countries to consider; tariffs and other methods of excluding foreign goods such as quotas by value or by volume are at work to reduce international trade. Tariffs impose a duty on imported goods to raise their price as they enter a country and therefore reduce the advantages of international specialisation. Quotas by volume limit the quantity of goods which may be imported (so many units, or so many tonnes). Quotas by **value** permit imports up to a certain value – say £1 million only. All such barriers reduce the advantages of international specialisation and protect home producers – however inefficient they are.

5 INTRA-INDUSTRY TRADE

Although the traditional theory of international trade concentrates on considering countries as specialists in the product where they have a comparative advantage, it is increasingly a feature of international trade that countries both import and export the products of a particular industry. This is particularly true of 'free-trade areas', which tend to form between groups of nations who are at a similar level of sophistication in productive techniques. Thus Germany both exports Volkswagens to the UK and imports British motor vehicles. This has been called intra-industry trade to distinguish it from inter-industry trade of the barley-steel variety described above.

The question is, can this type of trade be explained in terms of the traditional theory? It seems it can, because all that is needed is the relaxation of the assumptions which are made in the theory of comparative costs. For example, the theory deals with homogeneous products, like beef and aluminium. The term 'homogeneous' implies that all units of the product are exactly alike. While this may be true of rods of aluminium or even quarters of beef, we must relax the concept when we discuss manufactured goods. The fact is that a British Ford Fiesta from Dagenham, Essex, is not the same as a German Volkswagen or a French Renault. We should reduce the variety and choice available to us if we ceased to trade in such goods, but it is still true to say that specialisation is taking place. It is more economic to produce Ford Fiestas to cater for a high British demand (and a low French demand) at Dagenham, and leave it to the French to produce Renault cars in France and thus cater for a high French demand (and a minority British demand).

A second assumption in the theory is that transport costs are disregarded, and reference has already been made to the effect upon trade of transport costs. Not only do transport costs narrow the belt within which trading can take place (see page 226) but for certain goods they may make the use of domestic supplies quite uneconomic. Thus the domestic electricity generated in the North of England could easily be routed south to supply peak demands in Southampton, but not as economically as French electricity surplus to requirements in northern France. An hour later the peak demands in northern France are being met by imports from the UK because it is more economic than the use of domestic French supplies from southern France.

6 THE TERMS OF TRADE

In any overseas trade situation there are fluctuations from year to year in the prices of goods that are traded around the world. At times there are shortages of one good or another. For example crop failures occur due to the vagaries of nature, droughts, floods, frost and snow, hurricanes, tornadoes, etc. Political problems, wars, civil wars, closure of waterways such as the Suez Canal, etc., can all disrupt trade. Countries which supplied certain items may switch to other customers, and customers who formerly bought large supplies from us may increase home production and cease to buy. A rise in prosperity (a boom) in one country may raise the standard of living of its citizens and they may consume more and be unable to export as much as before. Similarly a depression may discourage home consumption and leave more for export. These changes alter the prices that must be paid for all sorts of items.

This whole general field is called the 'terms of trade'. If the terms of trade are favourable to us, then our exports are fetching high prices and our imports are costing us little. If the terms of trade are unfavourable then our imports have risen in price while our exports are not in great demand and therefore have to be sold cheaply.

Figures for the terms of trade are published in an official publication which appears each year in August. It has a pink cover and is called *The Pink Book – United Kingdom Balance of Payments*. The terms of trade are given in the form of an index number. Export prices and import prices are measured every year against a base year (1985). The resulting figures show how prices have changed over the years since the base year, which is taken as 100. The terms of trade are then found by the formula

$$\text{Terms of trade} = \frac{\text{Index of average export prices}}{\text{Index of average import prices}} \times 100$$

Thus in the base year (1985):

$$\text{Terms of trade} = \frac{100}{100} \times 100 = 100$$

This is what you would expect in a base year.

In 1986 the figures were:

$$\text{Terms of trade} = \frac{91.8}{96.0} \times 100 = 95.6$$

Both import prices and export prices fell in 1986 but as export prices declined more than import prices the terms of trade had turned against the UK and the Terms of Trade Index fell from 100 to 95.6.

If the index falls below 100 the terms of trade have worsened, but if the terms of trade have risen above 100 the UK is better placed.

In 1987 – the latest figures available at the time of writing – the figures were:

$$\text{Terms of trade} = \frac{95.5}{98.5} \times 100 = 97.0$$

Therefore 1987 was a slightly better year than 1986.

The reader should consult the latest Pink Book and fill in the figures for more recent years in Table 8.4.

Table 8.4 The terms of trade

Year	Export index	Import index	Terms of trade
1985	100	100	100
1986	91.8	96.0	95.6
1987	95.5	98.5	97.0
1988			
1989			
1990			
1991			
1992			
1993			
1994			

(Source: *The Pink Book – UK Balance of Payments*)

SELF-ASSESSMENT QUESTIONS

1 Give five reasons why we must export.

2 Distinguish between absolute advantage and comparative advantage.

3 State the law of comparative costs.

4 Why do nations not specialise completely, and cease to produce goods at which they have no comparative advantage?

7 THE PATTERN OF UK TRADE

United Kingdom trade is in two parts, **visible trade** and **invisible trade**. Visible trade can actually be seen going through our ports, usually these days as containerised cargo. The economic handling unit today is the standard container, 8 feet by 8 feet square, 20 feet long, and strong enough to be stacked seven containers high in so-called cellular ships – the holds of which are rectangular 'cells' which will hold a uniform number of containers in each 'cell'. Companies which are large enough to have export movements capable of filling a container send the goods as FCLs (full container loads) weighing up to 32 tonnes. Those whose export loads are not great enough for an FCL export them through a 'groupage' freight forwarder. The groupage forwarder takes goods from many exporters and makes them up into 'compatible' FCLs – full container loads of goods which will not damage one another. One does not pack paraffin oil with cheese.

Invisible trade cannot be seen moving through our ports and airports. It is the trade in services, such as shipping, air transport, insurance, banking, servicing and even education. Generally speaking, the more advanced a nation is the greater the proportion of its activities that will be in services (tertiary production) rather than in goods (primary and secondary production). The figures for overseas trade given later in this chapter (see Figs. 8.1 and 8.2) show that invisible movements totalled about one third of total movements in the year in question. Therefore they are a very significant part of total trade although the production of goods is still the more important part of total UK trade. Visible exports are vital to our national survival, and £250 million of exports pass through our ports and airports every working day. Even more, a strong home production of high class, good quality products would reduce imports, because home nationals would prefer UK goods. This is known as **import substitution** and it is a very desirable thing to achieve some reduction of visible imports (currently running at about £290 million every working day). Study the illustrations of visible trade and invisible trade in Figs 8.1 and 8.2, and the notes below them.

8   THE BALANCE OF PAYMENTS

A country's balance of payments is an accounting statement of all the economic transactions which take place between its domestic government, firms, companies and residents, and the governments, firms and companies and residents of those other countries with which it trades. Like any other account, the Balance of Payments must balance, even though in reality there is little likelihood of a balance between the import and export of goods and services being achieved.

Until the second quarter of 1987 it was usual for the Balance of Payments for the UK to be presented in the form of:

a) A Balance on Current Account, in two parts – a balance of visible trade and a balance of invisibles.

b) A Balance on Capital Account.

c) The net effect of these balances would give an overall Balance for Official Financing. This figure was arrived at by adding together the totals of the

Fig. 8.1 *Patterns of UK visible trade (by products) 1987 (Source:* The Pink Book *1988)*

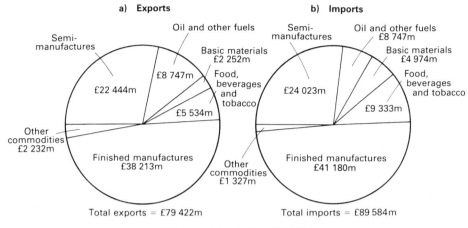

Total exports = £79 422m   Total imports = £89 584m

Deficit on visible trade = £10 162m

Notes
1 At one time the UK, as a great imperial power, had imports which largely consisted of basic materials for manufacture, coming in from colonial territories. Today they tend to come in far more as semi-manufactured goods.
2 Finished manufactures form a far higher proportion of imports today, partly because of a re-orientation of trade towards Europe, but also because many third world countries are now manufacturers, and some – the 20 or so NICS (newly industrialised countries) such as Korea, Singapore, Thailand, India, etc. – are particularly productive and highly competitive.
3 By contrast the proportion of UK exports which are fully manufactured has fallen (though not of course the actual value of exports which rises year by year). It remains a fact that basic material, and semi-manufactured exports have risen as a proportion of total exports. While some of this increase is due to North Sea oil, it is a reflection of UK decline as an exporting nation, in the face of severe international competition.

Fig. 8.2 *Patterns of UK invisible trade (by service) 1987 (Source:* The Pink Book *1988)*

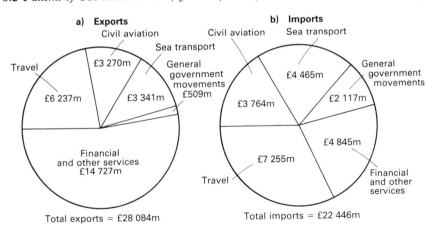

Total exports = £28 084m   Total imports = £22 446m

Surplus on invisibles £5 638m

Notes
1 Invisible trade is dominated by the activities of the City of London, shown under the general heading of 'Financial and other services' – for example insurance is included in this group.
2 Favourable balances in all other services have disappeared in recent years with the tendency of the UK public to holiday abroad. Travel, civil aviation and sea transport (now largely handled by foreign registered ships) are all adverse balances, while Government payments (largely to the European Community) are also mostly adverse payments.

previous two items, e.g. if the Current Account was in deficit by £275 million, and the Capital Account in surplus by £125 million the balance for official financing would stand at £150 million. This £150 million would have to be found from official reserves, or borrowed from abroad in order to square the account.

Since the spring of 1987 this format has ceased to be used and the present procedure takes the form of adding together the Current Account balance with changes in all the external assets and liabilities. In theory this should result in a zero balance. This is easy to understand. Since the items on Capital Account are already either assets or liabilities, and since the outstanding transactions on Current Account leave us as either debtors owing balances abroad or creditors awaiting payment from abroad, the total of all these must give a Balance of Payments. In practice information about the transactions taking place is always out of date, and the zero balance is never achieved, but a 'balancing item' is inserted to make the accounts balance.

The 1987 figures appear in *The Pink Book* as follows:

		£m
Balance on visible trade (adverse)		−10 162
Balance on invisibles (favourable)		7 658
Current Account balance (adverse)		− 2 504

Changes in UK assets and liabilities	£m	
UK external assets (acquiring an oversees asset is an adverse movement of funds)	−75 094	
UK external liabilities (A rise in foreign holdings in UK banks is a favourable movement of funds)	74 055	
		− 1 039
		− 3 543
Balancing item (items in the course of settlement)		3 543
The Balance of Payments must always come to zero		0

In recent years the large positive balancing item has called the accuracy of the Balance of Payments statistics into question. Further the balancing item is often subject to quite dramatic revision. For example, between January and March of 1989 the balancing item for 1987 was revised from £3.5 billion as shown above, to £12.4 billion. Even the Chancellor of the Exchequer when speaking of the preliminary Current Account deficit of £14.7 billion for 1988 said, 'Whatever the true figure, it is undoubtedly large!'

9 THE UK BALANCE OF PAYMENTS IN RECENT YEARS

We have seen that the Current Account falls into two sections, visibles and invisibles.

The visible balance (or the **balance of trade** as it is sometimes known) shows the net position after importing and exporting goods – tangible items such as cars, videos, washing machines, beef, etc.

The invisible balance deals with the net position after importing and exporting of services has been calculated, plus transfers and interest profits and dividends. The service element includes such items as tourism, sea and air transport, finance and insurance. Transfers are mostly related to what residents send overseas to their families and to Government payments to such institutions as the EEC. Interest, profits and dividends arise through the investments which UK residents make abroad, and those which foreign investors make in the UK.

The traditional picture of the UK Current Account from the middle of the nineteenth century until a few years ago was of a country exporting manufactured items and importing raw materials, foodstuffs and semi-finished products. Often the visible account would be in deficit, but this would generally be compensated for by an invisible account which was always in surplus. Recent developments have rendered this view of the UK Balance of Payments obsolete.

Since 1983 the manufacturing sector of the visible balance has been in deficit – the UK is now no longer a net exporter of manufactured goods; she imports a greater value than she exports. A further change has arisen as a result of the discovery of North sea oil – the UK is now a significant exporter of primary products. These changes have resulted in the steady growth of a Balance of Payments deficit for the UK from 1984 onwards. The export of oil has failed to keep pace with the growth of manufacturing imports resulting in a deficit on visible trade, and the invisible element has been unable to grow at a rate sufficient to cover the deficit on visibles. As the UK emerged from the depths of economic depression in 1981 the recovery meant heavy imports of raw materials, semi-manufactured goods and manufactured goods (especially tools, machines, etc.). This meant a deteriorating Balance of Payments position.

10 DEFICITS AND SURPLUSES

Earlier in this chapter attention was drawn to the fact that while the Balance of Payments Account will always balance, the actual trade relationships will either register a deficit – more bought from abroad than sold, or a surplus – more sold abroad than bought. Suppose a country has a persistent deficit year after year. This simply means that foreign suppliers are being forced year after year to accept debts on their books (there is an increase in foreign assets – claims on foreign residents) as far as they are concerned. Naturally, like any business with a persistent debtor, the time must come when further supplies are refused. It has been argued that it is just as bad to be a persistent creditor as it is to be a persistent debtor. Even if persistent surpluses or deficits are to be avoided, and governments should take action to counteract these, the presence of persistent deficits causes them to act with greater urgency. Most countries pay lip service to the idea that persistent surpluses are disruptive to international trade – being achieved as a result of deficits elsewhere. Some though, such as Japan and West Gemany, manage to run such surpluses with monotonous regularity and without, it appears, inflicting much damage on their own economies. One German Chancellor was heard to mutter under his breath when remonstrated with about Germany's persistent surpluses that 'it is for the sick to take medicine, not the healthy'.

Countries with deficits of a persistent nature are eventually forced to act to correct or reduce these imbalances and the range of measures open to them tend to fall into two distinct stages as follows.

Enabling or allowing measures

These are taken almost as soon as a signicifant deficit begins to develop and are those measures which allow a country to cover the deficit, rather as a bank loan might be used to cover the liability built up by a series of unauthorised overdrafts in the case of an individual. These measures in themselves are unlikely to cure the problem – they only buy time. Amongst the most frequently used measures of this sort in the UK are:

1 Delving into official reserves of gold and foreign currency.

2 Borrowing from central banks or the International Monetary Fund. As a lender of last resort this body is assuming an onerous responsibility; to lend money to a nation which is heavily in debt already. Naturally it can only do so if it has a firm undertaking from the government of the nation concerned that it will put its house in order. The IMF sets targets for Domestic Credit Expansion (DCE) which limit the standard of living of the people to the wealth they are creating, less an amount for the repayment of the debts they have incurred. If these targets are met the nation will recover its former solvency and be restored to the ranks of creditworthy nations.

3 Increasing domestic interest rates on UK investments, (e.g. sterling deposits) in order to attract 'hot' money into the country. 'Hot' money is short-term money, which seeks a high rate of interest wherever it can be found around the world. If hot money flows in it makes funds available to pay foreign debts, at least temporarily.

Measures designed to solve the persistent imbalance problem

If the private individual cited above takes the bank loan and continues to draw unauthorised overdrafts every month the situation soon deteriorates further. The same holds true for countries with a prolonged balance of payments deficit. The time bought with borrowed money must be put to good use in terms of a real solution if the country is to avoid a mill-stone of debt. The measures which countries can take to solve their deficit problems fall into four main groups:

1 LONG-TERM RESTRUCTURING OF THE ECONOMY

Many economies develop deficits because they don't produce the kind of items required by their own and/or other populations at a competitive price on a regular or reliable basis. The answer is to change what the economy produces and probably how it produces. For example, many people who have castigated the Conservative Government of the UK for the decline of British Industry between 1979 and – say – 1985, overlooked the fact that it was largely obsolete 'smoke-stack' industry that was going to the wall. This industry was not only not producing what the export market needed; it wasn't producing what the home market needed either. While the German or Japanese citizen was happy to buy home-produced goods the UK citizen wanted imported goods because they were generally speaking better in every way. To change people's attitude to design, quality and value-for-money cannot be the work of a day – or even of a single administration. Known by the general name of 'supply-side measures' such changes must be a long term answer and other measures need to be taken whilst the economy becomes more efficient or is re-orientated.

2 DIRECT MEASURES

Direct measures are measures taken to influence trade, either visible trade or invisible trade, to halt the persistent deficit. They include:

a) **Embargoes** – physical controls on imports which ban the import of an item altogether.

b) **Quotas** – these are limited embargoes – imports are allowed but only a certain volume or value per time period.

c) **Import tariffs** – here a tax is imposed at the border, making the price of imports higher than they otherwise would be. This reduces the amount demanded for the product concerned.

d) **Exchange controls** – limits upon the release of foreign currency with which to pay for imports.

e) **Subsidies** – these may be either general in nature (e.g. cheap power to manufacturers) or specific (e.g. a payment to a manufacturer for each car exported).

The criticism that can be made of these direct measures is that they have an adverse effect upon foreign countries, since they aim to reduce imports and encourage exports. They invite retaliation, and may not therefore prove in the end to be as beneficial as was at first hoped. Even worse, a rich and powerful exporting nation may be able to retaliate harder than a weak, third world country, and therefore the measures may be biased to hit the third world country rather than the advanced nation. If foreign governments can be persuaded not to retaliate to help a nation in difficulty this is of course helpful.

3 DEFLATIONARY POLICIES

These take the form of depressing the level of aggregate demand and will almost certainly lead to reduced economic growth and growing unemployment. They take the 'heat' out of the economy and achieve this by causing the population to spend less. Some of this reduced spending will be on imports, and fewer imports should help the Balance of Payments situation. They also reduce the demand for some produced goods, thus leaving more of them available for exports. Sometimes exports of good quality products are reduced because home demand is so strong, and deflationary policies strike at that demand and reduce it.

The commonest types of measure to deflate the economy are:

a) Fiscal measures Fiscal measures are tax measures. They get their name from *fisces* (the Latin word for the Roman Emperor's privy purse, which was replenished by taxation). If Government policy raises taxes it leaves the populace with less money to spend and reduces demand in the economy.

b) Reduced Government spending State expenditure is part of the demand in the economy, and careful control over it is essential, especially at times when it is desirable to reduce demand. There is a dilemma here. Governments do many things which are deemed desirable – education, health services, social security services, etc. If the policy is deemed all-important, and expense is no object, the suppliers of services will constantly come back to the budgeting authorities for 'supplementary estimates' – yet another allocation of funds to provide the service. To counteract this a system of 'cash limits' has been instituted in the UK. A cash limit is a budget within which the service must operate – and claims for a supplementary estimate will not be conceded except in the most desperate circumstances. For example, if a sudden bulge in the birth-rate requires more midwives we shall have to provide them – but we need not take emergency action to build more bus shelters – people can buy umbrellas perhaps.

c) Restrictions on credit At one time hire purchase controls were a formidable weapon in the armoury of any Chancellor seeking to deflate the economy. Raising the deposit rate, or reducing the repayment period, checked demand drastically, since people had to save more before they could begin to purchase and the instalments were higher – being spread over a shorter period. Today credit is instantaneous for many credit-worthy people, and it is more difficult to restrict credit. The chief restriction perhaps is the high interest rates payable. For some credit cards the APR (Annual Percentage Rate) is as high as 35 per cent per annum.

d) Constraints on bank lending Today bank lending is just one more aspect of the general credit scene, and direct controls over it have become very rare events. In former times restrictions were severe, the granting of loans and overdrafts was severely restricted and it was easier to get money from less reputable organisations. Today the chief restraint on bank lending is the general control exercised by the Bank of England over the 'prudential' policies of individual banks. This means that bank records, submitted at regular intervals, are scrutinised by the bank for any situation which might lead to financial difficulties. A stern (but quietly delivered) reprimand to a particular bank will soon correct adverse trends, but this can do little for the level of demand in the economy – it is purely an internal affair.

e) Higher interest rates This is the chief weapon available today to reduce the demand in an economy. By making the cost of borrowing high demand is reduced. However it cannot be a perfect weapon. Consider:

(i) It may damp down consumer demand and thus prove beneficial.
(ii) It may not damp down business demand if the higher cost can be pushed through in price rises on the final product. Thus it may generate inflation.
(iii) The best way to cure the Balance of Payments problem is to make home goods better, and cheaper and therefore increase the demand for them abroad. Suppose business people want to do this, but need to buy foreign machine tools, etc., to do it. We don't help efficiency if we make it more difficult to buy the very things needed to solve the problem of low productivity and poor export achievement.

The objection to all these deflationary measures is that they mean real hardship for some people. A general rise in tax levels and a tighter grip on credit is not going to affect the well-to-do very much – a slight tightening of the belt is all it amounts to. For other people it may be the difference between reasonable comfort and actual survival. For example tight control over welfare policies hits the very poorest people, who have to explain in great detail why they need what is really a paltry hand-out. An alternative policy which reduces the adverse effects on home populations is to use **exchange rate adjustments**.

11 EXCHANGE RATE ADJUSTMENTS

(*Note*: The theory of exchange rates is explained on pages 241–7.)

Exchange rates can be used to manipulate the prices of home and overseas goods as they cross frontiers, as exports and imports. The reason this can be done is that there are two elements in the prices of goods and services. Considering UK exports as an example the two elements are:

1 The domestic price – in other words, the price quoted in domestic currency. For example, a woollen sweater might have a price in the UK of £28.

2 The exchange rate calculation. Those who buy from other countries must normally take into account the exchange rate between their own currency and that of the country from which they are buying. Variations in the exchange rate can cause 'price' changes even though the domestic price does not change at all. Suppose a German purchaser wishes to buy a UK woollen sweater. The UK domestic price is £28 but the German purchaser is interested less in the sterling price than in the amount that has to be paid in Deutschemarks. If £1 exchanges for 4 DM, then the price of a sweater is 112 DM. If, however, the sterling price does not change but the pound sterling appreciates to £1 = 5 DM the same sweater now costs 140 DM. This clearly will be a factor discouraging German purchasers of UK goods, but it is likely to *encourage* UK purchasers of German goods. A German cassette recorder costing domestically 240 DM under the old exchange rate would cost £60 to a British customer but under the new exchange rate only £48.

One way around the balance of payments deficit might therefore be through the device of exchange rate adjustment. A reduced rate will make exports cheaper and imports more expensive and this *might*, in the medium term, improve the Balance of Payments situation. The most likely immediate effect though, is to make matters worse, a factor known as the J curve effect.

The adjustment process and the J curve

In general, a country whose charges for goods and services are low because of high productivity or low rewards to home factors will have little difficulty with balance of payments problems. Where a country has balance of payment problems and it allows its currency to depreciate (or devalue) against other currencies it will move back into balance. The speed with which it does so depends upon the elasticities of demand for and supply of its goods and services. In general the effect known as the J curve will be experienced. This is illustrated in Fig 8.3 and explained in the notes below it.

Some of the most important factors determining whether exchange rate adjustment will have a beneficial impact on a Balance of Payments deficit or not are the elasticities involved.

The impact of elasticities on curing a disequilibrium

The four elasticities to be considered here are: (a) the elasticity of demand for exports; (b) the elasticity of demand for imports; (c) the elasticity of supply of exports; and (d) income elasticity. Each of these will vitally affect the success of the depreciation of currency.

THE PRICE ELASTICITY OF DEMAND FOR EXPORTS

If we are reducing the prices of our exports in order to increase earnings of foreign exchange, it is vital that the demand for our exportss is elastic. Suppose

Fig. 8.3 *The J curve effect (Reproduced by courtesy of* Finance and Development*)*

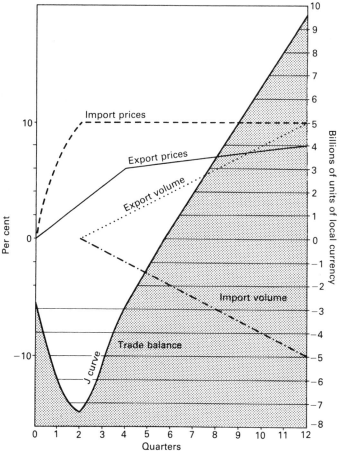

J curve: an illustration of the effects of a
10 per cent depreciation on the trade balance*

*The price and volume effects of the depreciation are shown as
cumulative quarterly per cent changes (left scale). The price and
volume effects of the depreciation on the trade balance are
expressed in units of local currency at an annual rate (right scale).

(reproduced by courtesy of *Finance and Development*)

Notes

1 The initial impact of the depreciation is negative. Import prices rise quickly to the full extent of the depreciation in terms of the home currency. In the illustration it was 10 per cent, but it takes time for demand to fall off. Exports do not increase at once, and those that are in the pipeline earn even less foreign exchange. The balance of payments actually worsens (the down stroke of the J curve).

2 Under the impact of higher import prices import volumes fall away. This is a favourable effect.

3 Export prices, because of the depreciation, are favourable to foreign buyers. Export volumes begin to rise as the 'trade effects' begin to come in – foreign customers switching their trading patterns to buy the goods of the nation that has depreciated its currency. If the elasticities are favourable this increased volume will more than compensate for the depreciation in value of the currency. The result is the longer, upward movement of the J curve in Fig. 8.3. (For an explanation of the effect of price and income elasticities on the success or failure of the depreciation in currency see pages 238–41.)

4 Export prices (in terms of home currency) begin to creep up as the trade unions succeed in winning wage increases for their members. These higher export prices further improve the balance of payments (but if too pronounced will eventually have trade-diverting effects once again).

we reduce export prices by 10 per cent, and the rise in export sales is exactly proportional – in other words, there is unitary elasticity of demand. The result will be that the earnings of foreign exchange have not altered. The greater volume of sales earning foreign exchange will be offset by the smaller amounts earned on each consignment. We shall even be worse off in other ways, for we will have had all the extra trouble of shipping larger volumes of goods for the same reward.

It will be even worse if the demand for our goods is price inelastic. Then our extra effort in selling a slightly larger volume of goods will have been worse than useless, for the smaller earnings in foreign exchange on each consignment mean we shall actually earn less total foreign exchange. The balance of payments may even deteriorate. Only if the demand for our exports is price elastic, so that greatly increased volumes of sales occur, will the depreciation result in larger earnings of foreign exchange. This is illustrated in Fig 8.4.

Fig. 8.4 *Effect of the elasticity of demand for exports on the earnings of foreign exchange after a depreciation.*

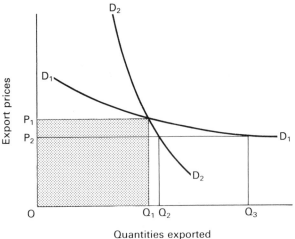

Notes
1 If the demand for exports is elastic the curve may be as in D_1D_1.
2 If the demand for exports is inelastic the curve may be as in D_2D_2.
3 Total earnings of foreign exchange (before depreciation) are shown by the shaded area.
4 In the case of exports where the demand is inelastic, quantities sold rise only to OQ_2 less than proportionately, and total earnings of foreign exchange decline.
5 In the case of exports where demand is elastic, quantities sold increase more than proportionately to OQ_3, and total earnings of foreign exchange increase.

THE PRICE ELASTICITY OF DEMAND FOR IMPORTS

Here the situation is very similar, but works in the opposite way. A country which is allowing its currency to depreciate wishes to correct its balance of payments by increasing exports and decreasing imports. How successful it will be in decreasing imports depends on the elasticity of demand for imports by its citizens. The depreciation will raise the price of imports to them. Will their demand reduce proportionately, more than proportionately or less than proportionately to the change in price? If the imports are basic raw materials which are essential to production, it may be impossible for the quantity demanded to decrease at all. Indeed, higher export sales could even require larger imports of basic raw materials. If the imports are non-essentials or if similar products are produced at home so that home products can be substituted for them then the decrease in the quantity demanded may be more than proportional. This situation is necessary if the depreciation is to be successful from the import point of view, but the position is not quite as crucial as with exports. Since the price of imports has not changed in their own currencies we are not having to pay out more foreign exchange per unit imported, even though the home consumer is paying more for it. Therefore any reduction is welcome, even the small reduction in the quantity demanded for goods which are in inelastic demand.

A further point, with regard to import substitution, is that if home-produced goods are in inelastic supply so that their volume cannot be increased easily, it may be impossible to reduce the quantity of imports demanded.

THE ELASTICITY OF SUPPLY OF EXPORTS

If exports are to be sold in increasing quantities they must be available to sell. This means it may be necessary to reduce home demand for them if the supply of exports is inelastic. Anything we do to reduce home demand will increase the supply of exports. Frequently a depreciation is accompanied by a 'credit squeeze' at home which seeks to reduce the demand for goods by home consumers and leaves the goods available for export.

INCOME ELASTICITY OF DEMAND

Although we usually think of income elasticity of demand (the response of demand to changes in income) as being something that only changes in the long term as the distribution of income varies among the various groups in society, there are short-term effects too. Thus if a balance of payments crisis leads to a severe stop in the cycle of stop-go policies, the incomes of all groups are reduced and some people will be put out of employment. The marginal effect of such changes can be quite pronounced, and the reduction of demand for imports and for home-produced goods can be more than proportional to the change in income. This will often be reinforced by a reduction in demand even from those who have not been directly affected by a reduction in income. Liquidity preference rises and demand falls as they prepare for the 'rainy day' which may be ahead by keeping extra reserves available.

12   THE THEORY OF EXCHANGE RATES

An exchange rate is the price of one currency in terms of another. Those who watch the televised business programmes will see and hear endless references

Fig. 8.5 *Determination of the rate of exchange for sterling against Deutschemarks*

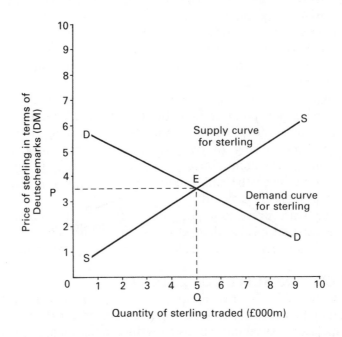

Quantity of sterling traded (£000m)

Notes

1   The demand curve for sterling slopes downwards towards the right. This means that when £1 costs a lot of Deutschemarks (say DM 6 to the £1) German customers do not want to buy the high priced UK goods, or to visit the UK. Consequently demand is small. When Sterling is cheaper, (only DM 2 to the £1) the quantity of Sterling demanded is much greater.

2   The supply curve for sterling slopes upwards to the right. Thus when £1 Sterling can be exchanged for DM 6 the supply of sterling is large as German goods and services are cheap and many UK citizens offer to buy them, or to travel to Germany on holiday. When £1 sterling will only exchange for DM 1 the supply of Sterling is small as German goods and services are expensive, and few UK citizens demand DM.

3   The rate of exchange is fixed at E, where the two curves intersect. The price of Sterling is DM 3.50 = £1 and £5 000 million of sterling is traded. At this price P supply and demand are in equilibrium.

to 'Sterling weakening against the dollar' or 'Sterling stronger against the DM'. How such rates are fixed is simply another illustration of the basic laws of supply and demand. Figure 8.5 illustrates the position, which is explained in the notes below the diagram.

Although an equilibrium price such as P in Fig. 8.5 is deemed to be stable, the foreign exchange market is volatile and a 'stable' exchange rate is not long-lasting. Like any other equilibrium price it will persist as long as the basic factors underlying it do not change. If some change in demand or supply occurs – such as an increased demand for UK exports due to the interruption of supplies from elsewhere around the world, the rate of exchange will change in response to the new situation. Fig. 8.6 shows a typical change in demand for sterling and the resulting effects on the rate of exchange.

Fig. 8.6 *A change in the price of sterling*

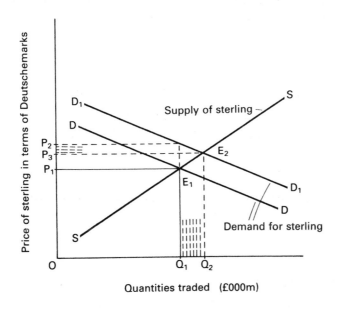

Notes
1 An increased demand for sterling is shown by a change in the demand curve from DD to D_1D_1.
2 The immediate result is a rise in the price of sterling from P_1 to P_2 DM.
3 The increased value of the £1 begins to have an impact upon UK families who see German goods and services as more accessible. The supply of sterling creeps up from Q_1 towards Q_2 as they increase their demand for German goods and services and as it does so the price of sterling begins to decline from P_2 to P_3.
4 Equilibrium is re-established at E_2, where Q_2 of sterling is sold at a price of P_3. The decline of sterling causes some German customers, frightened away by the earlier sudden increase, to take more UK goods.

5 The new equilibrium, in theory at least, equates the value of imports and exports to achieve a 'Balance of Payments'.

13 EXCHANGE RATES OVER RECENT YEARS

Fixed exchange rates

From 1945–1970, under the Bretton Woods Agreement, a system of fixed exchange rates applied. Each country agreed an exchange rate level relative to the United States dollar and apart from a tiny fluctuation of about 1 per cent either side of the agreed parity, no variation was allowed. A country whose exchange rate moved towards the 1 per cent limit was forced to correct it by changing the arrangements within its own territory. This became known as 'managed prosperity' but it involved a succession of go-stop policies, in which the economy was allowed to 'go' and expand as long as the exchange rate was stable, but as soon as the exchange rate showed that too high a standard of living was threatening the competitiveness of the nation's products the exchange rate sounded a warning and the economic brakes were applied.

The brakes used were many. They included:

1   Increased interest rates to reduce borrowing and cut demand in the home economy.

2   Higher taxes, to cut demand and take money out of circulation.

3   Hire purchase controls, to make it more difficult for people to purchase consumer durables (which thus became available for sale in the export markets).

4   Strict controls over bank credit.

All these measures caused unrest, because they meant unemployment for many people, and even bankruptcy for some firms.

Floating exchange rates

Reference has already been made to the fact that there are two elements in the price of exported goods; (a) the manufacturing costs included in the home price and (b) the rate of exchange into the foreign currency. 'Why not', said many politicians, 'change the system. Let us not attack the home market with all these measures to introduce hardships into what were otherwise prosperous industries. Instead, let the exchange rate find its own level, and achieve a Balance of Payments by letting the falling exchange rate encourage foreigners to buy our goods.' This introduced an era of floating exchange rates. Currencies were allowed to **float freely**; market forces prevailed in the foreign exchange market, and an automatic balance of payments was achieved. If sterling was weak on the foreign exchange market because foreigners believed UK goods were not good value for money, it simply floated down to the point where it could establish credibility as a currency worth holding, because at that lower price UK goods did seem to be value for money.

This concept sounds reasonable enough, but it proved to be unsatisfactory for two reasons. In the first place it is a 'begger-my-neighbour policy'. If a country is producing high-cost uncompetitive goods which are too expensive on world markets, it should put its own house in order and get its production system into better shape. If it takes the easier free-float method and lets the exchange rate fall to undercut the low-cost producers in other countries who really are turning out good products at fair prices it beggars them to no real advantage to itself. The policy also proved to be naive because of the presence of speculators on the foreign exchange market. Speculators are always ready to sell a currency that is falling – so they can buy it back cheaper later on. Many holders of foreign exchange for proper purposes (for example as part of their national reserves) cannot stand by if speculators are lowering the value of a currency to make a quick profit.

Everyone who holds a foreign currency, for whatever reason, is liable to become a speculator if the value of the currency changes. It would be sheer madness if sterling was falling in value to hold it while it fell. The only sensible thing to do is to sell it and buy it back later at a cheaper price. To allow a perfectly free float would be to damage all those who are holding the currency and giving it validity in the world's eyes. Someone must manage the currency if speculation is to be defeated and after a few years of 'free floating' the International Monetary Fund altered its rules to prevent 'beggar-my-neighbour' policies and encourage more sensible behaviour. The new rule on this point, part of the General Obligations of Members, reads:

Article IV, Section I. General obligations of members
Recognizing that the essential purpose of the international monetary system is to provide a framework that facilitates the exchange of goods, services, and capital among countries, and that sustains sound economic growth, and that a principal objective is the continuing development of the orderly underlying conditions that are necessary for financial and economic stability, each member undertakes to collaborate with the Fund and other members to assure orderly exchange arrangements and to promote a stable system of exchange rates. In particular, each member shall:
(i) endeavour to direct its economic and financial policies towards the objective of fostering orderly economic growth with reasonable price stability, with due regard to its circumstances;
(ii) seek to promote stabilty by fostering orderly underlying economic and financial conditions and a monetary system that does not tend to produce erratic disruptions;
(iii) avoid manipulating exchange rates or the international monetary system in order to prevent effective balance of payments adjustments or to gain an unfair competitive advantage over other members; and
(iv) follow exchange policies compatible with the undertakings under this Section.

The situation is that most countries now practice a system of **managed floating**, in that the currency is allowed to float freely according to market forces, except where a rise or fall in the currency is deemed not to be in the national interest because it is being engineered by speculative forces at work to make a profit out of an exchange rate fluctuation. At such a time the Central Bank of the nation concerned will buy its own currency (to 'support the £' for example) or sell its own currency (to prevent it rising too high). At certain times other Central Banks will support a Central Bank whose currency is unjustifiably under pressure, by buying or selling the currency as required to defeat the speculators. The speculator only sells to buy back later at a cheaper price, and only buys to sell later at a higher price. To defeat the speculator we have to take the currency he/she is selling, and keep buying no matter how much is offered. If we can do that without the price falling the speculator will have to buy back at the same price (or even better – at a higher price). A speculator caught in this way is said to 'burn his/her fingers'.

The effect of managed floating can be followed in Fig. 8.7, and is explained in the notes below the figure.

Fig. 8.7 *Managing the exchange rate*

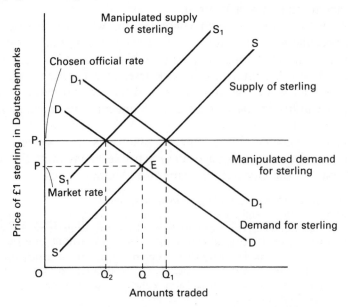

Notes

1 Three situations are shown on the diagram. The first is the market rate for sterling (£1 = DM *P*), with equilibrium being reached at E, with Q amounts of DM and £ sterling being traded at the price £1 = DM *P*.

2 If the authorities are not happy with this exchange rate, believing it is being achieved by unjustified speculative pressures they can take two actions. They can decide upon an 'official' rate and achieve it by influencing the demand for sterling, in this case by buying sterling on the markets (paying for it with official reserves of other currencies). The demand by the Central Bank will change the demand curve to D_1D_1, forcing up the price to the chosen rate, with Q_1 amounts being traded.

3 Unfortunately managing the exchange rate as in **2** above is not always possible, if the adverse trend of market rates is long term and not purely speculative. If it represents a fundamental imbalance the authorities must operate in a different way, and achieve the chosen rate by operating on the supply of sterling. This means reducing the standard of living at home to shift the supply curve of sterling to the left by making it harder for people to enjoy foreign goods, foreign travel, etc. The measures are: (a) to cut real incomes by fiscal (tax) measures; (b) squeeze credit by high interest rates, hire purchase controls and directives to the banks about overdraft and loan policies; (c) reduce government spending, including social security benefits, education cuts, etc. The suppply curve shifts to S_1S_1 and the chosen rate is at P_1, with Q_2 amounts of currency being traded at the chosen rate of £1 = DM P_1.

PEGGED EXCHANGE RATES

The term 'pegged exchange rates' means fixed exchange rates, where a currency is fixed against other currencies (usually by reference to the United States dollar). No variation is allowed – an absolute fixed peg – and exchanges can only be effected at the official rate. This is unsatisfactory because a country's trading state varies from time to time and very fierce controls are necessary to enforce exchanges at an unrealistic 'official' rate. Communist countries show examples of the fierce measures taken – for example foreign travellers may be forced to change all foreign money at the official rate as they cross the border. In some African countries it takes two or three hours to get out of an airport because it is necessary to list all foreign currency held, and it must be produced, unchanged, on leaving the country again.

A CRAWLING PEG
A crawling peg is one where an official rate is allowed to vary by an agreed percentage – but the change per annum is always less than the market exchange rate change.

DIRTY FLOATING
Dirty floating is allowing a currency to sink down to a price where it enables the foreign customer to buy the exporter's products at such cheap prices that they undercut efficiently produced home produced goods. This is a 'beggar-my-neighbour' policy and is deemed unfair. In 1976 the International Monetary Fund changed its rules for members to discourage 'dirty floating'. The actual terms are quoted above (see page 245).

DUMPING
Dumping is selling goods abroad at a lower price than they are being sold at home, in order to earn foreign exchange. It is an unfair practice, because an inefficient producer, who should in fair competitive conditions go out of business, undercuts viable industries in the country to which the exports are going. The loss on the exported items is made up by high prices charged to home consumers. If dumping occurs it is usual to charge an anti-dumping levy to force the price of the goods coming in up to the price at which they are being sold in their home country.

14 THE EUROPEAN MONETARY SYSTEM (EMS)

The European Monetary System is a system designed to promote currency stability within the European Community. It is really a return to the fixed parity system which was used between 1945 and 1970 after the Bretton Woods Agreement held during the Second World War. The idea is that currencies should be kept reasonably stable, since floating currencies are always to some extent 'beggar-my-neighbour' policies. The only member of the European Community not to be fully committed to the EMS system is the UK, which is endlessly waiting for the right moment to join the ERM (the exchange rate mechanism). As with all such hesitations, it is difficult to know a right moment when we see one.

There are three elements in the system:

1 Each member currency is tied to every other currency by a fixed parity – an agreed rate of exchange with every other member of the group. If market rates fluctuate away from these parities, as they are bound to do with the ebbs and flows of trade in goods and services, no action need be taken until the market rates are 2¼ per cent either side of the fixed parity. In the case of Italy the fluctuations are allowed to vary by up to 6 per cent. When the maximum variation is reached corrective action has to be taken, but how

do we know who is at fault? Under the Bretton Woods System both parties had to take corrective action, but this led the German Chancellor, as stated earlier, to claim, 'It is for those who are sick to take medicine'. If two currencies are drifting apart someone is at fault, but who is it?

2 The answer was found by inventing a new kind of money which was a 'currency basket'. This new money is called the ECU – the European Currency Unit. The composition of the ECU is revised every five years and is due for revision in 1990, but at the time of writing it is as shown in Table 8.5.

Table 8.5 The European Currency Unit (ECU)

Currency	Weight (Total 100)	Amount (in units of each currency)
Deutschemark	34.93	DM 0.719
Pound sterling	11.87	£0.0878
French franc	18.97	Ffrs 1.31
Italian lira	9.44	Lir 140
Dutch guilder	11.04	Fl 0.256
Belgian franc	9.07	Bfrs 3.71
Luxemburg franc	– (linked to Bfr)	Lfrs 0.14
Danish krone	2.79	Dkr 0.219
Irish punt	1.13	£IR 0.00871
Greek drachma	0.76	Dr 1.15

We can see from the table that as two more states have joined the Community since this structure was laid down the revision in September 1989 will need to take Spain and Portugal into account.

An ECU is made up of 34.93 per cent Deutschemarks, 11.87 per cent is made up of £1 sterling, 18.97 per cent of French francs, etc. This seems a strange idea, but what it actually gives is a currency unit which is more stable in value than any of the component currencies. Suppose Sterling falls in value, then the ECU will fall in value – but only 11.87 per cent of the Sterling fall will fall in the ECU. Since, when Sterling falls, all other currencies tend to rise, the drop in value of 11.87 per cent of the ECU will be counter-balanced by a rise in the 34.93 per cent that is Deutschemark, the 18.97 per cent that is Ffrancs, etc. So the ECU will be stable, much more stable, than any of the currencies from which it is founded.

Now, how does this show which currency is at fault when the market rates move away from the fixed parities? The answer is that all the currencies have a fixed parity against the ECU too, and the divergence from that parity is more tightly set than the 2¼ per cent range against the other currencies. If the sterling rates of exchange are falling because of adverse aspects of the British economy – poor productivity making our goods too expensive, etc., the ECU will be the first currency to signal the danger mark. This is called the '**divergence indicator**, and it pinpoints the party at fault. If the ECU 'alarm bell' rings, meaning that Sterling is getting too weak, or too strong, the UK, if it was in the EMS, would have to take corrective action to bring its economy under control. The sick nation must take the medicine, and bring its currency back into line by influences upon its domestic economy. As it improves its performance it will come back into parity with the ECU, and of course with all other currencies.

Full membership of the European Monetary System envisages the eventual adoption of the ECU as a single currency for Europe, and the discontinuance of Sterling, along with all other EC currencies. This will involve a considerable loss of sovereignty and a re-orientation of many nationalistic ideas. The ECU will no longer be a currency basket, with a trade related component of 12 nationalist currencies entering into it, but a currency in its own right. As such it will need a European Central Bank which must, of necessity one would think, be in Brussels. Much of the assets of national Central Banks, such as the Bank of England, would need to be transferred to it, and the European Central Bank would then operate in the interests of the community in general and not in the interests of a single nation only. It would also make secession at some future date very difficult to achieve, and indeed wholly undesirable. Small wonder that there is some hesitation about a full commitment to the EMS by the British Government. On the other hand, do we want to be a leading figure in Europe or do we not? The fears that we shall become an offshore island divorced from the mainstream of European life are probably groundless. Hawaii does not seem to suffer from its full membership of the United States. We are moving across the boundary which separates politics from economics; but these are economic subjects we can hardly disregard.

SELF-ASSESSMENT QUESTIONS

5 What are visible exports and imports?

6 What are invisible items?

7 The Balance of Trade never balances; the Balance of Payments always balances. Can you explain?

8 Explain how an exchange rate is arrived at in a free floating foreign exchange market.

9 Explain how an exchange rate that is believed to be right for a particular currency can be 'managed' under a system of 'managed floating'.

REVISION TEST

Answers	Questions
—	**1** Why do we trade with foreign countries?
1 To enrich the variety of goods and services available to us.	**2** Why can we not produce everything we need ourselves?
2 (a) Nature has distributed her blessings haphazardly; (b) climates vary; (c) population density varies; (d) strategically it may not be advantageous; (e) because of comparative advantage.	**3** State the doctrine of comparative advantage.
3 Generally speaking, it will be advantageous for mankind if people specialise in those occupations at which they have the greatest comparative advantage, or the least comparative disadvantage, leaving others to produce the goods and services for which they have no special aptitude.	**4** What is the law of comparative costs in international trade?
4 Nations will find it profitable to trade: (a) when they have different alternative cost ratios and (b) when the international terms of trade lie within the limits set by their domestic alternative cost ratios.	**5** What is the pattern of UK trade?
5 (a) A large volume of **visible trade** (trade in goods) which often results in an unfavourable balance. (b) A smaller volume of **invisible trade** (trade in services) which usually brings a favourable balance, but not necessarily a big enough balance to offset the adverse balance on visible items. (c) A substantial movement of capital items, loans, grants, subsidies, investments, inheritances, etc. Today these capital movements are rolled in with foreign debtors and creditors to give an overall	**6** Who actually arranges foreign currency receipts and payments?

balance. (d) Since this overall balance must balance (but never does because of items in transit) a balancing figure is inserted which represents the total uncertainties in the system.

---

6 In the UK it is the banking system, now that exchange control has been ended, but the Bank of England collects statistics to review the general trend in receipts and payments.

7 List the elements of the balance of payments account.

---

7 (a) The balance of visible trade; (b) the balance of invisibles; (c) the balance of capital items; (d) since all outstanding balances must finish up as either debtors or creditors the Balance of Payments must always balance, since unpaid bills (in either direction) finish up as 'capital items' held over until the next year as debtors or creditors.

8 What is a 'balancing item'?

---

8 It is the final figure added to a Balance of Payments Account to make it balance. It represents all the unknown items in transit in both directions.

9 What measures can be taken to cure an imbalance on the Balance of Payments?

---

9 (a) Enabling measures (which solve the problem in the short-run and enable the country to cover the deficit and carry on trading); (b) measures designed to solve the long-term problem of an imbalance of overseas trade.

10 List the enabling measures.

---

10 (a) Use of the official reserves; (b) borrowing from foreign Central Banks or the IMF; (c) increasing interest rates to attract foreign 'hot money', looking for a high rate of interest.

11 List the long-term measures to solve the Balance of Payments problem.

11 (a) Direct measures to influence trade in either visibles or invisibles, such as (i) embargoes on imports, (ii) quotas (limited embargoes) by volume or value, (iii) import tariffs, (iv) exchange controls, (v) subsidies and other aids to exporters, (b) deflationary policies to depress aggregate demand such as (i) fiscal measures, (ii) reduced Government and local Government spending, (iii) restrictions on bank lending and credit generally, (iv) raising interest rates to make the cost of borrowing higher.

12 What is the objection to these policies?

12 The direct measures harm other countries and may invite retaliation. The deflationary measures cause real hardship to some people at home, raise unemployment and may be socially and politically unacceptable.

13 What is the long-term solution?

13 A complete re-appraisal of the climate of production; overthrow of vested interests and any forces tending to preserve out-moded methods; a complete revitalisation of the whole scene. The measures necessary have been called 'supply-side measures' because they operate to improve the supply of good quality goods and services.

14 What elasticities affect our ability to improve the Balance of Payments position?

14 (a) The elasticity of demand for exports; (b) the elasticity of demand for imports; (c) the elasticity of supply of exports; (d) income elasticity of demand.

15 What is the J Curve effect?

15 It is the shape of the curve of a trade balance under the impact of a depreciation of the currency. At the start the balance of payments actually gets worse. The depreciation raises the price of imports but it takes time for the demand for imported goods to decline. Exports are cheaper, but it takes time for new orders to come in and orders already in the pipeline earn even less foreign exchange. This is the downslope of the J. Then the imports fall away and exports rise to cure the adverse balance.

16 How is the exchange rate of one currency in terms of another arrived at?

16 By the ordinary rules of supply and demand, with the demand of a foreign country's citizens for the currency of the home country being set against the home country's citizens' willingness to supply it.

17 What is a floating exchange rate?

---

17 An exchange rate decided upon by the free flow of market forces – a currency which is not in demand floats down against other currencies until it reaches a point where its purchasing power does represent a fair value for the foreign currency surrendered to purchase it.

18 What is the EMS?

---

18 The European Monetary System.

19 What does it do?

---

19 It gives stability to the exchange rates of member countries, since they declare a parity against all other member currencies and also against the ECU – the European Currency Unit, and diversion in excess of 2¼ per cent (Italy 6 per cent) calls for corrective policies on the offending country's economy to restore its currency to the parity position.

20 How do we know which currency is the offending one, when two currencies drift apart.

---

20 The 'divergence indicator' of the ECU sounds a warning *before* the actual currencies reach the danger level, and the currency that is changing value must then take action.

Go over the test again until you are sure of all the answers. Then try the questions below.

ANSWERS

(See Self-assessment questions on pages 229 and 249.)

1 We must export to pay for the primary imports we need, since nature has not provided us with everything we require. Similarly we need many foreign secondary goods to enrich the variety and choice in our lives. We need many foreign capital goods, since inventions are made worldwide today. We need to travel abroad and must earn foreign exchange to pay for it. Strategic considerations often enter into exporting – giving support to friends abroad and maintaining bases for defence purposes.

2 Absolute advantage is a situation where a nation can produce, with a given set of factor inputs, more outputs than another nation. Comparative advantage is a situation where, by specialist knowledge and skill, high quality factors, etc., a nation can do so well at some things that it pays to specialise and use its factors in producing the things it is best at producing – leaving other less efficient nations to produce the other things it needs.

3 See Question 4 in the Revision Test above.

4 Nations do not specialise completely for the following reasons: (a) Since factors are not homogeneous, there comes a time when the very best domestic factors are more efficient than the very worst of the foreign supplier's factors, despite their natural advantages; (b) strategically it may be unwise to cease production of any item completely; (c) the specific nature of some assets means we cannot cease to use them until they are totally obsolete – it would be wasteful (d) transport costs narrow the band where a foreign competitor can produce more efficiently than ourselves.

5 Visible imports and exports are goods, which we can actually see, passing through our ports and airports. They include raw materials, semi-manufactures and finished goods.

6 Invisible items are services, of which the most important are banking services, insurance, shipping, aviation, travel and tourism.

7 The balance of trade is the balance of visible trade and invisible trade, imports and exports. In any given financial year it is most unlikely that these will exactly balance. We shall either have a deficit on current account, or a surplus on current account. However, to set against the deficit or surplus, whichever it is, we do have a great many capital movements. Capital movements include investments by UK firms abroad, and by foreign firms in the UK. They also include funds transferred by foreign Governments and the International Monetary Fund. However, these capital movements may not cancel out any imbalance on Current Account. The rest, whether it is a surplus or a deficit, becomes either a debit balance – we owe foreigners money – or a credit balance – foreigners owe us money – somewhere in the book-keeping system. The final result of the Balance of Payments must be a balance – the sum total of assets and liabilities sums to zero.

8 In a free floating foreign exchange system the exchange rate is decided at the point where demand for a particular currency is in equilibrium with the supply of the currency. The demand for a currency is the quantity foreigners are prepared to buy at a given price (rate of exchange). The supply of a currency is the quantity home nationals are prepared to bring to market at a certain price to exchange for all other currencies. If demand is strong and supply is weak the price will rise. At this higher price demand falls (some foreigners cease to demand) and supply increases (more home citizens are prepared to trade and travel abroad now the exchange rate is favourable. When the price rises enough to bring demand and supply into equilibrium the exchanges take place at the market price for the day.

9 We can manage a currency as follows:

a) Market price is below the perceived 'right price'.

b) Official buyers step into the market and buy the currency, thus shifting the demand curve to the right. Under this extra demand the exchange rate (the price of the currency) rises. If the Central Bank keeps on buying it will push up the market price to the perceived 'right price'.

c) If the Central Bank has insufficient reserves to keep buying the market cannot be managed by working on the demand curve. Instead measures must be taken to influence supply, by reducing the home demand for imports, foreign travel, etc., and increasing exports. This shifts the supply curve of the currency to the left, thus forcing the price up to the perceived price. (See Fig. 8.7 to revise this point.)

QUESTIONS ON CHAPTER 8

1 'The cost of the steel we decided to make is the cast iron we decided not to make.' Explain.

2 Outline the gains to be expected from free international trade. How are these gains shared between the trading countries?

3 What are the 'terms of trade'? How may these terms of trade be measured?

4 What are the basic elements in the balance of payments statistics? How is a deficit on the balance of payments cleared in the short term?

5 Why is export trade of importance to a country like the UK? Explain the advantages of export trade to a firm contemplating venturing into the export field.

6 What are the effects of price elasticities upon the balance of payments when a currency floats downward on the foreign exchange market?

7 'Go-Stop policies are unacceptable.' 'Go-stop policies are inevitable unless firms raise productivity and meet contractual commitments to the satisfaction of foreign customers.' Discuss these two attitudes to go-stop policies.

8 Why is increased productivity the ideal solution to balance of payments problems? Analyse the part your own firm could play in assisting balance of payments difficulties.

9 Explain how floating exchange rates affect balance of payments problems. What is 'dirty floating'? When does 'floating' become 'dumping'?

10 What is a 'beggar-my-neighbour' policy? Why are such policies unfair? How could a nation retaliate when faced with unscrupulous policies of this sort?

TIPS FOR STUDENTS: A SPECIMEN ANSWER TO QUESTION 10

A 'beggar-my-neighbour' policy is a policy which passes the burden of an adverse balance of payments over to the citizens of another country, by allowing the exchange rate to sink on the foreign exchange market. If our goods are not in demand by foreigners because they are a poor buy at their present prices, we shall not be able to earn foreign exchange by selling them and consequently will have an adverse balance on the Balance of Payments. If we allow our currency to float down on the foreign exchange market until our goods do become value for money we shall achieve sales in other countries which we would not otherwise achieve, and this will adversely affect home producers in all the other countries. We shall be exporting unemployment to them unfairly, for their efficient, low-cost industries are being undercut by our inefficient high cost ones. This is against the IMF rules which require member nations not to manipulate exchange rates to gain an unfair advantage over other nations.

A nation faced with unscrupulous policies liike this could (a) introduce an embargo on goods from the offending nation (b) impose a tariff which will raise the price to the true cost price in the exporting country (c) bring in exchange controls to delay and even prohibit payment for the goods suppled until the offending country ceases its unfair practices.

9 The national income

1 WHAT IS THE NATIONAL INCOME?

Every nation creates wealth which it uses to support its people in their everyday lives. How much wealth is created and how it is shared out among the people is of crucial interest to every citizen. Obviously the bigger the cake that can be shared up the larger the individual slices that a family or an individual can hope to enjoy. However, if the shares are unfair, and some enjoy a large slice while others are reduced to collecting crumbs from the rich people's tables social unrest will inevitably arise. If some are privileged and others are underprivileged resentment will grow and even the fiercest repression will not contain the frustration in the end.

The total wealth created is called the 'National income' which was defined by the celebrated English economist Alfred Marshall as *'the aggregate net produce of, and the sole source of payment for, all the factors of production'*. We are back to Fig. 1.2 (page 14) with the factors of production, land, labour and capital being organised by the entrepreneurs into a wide variety of production activities. The goods and services created by this activity, when counted, valued and added together give us the *aggregate net product* which we can all enjoy.

The word 'net' in the definition refers to the fact that in creating all these goods and services we do wear out a great deal of capital assets created in earlier years. These have to be replaced or we shall be 'living on our capital' and in a few years all our assets will have been worn out and have ceased to exist. To put some figures on this, and to make it clearer, in 1987 the UK had:

			£m.
	a)	Gross national product	357 760
Less	b)	Capital consumption	48 238
		Net national product	£309 522 m.

£48 000 million of capital worn out in one year seems a very considerable quantity of assets to have wasted away, but those were the figures collected by the 'national income' statiticians.

Continuing with our definition – the aggregate net product of £309 522 million is *the sole source of payment for all the factors of production*. Of course, we actually reward the people with payments in money form, but as the value of the goods and services produced was £309 522 million there is no point in giving them any more money than that. We can't eat money, or drink money, or be educated or entertained by money. All our pleasures in life have to be achieved by the goods and services we enjoy. If we do pay our factors more than £309 522 million all that will happen is that the prices of the goods and services will go up. This is inflation, more money chasing the same amount of goods simply means that prices rise. We can't have any more goods and services as a nation, because that is all we have made. It is worth while learning Alfred Marshall's definition by heart.

> The national income is the aggregate net product of – and the sole source of payment for – all the factors of production.

2 MEASURING THE NATIONAL INCOME

If the government is charged with the responsibility of organising the prosperity of the nation it must be helpful to attempt to make some sort of estimate of the total national income, and from that knowledge we should be able to achieve some sort of fair balance when it comes to sharing out the cake. There are some inherent difficulties in such a statistical exercise. For example we have to collect figures for output from thousands of different enterprises. Many of these enterprises hesitate to let their competitors (let alone the tax inspectors) know how well they are doing, and may not send in a return at all, while others may deliberately understate the figures. To get totally correct figures is perhaps impossible, but by collecting the figures in three different ways a bit of a check can be made to detect errors in the figures, and the odd penalty (a fine or imprisonment) may encourage traders to try harder next time.

The three methods of collecting the figures are:

1 **The output approach**, in which we add up the net outputs of all the producers, i.e. the value they have added to the inputs of the industry to produce the outputs.

2 **The income approach**, in which we add up all the incomes received by everyone in the nation, i.e. the rewards paid to the factors employed.

3 **The expenditure approach**, in which we add up all the expenditures of everyone in the nation, either by consuming goods and services or adding to wealth, i.e. savings.

Certain adjustments have to be made to these figures, for example for incomes coming in from abroad, and capital consumption, and these are revealed in the following tables. The three main concepts in all these approaches are as follows:

1 **Gross domestic product** – which is the sum of all the incomes earned in producing current goods and services within the economic territory of the UK, wherever the earner of the income resides. None of this income comes from abroad (it is all domestic) but some of it is earned by non-residents.

2 **Gross national product** is the same as the above, except that we add in any income earned from abroad and leave out any domestic income that goes to non-residents. So gross domestic product plus net national income from abroad gives us gross national product.

3 **National income**, which is the Gross National Product (GNP) less capital consumption. This is the final figure for national income which is useful to the Government in keeping a general perspective of the nation's wealth and progress.

The tables for presenting these figures are long and complex, but in theory whichever method is used they should all come out to the same answer. In fact they do not agree exactly, and to get as accurate a figure as possible we take an average of the three results. The adjustment is shown in Table 9.1 as 'Statistical discrepancy'.

Note The reasons why the three sets of figures must come to the same answer is because they are basically exactly the same figures. For example, national output is valued at the figure we paid to all the factors who helped produce the output, in other words it is valued at factor cost. Since the amounts paid to these factors, land, labour, capital and enterprise are the incomes of the persons who control the use of the factors, the value of all these incomes together (using the income approach) must be the same as the figures found by the output approach. Similarly, since the incomes are then spent to purchase a balanced basket of goods and services for the families of the income earners, the expenditure method, in which we count all the expenditures of the various families must come to the same figure again. Any savings (moneys not spent) appear in the account as 'capital formation'.

These figures are published annually in August showing the figures to the end of the previous year. The publication is called *United Kingdom: National Accounts* and has a blue cover, hence its popular name '*The Blue Book*'. Study Table 9.1 now – and if you are able to obtain *The Blue Book* for the current year fill in the up-to-date figures for the year to 31 December last in the spare column provided.

Table 9.1 The National Income, 1987 (£millions)

Industry	Value of product in year (at factor incomes valuation) £m.	You may enter more up-to-date figures here
Agriculture, forestry & fishing	5 901	
Energy & water supply	24 184	
Manufacturing	85 552	
Construction	21 524	
Distribution, hotels & catering	48 963	
Transport	16 227	
Communication	9 688	
Banking & business services	43 358	
Ownership of dwellings	20 180	
Public administation, defence etc.	24 895	
Education & health service	31 681	
Other services	22 366	
Gross domestic product by this method	354 519	
Less statistical discrepancy	2 282	
Gross domestic product	352 237	
Add Net income from abroad	5 523	
	357 760	
Less capital consumption in year	48 238	
Net national income at factor cost	£309 522 m	

(Source: *The Blue Book 1988 Edition*)

3 THE BASES OF THE NATIONAL INCOME

In Table 9.1, using the output approach in which the outputs of all the industries and other institutions are aggregated we see that the UK's national income in 1987 was £309 522 million. What are the bases for the national income of any country? The crucial elements in national income are the factor endowments on which a nation can rely. Thus if a country is blessed with a wide variety of natural resources, as for example the United States or the Soviet Union are blessed, it should be easy to achieve national prosperity. Compare these countries with Singapore, or Hong Kong, with tiny specks of land without any natural resources at all and one is left to marvel at the prosperity achieved by such tiny countries. Clearly, natural resources are not everything. Factor endowments is a wider term. The chief factor endowments are:

Natural resources

We know that these are the minerals of the earth, the gases of the atmosphere, the plants, trees and other vegetable products, the animals both wild and domesticated, the produce of the seas and the energy resources of the country. Those nations which are generously endowed with most of the resources the country needs should be largely self-sufficient. A nation which is largely self-supporting is always in a relatively happy situation. A nation which is dependent on foreign supplies is always to some extent balanced on a knife-edge, and can be affected adversely by any disturbance of the economic situation – a war, or the closure of a canal, or something of this sort can seriously affect its national income.

Human resources

The second great resource is the population of the nation. Populations vary. They can be sober, industrious, intelligent, knowledgable, skilful and energetic. They can be intemperate, lazy, boorish, ignorant, untrained and somnolent. Nations which lack natural resources must usually make up for this defect by achieving very high standards from their human resources. Wealth has to be created by the skill of the people, which can add value to the imported raw materials which the nation lacks and sell the resulting output to both pay for the imports and support the people, with a good standard of living. In Singapore, for example, the quality of life is a constant concern of the Government, and its support of some 3 million people on an island the size of the Isle of Wight reflects its success in achieving high levels of skill and enterprise from its people.

Capital resources

Capital is the stock of producer goods which is available at any given time in a nation. Where these are in short supply they have to be created. This can only be done by using factors to create capital assets instead of goods for current consumption. It is a delicate managerial art by any government to create capital assets and restrain public demand; denying current consumption to a public who find it difficult to see why their efforts should be so poorly rewarded.

The situation is aggravated if unwise decisions are made by central planning bodies, or if excessive speculative zeal leads to a proliferation of projects many of which prove to be abortive. In the nineteenth century 'canal manias' and 'railway manias' soaked up capital to such an extent that ordinary projects for consumption goods were totally starved of capital, sometimes for years at a time. By contrast, prudent use of capital to create wealth-creating assets leads eventually to a higher standard of living all round, and to levels of prosperity undreamed of by our ancestors.

Enterprise

Enterprise is not a separate resource – it is simply one of the skills possessed by human resources. The ability of some people to lead the way in wealth-creation is a very important factor in the national income. Above all the political climate must be right. In the UK, for example, the legal rule that 'there is always a presumption in favour of development' holds that everyone is free – so long as it does no harm to others – to spend his/her money, time and energy in wealth creation. Petty bureaucracy must not be allowed to prevent this; nor must vested interests like powerful rivals or powerful trade unions exert more than a reasonable restraint on enterprise. Unbridled capitalism has been proved in the past to be a bad thing, because it heaps costs like polluted air, polluted rivers, derelict land, etc., upon the general public to be borne as 'social costs'. On the other hand excessive restraint on enterprise reduces the use of native wit and energy to the detriment of the nation too, preventing wealth creation and driving enterprising individuals abroad in a brain-drain or skill-drain or talent-drain.

4 DIFFICULTIES IN MEASURING NATIONAL INCOME

It is not easy to measure the national income, and since we measure it in three different ways the difficulties are also tripled.

The chief problems are:

1 accurate definitions
2 double counting
3 collection procedures
4 analysis of the raw data, and their interpretation and validation
5 publication of the final data.

Accurate definitions

Every quantity to be collected must be specified in a careful way so that when the figures come in we are quite sure we are grouping like with like. For example in Table 9.1 we have a list of industries whose output of wealth is to be measured. Under the heading of manufacturing (the largest creator of wealth) there are many types of manufacturing firms, but whether a particular firm is to be classified as a manufacturer, or a construction firm, or a transport firm might be a matter of doubt. If a garage manufactures some spare parts should it be classed under transport or manufacturing, or a bit of each. A special publication *National Accounts, Statistics, Sources and Methods* (revised frequently) is available from Her Majesty's Stationery Office, and gives a great deal of background knowledge about national income statistics.

The Blue Book also has a useful glossary of terms. For instance it defines capital consumption as follows:

Capital consumption This item is a measure of the amount of fixed capital resources used up in the process of production during the year. Capital consumption is not an identifiable set of transactions: it is an imputed transaction which can be measured only by a system of conventions.

Such definitions are helpful in understanding national income statistics.

Double counting

Here are many situations where we might be tempted to count things twice. For example if a man earns £20 000 per annum and uses £2000 of it to send his daughter to university we cannot count the incomes of both father and daughter as 'national income'. If we count the daughter's £2000 as her income we must reduce the father's income to £18 000. If we tax £1000 million away from rich people to pay out social security money to the very poor then the incomes of the rich must either be reduced 'net of tax' or the incomes of those receiving welfare benefits must be given at the figure before the benefit is added.

Similarly, the wealth created by any firm must only be given at the 'value added' figure. Suppose a farmer fells a tree (a gift of nature) and sells it to a furniture manufacturer for £1000. Suppose the furniture manufacturer turns it into 100 coffee tables at £100 each, which is £10 000 of coffee tables. We cannot add them together and say the aggregare wealth created is £11 000. The final result is £10 000 of coffee tables. The farmer created the tree (with nature's help) £1000 and the furniture manufacturer added £9000 more value as it was turned into coffee tables. The 'national income' is £10 000 because we must not 'double-count'.

Collection procedures

Some statistics for national income purposes are collected by the tax officials – for example, income tax figures are largely used for the 'income approach' (page 258). However many people do not pay taxes – they are too poor. Clearly we cannot leave them out of our calculations. As everyone who is in employment pays National Insurance contributions we can use these figures to find out how many people are in employment and by taking away the number with income tax records we can find the missing numbers. We still don't know how much they earn – so we shall have to take a sample and ask them what their earnings are. This could then be used to find an average figure and the average earnings, multiplied by the number of people, gives us the earnings of the whole group of untaxed people.

Obviously there are many problems with collection procedures – with over 55 million people to check on it is not easy to get completely accurate figures for output, income or expenditure.

Analysis

It is usual, where questionnaires about earnings or output are concerned to use both 'the stick and the carrot'. We ask people to cooperate and give accurate figures, explaining the purpose of the exercise, its use to the nation, etc. We also tell them quite clearly that it is an offence punishable by a fine and/or imprisonment to give false answers. One occasionally sees cases reported where a person who refuses to answer an official request for information is sent to prison – as much as a warning to others as to punish the person concerned. All results of enquiries have to be analysed, tested for errors, all calculations checked and double checked, etc.

The use of these statistics is to study trends within the economy and many statistical processes are helpful in this respect. For example we may find it helpful to look, not at the actual figures collected, but at the figures adjusted to take account of inflation. For example the year 1985 has been chosen as the base year for national income statistics and if the 1987 figures of £309 522 million are adjusted to take account of inflation we find that at 1985 prices the national income was only £289 074m. The index of retail prices, taken as 100 in 1985 had risen to 107.07 by 1987. Therefore in real terms the national income had risen much less than appeared from the figures collected in 1987.

Publication

The actual preparation of the tables for publication is a lengthy task, and calls for personnel of high quality. Since decisions are going to be made on the basis of the published figures it is essential to have them as accurate and as well presented as possible.

SELF-ASSESSMENT QUESTIONS

1 Define the national income.

2 What are the three methods of calculating national income? Why must they come to the same result (except for statistical discrepancies)?

3 What are the difficulties in measuring national income?

4 Why are some nations rich and others poor?

5 THE GOVERNMENT'S SHARE OF NATIONAL INCOME

The Government, with its ability to tax away such funds as it requires, and to compel the payment of taxes if necessary, is able to obtain vast sums of money which can be used for its general purposes and the implementation of what it conceives to be desirable policies. This power is limited in a democratic society by the prospect of dimmissal at the next election if too large a share of national income is demanded by taxation. A non-democratic government if despotic enough, may remain in power for many years, but eventually popular discontent will overthrow it.

Why do we need to be taxed?

Reference has been made already to many things that Governments do, but if we recapitulate them in order of importance we may list:

1 Measures to preserve the framework of society; defence, law and order, the courts, prisons, administrative controls, security, international treaties, etc.
2 Measures to promote prosperity, assistance to production, distribution, overseas trade, enterprise, etc.
3 Measures to promote the well-being of the nation, health, education, social security and welfare of all sorts.
4 Measures to enhance the quality of life; including all manner of environmental activities, recreational activities, etc.

Clearly all this costs a great deal of money, and in the year 1987 where national income totalled £309 522 million (see Table 9.1) the Government's share amounted to £164 966 million. This was 53 per cent of all the wealth created.

The Government has three main sources of funds; taxation, trading income and borrowing. Trading income is a relatively minor source of funds, and may be negative in some years. For example, in 1987 a trading deficit of £177 million was suffered, even without taking depreciation into account. By contrast in that year taxation raised revenues for the Government as follows:

	£m.
Taxes on income	55 601
Taxes on expenditure (VAT, etc.)	67 980
Social security contributions	28 449
	£152 030 m.

This was 92 per cent of all the money required by Government. There was no borrowing in that year (in fact there was £108 million surplus on the General Government Account). The other 8 per cent of the Government funds came from such things as interest and dividends on money and shares held temporarily by the Government and rents from official properties.

Changes in the Government's share

In the nineteenth century Gladstone declared the chief aim of the Government should be the saving of candle ends; the Board of Trade consisted of two people, the President of the Board of Trade and his Clerk and the total Government expenditure was £69 million. Income tax raised £21 million, beer and spirits £31 million and the rest was raised by taxing the 'poor man's luxury – tea'. Today's income taxes at £55 601 million are nearly 3000 times as great as in 1881, and the Civil Service has over 4 million members. In 1987 Government spent 2300 times as much as it spent in 1881, yet this is at a time when the Government is seeking positive reductions in public spending and the privatisation of socially-owned industries to boost the private sector. Clearly huge changes have taken place in the share of the national income which is spent by central and local government, and almost all of it is financed by taxation.

6 PUBLIC FINANCE

Adam Smith, the first great economist who published the *Wealth of Nations* in 1776 held that taxes should be levied on people according to their ability to pay – in other words that the fairest form of direct taxation is progressive taxation, falling progressively more heavily on the taxpayer as income levels rise. Other forms of direct taxation are to some extent regressive, that is, they fall most heavily on those who can least afford to pay. The best example is the poll tax (or per capita tax) where every citizen pays the same tax per head of the population. In South Africa, many years ago, the British introduced a poll tax. Those with money just paid up. Those without incomes, and without a cash crop, were forced to leave their kraals and go to the mines to earn their poll tax. Much of South Africa's problems began with that poll tax, the burden of which fell very unevenly. The third form of direct taxation is proportional taxation, where tax is a percentage of total income.

Direct taxation is taxation levied on the citizen directly, which cannot be avoided except by emigration from the country which is levying the tax. We can see how these methods vary by considering Table 9.2.

Table 9.2 Methods of taxation

| | Income per annum | | | | | |
| | Mr A (£5 000) | | Mrs B (£25 000) | | Mr C (£250 000) | |
	Tax payable	Balance left	Tax payable	Balance left	Tax payable	Balance left
Type of tax						
Per capita (£1 000 per head)	£1 000	£4 000	£1 000	£24 000	£1 000	£249 000
Proportional (20%)	£1 000	£4 000	£5 000	£20 000	£50 000	£200 000
Progressive	–	£5 000	£3 000	£22 000	£100 000	£150 000

There are a number of problems with various methods. For example the poll tax is the most unfair, with the poorest sections of the population paying the same as the richest sections. It will usually be necessary to make exceptions for certain disadvantaged groups, and a good deal of administrative costs in supervising the system will be incurred. With progressive taxation, by contrast, all are taxed, in theory, but the rich are taxed more heavily. In practice, many of the population, having low incomes, pay no tax at all (and hence do not need supervising for evasion of their tax liabilities). The few people who are rich enough to pay are usually financially sophisticated and easily supervised. Unfortunately they are few in number, and may 'vote with their feet' and leave the country if taxes are too repressive. It is usual to have a wider group paying tax, at more reasonable levels, so that sufficient income is generated without creating either popular unrest from the poorer sections of the population or evasive action from the richer sections. For some years after the war the top rate of tax on unearned income (income from investments) was 98 per cent, which did encourage many rich people to move abroad.

Indirect taxes

These are taxes imposed on goods and services, rather than on the citizen directly. They are nearly always taxes at the point of consumption – in other words if you wish to enjoy the good or service you are automatically caught by the tax, which you must pay as you purchase the good, or pay for the service. Thus a purchase tax is paid at the point of purchase of the original good, either by the wholesaler or the retailer, who then passes the tax on in his/her prices to the final consumer. A sales tax is paid at the point of sale, where the final consumer purchases the good or service. The supplier who supplies the final consumer collects the tax and is liable to pay it over to the authorities. This sort of tax is widely used in America, where many states impose this type of tax (at around 5–7½ per cent) at the point of sale. In the UK a more complex tax is called Value Added Tax (VAT) and is imposed at every level where value is added. A pause to discuss this tax is worthwhile, and a full example is given in Table 9.3.

The basic idea of VAT is that tax is added at every stage of production as value is added to the product. The word 'production' is being used here in its economic meaning. We say that an article has not been completely 'produced' until it reaches the final consumer. Thus a typical chain of production might read as follows:

GROWER MANUFACTURER WHOLESALER RETAILER CONSUMER

Let us consider a tree cut down in a Forestry Commission plantation and made into a ladder which eventually is purchased by Jones, a do-it-yourself enthusiast. The ladder costs Jones £40, but in fact the Forestry Commission charged £8 for the tree; the Upright Ladder Co. charged £20 for the ladder to Distribution Ltd, who charged £30 to Paylittle DIY Stores for it, and they charged Jones £40. The value added in each stage was therefore £8, £12, £10 and £10 respectively. Notice in Table 9.3 that the tree which was originally a free gift of nature was increased in value at each stage, though one might think some people's work was more valuable than others. The Forestry Commission did little to the tree and it rose in value £8. The manufacturer turned it into a ladder and it rose in value £12. The distributor changed its geographical position and it rose in value £10 and the DIY store simply displayed it and it rose £10 in value. It shows how difficult it is to say what real value is!

Tax was added, let us say at 15 per cent, at each stage. Therefore the Forestry Commission charged £8 + VAT = £8 + £1.20 = £9.20. They are therefore liable to HM Customs for £1.20 tax they have collected. This is called **output tax**, a tax on the Forestry Commission's output. The manufacturer charges £20 + VAT = £20 + £3 = £23. It is liable for output tax of £3 collected as output tax, but is allowed to keep back the **input tax** it paid, of £1.20. It is therefore liable for £3 − £1.20 = £1.80. The whole situation can be seen in Table 9.3.

Table 9.3 How VAT is collected in the UK

	Forestry Commission	Ladder Co.	Distribution Ltd	Paylittle DIY	Jones (consumer)
Cost price without tax	£0 (gift of nature)	£8	£20	£30	£40
Selling price without tax	£8	£20	£30	£40	–
Value added	£8	£12	£10	£10	–
Selling price with tax	£9.20	£23	£34.50	£46	–
Cost price with tax	£0	£9.20	£23	£34.50	£46
Output tax	£1.20	£3	£4.50	£6	Tax paid
Input tax	£0	£1.20	£3	£4.50	£6
VAT payable to	£1.20–£0	£3–£1.20	£4.50–£3	£6–£4.50	–
Customs & Excise	£1.20	£1.80	£1.50	£1.50	–

Notes

1   The only person who paid any tax was the final consumer, Jones, who paid £6 tax to Paylittle DIY.
2   However this tax reached Customs and Excise in four bits, £1.20 from the Forestry Commission, £1.80 from Upright Ladder Co. £1.50 from Distribution Ltd and £1.50 from Paylittle DIY.
3   None of these firms paid tax, they just collected it and handed it over to Customs and Excise.
4   All the firms had to keep VAT records – a very cumbersome way to collect tax.

It is worth stating here Adam Smith's four 'canons of taxation'; the rules for a good tax. These were:

1 Taxes should be equal – by which he meant that they should fall proportionately on all the population, and thus be seen to be fair.
2 They should be certain, so each person knows what he should pay. They should not be at the whim of the tax collector, who could treat some people more harshly than others.
3 The tax should be collected conveniently. The PAYE scheme, used in the UK, to 'pay as you earn', has been a very good scheme because it removes

the tax before most people get their wages, and hence they cannot get into debt for taxes. By contrast businesses pay tax after the financial year is over, and often get into difficulties. The vast majority of bankruptcy cases involve sums owing to the Inland Revenue.

4 Taxes should be economic, i.e. they should raise much more money than the costs of collection. In the UK the costs of collection are rarely more than about 5 per cent (especially as much of the cost involved has to be borne by the employer). This is called the 'costs of compliance', and every attempt is made by a good Chancellor to keep these costs as low as possible.

We could add other rules – for example impartiality between citizens is a good rule. This means that taxes should fall equally on all people in the same situations, for example, if two people earn the same salary they should pay the same tax. This is possible for direct taxes but impossible for indirect taxes. If Mr A has the same income as Mr B, but smokes, likes a glass of wine or spirits, frequently bets on a racehorse, does the football pools and drives a car, but Mr B does none of these things, Mr A will pay a lot more tax than Mr B.

7 FISCAL POLICY

Although governments have been raising revenue through taxation for centuries, fiscal measures (tax measures) as a means of economic control are a comparatively recent phenomena. Only when the ideas of Keynes were accepted by the UK government in 1941 (see Chapter 11) did fiscal policy assume a significant role. During the period when governments felt that Keynesianism had *every* answer to economic problems, fiscal policy became dominant. Although less important today, when monetarist policies to keep control of the economy by influencing the money supply are in greater favour, fiscal policies still have some part to play.

Fiscal policy concerns the raising and spending of government revenues, in particular the *amounts* involved and the *timing* of variations. During the early part of the twentieth century taxation was a relatively straightforward matter. The government had certain expenditures to make, it therefore needed certain revenues to 'balance the budget' and taxation was a prime source of income. There is, though, much more to modern taxation than a simple attempt at keeping government books in balance. From 1945–1979 taxes were frequently varied in order to influence the level of aggregate demand. A rise in direct taxes, e.g. income tax, reduces the population's disposable income and hence aggregate demand (assuming that the government does not itself spend all of the tax take). A reduction in direct taxes has the opposite effect. In theory direct taxes can be changed easily, but the mechanics of actually doing so with a hard-pressed revenue service effectively means that only infrequent changes occur (usually in the March budget). The brunt of tax variation falls upon indirect, particularly expenditure, taxes. This is because any administration costs involved in a change are borne by traders and distributors, and not by the government service. There tends, therefore, to be an absence of administrative bottlenecks. Variations in indirect taxation affect the level of aggregate demand in a similar way to changes in direct taxation. When indirect taxes rise the population has less income to spend on other items once it has purchased the items which have been taxed. When rates fall it has more income left to spend on other items once it has purchased the taxed items. There is, of course, always the argument that consumers need not buy goods which have indirect taxes upon them. While this is true, the Chancellor does tend to choose goods with a high level of price inelasticity of demand – consumers, on the whole still buying the good despite its tax (price) increase.

The reaction of the population to tax rates is an important and topical consideration. While almost everyone who pays tax would like to pay less (presumably while enjoying the same level of services!), debates over tax rates concentrate less upon a *reduction* of tax than they do on the distribution of the tax burden between direct taxes (such as income tax) or indirect taxes (such as value added tax, VAT). On the one hand, those of Socialist leaning claim that direct taxes are preferable since they take a higher proportion of a rich man's income than they do of a poor man's income. The rich, having more to spend, presumably find the indirect tax burden easier to bear than the poor. On the other hand are those (usually of free-enterprise leanings) who argue for higher indirect and lower direct taxation. This argument centres around the disincentive effect of high levels of income tax, especially upon higher and middle management, private investors and dynamic firms. The argument is an inconclusive one since no one can furnish proof that high levels of direct taxation do adversely affect output. In the final analysis ideas of what is regarded as fair hold the day, and such ideas are a matter of political ideology rather than of economic theory.

After the General Election of 1979, which was won by the Conservatives precisely about the question of tax disincentives to high production, the chairman of one major company earning a salary of £106 000 per annum and other emoluments of £30 000 was left with £61 000 after tax (previously £32 000). He commented that it would make little difference to the output he achieved, but if it created a climate where people had more money in their pockets and a free choice of how to spend it there would eventually be some improvement in the effort put into the economy.

Local taxation v. taxation from the centre

The nation state is the logical unit for taxation purposes. Fiscal policy (like the Roman Emperor's privy purse) is usually arranged by the Central Government under the authority of the sovereign power, but since much of the actual expenditure is disbursed in the localities the UK has always had a strong element of local taxation. This has taken the form of 'rates', a system of taxation based upon the property in any given area. Every property is given a rateable value by a Rating Valuation Officer, and a charge is then levied on each property at a given rate in the £1 of the valuation. Presumably a well-to-do person has a large house, and a more impecunious person a smaller house, and the system has been reasonably satisfactory for many years.

More recently this rating system has proved unsatisfactory for several reasons. First, if central government is seeking to control the economy by strongly monetarist controls designed to reduce inflationary pressures it is a great nuisance if there is a large sector of the economy (the local government sector) which is insusceptible to control because it raises local taxation and refuses to abide by central government guidelines. Second a great many people, because of concessions made in the interests of relieving hardship, pay no rates at all, or only make a minimum contribution to the rates. For example young people living in the family home and sometimes earning excellent incomes pay little towards rates which are paid by the householder. For this reason the system has been changed from a rateable value system based on property to a community charge based on citizenship. The term 'poll tax' has been applied to this new charge, since it is intended to be a charge on every person (poll is an ancient word for head), although not everyone is expected to pay the full amount.

The resulting unrest has been considerable. The tax does appear to be flawed to some extent, since it does not meet some of Adam Smith's canons of taxation. It does not fall 'equally' on all, especially if ability to pay is taken into account, so that it will not be seen to be fair. The costs of collection are high and therefore the tax is less economic than the rates. The tax is not convenient for collection (for example it cannot be collected on a Pay As You Earn basis), and people who find it difficult to put away money to find the lump sum required will face difficulties. It remains to be seen whether the tax proves to be a viable system of local taxation, but the central government seems to be facing considerable difficulties in extending central fiscal policies into the localities.

Taxation is a relatively easy way of removing funds from the pockets of the public, and it is easy to compel payment of direct taxation. The tax moneys coming into the public purse are however at risk. There is always a temptation for the public to demand levels of services well above what is essential, and some calls for increased social services have been very well orchestrated. There is little point in a Government which advocates a 'managed' economy, and to that end removes money from the pockets of the public, then spending all the tax taken. Yet, if money is available in the public purse, cries for extra expenditure are difficult to resist, and it requires a will of iron to enforce sound restraints on expenditure in the public sector. The system of **cash limits**, which set strict limits beyond which expenditure would not be allowed to go, causes much unrest.

Whereas in the days of the 'managed' economy governments rarely met all their expenditure needs by taxation and were forced to balance the Budget by borrowing, today the Chancellor is in the happy position of having surplus funds, and is even able to reduce the National Debt to some extent.

8   THE DETAILED PATTERN OF TAXATION

In 1987 the detailed pattern of taxation was as shown in Table 9.4.

Table 9.4 Taxes collected in 1987

		£m.
Personal income tax		44 074
Less tax credits		3 646
		40 428
Corporation Tax (companies)		11 151
Public corporations		77
Non residents		3 945
		55 601
Social Security contributions		28 449
		84 050
Taxes on capital		3 361
Taxes on expenditure	£m.	
Beer	1 946	
Wine etc	2 283	
Tobacco	4 867	
Hydrocarbon oils	7 556	
Customs duties	1 451	
VAT	25 192	
Car tax	1 063	
Betting	835	
Road haulage	2 601	
Rates	16 648	
Other	3 538	
		67 980
Rents and other income		9 683
		£165 074 m.

(Source: *The Blue Book*, August 1988)

SELF-ASSESSMENT QUESTIONS

5 Why do we need to be taxed?

6 Explain *per capita* tax, proportional taxation and progressive taxation.

7 What are the advantages of direct taxation?

8 What are the advantages of indirect taxation?

9 How does VAT work exactly?

REVISION TEST

Answers	Questions
—	**1** What is the national income?
1 It is the aggregate net product of, and the sole source of payment for, all the factors of production.'	**2** Why is the word 'net' included in 'aggregate net product?
2 Because we use up capital assets in the course of production and these have to be replaced by new investment before we can start enjoying the wealth we have created. We cannot consume the aggregate product of the nation – only the aggregate net product (net of capital replacement).	**3** How is the national income shared up?
3 As rewards to the factors that created the wealth, but some of those incomes get taxed away to help those who were unable to supply any factors (either because they did not have any land or capital, or could not find employment for their labour power).	**4** What are the three ways of measuring national income?
4 (a) The 'national output' method in which we count up the 'value added' to wealth in the period under review; (b) the national income method in which we count up the incomes of all the citizens (c) The 'national expenditure' method in which we count up all the expenditures of all citizens (taking savings into account).	**5** Why do the three figures all come to the same result?
5 Because basically they are all the same thing. The output is valued at factor cost; the factor costs are the incomes we earn and the incomes we earn are spent on goods and services (apart from any savings – which appear in the table as 'capital formation').	**6** What is the gross domestic product; GDP?

6 It is the wealth we actually produce in our own country?

7 What is the gross national product; GNP?

---

7 It is the gross domestic product and earnings from overseas (but less transfers to foreigners).

8 What is national income?

---

8 It is GNP less sums incurred in replacing the capital consumed in producing the wealth created (i.e. replacing the depreciation of assets).

9 What are the bases of national income?

---

9 (a) The factor endowments provided by nature to the nation in various forms, minerals, land for agriculture, water, gases of the atmosphere, etc. (b) The human resources, including the enterprise shown by some people in organising production, (c) The capital assets handed on from the previous period to the present period.

10 What are the problems in calculating the national income?

---

10 (a) The need for clear definitions of the statistics collected; (b) The dangers of double counting; (c) Collection procedures; (d) The analysis of the raw data; (e) Its final published form.

11 What are the chief types of tax?

---

11 (a) Taxes on personal income (income tax, corporation tax); (b) Taxes on expenditure (VAT, petrol tax, beer, wines and spirits, car tax, betting); (c) Taxes on capital (capital gains tax, inheritance tax); (d) local taxation (community charges and rates).

12 What were Adam Smith's canons of taxation?

---

12 (a) Taxes should be equal (proportional); (b) they should be certain (not at the whim of the tax collector); (c) they should be collected conveniently (like the PAYE scheme); (d) They should be economic (collecting much more than the costs of collection).

Go over the test again until you are sure of all the answers. Then try some of the questions below.

ANSWERS

(See Self-assessment questions on pages 264 and 272.)

1 The national income is defined as the aggregate net product of, and the sole source of payment for all the factors of production. This definition goes to the root of economic thinking about any economy. Only the factors of production, land, capital and labour can create wealth (in the form of an abundance of goods and services. Not all the wealth created can be enjoyed as income – we must replace the depreciation as capital assets are worn out. Hence, the word 'net' in 'aggregate net profit'. Finally, we can enjoy the rest, and it must be shared out as rewards to factors (but whether the rewards are fair is a matter for human judgment).

2 We can calculate the national income in three ways. (a) By counting up the output (the output method) as the value added by all the enterprises in the country. (b) By counting up the incomes paid to all the citizens (the income method). (c) By counting up all the expenditure, and taking account of savings. They must all come to the same figure, since they are the same thing. Output is reached at factor cost, in other words what is paid for the output achieved. As this is the same as income, and as we can only spend (or save) what we earn, the expenditure and savings must be the same as the income. All three therefore come to the same figure. In practice they don't because of statistical errors and it is usual now to take the average of the three figures.

3 The chief difficulties in measuring national income are as follows: (a) double counting of factor incomes (as where a father gives his student son an allowance – we must not count both incomes); (b) double counting of expenditures (we only count final expenditures, not intermediate expenditures). Final expenditures are expenditures on goods and services not used up in production, i.e. consumption expenditures and investment expenditures on fixed assets and stocks and work in progress. Intermediate expenditures are things that are used up in production. They are not counted until they get to the finished state and someone definitely buys them for consumption use or as a capital asset; (c) difficulties in collection (i.e. clear definitions of the quantities required and compelling people to respond to the enquiries made); (d) difficulties in analysis and (e) in presentation.

4 There may be many reasons why some nations are rich and others poor, but the most important reason is that they have different factor endowments. Nature has provided some nations with many resources and other nations with few. She has made some resources accessible (for example close to seashores or with river access) while others are inaccessible and difficult to use. Another difference is in the skills of the people – some are sophisticated and diligent, skilful and knowledgable. Others are none of these things. The amount of enterprise shown is also a factor. For example the natural resources of the United States were the same before the settlers arrived, but the native population did not use them in the same intensive way as the settlers. They probably didn't need to anyway, but enterprise certainly affects wealth creation. Finally of course the capital assets available to a nation affect its prosperity – building up capital resources and infrastructure takes a century or two, and a fully developed economy can only take place when this has happened.

5 We need to be taxed to: (a) defend ourselves; (b) preserve law and order; (c) cater for those unable to create wealth for themselves; (d) achieve an egalitarian society by redistributing incomes where they are excessively uneven; (e) promote education, health and similar things to encourage a peaceful and just society.

6 *Per capita* tax is a tax per head – where everyone pays the same. It is regressive, falling most heavily on the poor. Proportional tax is tax levied at a percentage rate on all incomes. It thus falls equally on all, proportionately, but this does not mean that it is the most just tax. If a pensioner earning £100 a week and a millionaire on £20 000 a week pay 10 per cent in tax the millionaire has £18 000 to live on and the pensioner only £90. Progressive taxation falls most heavily on the rich, and is the fairest tax, so long as it is not so heavy that the rich person deems it unfair and emigrates to escape the tax burden.

7 Direct taxation falls directly on the person Parliament has intended to tax. It cannot be avoided and is therefore presumably fair (if Parliament has been behaving in a proper manner).

8 Indirect taxation falls on the taxpayer at the point of consumption and is usually levied on non-essential items. As such those who enjoy the items taxed must pay for their pleasures. Those who choose not to enjoy the taxed items can avoid the tax. Thus taxes on the 'poor man's luxuries', beer, tobacco, betting and (these days) personal transport have always raised good revenues because people hesitate to give them up. Demand is inelastic, and when imposing taxes it is always best to impose them on goods or services the demand for which is inelastic.

9 VAT works in the following way. The tax is imposed at every point where one person supplies goods to another. The supplier collects the tax, known as output tax because it is imposed on the supplier's outputs. For the person buying the good the tax is input tax. When this person in turn sells the goods (to which value has been added in the manufacturing, wholesaling or retailing process) tax will be added again, and will be the trader's output tax. The trader is now liable to Customs and Excise for the output tax collected, less the input tax paid earlier. In effect the tax paid over is the tax on the value added by each particular trader. The only person paying tax is the final consumer, but the tax is collected from all those in the chain of production, as a tax on the value they have added.

QUESTIONS ON CHAPTER 9

1 What are the three broad identities used to obtain a figure for national income? Explain how each is measured.

(Institute of Marketing)

2 Describe and explain the measurement of national income. Is it a reliable measure of the standard of living?

(Association of Business Executives)

3 a) Define the concept of national income and outline the ways in which it is calculated.
b) What is the effect of unrecorded employment and 'Do-it-Yourself' activities on the calculation of national income?

(Association of Business Executives)

4 By reference to any one country, examine the major objectives of its taxation policy.

(Institute of Commercial Management)

5 a) How does the economist define 'investment' for national income purposes?
b) Outline the major factors determining the level of investment.

(Institute of Commercial Management)

6 An individual's income may rise relative to other individual's incomes or rise as part of a general increase in the income level of the community. Discuss whether the effect of the individual's income increase on his consumption is likely to be different in the two cases.

(Institute of Marketing)

7 Explain what value added is and show how in a closed economy with no government the sum of the value added (GDP) equals the sum of factor incomes (GDI) equals the total of final expenditure (GDE).

(Institute of Marketing)

8 Analyse the main purposes of national income calculation.

(Institute of Commercial Management)

9 'The community charge can be justified on the grounds that taxation should fall equally on those that can afford to pay, and the rating system is manifestly inequitable.' Discuss this statement.

TIPS FOR STUDENT: A SPECIMEN ANSWER TO QUESTION 7

Value added is the increase of value that is experienced by any product that takes part in the production process – viewed as the change from raw materials to a finished product finally put into the consumer's hands. Thus the value added may be an actual improvement on the natural product or merely a relocation to bring the product over the gaps that separate it from the consumer, i.e. the time gaps (warehousing and storage) or the geographical gaps (transport and distribution). In a closed economy (that is one without foreign trade) and with no government (one without any redistribution of incomes by the tax system) the gross domestic product (GDP) must be the same as the gross domestic income (GDI) and the gross domestic expenditure (GDE). The reason is that gross domestic product is valued at factor cost, in other words the value added to goods is priced at what we have to pay the factors (in their human form as landlords, owners of capital and workers). Therefore the GDP must be the same as GDI, because we are valuing GDP at the value of GDI. Since GDE, the expenditure of the nation, is made up of all the expenditures of the nation + the gross capital formation (i.e. savings) this too must be the same as GDI, because all our income is either spent or saved. So, in theory at least GDP = GDI = GDE. In practice they don't quite agree because of all the difficulties encountered in collecting the statistics, but we take the average of the three as the correct figure for each set of statistics.

PART 4: **Macro-economics – the study of the whole economy**

10 The background to practical macro-economics

1 INTRODUCTION TO MACRO-ECONOMICS

Macro-economics is that part of the subject of economics which deals with the broad aggregates of the economy, national output, national income, national expenditure, the balance of payments, etc. As with other branches of the subject scientific method is applied to the study of the national economy in its real-world situation, to attempt to discover how the economy works, and to build up theories which will help in its control and management. Scientific method demands the following stages in building up theories about any aspect of the economy:

1 a definition of the feature to be studied so that we can know exactly what we are studying and can measure it with accuracy,
2 an hypothesis, that is an untested statement which attempts to explain a situation, and predict what will happen under varying circumstances,
3 testing of the hypothesis to see if it predicts results which are consistent with facts as we measure them.

In building up a workable body of knowledge economists suffer the misfortune of being 'social' rather than 'pure' scientists. Social science, as the name suggests, deals primarily with social rather than physical organisms; at the centre of our studies is man and his institutions. One of the problems with mankind is the degree to which his actions are unpredictable. It is possible to argue that, like other phenomena, men respond to the law of large numbers – that extremes cancel each other out and this makes group action more predictable than individual action. While this is so it is also true that the economic actions of individuals are not of equal significance; it takes a relatively small number of trade unionists in some key industries to cripple an economy, and the actions of a few military and political leaders can cause a world-wide energy shortage. It took only one Frank Whittle to develop the jet engine, and only one Alexander Graham Bell to put the 'hot line' through to Moscow.

Of greater disadvantage to the practical economist is the lack of control mechanisms when theories are put to the test. If a chemist wishes to ascertain whether a chemical stimulates the growth of, say, wheat, he might take 500 plants to which he adds the chemical and 500 plants to which he does not add the chemical. In all other respects the conditions in which the plants are kept will be identical. If the first 500 plants then perform significantly better than the second 500, it is reasonable to assume that the chemical is responsible for the beneficial effects.

An economist though, has to operate without the benefit of such precise controls. It is not possible to arrange for a duplicate society in order to find out what might have happened had certain economic policies *not* been applied. It is no real substitute to test ideas in different countries or regions, since there are national and regional differences, and in any case many of the most important economic ideas only work effectively at international or national level. The Chancellor of the Exchequer may *believe* that a reduction in the money supply has brought about a fall in the rate of inflation but he has no way of *proving* that this is the case, either to himself or to others. This has implications for the *next* period of inflation. If a tight monetary policy appeared to be successful on a previous occasion it could be used again, but it might prove particularly inappropriate if the new bout of inflation was due to a lack of investment caused by a shortage of funds for borrowing.

These are some of the practical difficulties which beset those who try to advise governments about the management of the economy. Another is that in a free society the government may propose but the general public disposes. If the Chancellor tries to raise revenue by a tax on smoking we may give up cigarettes; if he cuts the money supply we may all dis-save to leave the economy where it was before. We may refuse to invest in new industries even if he introduces capital allowances to encourage investment. The general public is more fully informed than the government on tax matters for as soon as the government announces its policy we know what it is up to. The economists advising the Treasury can never know what *we* will do about the taxes the Treasury imposes.

Macro-economics has been defined as the study of the whole, or of the aggregate, of a national economy. The few points raised above suggest that the application of economic theory to the aggregate level is a process subject to a reasonably high degree of uncertainty. No one can be absolutely sure what the outcome of a particular macro-economic policy will be (and this applies to the authors of books on Economics!). There is though, in practical terms, every reason for the study of macro-economics. That a point cannot be made 100 per cent clear ought not to detract from the achievement of a highly probable prediction. Business itself is founded upon the principle of exploiting uninsurable risk (and living with the consequences of such exploitation), and those who operate businesses ought to appreciate what is *likely* to happen within the national and international economy in order that they can reduce the risk element in their own businesses.

2 GOVERNMENT ECONOMIC POLICY AND MACRO-ECONOMIC THEORY

Macro-economics in a modern economy is to a considerable degree a study of government economics. Central and local governments play such a significant role in the formation and application of economic policies that it has become essential for businessmen to appreciate the bases of government economic policy.

At any given time government economic policy owes much to past economists and any appreciation of how it came into being involves a brief consideration of the history of applied economics. This also serves the useful purpose of demonstrating to sceptics how 'practical' men really are affected in their everyday lives by ideas emanating from the 'despised' theoreticians.

From the seventeenth to the twentieth centuries there have been three major schools of economic thought in the UK: mercantilism, classical economics and Keynesian economics. There is room for debate as to the exact period of influence of each, and it would be wrong to assume that there was no development within each school while it operated. The existence of this mainstream of economic thought should not suggest that there were (or are) 'blocks' of economists with identical ideas; it has also never precluded the existence and influence (though diminished) of those outside the mainstream.

Each of the three groups brought forward its ideas in response to the pressing practical issues of their day, and the policies which followed from their ideas were of the utmost importance for the business community. The following is a *brief* account of the development of macro-economic theory from the time of the mercantilists. In particular the way in which real problems gave rise to new explanations and policies is stressed, as are the very real implications of these developing policies for the business (and therefore ultimately the whole) community.

3 THE MERCANTILISTS

The group of statesmen and philosophers known as the 'mercantilists' had one preoccupation – national power. They were eager to explain *how* it was that nations became wealthy and powerful, in order that they could take action which would ensure that *their* nation became so. Their main concern in relation to economic policy was with the balance of payments. They believed that nations became powerful by accumulating precious metals. The reasoning behind such a belief was that supplies of precious metals allowed States to command military forces; allowed an expansion of the money supply (precious metals were almost the only circulating medium) necessary for an expanding economy; and in the process of accumulation the drain on the supplies held by rival nations had the effect of diminishing their power.

The message was clear: in the national interest there should be the maximum accumulation of gold and silver. This should be achieved by selling more abroad than was purchased, the balance being taken in precious metal. A desirable spin-off from the collection of precious metal in this way was that a surplus of exports over imports increased domestic aggregate demand. Even today Chancellors often refer to an 'export-led boom'. A strong export trade creates work for home industries.

Traders had, therefore, very much of a vested interest in mercantilism – it justified their exploitation of overseas markets and helped to expand the home market at the same time.

The operation of a state along mercantilist lines had great implications for the business community within that state. Governments in the UK, being convinced of the value of an export surplus and desirous of increasing national power, pursued a number of polices directed at promoting these ends.

One of the lines of attack was to develop and protect home industry. The UK passed the Corn Laws designed to protect agriculture. Only when the price of wheat was very high could imports afford to pay the (reducing) duty, and enter the country. In France, Colbert succeeded in convincing the establishment that manufacturing industry should be subsidised by the State. In one important respect such legislation as the Corn Laws operated against the interests of traders – it succeeded in driving up the cost of food and with this the demands made by workers for higher wages.

Low labour costs were essential to the other main line of government policy: the stimulation of an export trade. If wages could be held down then this did much to limit costs in total and helped in the competition against foreign rivals. Government also felt that the nation's best interests were served by a number of monopolistic trading companies such as the Hudson Bay Company and the East India Company. Such organisations had the strength of arms to defeat the foreign trader in what were eventually the colonies, and thereafter to regulate trade so that the UK was the main beneficiary.

Consistent with mercantilist policy, but not solely inspired by it, were the Navigation Acts (1651–96). The main concern of these was to ensure that goods to and from the colonies went in British ships. This swelled the size of the merchant fleet and provided trained seamen and potential warships, while at the same time undermining the main rival, the Dutch. It also had the effect of increasing invisible export earnings.

The economic climate in which mercantilism developed and operated was one of very slow growth. Contemporaries felt that there was a fixed volume of trade and that nations were competing with each other for that trade. They also believed that trade rather than manufacture was the real source of national wealth. Rapid economic growth in the latter part of the eighteenth century was to render this approach obsolete and bring such pressure to bear on Central Government that they were forced to accept an alternative explanation of how national prosperity could be achieved. This alternative explanation formed a part of what Keynes called 'classical economics'.

SELF-ASSESSMENT QUESTIONS

1 Why is it difficult to be scientific when attempting to experiment with the economy?

2 What is meant by 'the broad aggregates of the economy'?

3 What were the Navigation Acts?

4 Explain 'mercantilism'.

4 CLASSICAL ECONOMICS

Mercantilism worked well for traders and for those placed in positions of privilege by the system – so well that they fought hard to defend it. There were growing numbers of others, particularly manufacturers, who saw mercantilism as a check upon their development. They found a spokesman in Adam Smith, famous for his book *An Inquiry into the Nature and Causes of the Wealth of Nations*. He is often referred to as the first 'modern economist'.

Most of Adam Smith's work was concerned with what is now termed micro-economics (see page 57), but some of it was of the greatest importance in influencing the overall view of the economy for over 140 years. Smith and those who followed him (particularly Ricardo and John Stuart Mill) were aware that the pace of economic activity was quickening. They were especially concerned with an explanation of how the material wealth of an economy grew, and they were convinced that investment in capital equipment provided the answer.

They were equally convinced that State regulation was not the best way to achieve efficient capital accumulation and utilisation. Smith is famous for establishing the idea of *'laissez-faire'*. The words mean 'leave (people) to do their own thing' and amounted to a call for less State regulation and greater freedom for the individual to pursue business activity in his own way. In the free-enterprise society, Smith argued, individuals in pursuit of their own best interest become involved in activity which generates the maximum benefit for the State. Regulation was therefore unnecessary.

Not everyone supported this view. There were many – workers, merchants, even economists – who, through conviction or merely self interest, opposed the capitalist idea. The most difficult obstacle which the 'classicals' had to overcome was how to explain to supporters and opposition alike how a vastly increased output would be disposed of. Thomas Malthus (more famous perhaps for his Theory of Population) was not a lone voice when he suggested that capital investment raised society's ability to produce above its capacity to consume. He even suggested that the body of landowners who produced no tangible goods but were to the fore in consumption were providing a valuable service to the State!

It was David Ricardo who provided an acceptable explanation; an explanation which had both logical appeal and a remarkably long life. Ricardo felt that it was possible to have oversupply of some commodities, but this oversupply would only be of a temporary nature. A *particular* commodity might be in oversupply due to a change in fashion, in taxation, the threat of war, etc., but this would not persist for long. If people cut their purchases of one item they would expand the purchase of others. The machinery and men made idle by the initial change would be employed in meeting the extra demand for other products. Oversupply and unemployment would only be of a temporary nature.

The idea of general unemployment because of oversupply of a wide range of commodities was rejected as impossible. Ricardo used what has become known as 'Say's Law of Markets' to prove that there would always be full employment (with the exception of temporary unemployment mentioned above). Say's Law states approximately that 'supply creates its own demand'. It is attributed to the French economist Jean B. Say, who developed it in the context of the, largely barter, French economy. The law really means that production, which results in a commodity being placed upon the market, also gives rise to the income with which it can be bought. In other words, the returns to the factors of production, wages, rent, interest and profit paid to produce the total output of goods, are just sufficient to purchase the total goods produced. More production means more factor payments and an increased ability to purchase.

It was suggested that profit earners might not spend their share of the generated incomes, but that they might save it instead. Ricardo's reply was that those taking profits did so in order to make investment – they spent their accumulations upon buildings, machinery, etc. Even where profit-takers did not make direct investments in capital equipment and buildings they still would lend their money to those who did. The rate of interest would ensure this. Ricardo and the later classicals (sometimes termed 'neo-classicals') had great belief in the rate of interest. They felt that it regulated the supply of and the demand for loanable funds. At high rates those who had income would save and invest more, at low rates they would save and invest less. Those who demanded funds had the opposite reaction to the interest rate – at higher rates they took less money, at lower rates more. The rate of interest, like any price for any commodity, ensured an eqilibrium between supply (savings) and demand (investment). There could therefore be no *general* oversupply and no *general* unemployment. The natural tendency of the economy according to classical economists was to operate at the level of the full employment.

Ricardo had, in reality, only partially explained why full occupation of factors would be the norm. He had suggested that there would be no oversupply of goods or money but had only assumed that this would mean no oversupply of factors. Later 'classical' and 'neo-clasical' writers closed this loophole. In order to do so they utilised two pieces of theory which had been developed in the 'micro' field: the Law of Diminishing Returns and the Theory of Marginal Productivity. (These were explained in greater detail in Chapters 2 and 7).

Briefly, the Law of Diminishing Returns states that the more of a particular factor (say labour) which is, beyond a certain point, applied to a fixed quantity of another factor (say capital), the smaller will be the additions to the total output brought about by the extra units of labour. In other words, a smaller output will be added by each extra labour unit. What this means is that once a certain point is passed, the average output of labour must fall; but, of greater significance, the marginal output will fall even faster.

The Theory of Marginal Productivity suggests that each unit of a factor of production will be paid the value of its marginal product, i.e. what the *marginal physical product* will sell for in the appropriate market – the *marginal revenue product*. This means that the last unit employed will receive only an amount related to what its output sells for.

The two concepts combined imply that the greater the level of employment (particularly, but not exclusively, of labour) the smaller would be the output of the last unit; and that the last unit employed would receive only the (diminished) value of this product. Because the market for factors was thought of as competitive, what the last unit employed received, all the previous units also received. The more units (men) employed, the less the marginal output and the smaller the average remuneration (wage).

Using this approach, classicals could always guarantee full, or near-full, employment of labour. Those unemployed could always offer to work for less than the going wage rate; such action would allow the employment of more units since employers could afford labour even though the marginal output was diminishing. This gave rise to the claim, often misunderstood, that there was no involuntary unemployment – those who wanted to work could always secure work by asking less for their services. Those who were not prepared to work for less were voluntarily unemployed and as such hardly counted as unemployed at all!

It is not surprising that economists and politicians in a free-enterprise society found the above explanation of the economy appealing. If there was automatic clearing of all markets – no oversupply of goods, money, or factors – then there was no real need for government intervention to regulate the level of demand, etc. So convinced were economists' contemporaries of the value of the free market that they went even further and strongly advised against any government interference in the economy, on the grounds that such interference would be destabilising – it would upset the *automatic* mechanisms in operation. This view was adhered to even though the existence of the trade cycle was recognised.

5   THE TRADE CYCLE

Marx was one of the first economists to become concerned with the uneven rate of economic activity in industrial societies. He identified a regular pattern of uneven production which eventually became known as the trade cycle (meaning the cycle of production). Other economists soon took up the idea and towards the end of the nineteenth century it was believed that the trade cycle was well understood. Briefly, it was thought to operate as follows. The economy might be depressed – wages, prices, production and employment would be low, unemployment, for example, might be 9-10 per cent. There would then be a burst of expansion and employment, prices, wages, profits and output would rise; the rate of unemployment might be as low as 2 per cent. A peak would be reached, and perhaps kept for a short period before the downswing began – a fall back towards the depressed starting point. The whole cycle was believed to take about eight to ten years, and these short-term cycles were superimposed upon a rising trend, each peak being higher than the last.

Many explanations were advanced for the existence of trade cycles. One was by W.S. Jevons, who discovered a high degree of correlation between the sunspot cycle and the trade cycle. He felt that sunspots affected weather, weather affected agriculture and agriculture affected the whole economy. Some might feel this to be a prime example of spurious correlation; contemporaries certainly preferred an explanation which had an industrial, rather than an agricultural, bias – a reasonable enough preference in view of the declining importance of agriculture. Eventually, most economists agreed that trade cycles were largely caused by the investment cycle, often known as the 'accelerator'.

6   THE ACCELERATOR

The accelerator links relatively small percentage changes in purchases of consumer goods to large percentage changes in the demand for capital goods. Suppose that a firm sells £100 000 worth of plastic soldiers every year and that to do so it requires £50 000 worth of machinery. Every year 10 per cent of this machinery wears out and the capital goods industry is therefore required to supply £5000 worth of replacements. Imagine that for some reason the demand for plastic soldiers rises by 10 per cent one year. In order to produce enough to meet the extra demand the firm requires an extra input of capital goods amounting to 10 per cent of its existing stock – £5000 worth. In the year in question then, the capital goods industry faces a demand for its products which has doubled – the replacement £5000 *plus* an extra £5000 worth of completely new investment. A rise of 10 per cent in demand for plastic soldiers has brought about an *accelerated* rise in demand for capital goods of 100 per cent.

In reality, of course, there could be spare capacity in the capital goods industry, or a mere refusal to expand output fully which will render the effect of the accelerator much less than in an extreme example; but the effect will still be there. Further, once the accelerator has brought about expansion of the capital goods sector it also plays a large part in its contraction because it works in reverse: a small fall in the demand for consumer goods causing a larger fall in the demand for capital goods. Even if there is no change in the demand for plastic soldiers, our firm is going to require no more than 10 per cent of its stock of machinery the year following the expansion, i.e. it requires only £5500 worth of replacements. This represents a 45 per cent fall in demand for the enlarged capital goods industry in the following year.

7   THE BREAKDOWN OF CLASSICAL ECONOMICS

The attraction of such an explanation of cyclical activity was that though the downturn was inevitable, so was the upturn and the following boom. Left alone, the cycle would *automatically* play itself out, and any attempt to change the way in which the cycle operated might result in a prolonged, rather than a reduced, period of slump.

When very low rates of activity did persist for relatively long periods such as in the 1920s and 30s, the response of the majority of economists, politicians and businessmen was to assume that some factor or factors must be interfering with the operation of the automatic mechanism which always returned the economy to full employment. Eventually, the union movement became the scapegoat: among its aims the prevention of the reduction of wage rates ranked high and it was blamed for keeping rates of pay above the 'natural' level which would guarantee full employment. It is important to recognise the strength of this idea – the followers of Ricardo had argued that for more men to be in employment the average wage would have to fall.

In the early years of the twentieth century employers and government were so convinced that this approach was correct that they were prepared to become involved in the conflict of the General Strike. This should not come as a surprise. When theories cease to be adequate explanations of what is happening in the real world, one of the lines of action open to those who support such theories is to find some distorting or inhibiting factor, which they can then remove. It is much less likely that an alternative explanation will be found which proves acceptable to those in power.

During the period of mass unemployment in the 1920s and 30s the consistent approach of the government and their economic advisers was to make the 'classical' system work. They attempted to reduce wage levels in the hope that such a move would stimulate demand for products which could then be sold at a lower price. They kept interest rates low hoping to stimulate investment, and they cut out subsidies to agriculture, coalmining, etc., and reduced National Insurance benefits in order to maintain the balanced budget – the government by its own spending must not disturb the automatic processes operating in the economy.

The development of classical economic thought had provided a framework, acceptable to businessmen and to government, within which business (and particularly industrial) expansion had a virtually free hand. Cheap food kept British costs low and free trade meant access to a wide range of markets for British goods. Though the classical explanation was increasingly inadequate as the twentieth century progressed, few were inclined to search for an alternative theory given its seemingly satisfactory past record. The most outstanding of the dissenters was **John Maynard Keynes**, and the next chaper shows how his work revolutionised economics and the role of government.

SELF-ASSESSMENT QUESTIONS

5 What was the doctrine of *laissez-faire*?

6 What is the accelerator?

7 Why did the 'classical economics' of the nineteenth century break down in the twentieth century?

REVISION TEST

Answers	Questions
	1 What is macro-economics?
1 That part of the subject of economics which deals with broad aggregates.	**2** Why is the study of social science particularly difficult?
2 There are no efficient control mechanisms.	**3** Why does the study of modern macro-economics involve governments?
3 Because governments are responsible for taking a massive role in the planning and application of economic policy.	**4** The four main schools of modern economics have been?

4 Mercantilists, classicals, Keynesians and monetarists (neo-classicals).	**5** What were mercantilists concerned with amassing?
5 Precious metals.	**6** For what reason?
6 To promote national power.	**7** What did such a policy involve?
7 A great deal of government regulation of trade.	**8** Why did Adam Smith dislike this?
8 He felt that free enterprise was more efficient.	**9** What did he suggest instead?
9 That individuals should be left to pursue their own best interests.	**10** Why did the classical system not envisage persistent unemployment?

10 Because of the operation of 'Say's law' and the belief that by offering their servicecs for less, labourers could always secure employment.

Go over the test until you are sure of the answers. Then try to answer the questions below.

ANSWERS

(See Self-assessment questions on pages 285 and 290.)

1 The difficulty is that in dealing with social matters (which affect people) we cannot use control groups to test the validity of our experiments. We cannot have one group that pays high rates of interest and another that only pays low rates. We cannot impose taxes on one group and not on another. We cannot tell one group what we are doing and leave the others in the dark, to see whether the results achieved vary. All attempts to manage the economy have to be conducted under a searchlight of media attention.

2 The broad aggregates of the economy are the overall figures of production, income, expenditure, exports and imports, etc. We do not need the figures for individual citizens or firms, we need the figures for all citizens and all firms. The difficulties of collecting and verifying such statistics are enormous, and budgeting forward from the figures to envisage future growth etc., is a major economic exercise.

3 The Navigation Acts were a series of measures in the latter half of the seventeenth century and effective throughout most of the eighteenth century to tie UK trade to the use of British shipping. This ensured a strong merchant marine which could be used both to train sailors and to support military action in wartime. It also made colonies more dependent on the mother country, since their exports and imports had to be moved in British ships.

4 Mercantilism was a school of economic thought which linked economic development to the growth of the nation state. They believed that nations became powerful by accumulating precious metals, obtained as a result of exports exceeding imports, so that foreign countries had to make up the balance in gold or silver. The strong export trade kept home industries busy and encouraged further investment in manufacturing industry. The weaknesses of mercantilism was that it saw trade as the chief source of wealth and did not give sufficient credit to manufacturing and primary production. As the Industrial Revolution gathered pace after 1760 mercantilism gave way to classical economics, and controls yielded to *laissez-faire*.

5 The doctrine of *laissez-faire* held that people who were left free to operate without control by a bureaucracy, would labour to improve their own lot, and in the process would incidentally enrich the whole nation. The words actually mean 'let (them) alone to do (their own thing)'. It ushered in a period of uncontrolled capitalism which was highly beneficial to the entrepreneurs and the nation as a whole but unsatisfactory for many individuals. Thus social costs were heaped upon the public at large (accidents, air pollution, water pollution, diseases like silicosis, etc.). Wages were held down by laws to prevent trade unionism (the Combination Acts) and child labour was widespread.

6 An accelerator is any injection of consumer demand into an economy which has a more than proportional effect on the demand for capital goods. Thus if an industry retools every ten years it will be of such a size that one tenth of the total capital assets are produced each year. If there is a 10 per cent rise in consumer demand for the industry's products this will call for an extra 10 per cent of capital goods – which means the capital goods industry will double in a year.

7 Classical economics broke down in the first half of the twentieth century when it became clear that we could not just sit around and wait for an automatic mechanism to restore the economy. Whatever had been the nature of the automatic mechanism, and being on the gold standard may have been one influence at work, it manifestly was not operating to end the prolonged depression between the wars. The solution was to be found by Keynesian policies of managed prosperity, but before these could really be tested an older-fashioned cure developed – re-armament in the face of the rising power of Nazi Germany. Keynesian policies had to wait until after 1945 for a full testing period in the management of prosperity.

QUESTIONS ON CHAPTER 10

1 A Chancellor proposes to reduce the consumption of alcohol by imposing a heavy tax on beer, wine and whisky. Consider the various possible outcomes to such a policy.

2 What do you think are the likely effects of raising income tax to 40 per cent on earned income and 80 per cent on unearned income?

3 'In the mercantilist era trade followed the flag.' Explain.

4 'The true business of Government is the saving of candle-ends.' Comment on this attitude as far as macro-economics is concerned.

5 Explain why an economist is at a disadvantage compared with other scientists when carrying out experiments in the economic effects of various policies.

TIPS FOR STUDENTS: A SPECIMEN ANSWER TO QUESTION 5

The disadvantage that economists suffer is that they are social scientists, not 'pure' scientists. In pure science we do not carry out experiments without having a control group on which no experiment is being carried out. Thus if we were testing the effect of a new type of fertilizer on the growth of cabbages we should grow two plots of cabbages under exactly identical conditions, except that one group received the fertilizer and the other group did not. In economics we cannot do this sort of thing. We might think that it would be desirable to encourage the birth-rate by offering expectant mothers £5000 per live birth, but we could not offer it to one half of the population only and leave the other half as a control group to establish whether the money did improve the birth rate or not. We might think that a cut in the income tax by 50 per cent would increase enterprise, but we could not carry out a controlled exercise in which some of the nation enjoyed a tax cut – to test the effect on enterprise in that area – while the rest of the country remained with taxes at the original level.

What economists can do in certain circumstances is build up a mathematical model of the economy and then introduce changes in the model by asking 'What if' questions. Thus if our model represents accurately the various situations that exist in the real world we might be able to see what would happen if, for example, inflation increased by 2½, 5, 7½ or 10 per cent. The resulting information might be very useful, but it is a very difficult and time consuming job developing a satisfactory model. It is very difficult to predict the likely reactions of a large and sophisticated population to the policies proposed by economists, and their ability to evade any proposals made is legendary. One millionaire was reported as listening to the Budget Speech on the radio in his London hotel bedroom, flying home to Jersey that night, sitting up all night with a wet towel round his head to cool his teeming brain and flying back next day with a detailed plan to avoid the impact of every tax change proposed.

11 Keynesian economics

1 KEYNES' ATTACK ON THE 'CLASSICALS'

Keynes commenced his attack on the classical explanation of the economic system with a reappraisal of the role of the rate of interest. As suggested in Chapter 10, the rate of interest had a simple, but vital, role to play in the classical model. If the total of earnings was all to be spent savings must be made to equal investment and this was the task of the rate of interest. It was suggested that savings took place for reward – that savers abstained from consumption in order to take advantage of a return: the rate of interest paid. If the rate of interest rose, then more abstention from consumption took place as savers responded to the increased rewards. Borrowers, on the other hand, adjusted downwards their demand for loanable funds when interest rates rose. The rate of interest was therefore seen as a sensitive mechanism for regulating both the demand for, and supply of, loanable funds – it was responsible for bringing about an equilibrium between savings and investment. Fig. 11.1 illustrates this process.

The classical economists' view of the role of money was one which reinforced their attitude to the rate of interest. The feeling was that money was a medium of exchange – it was required because it gave command over goods and services but had no value in itself. Those who hoarded (stored but did not use) funds were regarded as irrational, especially when a reward for non-consumption in the form of the rate of interest was being offered.

Keynes' view of money was quite different. He agreed with classical economists that the stock of money held by the community at any time would depend upon their everyday trading needs (**the transactions motive**) and on provision for occurrences which could not be foreseen (**the precautionary motive**). But Keynes suggested one further reason why money might be held, even where this meant that a return (the rate of interest) would have to be sacrificed. This reason he termed **the speculative motive** for holding money, and its existence was due to the possibility of making future gains (or avoiding future losses) through the simple

Fig. 11.1 *Loanable funds and the rate of interest*

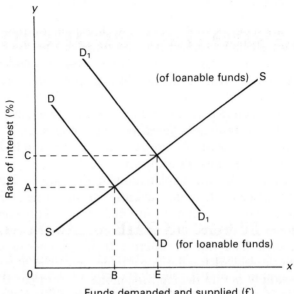

Notes

1 Imagine a situation where the demand for loanable funds is shown by curve DD and the supply of loanable funds by the curve SS. The equilibrium rate of interest is therefore A per cent.

2 Should the demand for loanable funds rise – shown by the new demand curve D_1D_1 – this will force up the rate of interest to C and bring forward extra lending in pursuit of the higher rate of interest.

3 The rate of interest always adjusts to settle at that level where those who wish to lend funds are lending the quantity they wish to lend *at the going rate*, and those who wish to borrow are borrowing just the quantity they wish to borrow *at the going rate*.

expedient of holding cash. The point depended upon the inverse relationship between interest rates and the value of paper assets. The following example should convey the essentials of Keynes' reasoning.

Suppose that a 7 per cent Consol (a negotiable perpetual bond) has been issued at par value of £100. This means that the interest rate on the bond is 7 per cent. Subsequently the rate of interest rises to 14 per cent on *new* debt of similar quality. This now means that the holder of the bond, if he were to part with his asset, would suffer a loss of 50 per cent of his capital outlay. No rational person would pay £100 for a 7 per cent bond when £50 on a 14 per cent bond gives the same actual return: £7 per annum. On this basis it became *rational* rather than irrational to hoard in circumstances when interest rates were low and expected to rise. Once a rational bssis for hoarding was established the assumption that all income would be spent lost its validity: it was no longer possible to claim, as classical economists did, that self-adjustment to levels of full employment would take place. Persistent hoarding could cause an underemployed economy to stagnate with income levels much lower than the economy's true potential.

2 KEYNES' ALTERNATIVE EXPLANATION OF THE ECONOMIC SYSTEM

There had been many critics of the classical explanation of an economic system; Keynes himself had attacked it many times in the 20 years leading up to 1936. However, prior to the *General Theory of Employment, Interest and Money*, published in that year, a major obstacle prevented critics making a serious impact. This obstacle was the lack of a reasoned *alternative* explanation of how an economy functions. In the 'general theory' Keynes set himself the task, not only of destroying long-believed portions of classical theory, but also of replacing defunct theory with a more realistic explanation of his own. That he succeeded in this task is now well known.

Having destroyed the classical explanation of the rate of interest, Keynes had to construct a replacement to link savings with investment. He did this by extending his interpretation of money outlined above. This commences with the view that money is desired for speculative as well as transaction and precautionary reasons. The rate of interest then becomes *a reward for not hoarding* rather than a reward for not consuming, and it is determined by the interaction of the supply of and demand for money – as opposed to the supply of and demand for loanable funds. The supply of money (currency and bank credit) is largely in the control of the government, but it is the public at large who determine what the demand for money will be. At any one time all the money in existence will be held by someone, but the important question is: do they wish to continue holding it? It might be that a proportion of those holding money would, in the near future, like to exchange their money for income-yielding assets. What is it, therefore, which will determine the public's demand for money, i.e. what can influence the community to exchange money for income-yielding assets?

Keynes felt that the public's demand for money depended upon two factors: (a) the level of aggregate income and (b) the rate of interest. He maintained that as the community's income rose so would its need to hold more money for transactions and precautionary reasons. He also maintained that the speculative motive for holding money would depend primarily upon the rate of interest and *the view the community took of the future movement of the rate of interest*.

If the community expected future rates of interest to rise they were likely to hoard as a hedge against capital loss; if they expected future rates to fall then dis-hoarding would be logical, in order to take advantage of capital gains. We have already seen that a 7 per cent bond valued at £100 falls to £50 if the rate of interest rises to 14 per cent. Clearly, if the rate of interest falls to 3½ per cent it will be worth £200. Therefore, when interest rates were low, hoarding would be much more likely than when they were high (on the basis that low rates can be expected to rise).

This rather startling conclusion was directly the opposite of what the classical economists would have forecast, since at low rates more people would – they believed – carry on consuming. Keynes termed the tendency of the community to hold hoarded funds when interest rates were low the 'liquidity trap'. He felt that the 'trap' would apply to institutions as well as private individuals. Banks are in the business of borrowing from the public but they normally do not hold large idle balances (hoarding); they lend to those who wish to borrow. When the economy is depressed, though, they may find their lending potential diminished by a lack of eligible borrowers. There is one way out, however: lend to the government at a secure rate of return. This seemingly attractive solution to the banks' problem of idle balances becomes much less attractive when the possibility of significant capital losses arises: banks, like individuals, may hoard for speculative purposes.

The essence of the mechanics of the Keynesian interpretation can be conveyed with an example. Imagine an increase in the supply of money (perhaps by government buying back securities). How can an equilibrium between the (increased) supply of money and the demand for money be arrived at? Assuming that there is no change in the size of national income there is no reason to suppose that the public will extend their transactions and precautionary balances. Those who received the extra cash balances (in exchange for securities) will have among their number some who would prefer to hold income-generating assets. As demand for these assets increases their price is likely to be bid upwards – a movement which will bring a reduction in the rate of interest. As the rate of interest falls, members of society are less unwilling to hold extra money balances. In this way, the rate of interest and the supply of money interact to bring about a new equilibrium which will allow the extra money to be absorbed into the system, partly as idle balances. This was a complete reversal of the 'loanable funds' approach of the classical economists, which stressed the importance of thrift and the productivity of capital without even considering the view that money could be held for speculative purposes.

A further factor in the Keynesian view of the economy was the importance of the level of income.

The importance of the level of income

In their approach to macro-economic problems the classicals paid a great deal of attention to the rate of interest, but dealt hardly at all with the level of income. This is not surprising in view of their belief that the level of national income would automatically tend towards the maximum possible, given the level of available resources. With such a belief it became superfluous to explain what determined the level of national income. By destroying the classical approach to the rate of interest Keynes made the level of income a burning issue. If there was no guarantee that all income would be spent (and with speculative balances and the liquidity trap there wasn't) then the level of national income could fluctuate quite widely over time *and* could become stuck at an underemployment equilibrium – producing *less* than the maximum possible output.

It was Keynes' belief that the level of income was the major influence upon saving. He firmly rejected the idea that people save in order to earn interest, and instead suggested that most saving was a residual, comprised of what was left after consumption had taken place. Most people, he maintained, first of all attempted to ensure an acceptable level of consumption. If this utilised all their current income then no saving took place (indeed, it is not unusual for consumption to outstrip current income and for dis-saving to occur, or the pledging of future income). Only where income was large enough to allow acceptable consumption and some residual for saving, would saving take place. Further, he believed that as a society became more affluent its propensity to consume (see appendix to this chapter – page 309) would diminish, and consequently its propensity to save would rise. Such a development has profound implications for the level of investment required in an economy. If income levels are to be maintained in situations where consumption expenditure becomes a smaller *proportion* of total income, the expenditure gap needs to be filled by investment expenditure.

In part Keynes rehabilitated the rate of interest when dealing with the determinants of investment. He believed that businessmen would compare the expected rate of return from the life of a project with its cost. One of the important elements in the cost calculation was the rate of interest – the price of borrowing money (or the alternative return on accumulated funds of the business). However, it is important to note that stress is laid upon *expected* returns. One of Keynes' major innovations was the introduction of the role of expectations into economic theory. Crudely put, when businessmen in aggregate are optimistic they will tend to make new investment; when they are pessimistic they will not (or they will make less of it). The important question then is to ascertain what it is which generates business optimism or pessimism. Keynes himself linked the matter of business confidence to the level of income. When incomes rose more consumption took place and, stimulated by a consumer boom, businessmen became optimistic about profit potential and were eager to make new investment. Similarly, if income and consumption fell this made the business community pessimistic and less likely to make new investment.

One implication of far-reaching importance to arise from this interpretation of investment related to the necessity for increasing absolute amounts of investment as incomes rose. Because affluent societies spend a smaller *proportion* of their rising incomes on the almost automatic consumption items, a significantly *increasing proportion* of their incomes must be devoted to investment expenditure. This is necessary even to *maintain* the higher levels of income. To push incomes even higher in future times still greater quantities of investment must be made. Keynes doubted the capacity of businessmen's expectations to provide the impetus for the required amounts of new investment; he felt that the business community were often likely to sink into pessimism. When this pessimism became prolonged then a situation of underemployment equilibrium such as that from 1922 to 1938 in the UK was likely to occur. His prescription for the defeat of pessimism and the regeneration of levels of output and income was to have the Central Government make expenditures to compensate for the lack of private investment. He suggested that when economies were very depressed the schemes upon which expenditure took place were less important than the expenditure itself. Money pumped into the economy would increase the circular flow of income and generate optimism among investors. These investors would then be moved to make investment decisions themselves, which would have the effect of further increasing the level of income. Eventually, it was hoped, the new equilibrium level of income which the economy arrived at would be that at which output, income and employment were maximised.

For an equilibrium level of income to exist it is required that all income generated is expended. If this is not the case the level of income begins to alter. If less is spent than is generated (net saving) then the level of income will fall as some groups within the economy find their personal incomes reduced. If more is spent than is generated by current incomes (net investment) then personal incomes rise and so does aggregate income. Only when the total of savings is equal to the total of investment will income neither rise nor fall – it will be in equilibrium.

One of the processes by which income was expected to grow was first introduced by a contemporary of Keynes. The process was known as the **multiplier** and its origination is credited to R.F. Kahn. It had a very important role in the Keynesian system since it was the multiplier which described by how much aggregate income would have to rise in order to generate enough saving so that the total amount saved once more equalled the total amount invested.

The multiplier is explained in greater detail in the appendix to this chapter but the essentials of it can be conveyed by a simple example. Suppose that the economy is in equilibrium, i.e. the total of savings equals the total being invested. Then, investors decide to increase the amounts which they have previously invested. Obviously, the level of income of those employed in the capital goods industries will rise – extra investment expenditure will make sure of this. However, other groups within the economy will also benefit from the investment; those who work in the capital goods industries, and those who provide capital and material resources for them, will pass on a proportion of their increased incomes in the form of increased expenditures. The extra expenditure then becomes extra income for those who provide the extra goods and services supplied to those working in the capital goods industries. They in turn pass on a part of their extra incomes in the form of extra expenditure, and so the income-creating process goes on. The process only stops when the aggregate level of income has risen sufficiently to allow the population a large enough residual after consumption once more to equate the level of savings with the new (higher) level of investment. This would then be a new equilibrium point where income would neither grow nor shrink, providing that savings and investment levels did not change.

The concept of the multiplier gives a precise indication of the extent to which income must grow before the new equilibrium level of income is reached. If the new injection (investment) amounted to £100 000 and the community was accustomed to withdrawing (saving) one quarter of its incremental income, then total income would have to rise by £400 000 before enough saving had taken place to offset the original investment. Obviously this is a much simplified example and in reality the total of withdrawals is likely to be greater than savings alone (for example, leakages in purchases abroad). Furthermore the time period over which the level of income will grow may be such that there is a significant lag between the initial investment and the total income generation. Such factors tend to result in the necessity for the generation of a larger increase in income than would be the case in a simple theoretical model.

It is also of critical importance to consider which groups within the economy receive the incremental income. The marginal propensity to save of affluent groups is likely to be much greater than that of poor groups. Should the former group receive the bulk of the extra income the multiplier effect will be less than had most income gone to the latter.

Keynes, then, supplied an explanation of how an economy works which rested upon the level of aggregate income, and the manner in which it grew and shrank. He was the first to consider the movement of income in this manner, because he was the first to believe that there could be serious long-term departures from the maximum income possible: his predecessors simply did not think it worthwhile to analyse a variable which they felt did not vary!

Using variations in income he attempted to demonstrate that the total withdrawals from the circular flow of income were capable of equalling the total injections at almost any level of economic activity, i.e. at almost any level of income and employment. When withdrawals are equal to injections there can be no 'multiplier' effect, and the economy will be stable at the existing level of national income.

The significant question which Keynes now felt able to answer was why the economy would become stuck in underemployment equilibrium. The key rested in the income-generating role of investment. If businessmen were pessimistic and would not increase the net levels of investment, income would not rise. If the feelings of the business community were such that 'replacement only' investment was entered into, a relatively low level of income could be maintained for a considerable period of time. Without the stimulus of new investment there was little that could be done to push the economy to full employment/maximum output equilibrium. *There was definitely no automatic mechanism driving the economy to maximum output as the classical economists had claimed for over a hundred years.*

The reader may find it easier to follow this rather long and difficult discussion by considering it again in diagrammatic form. This can be done by turning back to Fig. 1.2 (see page 14) and re-reading the notes on how the mixed economy works, but imagining oneself in Keynes' position before the flows round the economy were clearly understood.

Flow 1 in that diagram shows the flows of factors into production. However it does not tell us anything about what proportion of the nation's endowment of factors is actually being put to work. Classical economics assumed that the natural tendency was for national output to be at a maximum, but clearly the great slump of Keynes' day proved this was not so. There could be 3 million men and women idle, not to mention much land left derelict, factories in mothballs and liquid capital lying idle because investors were not willing to invest.

What determines whether the economy is in a slump, or booming, is the extent to which the taps in Flow 2 of the diagram are open. If people are confident and demanding high levels of consumption the incomes they spend will reach the organisations and they will gather confidence and start to produce more. If they are not spending (**Tap 1** closed) but saving, prosperity will still be achieved so long as **Tap 2** is open; and the investors are building new plant and factories. However if they are pessimistic the economy (as in Keynes' day) would be in a prolonged state of depression.

The injections into the circular flow of incomes may be listed as follows:

1 consumption expenditure: i.e. expenditure by UK households on UK consumption goods and services.
2 planned investment expenditure: is expenditure by UK firms and Government organisations on UK investment goods (and on services treated as capital expenditure.
3 Government expenditure, i.e. expenditure by central and local government on UK goods and services (but not the expenditure on planned investment referred to in 2 above.
4 export expenditure, i.e. expenditure by foreign households, firms and governments on UK goods and services.
5 unplanned investment expenditure, i.e. expenditure on stocks left unsold in the hands of producers who produced speculatively in anticipation of sales but were disappointed. Sometimes called the **physical increase in stocks.**

The withdrawals (leakages) from the circular flow of incomes are:

1 savings, i.e. that part of income that households do not spend,
2 corporate savings, i.e. that part of profits which firms and companies do not distribute and do not spend on expansion projects requiring planned investment expenditures.
3 taxation, local taxation, community charges, etc. The extent to which these funds diverted from the pockets of consumers actually are withdrawals depends upon government and local government expenditures and they may in fact be over-spent.
4 import expenditures, i.e. expenditures by home households, firms and governments on foreign goods and services.

During the great depression of the 1930s the withdrawals of spending power from the circular flow of incomes exceeded the injections, and recovery could not take place. Recovery only began when President Roosevelt's team of advisers, which included Keynes, showed that to cure a depression someone who did have the power to turn on taps must step in and solve the problem. The only power that can do this is the Government. It can open up the welfare tap (**Tap 4**) and let the unemployed have increased welfare. This will open up **Tap 1**, because after their long privations the unemployed are well placed to demand goods and services. It is no good giving to the rich – because they will withdraw the money from circulation and just add it to their savings. By contrast social security payments will open up **Tap 1** and encourage sales giving producers the confidence to expand production. Even more the Government must itself offer contracts to firms to increase the social capital being created. If investment in industry is low, encourage investment in schools, colleges, the infrastructure, etc. Opening **Tap 3** will give business confidence and it will open up **Tap 2** as well. To open up **Tap 3** it may be necessary to borrow through **Tap 5**, or we can increase taxation on the rich, and like Robin Hood 'persuade' the rich to help the poor. To repeat – there is no automatic mechanism driving the economy to maximum output. If we want prosperity we must manage it. In the 30 years from 1946–74 the management of prosperity was the chief purpose, and interest, of governments.

SELF-ASSESSMENT QUESTIONS

1 Explain the transactions motive, the precautionary motive and the speculative motive for holding cash.

2 Explain Keynes' liquidity trap.

3 List the elements injecting demand into the circular flow of incomes.

4 List the leakages from the circular flow of incomes which reduce demand and discourage entrepreneurs.

3 THE PRACTICAL IMPLICATIONS OF KEYNESIAN ECONOMICS

While working upon the 'General Theory', Keynes wrote the following in a letter to George Bernard Shaw:

> I believe myself to be writing a book on economic theory which will largely revolutionise – not I suppose at once, but in the course of the next ten years – the way the world thinks about economic problems!

In fact, Keynes' expectations were more than justified: not only did his book revolutionise the way in which the non-communist world thought about economic problems, it also changed drastically the way in which attempts were made to solve those problems.

In the two decades following the end of the First World War in 1918, the majority of governments attempted to influence their economies in the following ways:

1 by reducing the levels of wages and prices;
2 by reducing government expenditure;
3 by keeping interest rates as low as possible in order to stimulate investment.

In applying such economic policies they were following tenets of economic wisdom laid down in the preceding 150 years. The extent to which they intervened in the economy at this stage was, by modern standards, small, but at the time their activities were holding actions – the ideal towards which they worked was one of less, rather than more, government involvement in the economy. They hoped that their action would re-establish the workings of the 'automatic equilibriating mechanism'.

What was the probable outcome of inter-war government economic policy? Domestic investment was certainly not likely to be encouraged by reduced government expenditure since, in the absence of compensating private expenditure, it amounted to a reduction in demand for the output of private industry. Nor was it likely that lower wages and prices would cause a greater output to be produced. When wages are cut in aggregate, those who produce the goods and services are in turn able to *spend* less – in short, consumers' demand diminishes and businessmen are likely to sell *less* rather than more. (This is assuming that wage earners have the higher propensity to consume – see the appendix to this chapter.) Diminishing consumers' demand is not calculated to stimulate the level of business investment. Once an economy is depressed it is also unlikely that a low rate of interest will stimulate investment; the liquidity trap will operate and balances will be hoarded in expectation of a future rise in interest rates. The collective effects of these policies are probably going to be the *opposite* of those intended: they will actively depress the level of economic activity. Those who have direct experience of areas with high levels of unemployment will realise what this means in terms of human deprivation.

In order to shake an economy out of prolonged depression Keynes urged that the government take a major role; that if necessary it borrow or print money in order to make public expenditure. Where the private sector was pessimistic he saw government spending as the only way to revive the level of aggregate demand and bridge the gap which had developed between total income and the level of consumption. Once income and consumption levels began to rise, he expected that optimism would return to the business community, and they would once more increase their level of new investment. He did not, though, imagine a situation of maximum output/full employment equilibrium of a persistent nature without continuing government expenditures; as societies become more affluent it can be expected that their marginal propensities to consume will diminish. This will place increasing burdens upon businessmen to step in with extra investment as incomes rise. He believed government intervention on a large scale would be a permanent feature of the modern economy.

That Keynes' prediction about the impact of his theories was correct in timing as well as in content probably resulted from the Second World War. This brought the government into close contact with all branches of the economy, and Keynes became a senior adviser to the Treasury. By 1941 the logic of his arguments had convinced those in power. From the Barlow Report of that year, governments in the UK accepted that they held overall responsibility for the level of employment of resources, particularly labour – in effect, that they were responsible for regulating the levels of national income and output. The ideas of Keynes brought the UK in the space of 35 years from an economy of private entrepreneurial activity to one dominated by central government. Keynes had provided a more reasonable explanation of the workings of the economic system than his predecessors and had shown how to manage prosperity.

The objectives of macro-economic policy

Macro-economic policies are policies which act upon the broad aggregates of the economy, national output, national expenditure, etc. Such policies will not be the same at all stages of a nation's affairs. For example in Keynes' day the problem was mass unemployment and the objectives of macro-economic policy were to achieve full employment, a more egalitarian society, sustained economic growth, etc. In the 1980s and 90s the problems are rather different and need examining from the point of view of our affairs today. Since this chapter is about Keynesian economics we will examine the management of prosperity in the years after the Second World War, when Keynes' ideas were implemented in a sustained period of economic experiment. We can best study these in diagrammatic form, from the UK's point of view. Irish students will forgive the inclusion of Eire in the diagram for the sake of geographical simplicity.

The student will appreciate that some of these objectives conflict with others, or may do if they are not carefully managed. For example if we encourage full employment it means more factories must be built, more machinery installed, more raw materials must be purchased, etc. Some of these items will be imports and we shall have to earn more from exports if the Balance of Payments is to be maintained. If we tax the rich to help the poor and thus try to establish a more egalitarian society we may increase demand (the poor are strong demanders when they receive funds). This extra demand may force up prices and bring inflation. Economic growth will have the same effect. People who want a higher standard of living demand goods and services, making it difficult to export the goods which are being demanded at home, and sucking in imports. Once again the Balance of Payments may present a difficulty.

Those who tried to manage prosperity in the years between 1945 and 1979

Fig. 11.2 *The objectives of Keynesian macro-economic policies*

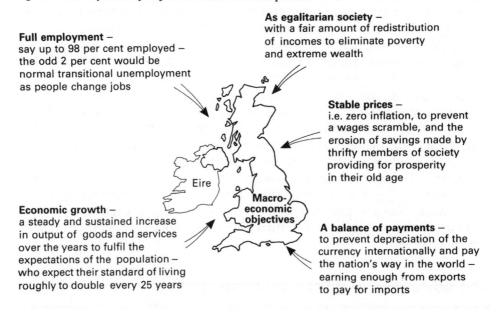

Full employment –
say up to 98 per cent employed –
the odd 2 per cent would be
normal transitional unemployment
as people change jobs

As egalitarian society –
with a fair amount of redistribution
of incomes to eliminate poverty
and extreme wealth

Stable prices –
i.e. zero inflation, to prevent
a wages scramble, and the
erosion of savings made by
thrifty members of society
providing for prosperity
in their old age

Eire

Macro-economic objectives

Economic growth –
a steady and sustained increase
in output of goods and services
over the years to fulfil the
expectations of the population –
who expect their standard of living
roughly to double every 25 years

A balance of payments –
to prevent depreciation of the
currency internationally and pay
the nation's way in the world –
earning enough from exports
to pay for imports

were endlessly performing a balancing act. This balancing act came to be called 'Stop-go' policies, but it would have been better to say 'Go-stop' policies. The economy was allowed to go until a problem presented itself, when the most appropriate set of brakes was applied to slow it down, while the Government steered itself out of the difficulty. What weapons could the Government use in this battle?

The weapons for waging battle on the macro-economic front

Once again we may study these most simply in diagrammatic form, as shown in Fig. 11.3.

In 1946, at the end of the Second World War, the great fear was that the 'prosperity' of the war years (largely financed by surrendering the overseas investments made in the previous 200 years) would be replaced by a long and enduring slump, repeating the experience of the inter-wars years. To prevent this, prosperity was to be managed by the Government, which also wished to implement a huge nationalisation policy as well as repay the debts incurred in war-time, chiefly in the form of 'blocked credits' held by Commonwealth and other countries who now wished to enjoy these accumulated rights to UK exports. The repayment of this debt took about 10 years, so that much of the national output in the post-war years could not be enjoyed by UK citizens, it was already promised to foreign creditors.

The chief weapon used to manage prosperity was high taxation, with taxes rising to very high levels on unearned income (92½ per cent for some years). This was a 'soak the rich' policy which gave the Government funds to finance

Fig. 11.3 *The weapons for fighting the battle for prosperity*

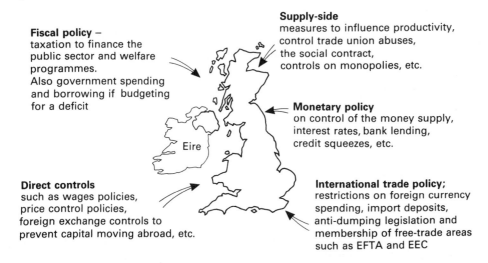

Fiscal policy –
taxation to finance the
public sector and welfare
programmes.
Also government spending
and borrowing if budgeting
for a deficit

Supply-side
measures to influence productivity,
control trade union abuses,
the social contract,
controls on monopolies, etc.

Monetary policy
on control of the money supply,
interest rates, bank lending,
credit squeezes, etc.

Eire

Direct controls
such as wages policies,
price control policies,
foreign exchange controls to
prevent capital moving abroad, etc.

International trade policy;
restrictions on foreign currency
spending, import deposits,
anti-dumping legislation and
membership of free-trade areas
such as EFTA and EEC

reconstruction programmes, rebuilding British industry, particularly nationalised industries and social programmes like the National Health Service. This
ensured full employment. Where programmes could not be financed by
taxation they were financed by borrowing, the Chancellor budgeting for a
deficit. This means that in the Budget each year he did not attempt to raise
taxes sufficient to cover all expenditure because too high a taxation level
discourages effort and enterprise. Instead he deliberately budgeted to be a bit
short of funds, and borrowed the rest by selling gilt-edged stock to those who
wanted to save money. Gilt-edged stocks are Government bonds (promises to
repay) bearing a known rate of interest.

To ensure that Government programmes were not interrupted by less
essential private activities there were many direct controls, for example over
the export of capital, over hire purchase, over the use of foreign exchange for
holidays abroad, over wages and prices, etc. Bank lending was under strict
control and interest rates were manipulated to discourage excessive borrowing.
Attempts by powerful trade unions to improve the lot of their members,
particularly the better-off skilled workers, were resisted, because of the
manifest unfairness when other groups such as unskilled workers, pensioners,
etc., would suffer from the rising prices that resulted. The idea of a 'social
contract' was widely discussed. It argued that if a Labour Government was
doing its best to maintain prosperity for all working people there must be
another side to the bargain – a social contract – by which the Labour
movement in return did not demand too high a share of the national income
for its more skilled workers. The appeal was especially made to workers in the
new nationalised industries, whose employment was relatively secure, and who
therefore, it was hoped, would show a more restrained and responsible attitude
to industrial unrest.

Monetary policies attempt to control demand in the economy by keeping money 'tight' – that is borrowing was restricted to essential needs like industrial expansion, hire purchase of essentials such as cookers, electric heaters, etc. Bank lending was actively discouraged whenever a boom developed, so that non-essential requirements would be beyond the reach of many families. Such systems as Barclaycard and Access, which make credit easy to obtain and funds available instantly to millions of customers, could not be introduced until much later. After many years of managed prosperity people grew accustomed to the use of money in a responsible way. The use of such systems is a sign of a sophisticated population with a good understanding of budgeting and money management.

International trade policies are policies which influence imports and exports. Thus the imposition of import quotas, either by volume or value, restricts imports to the specific number of items allowed (say 20 000 foreign cars) or the value allowed (say foreign cars not to exceed £50 million in value). Import deposits restrict imports until a heavy entry duty has been paid (one South American country imposed duties of 1400 per cent at one time). Foreign credit lines permit foreign countries to buy UK exports up to a certain figure – say £50 million to an Eastern bloc country – the Government paying the UK manufacturer and arranging repayment by the Eastern bloc customer, for example. Anti-dumping legislation seeks to prevent foreign goods being sold on the UK market at lower prices than home nationals are paying in the country of origin.

Conclusions about Keynesian economics

Keynesian economics was a considerable success in the years between 1945 and 1970 and to many of those who lived through the unemployment of the inter-war years it seemed at times a very heaven. Yet it had within it certain weaknesses not envisaged by its early advocates which led to its reduced use, particularly in the UK. Some of the policies in use today are deliberately aimed at undoing the systems installed during the Keynesian era, and the general term 'supply side economics' has been applied to these new policies. In Keynes's day the problems of society stemmed from an absence of demand in the economy, and Keynes showed how to manage the aggregate monetary demand to ensure that business boomed and a general prosperity was enjoyed. The day came when the demand for prosperity outreached the capacity of the UK economy to supply. The loss of the empire, the rise of the newly industrialised countries (the 20 NICS, such as Korea, Japan, Singapore, India and other highly competitive nations) declining productivity and industrial unrest meant that the situation had reversed – there was too much demand and too little supply. Keynesian economics did not fail, it was just too successful. It raised expectations beyond what could be achieved. That 'managed prosperity' became eventually almost unmanageable was no fault of Keynes. The pendulum had swung too far, and a new approach was required. Monetarism reared its lovely (ugly) head. Before leaving Keynesian economics to consider monetarism the student should study the appendix on some aspects of Keynesian economics, given below.

4   APPENDIX TO CHAPTER 11

Propensities to consume and propensities to save

It has already been suggested that as the aggregate level of income within the community rises, the *proportion* of income spent upon consumption is likely to decline. Fig. 11.4 helps to illustrate this process more precisely.

Fig. 11.4 *Propensities to consume and save*

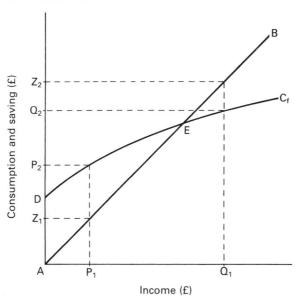

Notes
1   The line AB is the equilibrium line where income equals expenditure. (In mathematics it is the locus of points where income and expenditure are equal.)
2   If all income within a community were consumed the path of consumption as income increased would be described by the line AB. However, experience shows that as aggregate incomes rise, and the more basic needs of a society are met, the level of saving will rise. This causes the consumption function C_f, which plots the path of *actual* consumption, to depart from the total hypothetical consumption line AB.
3   The lower part of the C_f curve, DE, recognises the fact that at very low levels of income societies are forced to dis-save in order to help maintain consumption levels. Thus at an income of £P_1 consumption would be £P_2 and dis-saving of £P_2Z_1 would have occurred.
   By contrast, at higher levels, such as £Q_1, consumption of £Q_2 will take place and savings of £Q_2Z_2 will occur.
4   The relationship between the level of consumption and the level of aggregate income (Y) is known as the **average propensity to consume**. It is usual to express this as a fraction, e.g. if income is £80 millions and consumption £60 millions

$$APC = \frac{C}{Y}$$

$$= \frac{60}{80}$$

$$= \frac{3}{4}$$

That income which is not spent upon consumption is savings. The **average propensity to save** is also expressed as a fraction, e.g. if income is £80 millions and saving £20 millions

$$APS = \frac{S}{Y}$$

$$= \frac{20}{80}$$

$$= \frac{1}{4}$$

The APC and APS, when added together are, of course, 1.

5 Of greater significance than the average propensities are the **marginal propensities to consume and save**. The marginal propensity to consume describes the degree of consumption which takes place out of *extra* income, e.g. if income rises by £10 millions and *extra* consumption is £7 million, then

$$MPC = \frac{\Delta C}{\Delta Y}$$

$$= \frac{7}{10}$$

(N.B. The symbol delta merely means 'change in'. ΔC means 'change in level of consumption expenditure' and ΔY means 'change in level of aggregate income'.)

Similarly, if out of the *extra* income of £10 millions there is *extra* saving of £3 millions

$$MPS = \frac{\Delta S}{\Delta Y}$$

$$= \frac{3}{10}$$

The reason why marginal propensities are more significant than average propensities is that they tell us the likely proportion of any *extra* income that will be consumed, or saved. In economics it is often what consumers do with any *extra* income that has implications for the entrepreneur proposing to produce a new product, or expand output of an existing product.

6 The slope of the consumption function (C_f) in Fig. 11.4 gradually moves further away from the total consumption line (in relative terms) and this indicates that as incomes rise the marginal propensity to consume is declining and the marginal propensity to save is rising. This will not be unusual in an affluent society. There are, however, a number of other influences upon the propensities to consume and save, besides the *level* of income. These include the distribution of income, the structure of institutions and consumers' expectations of future behaviour of prices.

The multiplier

The multiplier is the mechanism which is responsible for bringing equilibrium between changed levels of investment and saving. It does this by altering the size of aggregate income. Should investment exceed saving (a net injection), the multiplier shows to what extent any given injection will be expanded (multiplied) before the savings process removes it from circulation and once again equates total savings with total investment. Obviously the size of increment in income required will depend upon how much of an increase in income the society in question is likely to retain in the form of savings, i.e. *the propensity to save*. If *all* of the increase in income is saved by those who receive it, there will be no necessity for a multiplier process at all – extra savings will almost immediately equal extra investment and income in total will rise by an amount equal to the extra investment only. However, in normal circumstances (the 1920s and 30s being exceptions) societies are not likely to save the *total* of extra incomes – the MPC is likely to be greater than 0, since consumers will respond to extra income by spending some of it. Once consumption spending takes place out of extra income, it in turn helps to generate further income.

For example, suppose a small builder is engaged to construct a storeroom for a local butcher. He is paid £10 000 for the job. From this he may obtain a personal income of £2500 (the other factors of production – labour, supplies of materials, capital etc. – receiving the remaining £7500). Out of this he may spend £2000 on personal consumption – food, heating, drink, holidays, etc. This means that his MPC is ⅘, i.e.   . If the MPC of the factors he employs (and of the groups he and they spend ⅘ of the £10 000 with) is also ⅘, then the calculation of spending in the next round becomes

$$\text{Original investment £10 000}$$
$$\text{MPC} = ⅘ = £8000$$

Generated income is therefore £8000. With an MPC of ⅘, only part of this £8000 (£6400) is likely to be passed on in the form of consumers' spending.

In this way consumers will continue to generate income for others until the effect of the initial injection has worked itself out (the figure eventually being passed on is reduced to almost nothing).

A shorthand way to arrive at a figure for the size of the effect of the multiplier is to use a formula. The easiest is one which relates the size of the multiplier – denoted k – to the size of the reciprocal of the MPS, in other words the MPS turned on its head. This formula clearly indicates that the expansion effect produced in total income depends upon the size of MPS.

$$k = \frac{1}{\text{MPS}} \text{ (really the MPS in its normal form is}$$

$$\frac{\text{MPS}}{1} \text{ ; its reciprocal is found by turning}$$
$$\text{it upside down)}$$

Where MPC is ⅘, the MPS must be ⅕ (the two together making 1), and therefore

$$k = \frac{1}{\frac{1}{5}}$$

$$= \frac{1}{1} \div \frac{1}{5}$$

$$= \frac{1}{1} \times \frac{5}{1}$$

$$= 5$$

This indicates that the *total* rise in income necessary to generate enough saving to equal the new investment of £10 000 is £50 000. This will be composed of the original investment £10 000, plus the secondary or generated increment £40 000.

Obviously, the process does not operate in practice as smoothly as suggested. Time lags occur and there are leakages (such as spending abroad).

The national income equilibrium diagram

The national income equilibrium diagram explains what happens in an economy as the circular flows of income and expenditure operate to promote or discourage prosperity. Expenditures are made up of the following elements:

C = consumption expenditure.
I = investment expenditure. This could be planned (I_p) or unplanned (I_u). The latter is the growth of stocks due to failure to sell the product invested in.
G = government expenditure.
X = export purchases by foreigners.

However, total expenditure may be reduced by taxation (if we counted the tax on consumption expenditure and investment expenditure as well as the Government expenditure we should be counting it twice). It is also reduced by import expenditures by home nations on foreign goods. These deductions are called T (taxation) and M (imports).

Therefore overall we may say

$$E = C + I + G + X - T - M$$

If a balance of payments in international trade is being achieved X and M will cancel one another out, and consequently do not appear in the diagram below (Fig. 11.5). The curves showing expenditure have been labelled to remind us that T has to be deducted.

What we have in Fig. 11.5 is the **national income equilibrium diagram**. The 45° line is the locus of points where income equals expenditure. There is a natural tendency for the economy to settle at an equilibrium position on the 45° line, and these points have been labelled E_1, E_2, E_3 up to E_f, which is the full-employment equilibrium at which all factors are fully employed, and the economy is producing all it can produce.

The reason why the economy moves to equilibrium on the 45° line is that the expenditures made react on the entrepreneurs to influence their activities and raise or lower output. Consider the consumption curve $C - T$. Suppose incomes of £7 billions were paid in a particular week to the various owners of factors as rent, wages, interest or profits. They could go out and purchase £7 billion of consumption goods, but in fact they do not, because the $C - T$ curve shows that they actually only spend about £6.25 billions. This means that in the next period the entrepreneurs who receive this expenditure can only pay out £6.25 billions in the next period. If the factor owners only get £6.25 billions in the next period they could spend it all on consumption, but the curve shows they only spend about £5.95 billions. The reader can see that at this rate the economy will slow down until we get to £5.8 billions – which is where the consumption curve cuts the 45° line. At this point the entrepreneurs get back the full £5.8 billions and can pay it out in the next period. Now look at Fig 11.5 and read the notes below it to see how Keynesian managed prosperity is managed.

Fig. 11.5 *Keynesian managed prosperity*

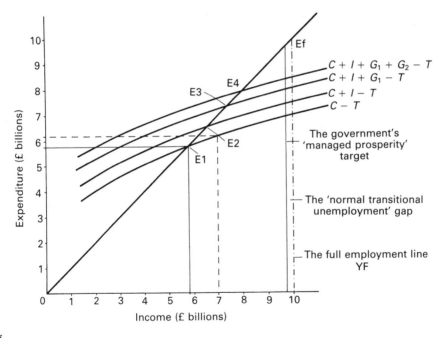

Notes
1   Looking at the $C - T$ (consumption less taxes on consumption) line we see it is in equilibrium at E_1. Entrepreneurs are getting back in sales all the incomes they paid out in the previous period. This is fine, but lots of factors are unemployed – we are nowhere near E_f on the 45° line which is the full employment line.
2   Actually investment, whether planned or unplanned (stock-building) increases incomes and expenditure to give an economy in equilibrium at E_2.
3   Also normal government expenditure on defence, education, etc., increases incomes and expenditures to give equilibrium at E_3.
4   There is still quite a lot of unemployment, so an extra injection of government activity is given to raise incomes (and therefore expenditure). It could be welfare payments to those in need, or armaments, or education, or subsidies (but the rich recipients might just save the increase). Because of the multiplier we

might find any injection does more than we expect so it is best to be cautious as we get closer and closer to full employment, with successive extra injections of government expenditure.

5 Actually no-one tries to get 100 per cent full employment – the usual target is 98 per cent – unemployment at 2 per cent. Actually when unemployment is only 2 per cent we have what is called **normal transitional unemployment**, which means no one is really unemployed – people are so prosperous they take a little break when changing jobs or moving over to a different field of activity.

6 So Keynesian prosperity is managed by Government action to raise incomes, which raises expenditure, which encourages entrepreneurs to think that the economy is on the mend. 'All we need is confidence' said President Roosevelt in the Great Slump – the confidence to raise aggregate monetary demand to get production going again. The Government must start the ball rolling, but once it does entrepreneurs will increase investment as well, and those who have been hoarding money in bad times will start to spend too. If the thing starts to go too fast the Government begins to rein in the galloping horses, and a light touch on the reins now and again will be all that is required.

7 Why can only the government get the economy going in a slump? Because no one else can do it. Consider:

 a) **The rich can't go on a mad spending spree.** They already look ostentatious enough with their present life-style. Social unrest might develop if they do.

 b) **The entrepreneurs can't do it.** They see little prospect of profitability. They can't sell the output they are making now.

 c) **The petty bourgeoisie can't do it.** They are bred to be frugal, and save for a rainy day. They don't realise the rainy day has arrived.

 d) **Only the Government can do it.** We need a spendthrift, to spend someone else's thrift. Keynes realised there was no-one like the Government for doing that.

SELF-ASSESSMENT QUESTIONS

5 What are the elements of macro-economic policy as used in the years 1945–79?

6 What are the weapons used in 'managed prosperity'?

7 Explain the multiplier.

8 Explain the national income equilibrium diagram.

REVISION TEST

Answers	Questions
	1 Which part of classical economic theory did Keynes first attack?
1 That part relating to the rate of interest.	**2** According to Keynes, what factors affected the level of saving?

2 The level of incomes and anticipated changes in the rate of interest.

3 According to Keynes, what factors affected the level of investment?

---

3 The expected rate of return on investments.

4 What is the 'liquidity' trap?

---

4 The tendency of society to hold idle balances even though the rate of interest is low.

5 Why does the 'liquidity trap' operate?

---

5 Because of the fear of capital loss if money is committed to income-earning assets and interest rates then rise, so that the asset values fall.

6 Why is it necessary for savings to equal investment?

---

6 In order that income will neither shrink nor grow, and we have a stable economic society.

7 What is the marginal propensity to consume (MPC)?

---

7 The tendency of society to consume from extra income.

8 What is the multiplier (k)?

---

8 A number which shows how the community's tendency to save influences the extent to which incomes grow as a result of investment (or contract as a result of savings).

9 What formula is used to calculate the size of the multiplier?

9
$$k = \frac{1}{MPS}$$

10 How did the acceptance of Keynesian economics affect the government economic policy?

---

10 It brought government from the side-lines to the very centre of economic policy-making.

11 What are the objectives of macro-economic policy?

---

11 (a) Full employment (b) an egalitarian society (c) stable prices (no inflation) (d) economic growth (e) a balance of payments.

12 What weapons are available to achieve these objectives?

12 a) Fiscal policy (taxation) (b) monetary policy (control of the money supply) (c) direct controls (d) supply side measures to increase the efficiency of production, market operations, etc. (e) international trade policy to influnce imports and exports.

Now try some of the written questions opposite.

ANSWERS

(See Self-assessment questions on pages 303 and 314.)

1 The transactions motive says that people need to hold cash to finance their day to day affairs, buying consumer goods, capital items, etc.; the ordinary transactions of everyday life. The precautionary motive says that people need to hold cash to meet emergencies, no-one knows when fate will knock on his/her door – we all keep cash balances in our current accounts to meet unexpected circumstances. The speculative motive was Keynes' addition to the pattern of motives for holding cash. He said people who expect interest rates to rise will hold cash rather than invest in income yielding assets now, because if they buy bonds now (yieldings say 8 per cent interest) and interest rates rise to – say – 10 per cent the capital value of the bonds held will fall and they will have suffered a capital loss. In the example given the capital value would fall to £80 (since the £8 interest on the original £100 bond is 10 per cent of £80). An investor buying the bond from the holder would not give more than £80 for it.

2 Keynes 'liquidity trap' said that a cheap-money policy such as was tried to encourage the economy to recover in the great slump between the wars would not work because if interest rates were as low as 2 per cent there was no way they could go but up. If interest rates were to rise, as prosperity grew, all those who had helped the nation to recover prosperity by lending their funds would suffer a capital loss, for example if rates rose from 2 per cent to 4 per cent a £100 bond would fall in value to £50. Therefore at such low rates those who had funds to invest would prefer to hoard it in liquid form rather than risk massive capital losses.

3 The elements of injecting demand into the circular flow of incomes are: (a) consumer demand (which may be stimulated by welfare payments) (b) planned investment expenditure by firms and government departments (c) current expenditure by central and local government (as distinct from investment expenditure) (d) export expenditure (by foreign households, firms and governments (e) unplanned investment expenditure (stock building).

4 The leakages from the circular flow of incomes are (a) savings by households (b) corporate savings (profits not distributed or re-invested) (c) taxation by central and local government (d) expenditure on imports.

5 The elements of macro-economic policy in the years 1945–79 were (a) the drive for full employment (b) the drive for sustained economic growth (c) the drive to a more egalitarian society (d) the control of prices to prevent inflation (e) the drive to secure a balance of payments.

6 The weapons used to manage prosperity were (a) fiscal policy, to secure tax revenues and thus pursue socially desirable policies (b) monetary policies to control the money supply and keep demand under control (c) direct controls such as HP controls, restrictions on bank lending, etc. (d) measures to influence international trade, quotas, import deposits, anti-dumping legislation (e) supply-side pressures designed to raise productivity and assist output for both home and export markets.

7 The multiplier is a mechanism which operates in the economy to achieve equilibrium between investment and saving. Any extra purchasing power (which is called an injection into the economy) will not only increase business activity by the amount of the injection but will be multiplied up to a much higher level, depending upon the marginal propensities to consume and save (the tendencies to consume or save extra income). Thus if £1 million pound is injected into the economy and the marginal propensity to save is $\frac{1}{4}$ (25 per cent) those who receive the original £1 million in the first time period will spend £750 000 of it in the next time period, and those who receive the £750 000 will spend £562 500 in the next period, etc. The final result will be:

$$k \text{ (the multiplier)} = \frac{1}{\text{MPS}} = \frac{1}{\frac{1}{4}} = 4$$

Thus an injection of £1 million boosts the economy by £4 million.

8 The answer to this question is given in the notes to Fig. 11.5.

QUESTIONS ON CHAPTER 11

1 Define consumption, saving and investment and explain how they are related. (Institute of Commercial Management)

2 What are the main injections and withdrawals from the circular flow of income? What are the effects of these injections and withdrawals? (Institute of Marketing)

3 'An increase in investment leads to an increase in employment via the multiplier'. Explain carefully what is meant by this statement, making clear the assumptions necessary for it to be true. (Institute of Commercial Management)

4 'The macroeconomic objectives of government, may not always be mutually compatible'. Identify and explain the possible conflicts which may arise. (Institute of Commercial Management)

5 How did the Keynesian approach to the rate of interest differ from that of his predecessors?

6 What is meant by liquidity preference? How does speculation affect this?

7 Why is the marginal propensity to save (MPS) so important in the Keynesian explanation of the working of an economy?

8 What is meant by the multiplier process? How is this process thought to operate?

9 What implications follow from the claim that the marginal propensity to consume (MPC) will decline as societies become more affluent?

10 What are the chief weapons which might be used by a chancellor in a slump situation to bring about recovery?

11 Why will an economy tend to adjust to a position where national income equals national expenditure?

12 'Keynesian economics proved to be a failure.'
'Keynesian economics was an undoubted success for the vast majority of lower income UK citizens.' Discuss these two views of Keynesian economics.

TIPS FOR STUDENTS: A SPECIMEN ANSWER TO QUESTION 3

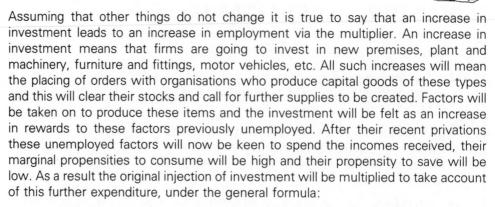

Assuming that other things do not change it is true to say that an increase in investment leads to an increase in employment via the multiplier. An increase in investment means that firms are going to invest in new premises, plant and machinery, furniture and fittings, motor vehicles, etc. All such increases will mean the placing of orders with organisations who produce capital goods of these types and this will clear their stocks and call for further supplies to be created. Factors will be taken on to produce these items and the investment will be felt as an increase in rewards to these factors previously unemployed. After their recent privations these unemployed factors will now be keen to spend the incomes received, their marginal propensities to consume will be high and their propensity to save will be low. As a result the original injection of investment will be multiplied to take account of this further expenditure, under the general formula:

$$k \text{ (the multiplier)} = \frac{1}{\text{MPS}}$$

The assumptions necessary for it to be true would be as follows:

a) The investment must be made with home firms, not foreign firms. If orders are placed to import capital items the leakage of funds away to foreign firms will not benefit the home economy and the multiplication of prosperity will occur in the countries of the foreign suppliers.

b) The investment constitutes a new injection of demand into the economy. If this new injection is offset by other, unconnected leakages from the system, for example savings by other firms, reduction in Government expenditure in other directions, reduced consumption expenditure for any reason (for example a reduction in foreign tourists to the home country) these will reduce the impact of the new investment.

c) There must be unemployed domestic factors available — otherwise price rises or extra imports (or both) may be the result. The economy is said to 'overheat' because the extra investment acting on an economy whose factors are already fully employed sucks in imports and leads to inflation, with too much money chasing too few factors.

12 Supply-side economics and monetarism

1 INTRODUCTION

In the years after the end of the Second World War, from 1945–1970, European economies were dominated by Keynesian ideas. These ideas also permeated the United States, though full acceptance was never finally admitted there.

The impact of the absorption of Keynesianism into government policy was immense. From a situation where governments were predominantly reluctant to take overall responsibility for the economy (before the Second World War), we now had a system where governments managed and planned economic activity, albeit within a capitalistic framework.

Very largely because of this movement towards government involvement, the great evil towards which Keynes addressed himself – mass unemployment and under-utilisation of other resources – was held in check. From time to time unemployment rose towards 6 per cent in the UK, but this was because governments were preoccupied with other economic objectives; by comparison 24 per cent of the working population were out of work in 1932 in the UK. That a range of economic objectives should be *pursued* by governments is a tribute to the wide applicability of Keynes' analytical methods. This is not to suggest that Keynesian economics has undergone no development since the time of Keynes. Indeed, the period from 1945 was one of unprecedented activity in the field of economics. Generally though, the bulk of those operating within the area of study were using Keynesian techniques and pursuing questions inspired by Keynes himself. Perhaps the best known of the large establishment of Keynesians was Paul A. Samuelson – the first American to win the Nobel Memorial Prize in Economic Science. More than any other single economist Samuelson helped to popularise the ideas of Keynes; he also performed much refining work upon them.

2 SOME DRAWBACKS TO KEYNESIAN ECONOMICS

Keynesian economic ideas were now widely used in the Western World, but this does not mean that they were without shortcomings. In particular, Keynesianism is a type of economic analysis known as macro-statics, which briefly means that it attempts to deal with the economy as a whole, but assumes that there will be movement from one state of rest to another – there is a search for a stable, equilibrium position.

Keynes claimed that his work was a 'general theory', presumably because it was capable of providing analysis to deal with a wide range of events. However, because of the widespread incidence of unemployment and the unemployment of resources current when the 'general theory' was in the process of preparation his book concentrates upon the 'unemployment' aspect of Economics. As suggested above subsequent theorists have extended the work so that it is applicable to a wide range of situations. Keynes himself, though, felt (and wrote) that once a full employment equilibrium had been established classical ideas might come into their own. This has been sufficient to allow an anti-Keynesian movement to develop – and claim authority from Keynes himself! Basically the new-monetarists (or new classicals as they are sometimes termed) feel that the Keynesian analysis is one which leads to too much state intervention and one which only works in *particular*, as opposed to *general* circumstances, the particular situation being, of course, unemployment!

The first move away from Keynesian analysis was a move from macro-statics to macro-dynamics.

3 MACRO-DYNAMICS: THE ECONOMICS OF GROWTH

Keynes was greatly concerned with the short-period – six to nine months. His work was therefore devoid of considerations of those factors which make economies grow over longer periods of time. In other words, it had little to say of macro-dynamics – of the forces which influence the rates of increase or decrease of broad categories of demand (for example, for imports or exports, capital goods, etc.). Even in the field of expectations – an area to which Keynes devoted a great deal of attention – there is no statement of *how* a desired level of expectations can be aimed at – no statement of what forces determine the level which expectations *should* be operating at to secure growth, in the short and long terms.

It was left to such distinguished economists as Sir Roy Harrod to point the way in dynamic macro-economics. He suggests that the move towards macro-dynamics owes less to Keynes than it does to the early classical economists such as Smith, Ricardo and John Stuart Mill: those writers who were concerned to find out how *progress* would affect an economy.

Dynamic economics was not allowed time to develop a *comprehensive* explanation of how economic systems function. Although a great deal of work was done in this field, and growth models such as the 'Harrod-Domar Model' were well established in economic literature, the pace of events was leading to a change in fundamental policies. Sideline effects of continuing Keynesian policies in an era when mass unemployment had ceased to be a feature of society began to appear and become increasingly important.

Some of these side-effects which became apparent in the 1970s may be listed as follows:

a) Since the Government was charged with managing prosperity the natural checks and balances recognised as being effective in a free-enterprise world ceased to be regarded. Any failure to achieve prosperity must be the Government's fault – irrespective of the fact that the Government only had the ordinary factors of production to work with in trying to achieve prosperity. It becomes more difficult to manage prosperity as those enjoying it come to believe that it was a right, rather than a benefit that resulted from hard work.

b) Businesses ceased to cut back production when a recession seemed probable – the Government would inject more demand if it was required. Bad times would never come, business believed.

c) Similarly labour grew to expect not only that the present prosperity would last for ever, but that its standard of living would rise. The expectation of the late 60s and 70s was that the standard of living would double every 25 years. That required a growth rate of 2½ per cent per annum, yet from about 1965 onwards growth was rarely more than 1 per cent per annum.

d) Social policies, such as equal pay, the abolition of sexual and racial discrimination, health and safety at work, compulsory training contributions from employers, social security payments, etc., heaped crippling burdens upon employers at a time when foreign competition from developed nations, NICs (newly industrialised countries) and developing nations was intense. The burden became impossible to bear, especially as productivity fell. Traditional industries collapsed as costs rose and competition ate into markets both abroad and at home.

e) As state responsibilities rose, and the duty to save industries in danger of collapse was added to other growing burdens, the Government's share of the national income had to rise. The tax burden became excessive, and a wages and prices scramble developed. Inflation moved into double figures. A cry arose for a return to market economics.

4   THE RETURN TO MARKET ECONOMICS

The move back to market economics was signalled by the revival of monetarism, led particularly by Milton Friedman and the 'Chicago School' of economists. Monetarists are, on the whole, committed to re-establishing the validity of much of the old classical theory. They are therefore committed advocates of the free market, and greatly dislike the state intervention which is such an important part of Keynesianism. Their present influence in the UK really began with the period of rapid inflation in the early 1970s. The policy prescriptions of the Keynesians – mostly fiscal in nature – were clearly seen to be incapable of restraining inflation. Perhaps, then, monetarists had the answer when they related inflation rates to the quantity of money available in the economy?

It would be a mistake, though, to regard monetarism as 'monetary policy'. Despite the fact that monetary policy is central to monetarism, monetarism itself is much wider than monetary policy alone. The benefits of monetarism can be listed as follows:

a) A minimum of state intervention. In the long run full employment, or nearly full employment, equilibrium will be established by market forces. These will be 'real' jobs instead of 'managed' jobs. There are many ways in which state intervention can be reduced and market forces can be encouraged. For example if a major strike occurs, instead of Government departments or quangos (quasi-autonomous non-governmental organisations, like ACAS – the Advisory Conciliation and Arbitration Service) stepping in to bring the strike to a speedy end (often by putting up Government money to meet the workers' demands) the strike can be left to settle itself. This will cost something in terms of disruption, but may be cheaper than the subsidies conceded under the conciliation method. The most extreme case was the miner's strike in the mid-80s, which lasted a full year, but ushered in a much more tranquil period in coal mining.

b) The minimum of state expenditure. The citizens will be allowed to spend their own money instead of it being removed by the Chancellor and spent for them. Under Keynesianism, Government expenditure crowds out private expenditure. One of the difficulties of liberal Government handouts is that appetite grows with feeding, and all sorts of vested interests get into the act. It is not solely the poorer members of society who learn how to take advantage of the system, though social security malpractices are often held up as examples. The farming community under the Common Agricultural Policy has been quick to exploit advantages offered by that system; hospital consultants have been criticised for 'legitimate' procedures which infringe the spirit of the National Health Service while keeping within the letter of the law. Training initiatives are another area where funds become available and advantage can be taken by alert managements to fund activities which would never be contemplated if the expenditure had to be financed by the firm itself. Reduction of official expenditure leaves market forces to decide the optimum way to spend money.

c) Control the rate of growth of the money supply since this has a direct impact on the level of expenditure in the economy. It operates through the 'transmission mechanism', the oldest expression of which is the quantity theory of money. This is explained below.

Monetary policy obviously is an important element in monetarism, but it cannot be regarded as a full exploration of this new body of economic theory. From the monetary policy viewpoint the monetarist approach aims at re-establishing the rate of interest as a sensitive tool in the regulation of economic activity (readers will remember that Keynes' own theory depended upon 'discrediting' the full role of the rate of interest). The 'liquidity trap' suggests that as the rate of interest falls capital assets rise in value and this prevents the spending of idle 'speculative balances' because the rate of interest can in the future be expected to rise (devaluing capital assets). The monetarist argument is that as an individual observes increases in the value of his capital holdings (his portfolio), he will tend to spend more freely, and this extra spending overcomes the liquidity trap. If this approach is accurate, classical economics has been re-established. To explain more fully what is occurring here monetarists utilise a modified version of the quantity theory of money as their 'transmission mechanism' – their link between the amount of money and total spending.

5 THE QUANTITY THEORY OF MONEY

This theory holds that the quantity of money in circulation plays an important part in determining the general price level. The belief was expressed very simply by an American economist, Irving Fisher, in what has become known as the 'Fisher Equation of Exchange'. This equation states:

$$MV = PT$$

Where M is the quantity of money, V is the velocity of money, P is the general price level, and T is the number of transactions within the economy.

The equation therefore states that the amount of money in circulation multiplied by the frequency with which it circulates within a given period, equals the aggregate value of transactions which take place within the defined period. Viewed in this way the so-called Fisher equation is not an equation at all, it is merely an identity – it only states what must be the case. The money we have, multiplied by the number of times we spend it, must be the same as the number of things we spend it on multiplied by their price.

The significance of this equation lies in the way it is possible to isolate the variables within it and then suggest a pattern of behaviour for them. For example, supposing the quantity of money M increases, but the velocity of money does not change, the left hand side of the equation grows bigger. That means that something on the right hand side must change too. There is no change in the number of transactions (because we have not mentioned that more goods or services are being created) so what must happen is that prices rise. An increase in the quantity of money causes higher prices. This certainly seems to have happened several times in history – for example when Spain discovered gold and silver in the Americas the increased precious metal coming into Europe caused a continent-wide rise in prices, to the benefit of Spain and the disadvantage of all other nations.

Similarly if the quantity of money stays stable but the velocity of money increases there will be an increase in prices, because there is effectively more money available in a given period of time.

There were many problems surrounding the Quantity Theory of Money. Some of these were:

a) In order for V to remain constant it was necessary for the population to have constant expectations, particularly as regards future price changes. Expectations of increases in prices might lead to accelerated spending as people tried to buy before the price rise. This increased V. Expectations of decreases in prices might lead to deceleration in spending and a decreased V. Once V is on the move, changes in M can be absorbed by V and not transmitted to P. (An illustration of this occurred in the late 1960s, when persistent attempts to control inflation by reducing the money supply were defeated by an increased velocity of money as factor owners refused to be robbed of their prosperity and pursued the higher standard of living they deemed they were entitled to enjoy.)

b) Full employment of all resources depends upon the flexibility of wages and prices, both in an upwards and downwards direction. Without such flexibility the volume of real output, T, will be subject to change, as the economy passes through varying levels of unemployment. T also could be capable of absorbing the effects of M and therefore forestall a potential change in P. Thus if there is more money about, but it leads to an increase in output of goods and services the increase in T will mean prices need not rise. This is what happens in Keynesian economics, when an extra injection of demand into the economy does not create inflation, because the previously unemployed factors now taken into employment start to create goods and services (thus increasing T).

Modern monetarism, while accepting the basic relationships of the quantity theory, go further in their explanations of the transmission mechanism involved. The argument goes that individuals try to maximise the satisfaction (utility) they can gain from the resources at their disposal. Some of these resources are in the form of money and this is largely held because it is convenient to have money balances. However, as the money supply grows so do the money balances of individuals, until the stage is reached where utility can be increased by converting some of these balances into the (many) substitutes which exist for them – financial assets, precious metals, jewellery, art, houses, etc. This is just a grand way of saying that the growing money balances are spent, and when spent in circumstances of no change in the supply of goods and services, are likely to lead to rising prices, more imports, or both.

Given that monetarists accept the likely stability of V and the long run tendency for T to arrive automatically at the full employment level, they believe that in the long run an increase in the money stock will not change the level of real output but will lead to increased prices – we are back to the Fisher quantity theory, though in a less rigid and more believable form.

Since monetarists believe that the money supply has a marked direct influence on the level of aggregate demand it would be reasonable to expect monetary policy to be put forward as a means of demand management. That such is not the case is due to more than monetarist dislike of state intervention. There are a number of drawbacks:

a) It is very difficult to identify precisely what is meant by the money supply (see Chapter 14).

b) Because the measures taken, e.g. a call for special deposits or an interest rate change, are at some distance from the **target variable** they are designed to influence, e.g. the amount of money in circulation, the results of such measures are likely to be unpredictable in their timing and exact magnitude.

Because of this monetarists favour not manipulation, but strict money growth rules – a steady and regular growth in the volume of money being seen as the best encouragement to the private sector that monetary stability will keep inflation at bay.

6   MONETARIST CONTROL OF THE ECONOMY

The money growth rules adopted by the UK Government are embodied in the medium term financial strategy. This was first introduced in March 1980 by the newly elected Conservative Government – a government much more monetarist in outlook than any of its post-war predecessors.

The Medium Term Financial Strategy attempted to chart the progressive reduction of the growth in both money supply and government borrowing – the public sector borrowing requirement – PSBR. It did this by setting target **ranges**, for up to five years at a time, for these and other variables. The policies the government than adopted were directed towards the achievement of these targets. The targets, in effect, were intended to bring into the operation of government policy some element of discipline – a definite position from which policy should not stray.

In terms of the PSBR the medium term financial policy has been exceptionally successful. Aided by record tax receipts, the sale of state owned assets, and massive North Sea oil revenues, the Government has managed to reduce the PSBR to a negative figure, i.e. past debts are being repaid.

The story in terms of the growth of the money supply is much less straightforward. It has already been mentioned that identification of the money supply in a country such as the UK is fraught with difficulty. The development of a single measure of money supply for medium term financial strategy control purposes has proved impossible. The various measures of the money supply have been targeted, defined, re-targeted and re-defined. They have proved to be poor indicators of the level of economic activity. Nevertheless, the rules of the game state that the medium term financial strategy *must* have a target for money supply growth and currently this is M0 (notes and coins in circulation, plus till money and the banks' operational funds deposited at the Bank of England – again see Chapter 14).

It is partly because of the difficulty of identifying what *is* the money supply that governments since 1979 have not attempted to control the rate of growth of the money supply directly. This original gangplank of monetarist policy has had to be achieved by indirect means (for example supply side measures – see Sections **7** to **10** below).

Besides the identification problem there has been the added difficulty of how control in a direct form might be achieved. Past governments have used direct controls. For example, they can use directives or requests to clearing banks to curtail their lending policies, or physical controls such as the Supplementary Special Deposits Scheme – the corset – to regulate banking business. (The *corset* gets its name in the following way: where a bank lends in excess of the Bank of England's guidelines it is required to make a special deposit of cash at the Bank of England. Since banks multiply up their cash deposits and 'create credit' several times greater than the cash itself, any removal of cash by the special deposit scheme means that lending must be cut by a much larger amount. Now if a bank lends aggressively and exceeds its permitted limits by greater amounts a far heavier special deposit is called for. Therefore a bank which chases quick profits, by lending to people unable to get loans elsewhere, is punished by having its lending activities squeezed tighter and tighter as it goes further and further beyond the point the Bank of England deems desirable. This is the corset.)

Understandably banks object to this kind of interference and put such objections to government, through the Bank of England which is charged under the Banking Act 1987 with controlling them.

With a government which itself dislikes the state intervening in the economy it is not surprising that the views of the banking community should prevail. Since 1981 there have been none of the restrictions on the volume of lending which prevailed for the previous 20 or so years.

For this reason, and because of the likely impact of controls on virtually any measure of the supply of money, current government policy on the control of money supply rests almost solely on the manipulation of the rate of interest. As interest rates rise it is argued that borrowers will be driven out of the market. The less they want to borrow the smaller the scope for the lending institutions to expand their businesses and the slower the growth of the money supply. Effectively the growth of the supply of money is being curtailed through action taken against the demand for money.

7 MONETARISM AND SUPPLY-SIDE ECONOMICS

While Keynesian economics was concerned with the demand side of the economy, and the feeling that the 'great depression' of the 1930s was caused by a lack of demand in the economy, monetarist policies are concerned with supply-side economics. Supply-side economics shifts the emphasis in economic policy away from demand management, and towards influencing what is happening on the supply-side. A strong centralised control of the economy can produce adverse developments. Chiefly these take the form of impediments to free activity, so that firms, companies and individuals cannot respond quickly to changing conditions. The role of market forces is reduced; regulations and bureaucratic controls clog up the arteries of commerce and the time comes when a return to old-fashioned *laisser faire* is required, the argument goes.

Supply-side measures are not macro-economic measures but micro-economic; They operate at grass-roots levels, where firms, companies, trade unions and entrepreneurs are wrestling with the problems of production, distribution and exchange. We may characterise supply-side measures as measures designed to make markets work better. The markets we are thinking about are the factor markets, where land, labour and capital resources are being put to work to create goods and services. They are designed to increase the creation of wealth (defined as an abundance of goods and services) and thus make the supply of goods and services greater. We are back to the equation:

$$MV = PT$$

If we can increase T, the number of transactions that are possible, we should be able to bring down prices, so long as the supply of money and the velocity of money do not alter.

We can list the supply side measures under three main headings; the market for labour, the capital market and the field of entrepreneurial effort.

8   SUPPLY-SIDE MEASURES IN THE MARKET FOR LABOUR

Some of the chief problems in the market for labour are mobility, disincentives to take employment and the disinclination of employers to employ. Looking at these in turn we have the following possible measures:

The mobility of labour

Labour tends to be immobile, because problems associated with housing, pensions, skills and trade union restrictive practices present themselves. Housing problems can be eased if more people own their own homes, because then it is just a case of the sale of one property and the purchase of another. Even then movement is inhibited if great differences in house prices from region to region exist. Those in council-owned accommodation may hesitate to move if they cannot exchange to comparable accommodation in another area. Those on waiting lists near the top will not move for fear of losing a housing opportunity. There is now a Tenants Exchange Scheme and a National Mobility Office to help those in council accommodation, new towns and housing associations move to areas where jobs are available. Stamp duty on the sale of houses has been cut and the solicitors' monopoly on conveyancing is to be ended.

Pensions often tie an employee to a named firm. If the employee moves the loss of pension rights can be serious. Legislation is in hand to permit pensions to be transferred from one employer to another.

Skill training promotes mobility. Changes in education (to make it marginally more work orientated) and in training (to encourage young people and adult returners to retrain) can make transfers more simple and more acceptable. Traditional apprenticeships lasting many years are inappropriate as work becomes more computerised with the operative able to learn in a few hours what previously required years of experience.

Trade union restrictive practices are a block to the promotion or engagement of many young people. A particularly blatant example is the conduct of the Equity trade union in the entertainment industry, where young actors often cannot get a job without an Equity card and cannot get an Equity card until they get a job. A great many new regulations to restrict the worst abuses of trade union power have been introduced in recent years – but they have not been universally welcomed. There is a fine dividing line between greater freedom and the ability of the employer to exploit the employees.

Disincentives to employment

The chief disincentive to employment is the 'poverty trap'. This stops people taking employment because they will be worse off if they do than if they were unemployed and drawing the full range of benefits that are available. It also prevents low-paid people re-training and learning new skills because they can rarely command a reasonable wage using their new skills until they get experience in that new trade. One of the troubles is that present tax rates and national insurance contributions are too high at the lower end of the wage spectrum. Such reductions as have taken place, apart from a small cut in the basic rate of tax, have tended to benefit the well-to-do and the employer, rather than the low paid.

Despite this there have been some measures to improve the lot of the low paid, for example the unemployed have been guaranteed £10 more in employment than they get when unemployed. The Enterprise Allowance Scheme of £40 per week (£80 for a married couple if both were genuinely unemployed) for one year after setting-up in business has encouraged many people to try self-employment.

The employer's disinclination to employ

This problem has been tackled in several ways. First the employer's side of national insurance contributions has been reduced slightly, and taxes on profits have been cut so that the employer has more money available. The investment allowances, which allowed an employer to claim 100 per cent allowances against new capital expenditure in the first year has been reduced to only 25 per cent. 100 per cent allowances were encouraging employers to buy a machine rather than take on labour, and this was a disadvantage (especially if the machine was imported). A wide variety of laws designed to protect employed labour, such as minimum wage regulations, minimum hours regulations, security of employment, etc., discouraged the hiring of labour because there was no way of firing it. Countless plumbers without a plumber's mate, and plasterers without a plasterer's mate, were forced, for fear of petty legislation, to refrain from taking on a mate (except on the 'black economy', with no proper employment status for the person given work). These matters have now been taken in hand, and many of the controls are being swept away. The worry is that in so doing we may lose some of the protection given to the less well-placed in society; though it could be argued that anything that encourages the employment of the weaker members of society is actually in their best interests. The principle, from the point of view of a Government wishing to encourage market forces is 'government regulations should not impose such a burden on employers that they prefer not to employ'.

9   SUPPLY-SIDE MEASURES IN THE MARKET FOR CAPITAL

Here the measures are much easier to implement than in the labour market. For example:

a) Foreign exchange controls have been abolished. Capital can be exported, and imported without restriction.

b) Dividend controls have been abolished. Forcing companies to keep profits within the company only leads to wasteful use of the moneys thus accumulated. Distributing the dividends enables capital to be re-deployed to help penniless inventors find the funds they are looking for to exploit their ideas.

c) Controls on bank lending have been abolished.

d) Hire purchase controls have been abolished.

e) Building societies, trustee savings banks and other institutions have been allowed greater freedom, and commercial common-sense rather than regulation has been the standpoint from which many lending and borrowing activities have now to be judged.

f) The stock exchange has been streamlined, and has become fiercely competitive. This is explained elsewhere in this book.

The general conclusion we can draw from all these measures is that, while this release of competitive energies in the capital markets has been traditionally a game which rich people play better than the generality of mankind, so much of the wealth these days is in the hands of institutional investors such as insurance companies, investment trusts, etc., acting on behalf of the general public that the broad generality of the population do in fact benefit from the financial activities taking place.

10 SUPPLY-SIDE MEASURES TO ENCOURAGE ENTERPRISE AND COMPETITION

Those who believe in market forces believe that the market place is the natural centre for business activity and anything that restricts free entry to the markets is *prima facie* undesirable. Enterprises by their very nature start small, but may grow to play a useful, and eventually a significant part in the economy. Therefore any official measures taken at a grass-roots level to encourage enterprise are justified. They are also usually quite inexpensive. For example the services of an organisation like the Small Firms Service do not cost anything like the subsidies that have been given over the years to such declining industries as shipbuilding, coal mining, railways, etc. The Enterprise Allowance Scheme, which only lasts one year, costs less than the social security money it replaces, and since about 70 per cent of those who set out to take up self-employment actually succeed it is well worth while spending the tiny sums involved.

Other measures are the reduction in red-tape bureaucratic procedures, such as planning permission for small developments. The release of publicly owned land (often near derelict land) encourages development. Office development permits have been abolished so that development can take place in any area where the developers see a commercial opportunity, rather than where bureaucrats deem development desirable.

By definition the market is a place where competition thrives, and measures taken to improve competition assist enterprise. Any system where privilege and vested interests can resist the intrusion of new enterprises is undesirable. A number of measures to strengthen competition have reduced the privileges of some professions – for example solicitors, accountants and opticians now operate in a more competitive environment. The privatisation of many industries has certainly reduced feather-bedding of both management and trade unions, and the ability of trade unionists to operate closed shops and prevent the introduction of new technology has been greatly reduced. All such measures are aspects of the general policy of which monetarism is the central core.

11 THE IMPLICATIONS OF MONETARIST POLICIES FOR ENTREPRENEURS

The change from Keynesian economic policies to monetarist policies has important implications for entrepreneurs. The whole climate of enterprise has changed to a more market-orientated approach. The market place becomes more free, but freedom brings responsibility. Government interference is reduced, but the entrepreneur can no longer assume, as he came to do in the Keynesian era, that 'hard times' would never return. The certainty that the government will prime the pump anew in any deteriorating situation, so that the 'Go' part of the Stop-Go cycle would return within a very short time, has disappeared. Indeed, so long as inflation is present the probability is that demand will not be stimulated and that money will remain tight. The opportunities to show enterprise are increased but government rescues to save the collapse of firms are no longer available, and management must return to managing its own affairs. Those who concede wage increases not justified by productivity will face bankruptcy, and the spate of take-overs that resulted in the 1980s led to a considerable shake-out of surplus labour and to the creation of leaner, fitter, industrial firms. That a great deal of industry has yet to recover is only evidence of its uncompetitive state under Keynesianism.

A further point is that 'freedom' in the market for factors does not mean the same sort of freedom that prevailed in former times. Monetarists do not propose a return to *laissez faire*, which would be quite impossible in the present social climate. Businessmen will still have to bear the true burden of costs that they should bear as a result of their activities. The burdens of polluted atmosphere, polluted rivers, uncompensated workers, etc., which early capitalists heaped upon their fellow men as socially-borne costs will not be tolerated today. Consequently, business costs remain high at a time when money is short because of monetarist controls. Between the two forces some firms have faced cash-flow problems and many have gone out of business. Those who have survived have had to become extremely cost conscious, and sound measures of budgetary control have been necessary to ensure survival in the face of tight money policies and foreign competition.

SELF-ASSESSMENT QUESTIONS

1 Why did Keynesian economics fall into disfavour in the 1970s and 80s?

2 Why is monetarism thought to be particularly capable of dealing with inflation?

3 What are the basic beliefs of monetarism?

4 Why must V and T be regarded as stable in the long run?

5 Why do monetarists reject the idea that you can fine-tune the money supply?

REVISION TEST

Answers	Questions
—	**1** What ideas prevailed in Economics from 1945 to 1970?
1 Keynesian ideas, and Keynesian policies.	**2** What are the chief aims of Keynesian policies?
2 Full employment and managed prosperity.	**3** What criticisms could be made of Keynesian economics?
3 It is better at curing a slump in the short term than sustaining and controlling growth in the long term.	**4** What is the science of macro-dynamics?
4 The branch of economics which seeks to discover how long-term growth may be achieved and managed.	**5** What is the 'new-monetarism'?
5 A movement in economics which seeks to control inflation by a tight-money policy and the re-introduction of stern market forces to control economic activity.	**6** What are the basic beliefs of monetarism?
6 (a) State intervention should be kept to a minimum, (b) State expenditure should be kept to a minimum, (c) control should be exercised over the rate of growth of the money supply.	**7** In practical terms, what do monetarist policies require?
7 Supply side measures, rather than demand management.	**8** How would you characterise supply side measures?
8 As measures designed to make the markets work better.	**9** What markets are we talking about?

9 The factor markets, where land, labour and capital are being combined by entrepreneurs to create goods and services.

10 How can we free the market for land?

10 By reducing bureaucratic controls; planning regulations, zoning regulations, direction of enterprise into special areas etc. Also the release of hoarded land held by nationalised industries, quangos, government and local government departments, etc.

11 How can we free the market for labour?

11 By curbing trade union power. By encouraging labour mobility. By removing well-intentioned but restrictive legislation on such things as low pay, employment of young people etc etc.

12 What is the monetarist view of regulations upon employers?

12 Government regulations should not impose such a burden on employers that they prefer not to employ.

Go over the questions again until you are sure of all the answers.

ANSWERS

(See Self-assessment questions on page 332.)

1 Keynsian economics fell into disfavour because of its inability to solve the inflation problems that developed in the 1970s. For a variety of reasons productivity was low, the burdens placed upon enterprise were great, money supply was expanding in an uncontrolled way and an increasingly sophisticated population knew how to increase the velocity of money to defeat any measures introduced to control the economy.

2 Monetarism is thought to be particularly capable of dealing with inflation because it emphasises the link between the money supply and the level of prices. It believes that increases in the money stock are bound to be transmitted through to prices, since those who have more money to spend will seek to increase their satisfactions by spending some of the money, and since extra supplies of goods are not available they will bid up prices.

3 The basic beliefs of monetarism are: (a) minimum state intervention, (b) minimum state expenditure, (c) control of the rate of growth of the money supply.

4 V and T, monetarists believe, must be regarded as stable in the long run if a direct link between M, the money supply, and P, the price level, is to be established.

5 Monetarists reject the idea that you can manipulate the money supply finely, because there are difficulties in the timing and magnitude of the measures to be used, and undershooting and overshooting are almost inevitable in trying to regulate an item which is itself very difficult to measure and identify.

QUESTIONS ON CHAPTER 12

1 Account for the Monetarist School's return to market economics, and rejection of Keynesianism in the 1970s and 1980s.

2 In what ways is a tight-money policy more difficult for entrepreneurs than a Keynesian policy?

3 What are the implications of monetarist policies for businessmen?

4 On what grounds is it argued that in a developed economy all suggested cures for inflation lead to increased unemployment?

(Courtesy of the Institute of Marketing)

5 In what ways may the government encourage enterprise at a time of high unemployment?

6 How would you recognise whether a government is pursuing a monetarist policy?

(Courtesy of the Institute of Marketing)

7 Compare and contrast the monetarist and Keynesian views of inflation.

(Courtesy of the Institute of Marketing)

8 What are supply-side measures? How do they operate to restore an economy to good heart?

9 'Monetary policies have destroyed the broad basis of British industry.' 'Monetary policies have led to the regeneration of British industry and national prosperity.' Assess the validity of these two statements in the light of British experience in the 1980s.

10 Why is it that governments following monetarist policies often choose to influence the price of money, i.e. the rate of interest, rather than the supply of money, even though the latter would seem to be a more direct method?

TIPS FOR STUDENTS: A SPECIMEN ANSWER TO QUESTION 10

The answer should include the following points:

a) The realities of a sophisticated economy make (i) the identification, and (ii) the manipulation of the money supply, much more difficult than cursory consideration would suggest.

b) A great deal of extra money (money supply) is created by the banking network. The banks do not create this money at random, they create it in response to demand. Customers demand such borrowing because they wish to spend more, but they are unlikely to borrow regardless of price. The price of money is the rate of interest charged, and a government wishing to slow down the rate of growth of the money supply would do best to raise the rate of interest to such a level that it dampens demand for created credit. The best way to restrict the money supply is to persuade those who wish it to be extended that it is in their best interests to hold back and restrain their own demand.

13 A survey of technology

1 INTRODUCTION

Most economic theory, especially that defined as micro-economics, ignores the existence of technical change. This is so even when dealing with the factor capital where it is admitted that there can be changes in quality, as well as in quantity. In reality, technical (or technological) change is so important in a modern economy as in itself to qualify as a separate factor of production.

For the most part, efforts to advance production techniques before the First World War were amateur affairs. The individual 'improver' or 'tinkerer' working in his shed or basement was just as likely to stumble across a major invention as was the large industrial enterprise. This was because large firms tended not to have teams of scientists and engineers working on formal research and application projects: they depended upon the discoveries of individuals who not only worked alone but were also self-financed.

Today, although there is definitely room for the individual innovator, most research is undertaken by large firms and institutions. The larger industrial firms tend on the whole to direct their formal research programmes towards areas which they might themselves 'apply', the object of the exercise being to generate greater profits. This is not to say that private firms do not undertake 'basic' research, but it is no surprise that most basic research takes place within institutions such as universities – there is no guarantee that basic research will ever benefit anyone, although there is a general expectation that it will prove useful.

A really rapid development is the way in which UK governments have become involved in expenditure upon research. It is true that even late nineteenth-century governments encouraged inventors, especially where their inventions might have a military application. The Royal Navy tried out many types of iron-clad steam-driven warships before eventually settling upon the Dreadnought pattern in the early 1900s. Military applications apart, in line with pre-Keynesian attitudes to government there was no massive direct employment of research teams and very little government money available.

Today, of course, the situation is quite different, particularly in the fields of agriculture, public health and defence, where the bulk of expenditure is made directly by government departments. In addition, many of the funds available to universities come directly from government grants, and private firms' research activities are in part subsidised by government tax concessions.

Broadly, technical progress takes two forms: improvements in *methods* of production and improvements relating to *new products*. Obviously, while it is possible to identify these two aspects of technical progress, it is also true that there is a great deal of interrelation. Quite often a new product requires new methods of production if it is to go onto the market at all. Similarly, it is not unknown for a new product to be devised precisely to take advantage of new methods of production.

2 IMPROVEMENTS IN METHODS OF PRODUCTION

It is possible for inventions to be thrown up by chance; alternatively a definite programme might pursue the invention of a particular process relentlessly until near perfection is reached.

Quite often an idea must 'sit around' until a discovery in an unrelated area makes its application possible. In addition, some discoveries are spin-offs from a main research programme and are almost fortuitous. Whatever the method of discovery, inventions really become of major importance within an economy only when they are applied, i.e. when they become innovations. The word 'innovations' is used here to mean the practical application of an idea that has already been discovered or invented, but is only now to be exploited.

At any time there will be a backlog of potentially usable inventions waiting to become innovations. When these inventions are embodied in innovations then technical change has taken place; in relation to methods of production this technical change might mean new designs of equipment, new materials, or new processes.

3 CAPITAL ACCUMULATION AND UNCERTAINTY

No investment lasts for ever. Even if there is physical durability attached to equipment, the range of products and methods of production associated with them are constantly changing. In order to continue in existence firms therefore have to keep abreast of technical developments. They have to replace old equipment with new, even if that old equipment is not completely worn out. In order to provide new equipment firms have to maintain their capacity to earn profits. There are periods where the prospect of profits being opened up by innovations is greater than at other times and this will encourage firms to innovate. The rate of innovation is, in fact, likely to be greatest when the rate of investment is high, because it is obviously advantageous for entrepreneurs to install the most up-to-date line in plant when investment is being made.

The relationship between the accumulation of capital and the rate of innovation was forcefully put by an Austrian (and eventually an American) economist, Joseph Schumpeter. He felt that variations in the rate of technical change were sufficient to explain observed fluctuations in activity known as the trade cycle. He suggested that occasionally an innovation is made which promises great profit for firms which adopt it. Forward-looking firms seize the opportunity presented and other firms follow. During this period of intensive investment the economy is characterised by high employment, high consumption and high profits. From these high profits a surplus of funds is generated which can be devoted to adapting a backlog of innovative ideas in industries not affected by the initial innovation. Eventually, though, all the equipment associated with the initial innovation has been installed and the level of investment falls, causing a general depression. There are still discoveries being made and potentially useful innovations available but because the level of investment is low they largely go into 'cold store' until one generates enough interest to spark off a new boom. Such an explanation of fluctuations is quite consistent with the ideas of the accelerator (see Chapter 10, pages 288–9) and the multiplier, (see Chapter 11, page 310) and might provide some clue to the state of optimism or pessimism of businessmen.

Alternatively, there might be a much simpler explanation: capital starvation. Once available stocks of capital are committed no further innovation can take place. This is so even though the innovations waiting in 'cold store' may contribute more to economic growth and further accumulation than the innovations which have just taken place. This problem was particularly felt in the eighteenth and nineteenth centuries when a series of 'manias' – such as the canal and railway manias – swept the country. In 1845, besides 118 railways in the process of construction, there were 1263 seeking £566 000 000 in capital, and this at a time when the financial system would have been hard pressed to raise a tenth of that amount.

In a modern economy, though, some role in the accumulation/innovation exercise must be found for government. Section 8, page 345, deals more fully with this.

The discussion of technical change and the amount of investment required to absorb it into productive capacity often takes the form of a distinction between *neutral* and *biased* accumulation. These terms are part of an extremely involved body of economic knowledge, but briefly innovations are said to be neutral when over a period of time the cost of equipping a workforce with machines does not change, i.e. the amounts of labour and capital required to provide the latest machine are the same as those used to provide earlier, less technically advanced machines. Innovations are biased when they allow production processes to be equipped while using less capital in *providing* the equipment (known as capital-saving bias), or where the *provision* of equipment uses more capital than did the machines being replaced (known as capital-using bias).

Techniques which can offer capital-saving or neutral innovations are superior to those they replace since they will bring forth a greater output from less, or the same, investment. This does not mean that capital-using techniques cannot be superior to those which they displace – they can. Providing that the cost of adopting the new equipment does not amount to more than the value of the extra output from the equipment when it is in use, the capital-using innovation will still be worthwhile.

There are instances, of course, where there are no superior techniques available, and the existing stock of machinery is the best available. Even so, firms may still be eager to increase productive capacity and might therefore be prepared to raise the cost of investment per unit of output because they can conceive of no other way of raising output. Such a process is known as **capital deepening**. One special kind of capital deepening is the increase in the proportion of the labour force re-equipped year by year. This means that the active life of each machine becomes less and the proportion of the capital stock which is new, and therefore more reliable and productive, is increased.

One of the uncertainties associated with an investment in capital equipment is the lifetime earnings of such an investment. Firms which own machines do not want to see the value of such machines disappear as the machine wears out. They must provide for depreciation – it is necessary to recover from the lifetime earnings of the machine sufficient to allow investment to take place in another machine of at least equal value when the useful life of the first machine comes to an end. In order to do this two things are necessary. First, a deduction must be made from the profits earned to reduce the profits available for distribution to the shareholders or other owners of the firm. Secondly, the money thus released must be safely invested until the time that it is needed to replace the asset. If left in the system it may be used on non-essential items. It could be stored away in a balanced portfolio of shares to be realised when the new asset is required, or it can be used to purchase an endowment assurance policy which will provide the capital sum required. This sum should be large enough in inflationary times to provide for the purchase of a new asset at the increased price. Successful businesses tend to do this as a matter of course; the finance they invest is continually being recovered and reinvested in fresh types of physical capital.

Inflation makes provision for depreciation very difficult, but so does technical progress. The lifetime earnings of any machine lie in the future and cannot be known precisely. Informed estimates can be proved drastically inaccurate by the sudden emergence of a technically superior article which renders the existing stock obsolete.

4 WHY FIRMS DECIDE UPON NEW TECHNIQUES OF PRODUCTION

Firms invest in new techniques because they expect to earn profits from such investment. However, even if a firm does succeed in reaping benefits from investments in new techniques, it knows that eventually such profit is likely to be eroded by the appearance of some improvement in the hands of a competitor. Despite this, the investment will still be made and the basic reason is fear; fear that if a firm fails to take advantage of new techniques as they come along, other enterprises will.

There will always be some firms that are ahead of others in their particular line of business. When they have made new investment other firms are often forced to follow, since they cannot compete with the obsolete methods of production at their disposal. Failure to invest in new techniques would mean they would gradually go out of business. These less inventive firms are also forced to *continue* the process of innovation, since the leaders tend not to stop once a new technique has been introduced – they employ research staffs to think up and develop further improvements. They also take over experiments made by the host of innovators who have good ideas but little capital with which to develop those ideas. By being adventurous in an innovative sense, the leaders in any line of production manage to stay 'one jump ahead' of the competition and in doing so earn for themselves a higher return on capital employed – from this they are then able to pay higher wages. Because the firms which follow cannot afford to pay such wages while using the old techniques they are forced to discard their obsolete methods of production. The pace of innovation then in part reflects the degree of competition involved. Productive capacity is built up, in Schumpeter's words, in 'a gale of creative destruction'.

The leading firms make great use of patent laws in their search for continued supremacy. Even classical economists in the nineteenth century, while supporting the ideas behind perfect competition – free entry into an industry and free access of information – were generally also in favour of patent laws. They recognised that firms are less willing to innovate if they feel unsure of reaping the rewards of the innovation. Patent laws were therefore suggested as a means of extending the short-run period within which the discovering firm could, in effect, enjoy its 'patent monopoly'.

Some 50 000 patents are applied for each year in Great Britain alone, of which about 40 000 are granted. In addition, separate registers of European patents and PCT patents (under the Pattern Cooperation Treaty) also exist.

It might be thought that patents are of importance only in relation to the introduction of new products, but this is not so. There are many processes which are protected by patent and from a businessman's point of view a great advantage is conferred if some cost-saving technique is denied his competitors. In many countries the patent fee payable (to maintain a monopoly) is reduced if the patent-holder agrees to general licensing of the invention to make it freely available for a licence fee. This is the case in the UK and in Germany.

In developed countries patents are normally very important and have the following economic consequences where they lead to patent monopolies:

1 While the 'extended' short-term period is operative firms can charge very high prices which need not bear any relation to the costs incurred in producing the product or adopting the technique.

2 Eventually new firms will innovate in order to find a way round the patent and this will have the effect of competing away 'patent profits'.

3 During the period in which the patent monopoly does operate (even if this is only some months) extremely large profits *may* be made.

The classic patent case is that of the ball-point pen, where the profits made by the original firm were so large that a host of breaches of the patent followed one another in quick succession and a whole series of law suits resulted.

It is estimated that the Reynolds International Pen Company earned more than $500 000 profits in only one month, soon after introducing the first ball-point pen in 1945. (The capital of the Company when established was only $26 000!)

SELF-ASSESSMENT QUESTIONS

1 What is technology?

2 What brings about technological change?

3 What is a patent? How does it help the inventor of a new machine or component?

4 A firm is considering the replacement of its machinery by the latest equipment. What considerations enter into the decision?

5   THE DEVELOPMENT OF NEW PRODUCTS

Most of us are more familiar with technical progress than we realise, even though we might not work in an industry which is regarded as being in the forefront of the 'technological revolution'. As consumers most of the products we purchase reach us as a result of some technological development. Many such developments have been so absorbed into economic life in developed countries for so many years that we cease to think of them at all. For example, we take for granted the great advances made in the movement of goods and information, which are so vital if an economy based on specialisation is to function. What is perhaps even more surprising is the rate at which we absorb the new products made available by technology. In the normal UK home there are likely to be at least a dozen goods which were unknown 25 years ago. The most pervasive of these is the colour television set; but others include items made from mineral-oil derivatives – non-burn surfaces, non-stick surfaces, home insulation, radio telephones, satellite dishes to collect entertainment beamed from space, etc.

The development of new goods not only encourages the level of investment but it also stimulates spending. There is status to be gained by being one of the first possessors of a compact disc player, personal stereo, solar-powered calculator, car telephone, etc. Wherever possible, manufacturers invoke the patent laws mentioned in Chapter 7 in order to prolong the advantage of having introduced a new product.

The development of new products and new services is an essential element in the forward planning of all companies who are seeking to stay ahead of their competitors. Some of the developments will be complete innovations; others may be re-vamped versions of existing products using new materials; some will be re-styled models or perhaps the same old model presented in new packaging. A great many new products are 'me-too' items; imitations of lines developed by other companies designed to capture some of the market. A recent example is the Filofax® a clever pocket-book collection of personal records and effects which became so popular that almost every major stationer and many professional bodies jumped upon the bandwagon and produced an imitation of the Filofax, claiming that they too, had a product in the Filofax style. Many 'me-too' products may not be in direct competition with the original product, but eat into the general market to erode away the original product's profitability. Thus imitation products directed specifically at teachers, engineers, doctors, etc., eat into the general market for the Filofax product in what the original producers can only regard as an unfair way; yet it is doubtful whether a legal action for infringement of copyright would be upheld by the Courts.

6   CAPITAL ACCUMULATION AND TECHNOLOGY

Traditionally capital accumulation and technology have tended to go hand in hand. New equipment could not be afforded unless the capital was available to invest in it, and starving inventors scoured the world to find those prepared to invest in the development of a new technology. The failure of UK companies to risk investment in British ideas is one of the commonest complaints in the British press, and such examples as the hovercraft have become world-famous. Invented by Christopher Cockerell, an electronics engineer with Marconi, who left them to set up his own boat-building and hiring business on the Norfolk Broads, the hovercraft was his solution to reducing the resistance encountered by a hull as it travels through water. Despite the manifest advantages to be gained by 'flying' a boat over the water, Cockerell could not find risk capital in the UK to develop the idea, and its fullest development came only from abroad, for military uses.

By contrast, where a new technology is taken up it can generate enormous profits for re-investment. These profits take the form of cash balances, generated by the new methods of output as sales grow and costs of production are reduced. In one recent year a severe setback in the United States economy which created serious unemployment and lowered wages generally enabled profits of America's top 500 companies (those most advanced in using new technologies) to rise by 25 per cent. In an era where takeover threats are certain to arise if a company has unused cash balances the companies were faced with a problem. What should they do with the money? They could (a) plough it back into existing businesses or (b) diversify into new areas or (c) pay it out as increased dividends. While the latter may be theoretically the best solution in economic terms (enabling the shareholders to re-cycle it to penniless inventors in search of capital) managements rarely sought this solution. Diversification has proved to be an unsatisfactory policy in recent years because it means taking over companies whose technology we do not understand and trying to run them better than their original owners who did understand it. The popular solution was to re-invest in one's own industry, and grow.

7 HOW INNOVATION AFFECTS EMPLOYMENT AND WAGES

It is not difficult to form the impression that technological advance of an applied nature is to the advantage of everyone – that it brings us nearer to a society where drudgery and toil might disappear with no corresponding reduction in the availability of goods and services. However, there are a number of drawbacks associated with technology and one of these manifests itself in the area of employment.

When technical advance occurs one of the normal outcomes is a rise in output per person employed. This might easily be absorbed without any displacement of labour if there is rising demand for the production or if the amount demanded can be expected to respond to a reduction in price brought about by introducing the technique. Suppose, though, that it is not anticipated that a great deal of extra output can be disposed of. Here there is every likelihood that at least some of the labour force will become 'technologically unemployed', i.e. will have to leave the industry and find employment elsewhere.

Not all labour forces, though, have been prepared to accept technological unemployment. Where there is a relatively small, highly concentrated and well organised labour force – as in the Fleet Street printing shops – an alternative to technological unemployment was, for a long time, negotiated overstaffing, i.e. continuing to operate advanced machinery with as many people as were required to operate earlier, inferior machines. Such overstaffing is a logical reaction from the point of view of those who may lose their jobs, and might also appeal, to some extent, to manufacturers; the gains from the new technology could be sufficient to enable them to 'carry' the 'disguisedly unemployed' labour. Where foreign competition cannot be excluded the duration of 'carrying' under-employed labour may be limited, or imports may be sucked in to the general disadvantage of the home industry.

In a situation where technology is advancing and there is a fairly large 'pool' of unemployed labour it might be possible for businessmen to keep the real wage rate at a constant level and to take the fruits of technology in the form of higher profits per man employed. Such a policy would contain dangers, though, since if the real value of wages does not change, even to keep a constant labour force employed as income rises assumes that an increasing share of income must be going in investment. As the ratio of savings to income then rose, and investment failed to expand fast enough to maintain the level of employment, the full benefits of technological advance would be lost through unemployment. That such an outcome from technical advance is not widespread has tended to depend upon the rise in the value of real wages, particularly over the last 35 years or so. These have risen in part because:

1 Workers have combined to force, where possible, an increase in the real value of wages.
2 Businessmen who install technically advanced equipment are prepared to 'buy off' a potentially troublesome labour force in order to take advantage of some of the benefits from such equipment.
3 As goods are increasingly manufactured for a mass market (as a result of the economies of scale associated with some technical advances), prices have to be kept low to tap such a market. This tends to raise real wages, even if money wages remain stable.
4 Increasing real wages in the advanced countries have often been at the expense of low incomes in those parts of the world supplying primary products.

When real wages rise in value in step with output this removes some of the problems associated with growing saving, since wage earners on the whole tend to consume most of their incomes. The problem of withdrawals from the circular flow of incomes becomes correspondingly easier to deal with and the danger of mass unemployment is averted. (The circular flow of incomes is explained more fully in Chapter 11, pages 302–3).

One final point is this. A trade union's attempts to negotiate overstaffing can only be pushed so far, since the continued employment of their privileged members is being made possible by the sacrifice of consumers generally – forced to pay higher prices than they should. Many of these consumers are worse off than the privileged trade unionists, and an increasing number of them will be unemployed. The government may step in to redress the unfairness, or the misuse of the new technology may be so blatant that it arouses popular unrest. Sooner or later the industry will be rationalised and a more sensible and just system will be applied to reduce the labour force to the logical level in the new technological situation.

8   THE GOVERNMENT AND TECHNOLOGY

Government in the UK currently spends around £5 billion on science and technology. About half of this is for defence purposes and around about one quarter for research by universities and research councils.

The Government's approaches to this expenditure are set out in two major white papers: CMND 8591 (1982) and CM 185 (1987).

CMND 8591 states that 'Excellence in the development and exploitation of science and its applications is essential if the economic prosperity of the country is to be advanced in the coming decades, and if companies based on science and technology are to play their part in providing new employment opportunities'.

CM 185 states 'Advances in science and technology, and the early exploitation of those advances, are essential to national success.'

These broad statements, while most desirable, need much detailed work in order that their objectives can be achieved. To this end four major areas can be identified.

a) Efforts to bring about better industrial and commercial exploitation of scientific discoveries.
b) Efforts to achieve technology transfer.
c) A more international approach to research and development.
d) Contracting out of Government research and development requirements.

a) **Better exploitation**   It has long been recognised that while the UK is a leader in many fields of research and discovery, it lags behind when its discoveries come to the stage of application. To overcome this poor performance in the area of exploitation the Government has introduced the following measures:

(i)   It has allowed universities *to retain sums* earned from outside sources without losing any of their government grant. This is intended to bring the sponsors (industry) and the academic world closer together.

(ii)   Relaxation of ownership of discoveries. Discoveries financed by research council funds used to belong (unless ownership was waived) to the British Technology Group. Since September 1984 this has ceased to be the case. This relaxation of restrictions brings together researchers and those companies interested in exploiting their ideas.

(iii)   The development of science parks by English Estates – a government funded body.

(iv)   The Teaching Company Scheme. Under this scheme high quality graduates are appointed on two year contracts to work full time in a company on agreed projects.

(v)   LINK. Under the LINK programme the government intends to spend £210 million over the next five years in order to foster strategic areas of research directed towards new products and processes in industry. LINK is prepared to pay up to half the cost of collaborative projects between the scientific community and industry, and has, as one of its main aims, the object of getting industry itself to spend more on research and development.

b) **Technology transfer**   This can be sumarised as an attempt to make sure that all firms and companies which might benefit from the existing (and growing) pool of technology are aware of its availability in order that they can evaluate its possible applicability to their own field. Two significant Government developments were:

(i) The Department of Trade and Industry spent over £70 million on technology transfer activities; for example industrial training and education, consultancy and advisory services etc.

(ii) The Government established Defence Technology Enterprises Ltd in 1985 (in conjunction with City of London instututions) as a means of scouring Defence Research Establishments in order to expose commercially exploitable ideas.

c) **A more international approach** In addition to the defence field, where Government has long recognised the savings from collaboration with other defence establishments abroad, there has been increased interest in collaboration in areas suitable for commercial exploitation. The most important of the current projects of this latter type is EUREKA, where industrialists throughout Europe are acting together, backed up by Government encouragement and support. There are about 165 EUREKA projects currently operating and the UK is involved in around one-third of these.

d) **Contracting out of Government research and development** The Government is a major spender in the field of R&D and in order to stimulate private firms' R&D efforts further, it is believed that the Government should become a 'customer' of some firms for its R&D requirements. The thinking behind this is the stimulation of the private sector's efforts – less than 1 per cent of GNP was spent by industry funding R&D in 1985. This compares with 1.3 per cent for the USA, 1.6 per cent for Germany and 1.8 per cent in Japan.

9 COMPUTERISATION AND TECHNOLOGY

The most dramatic development in the technological field has been the computer. It has been calculated by one American economist that it takes about 60 years for a new technology to develop to the point where it permeates the whole of society. Taking 1940 as a rough starting point for the development of the computer we are moving into the last decade of its 60 year development and it has certainly borne out the calculation. Even toddlers punch keys these days and are more familiar with visual display units than with dolls and teddy bears. The miniaturisation of computers, which has been made possible by the development of silicon chips, has made it possible to include computerised circuits even in toys.

The so-called 'silicon chip' is a silicon integrated circuit, and it is manufactured by taking as a base a thin wafer of silicon (about the size of a child's small fingernail) and building upon it a series of circuits and desired inter-connections. The circuitry and interconnections are constructed using photographic masks and electron beams, and a single chip can have thousands of separate circuit components upon it. The chip is, in fact, an extension of the miniaturisation process in electronics which received such a boost with the transistor. Compared to the transistor the circuits on a silicon chip are microscopic.

The importance of the silicon chip is quite simply low cost. Relative to their output silicon chips are not expensive. Their small size also means that miniature versions of familiar items can be built inexpensively. The multi-million pound mainframe computer was not only expensive in itself – its bulk meant that special buildings were often required, usually equipped with air-conditioning and dust-filtration plants. A computer built around silicon chips (and known as a microprocessor because it is so small that it sits on a desk top!) can perform most of the tasks of a mainframe computer, and at a tiny fraction of the cost (hundreds rather than millions of pounds). The micro circuit thus makes available computer facilities on a much wider basis. In addition it opens up the possibility of automatic, electronic control in countless applications where previously either price or bulk, or both, militated against this. What will be the impact of micro-technology upon UK industry?

A great deal of the debate surrounding the application of silicon chips involves the effects upon the level of employment. In the UK both government and trade unionists are anxious that already high levels of unemployment should not be increased by the 'technologically unemployed'.

At the simplest level arguments relating to the new technology and employment polarise around two positions: one which states that silicon chips will lead to further unemployment, and one which states that they will not! As justification for their pessimism those forecasting high levels of unemployment point out that high levels of capital intensity coupled with high output must necessarily lead to a reduction in the workforce. Particularly disturbing to those who favour this line of argument is the way in which silicon chip technology is likely to eat into those areas where there has traditionally been absorption of unemployed – private service industry, and central and local government. Countering suggestions that extra labour can be absorbed producing large outputs for overseas markets, pessimists point out that within the developed world many products are already reaching saturation level, and besides the UK's record in selling high technology goods abroad is not an encouraging one.

Optimists feel sure that silicon chip technology is likely to lead to more rather than less employment. To support this view they point out that there is no necessary link between productivity and the rate of unemployment.

Indeed history, both in the UK and other countries seems to show that technological change is a pre-requisite for generating economic growth and increasing real incomes. It seems almost certain that without some increase in productivity in the years ahead there will be increases in unemployment, rather than decreases. Many of the supply-side measures introduced in the 1980s (see Chapter 12) have been designed to raise productivity by setting industry free from restrictions designed to 'protect' privileged sections of the labour force.

From the point of view of a high level of traditional employment there are some disturbing facets to silicon chip technology. Technological change has not suddenly burst upon the economy in the latter half of the twentieth century – it is a process which is of a continuous nature, though there are periods where technological developments accelerate. We have had a 'Steam Age', an 'Electrical Age', a rather short 'Electronic Age' and we are now in a 'Microelectronic Age'. In the past though, the main impact of technology has been felt by manufacturing industry and agriculture. These are both areas which have traditionally shed labour as technological advance has occurred (in this respect agriculture has experienced a dwindling labour force since the 1780s), and in this they have been assisted by the existence of other employment opportunities. In the early part of the nineteenth century the surplus agricultural labour force found employment in expanding industries; later when industry itself needed fewer labour units, expanding private and government services absorbed them with little trouble. One of the most marked characteristics of advanced industrial nations in the twentieth century is the extent to which their service sectors have grown.

However, the applications to which silicon chips can be put lend themselves to service as well as industrial areas. The National Westminster Bank estimates that since 1970 the business it has handled has increased by about 7 per cent per annum, while staff has increased by only 7 per cent overall. Much of the extra workload has been taken on by the computer and micro-processor, allowing the staff employed to pursue more interesting, less mundane tasks. The plain fact is, though, that many more extra staff would have been taken on had it not been for the advance of technology. As the silicon chip comes into increasing use such service areas as banks, insurance companies, brokers, etc., will be able to manage, not with the same staff, but with many less.

An identical argument applies to another safe area of employment which has seen recent expansion in the numbers employed: the 'office' sector of manufacturing industry. How many jobs are computerised systems of costing, purchasing and filing saving in the average large firm? Education is yet another area where computerised learning systems could be used to replace at least some teachers; provided that such systems are cheap enough there could be strong incentives for local authorities to adopt these salary-saving devices.

It is for reasons such as those outlined above that the level of unemployment can be expected to rise if silicon chip technology is vigorously applied. It is true that new industries will be formed to take advantage of the silicon chip and that such industries will need a labour force, but past experience suggests that technologically-based industry tends to be capital-intensive.

It would be surprising if vigorously applied chip technology created as many jobs as it destroyed. What it will do is release people from the boredom of routine work to do more creative things. Such a massive re-direction of effort needs enlightened guidance from political and economic leaders. Whether we have them remains to be seen. One aspect of the new world though, is going to be distressingly familiar – the threat of foreign competition. Production by new methods in those countries where there is little resistance to change will increasingly dominate world markets. It could easily reach the stage where we either compete wholeheartedly, or sink in a sea of foreign products. Recent increases in adverse balances on the Balance of Payments Account seem to suggest the new era has already arrived. Countries such as Korea, Singapore and Taiwan, the so-called NICs (Newly Industrialised Countries) are able to compete very strongly with the established UK industries with higher wage scales and shorter working days.

10 TECHNICAL DEVELOPMENT – THE UK AND ITS MAIN COMPETITORS

A great deal is made of the change since the nineteenth century, when Britain had what seemed an unassailable lead over her competitors in industry. It is suggested that she might have been able to retain industrial supremacy if only she had planned things better, and in particular if the country had devoted more resources to engineering. In other words, the argument is that the British are poor innovators (even though they might be good inventors).

It is well documented how Britain became the world's first industrial power, and how her industry and technology came to dominate the world and help her accumulate an Empire in the process. There can also be no doubt that once other nations adopted manufacturing techniques in line with those used in Britain, she could not expect to keep her industrial lead for very long. Britain is a small nation, poorly endowed with resources and geographically on the margin of the Old World (and far removed from the 'New World'). It is rather surprising that she managed to maintain her position as a major industrial power well into modern times, given that other countries could bring superior resources into operation.

In one sense the early, and enduring, lead built up in the early part of the nineteenth century probably helped accelerate the relative rate of decline of Britain as an industrial power. This is because she was so successful in those early, pioneering days that she tended to continue the methods which were the norm *then*. A great deal of early technical advance in the UK was brought about by practical men with little scientific training. This led later generations to feel that there was little point in gaining scientific training when common sense would prevail. This feeling persists to the present day; many parents still question the value of a formal education for their children on the grounds that they didn't have one themselves!

Britain's competitors, particularly Germany, tended to be more systematic and scientific in their approach to innovation in industry, in part because they realised they would never overtake Britain by applying her common sense methods to their own problems. Because of this they concentrated fairly heavily upon technical universities and colleges, even in the nineteenth century. Yet to claim that the provision of technical education is the whole explanation is too simple. Closer examination of the facts suggests that there may be other significant reasons for the relative decline, and emphasises that Britain does have historical links with Mathematics, Science and Engineering at least as ancient as that of her main competitors. Lectures in Engineering were taking place as early as 1785, which was a full nine years before the 'École Polytechnique' commenced operations in Paris. The first examinations in Engineering were taking place in Cambridge in 1865, only four years after the founding of the Massachusetts Institute of Technology. Unfortunately Mathematics was dropped from the classics tripos at Cambridge in 1894, on the grounds of increasing difficulty as the discipline developed, and it was never reinstituted. Leading schools and universities founded during the next century tended to follow this lead and did not give Mathematics a reasonable degree of emphasis. The basic study for a scientific or engineering-orientated career was, and still is, therefore missing from the backgrounds of most of Britain's most able and best educated men and women. The classical courses followed by the majority of those in the Civil Service in fact encourage the study of a type of society where, by our standards, technological advance is almost completely lacking.

There is evidence to suggest, though, that despite the non-scientific stress given to education, the British are nevertheless a very inventive people. Where the Nation seems to fail most noticeably is between the invention and its application – as the above sketch of the development of the hovercraft illustrates.

One of the problems which Britain faces is probably a result of her history of inventiveness; the reluctance to adopt technology which originates from elsewhere – the NIH ('not invented here') syndrome. There is a definite reluctance within British industry to purchase licences (Cockerell only had four original licensees for his patents) and a marked preference for doing one's own research and development. As a nation Britain only expends approximately as much on licences as she receives from abroad – in 1987 overseas earnings from this source were £900 million but only £750 million was paid out. In contrast, Germany pays out more than four times as much as she receives. In relation to the size of the economy Britain ought to be paying out about eight times as much as is received, unless of course the aim is to set up the economy as a research workshop, providing technology on a worldwide basis which others then develop into commercially viable products.

SELF-ASSESSMENT QUESTIONS

5 Why must a firm develop new products?

6 A firm whose new product has proved to be very lucrative has made considerable profits in the year just ended. What can it do with these profits?

7 A new technology is about to replace well-tried techniques. What are the likely problems of transfer to the new technology?

8 Explain the term 'improved exploitation of new technology.'

REVISION TEST

Answers	Questions
—	**1** How has the process of technological discovery changed in recent years?
1 Through the growth of large-scale research operations attached to firms or governments.	**2** What is basic research?
2 Research undertaken for the sake of knowledge gained rather than with specific applications in view.	**3** What forms can technical progress take?
3 Improvements in methods of production and improvements leading to new products.	**4** How is the accumulation of capital important in the application of technology?
4 Discoveries can be applied more readily when investment is taking place on a regular basis. Investment depends upon accumulated capital.	**5** How did Schumpeter account for the trade cycle?
5 By referring to the rate at which investment responded to new technology.	**6** What is neutral capital accumulation?
6 Where new technology does not change the amounts of capital and labour required to provide workers with new machinery.	**7** What is meant by capital deepening?
7 The provision of more capital equipment per unit of the labour force, without any change in the quality of such capital.	**8** What compels firms to invest in new technology?

8 The pursuit of profits and fear of possible competition.

9 What is the UK's main weakness regarding technology?

9 The failure to turn discoveries into products.

10 What is a silicon chip?

10 A silicon integrated circuit.

11 Why are silicon chips so important?

11 They are the essential components in low-cost electronic products.

12 What is the major fear associated with 'chip' technology?

12 That of rising unemployment.

13 Does everyone feel this fear to be justified?

13 No; there are those who feel that greater productivity will *generate* more employment.

14 Is this optimism justified?

14 It might be but silicon chip technology is special in that it will affect all areas of manufacturing *and* service industries.

Now try the written questions below.

ANSWERS

See Self-assessment questions on pages 342 and 351.

1 Technology is the science of practical and industrial arts. The essence of technology is the systematic treatment of the gifts of nature (primary products) to give improved (secondary) products which are more useful and more convenient.

2 Technological change comes about in several different ways. It may be a fortunate discovery by some perceptive individual, or the result of amateurish tinkering in some garden shed. It may be the result of problem-based research, or 'pure' research which is seen to have some practical application. It may be the result of systematic research over an extensive field by some well-organised Research and Development Department.

3 A patent is a legal protection given to some invention or discovery over a period of years – 20 years in the case of the UK. It gives exclusive use of the invention to its owner for this period. The advantage of the system to the inventor is that he/she can earn profits from the sale of the invention or by licensing others to use it. Patents encourage inventiveness, and are therefore beneficial to the nation as a whole.

4 The chief considerations are: (a) the cost of the new machinery; (b) its likely earning power in terms of improved output over its working life; (c) the possibility of it being rendered obsolete by new technology; (d) the costs and disruption of re-training staff; (e) the possible impact on staffing, redundancy, etc; (f) loss of production during re-fitting of the factory and solution of any teething problems.

5 Firms must develop new products because: (a) we must always anticipate that present products will prove of declining interest to customers as the years pass (every product has a life cycle); (b) continued employment for staff and senior management therefore depends upon periodic revitalisation of the firm's products and services; (c) changing technology will render present products out of date; (d) new materials will often enable competitors to imitate our products in a different form or format; (e) changes in administrative requirements will render present products obsolete and call for new products to meet new standards specified by the administrative bodies.

6 There are three choices: (a) distribute the profits as dividends to the shareholders (who will use or re-invest them as they wish); (b) invest them internally within the firm to increase output; give a more complete market coverage, etc; (c) invest them in other industries (diversification) by taking over existing companies or setting up completely new subsidiary companies in the new field.

7 The most likely problems are (a) purchase and installation of the new technology; (b) induction of existing staff into the new practices; (c) lack of communication with existing staff. When uncertainty develops it is the good people who leave; it is important to let the people we need to keep know that their jobs are safe; (d) teething problems during the transition period; (e) dealing with any redundancy situation.

8 The term draws attention to the fact that the people who invent a new process or procedure may not be the best people to exploit it; indeed they may not be at all interested in practical applications of the discovery they have made. We need to link those who make discoveries with those who can exploit the discovery so that a higher rate of return on our research work is obtained.

QUESTIONS ON CHAPTER 13

1 In the Industrial Revolution the UK's economic progress depended upon iron and steam. Discuss what materials and what sources of power are crucial to the development of your own country today.

2 How does technical progress affect the level of employment within an economy? Refer in your answer to: (a) the UK (b) India.

3 What is the link between capital accumulation and the application of technology?

4 In what ways could the UK ensure the best possible contribution to economic growth through technical progress?

5 Why might silicon chip technology lead to both higher levels of employment and output?

6 Assess the likely impact upon the service sector of the UK economy of widespread application of silicon chip technology.

7 One of the arguments in favour of protectionism that has been generally agreed internationally is that an infant industry may be protected. Since micro-electronics is in its infancy, is there a case for excluding foreign chips until a sound home-based industry has been established? What would be the 'private' and 'social' costs of such a policy?

8 Account for the relatively rapid growth of the UK economy in the 1980s.

TIPS FOR STUDENTS: A SPECIMEN ANSWER TO QUESTION 4

Generally speaking, growth in an advanced economy can only come from technical progress. While an under-developed country can achieve economic growth by a wider use of its under-utilized natural (and human) resources, in the advanced nations the movement of people out of primary production into secondary and tertiary production has already taken place. Consequently growth can only be achieved by more intense utilisation of existing resources and that means we must have improved technology.

There are two aspects of this need to improve technology: (a) we must do everything we can to encourage inventiveness and research, so that new developments do actually occur. If they occur abroad we should evaluate them quickly and obtain licences to use such as seem to be worthwhile; (b) having achieved advances we must then exploit them fully by ensuring that they are drawn to the attention of those who might use them.

Possible measures to encourage inventiveness and research are as follows:

a) A patent system, which should not be too expensive but which gives watertight control of an invention or process to the inventor, and enables actions for infringement to be brought in the Courts.

b) Encouragement of research and development work in firms and companies by making such expenditure tax-deductible.

c) A system of grants in aid to institutions undertaking pure and applied research; allocated by a panel of knowledgable people in the field concerned.

d) To provide further funds charitable donations to research foundations could be made tax deductible (they are in many countries). Money from such funds can be used to pay research workers. This gives security to research workers and releases them from dependence on official funds.

e) A central agency should be set up to monitor world-wide publications in all fields and discover licensing opportunities for foreign inventions. It would also market UK inventions to foreign customers. An information system should alert all firms to the potential sources of (or markets for) new discoveries.

Possible measures to improve the exploitation of new technical procedures are:

a) The provision of information services to the general public about new developments and discoveries.

b) The setting up of industry-wide committees to review and draw attention to advances being made. This may require some recognition of achievements to reduce secrecy about developments.

c) The setting-up of cross-industry links, so that developments in one industry that may be of benefit to another industry can be featured and considered.

d) Extensive re-training facilities should be available to reduce fears of technological advance, and promote the idea that new developments are not likely to have adverse effects on employees.

14 Money, credit and banking

1 THE ROLE OF MONEY IN THE ECONOMY

The complex economy of a country like the UK is dependent upon the existence of a sophisticated money system, so that the millions of transactions which are taking place at all levels can be settled expeditiously in generally acceptable units of currency. The nature of money, its qualities and attributes are discussed below, but first let us appreciate how simple it makes all the transactions of everyday life. Without money the employment of factors (land, labour and capital) would be difficult to arrange, for the rewards the factors require, rent, wages and interest would have to be negotiated by some sort of barter arrangement, e.g. a dozen eggs for an hour's labour at the work-bench. Without money the purchase of the many items we need in everyday life would be a difficult business of bargaining with goods exchanged for goods in an endless succession of tedious and time-consuming discussions.

The problems with barter are as follows:

a) **We need a coincidence of wants** That is each party must want what the other has, and have what the other wants. If A has wheat and wants a horse, and B has a horse and wants wheat they can trade. If B has a horse but does not want wheat in exchange the parties cannot trade.

b) **We need to strike equations of value** How much wheat for a horse? Is a fat goose worth a tin kettle? People's perceptions of value change from hour to hour and even minute to minute. Barter is not as convenient as a money system, where we decide the price of an article in money terms and then the seller uses the money so recently acquired to buy his/her own needs at some other point in the market place.

c) **Indivisible large items present problems** For example we can sell a cow, but not half a cow (without spoiling the cow). Where the buyer has insufficient funds to pay for an article required immediately it may be necessary to carry the balance over to a later date. In primitive societies debts are sometimes carried on to the next generation – a practice requiring a considerable sense of respect in honouring the debts of parents and ancestors.

The existence of money dispenses with such barter arrangements and simplifies commercial transactions in sophisticated societies where production is carried on by a variety of specialists. It is probably no exaggeration to claim that without some form of money the extent of specialised activity in advanced nations would be far less – the greater the degree of specialisation the more cumbersome barter becomes. In communities where individuals provide most of the things they require for themselves, the process of bartering for the residue of requirements (usually luxury items) can be an enjoyable break from every day tedium. Where every single thing we require comes from over the hills and far away the ceaseless bartering that would be necessary would become unbearable. What is it, then, that money is required to do to diminish barter to an absolute minimum and make occupational specialisation a real possibility? Money is traditionally regarded as having four main functions. These are:

1 it is a medium of exchange,
2 it acts as a store of value,
3 it is a measure of value,
4 it is a standard for deferred payments.

A medium of exchange

In all but the most primitive of economies the process of exchange is the life blood of the economic system. Very little is produced which can be consumed in total by the producer, and very few producers provide all the things they wish to consume. Trading of surpluses of one good to satisfy shortages of another *must* take place. This process of exchange takes place via the medium of money. All economic items can be converted into money and that money can then be used to purchase other economic items. Essentially money converts a two way exchange into two one-way exchanges. For example labour is provided by the worker, and its value is taken as a money reward from the employer. That money is then spent on a balanced basket of goods and services, groceries, shelter, light and heat, etc. Money has broken down the two way exchange-labour for food etc., and turned it into a number of separate exchange activities. Money is the common denominator entering into them all. The double coincidence of wants which makes barter such a cumbersome procedure has been avoided.

A store of value

In good years farmers might accumulate surplus stores of wheat which they can use to help them over bad years. In a similar way those operating in a money economy might choose to build up surpluses of money and hold such surpluses (savings) for use in other times when their income is for some reason inadequate. When a money system is operating efficiently one of the options open to those participating in it is to hold their surplus wealth in money rather than material form. This confers some advantages, one being that materials can deteriorate whereas money should not. Another is that money confers greater flexibility in terms of future action, than its material alternative. For example a store of wheat can only be used to make bread, and can only be exchanged with someone who wants wheat for milling and baking. Money as a store of value can be changed into anything else; it can flow into any market to purchase our needs. It is often called a 'liquid asset' because it can flow anywhere in the economy, and command the use of goods and services.

A measure of value

When we seek to exchange a fur coat for a car, how should we value each? There are many problems. What kind of fur is it? What length is the coat? What condition is the fur in? How old is the car? What model is it? etc.

Money is capable of taking into account all these factors and more. When we seek to value different items and services we avoid problems of comparison by using the common measuring rod of money. All items are assigned a monetary value and this greatly simplifies the process of exchanging them. No longer are we exchanging a moth-eaten fur coat for a rusty car, but these items for sums of money – and one sum of money is very easily compared with another one.

Money as a standard for deferred payments

Advanced specialised societies give rise to a great many contracts where future payment is specified; mortgages, bank loans, hire purchase agreements, etc. Money is the agreed means of payment for such contracts, and because of its special characteristics it greatly simplfies them.

2 THE FORMS OF MONEY

The functions of money as outlined above could be performed to a greater or lesser degree by a wide range of items. Many things have served as money; nails, screws, sea shells, bricks of tea, cigarettes, feathers; the list is almost endless. To be used as money an item has to be something that is readily acceptable to all those who wish to buy or sell goods or services. Some things are always acceptable because they have value to everyone; gold and silver for example. This is called 'intrinsic' value, and early coins were made of gold and silver for this reason. Later copper became the third 'coinage' metal for less valuable coins. Today most money is either in printed form, as banknotes, or in 'token' coins – that is coins made not out of the coinage metals, but of other metals which do not have intrinsic value. The metal in the coin is not worth the value placed upon it. To persuade people to take such money it has to be declared 'legal tender' – that is the sovereign body in each nation declares the currency to be a proper way of paying for goods and services, and compels those being paid to accept the payment offered, because it is a 'legal tender'. If A owes B £500 and offers to pay with 100 £5 notes that is a legal tender in the United Kingdom. If the creditor who is owed the money refuses to accept it the buyer need not tender the money again. The debt is not paid, but the buyer has done his best to pay, and it is now up to the creditor to ask for the money and take the payment tendered.

Although notes and coins are the only 'legal tender' we have invented many other ways of paying money to one another which depend upon the confidence of the parties in the honesty and integrity of the payer. Thus we often pay by cheque – which is an order to a banker to pay money. The danger is that the payer may not have the necessary funds in his/her bank account, and the cheque may be **dishonoured**. Most of us these days have cheque cards which are provided by our banks as a guarantee to shopkeepers and others that the cheque will be honoured. Most of them are only valid up to £50, but Eurocheque cards and some others are valid up to £100. Cheques above these values are widely used, but the parties must know one another and have confidence in one another's business honesty. Other payments may be made with credit cards and other forms of plastic money – some of which are capable of releasing money from ATMs (automated teller machines) or penetrating into bank computer databanks to deduct money from the payer's account. Few cards actually penetrate that far – the nearest most of them get is to queue the demand for money in a storage tape which will be processed after the bank closes for the day – the money being transferred from buyer to seller during the night.

What is it that distinguishes these various forms of money today from some things that have served as money in the past? It is whether or not an item has a number of characteristics regarded as desirable (and in some cases essential) in money.

3   THE CHARACTERISTICS OF MONEY

A good money should have the following characteristics or properties. The extent to which an item has these characteristics will determine how effective and long-lasting it is as money.

Universal acceptability

The most important property of money is undoubtedly that of universal acceptability. We all take money because we know we can exchange it for goods and services. We don't want it if others will refuse to give us goods and services in exchange. It is absolutely essential then, that the money we use is acceptable everywhere within the normal boundaries of the commercial world in which we operate. It is of little use if money acceptable in York ceases to be so in Leeds.

Stability of value

A close second in importance and having a great bearing on acceptability is the property of stability of value. There is hardly anything which can undermine the performance of the functions of money like loss of value. This situation is called by the general name of 'inflation'. The term actually refers to an increase of the money in circulation in relation to the quantity of goods and services available. The result is that prices of goods and services rise and consequently the money is effectively devalued. Those who have been saving money (using it as a store of value) find that their savings are declining in value. Later as inflation becomes more chronic (galloping inflation) even the use of money as a medium of exchange ceases to be possible – a wheelbarrow of bank notes is necessary to buy lunch, and exchange becomes nonsensical.

Recognisability, portability and homogeneity

Amongst the other main characteristics are recognisability – money must be recognised as such if it is to be acceptable; portability – a mobile society needs a form of money which is easily transported; homogeneity – each monetory unit (e.g. each £1 coin) needs to be identical with all others. An example of lack of homogeneity is the debasement of the currency that took place in Henry VIII's reign when coins were issued with a lesser value of intrinsic metal than coins already on the market. Sir Thomas Gresham, Queen Elizabeth I's finance minister, stated '**Gresham's Law**', 'that bad money drives out good money'. A person receiving one of the original coins will profit by taking it out of circulation, melting it down and using the resulting metal to buy more than one of the debased coins. Similarly units identified by the population as superior may be hoarded and the inferior ones passed on.

Divisibility and difficulty of imitation

Since transactions vary in value the monetary system must take account of both large and small transactions. The units chosen must have some simple link with one another, and the decimal linkage is one of the simplest to understand.

Coins and notes must be difficult to imitate, otherwise coining and counterfeiting will become common practices. The reprehensible aspect of such activities is that they permit those who have played no part in the productive process to participate in the fruits of production. Such enjoyment of resources can only take place at the expense of genuine people who have supplied factors, land, labour or capital, and are entitled to a reward for doing so. Since the coinage and the note issue invariably lie with the sovereign power, coining and counterfeiting are usually heavily punished both for the actual wrong done to society and the contempt shown to the sovereign power.

Finally money must be durable, particularly the lower denominations which are used more frequently than higher value notes. Inflation in recent years has seen both the 50 pence note and the £1 note discontinued and reissued as coins because of the long life associated with coins (about 50 years) compared with notes (3–6 months).

4 MONEY IN A MODERN ECONOMY

Most people, when they think of money think only of notes and coin, but by far the greatest proportion of money in the UK has no physical existence at all and is created by banks in the form of accounts. At first this is not an easy point to grasp, but a simple hypothetical example might help. Imagine that you wish to purchase a new car but don't have enough money; you don't want to take out hire purchase because you feel the rate of interest is exorbitant – so you approach your bank and ask for a loan. The loan is forthcoming – but where does the money come from and in what form. Contrary to popular belief banks are not great repositories of cash; buildings where millions are in reserve as notes and coins. Banks in fact hold very little cash in proportion to the business they transact. Where does the money come from? The answer is that it comes from the bank's ability to create credit. A bank can create money in response to customers' demand for it (within certain restraints which are explained later). The form taken by this created credit is that of a balance on a bank account. It may be a new account or an addition to an existing account. The loan that is granted is entered on the credit side of the borrower's current account, and hence the use of the word 'credit'. When a loan is taken it is unusual for cash to be involved; rather the customer is given the facility to draw on an account using a cheque, standing order or some other means of money transfer. The customer is effectively making payments by transferring balances from a bank account.

To understand how the system works we can consider the following case, illustrated in Fig. 14.1.

How loans are made and how they make deposits

Suppose that the cashier of a customer, The Beautiful Garden Centre Ltd, comes into the bank to deposit the day's takings of £1000. The bank now has £1000 cash which the company is entitled to withdraw and use at any time. However, experience has shown that in terms of the total business done the amount of cash that is likely to be requested is very small – less than 5 per cent. If we take the cash figure required as being 5 per cent, for the purpose of illustration we can see that the bank only needs to keep £50 out of the £1000 in cash form. It might be thought that the bank would keep £50 and lend out the remaining £950, but this is not the most profitable avenue open to the bank. Suppose instead that the bank keeps all the £1000 cash, and uses it as a 5 per cent cash ratio for much bigger loans. The probability is that only 5 per cent of the bank's deposits will be demanded in cash. That means that with a 5 per cent cash ratio the bank can have deposits of £20 000 (£1000 is 5 per cent of £20 000). At present the bank only has deposits (from the Beautiful Garden Centre Ltd) of £1000. Therefore it can in theory lend £19 000 to any customer who wishes to borrow such a sum, by putting it on the credit side of the borrower's current account. The loan is effectively a deposit in the customer's account. Suppose it does this for a customer called A. Borrower. Borrower now spends the £19 000 on a car from A. Dealer. It is totally imaginary money, which the Bank has created, but A. Dealer does not know this. He pays the cheque into his bank account, believing it to be good money. Borrower's account is now clear again (he/she has spent the loan) but the loan has returned as a bonafide deposit from A. Dealer. The bank now has deposits totalling £20 000. The probability is that these depositors will only ask for 5 per cent in cash, and if they do the bank can offer the money requested at once, for it has £1000 in cash. Follow this description of the creation of credit in Fig 14.1 now,

Fig. 14.1 *How loans of created money become deposits*

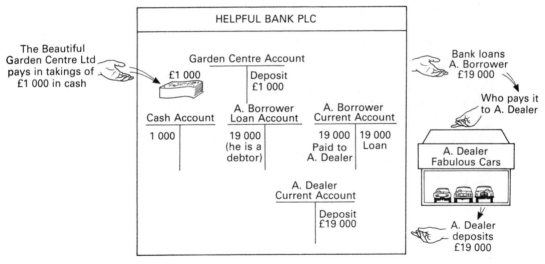

Notes

1 Those who understand double-entry book-keeping may enjoy following the double entries through. At first the £1000 deposit becomes a credit in the Garden Centre account of £1000, balanced up by the cash on the Cash Account, which is debited as one of the assets of the business.

2 Then the bank lends £19 000 to A. Borrower. This is credited in his Current Account but debited in a Loan Account opened in Borrower's name, which will of course earn the bank interest. The entries in these two accounts balance one another.

3 As soon as Borrower spends the money, the £19 000 is debited in Borrower's Current Account, which is consequently cleared, but credited in the account of A. Dealer, who deposits it the same day.

4 The final result is that the bank has £20 000 of assets – £1000 cash and £19 000; a debt from a debtor A. Borrower. It also has £20 000 of liabilities; deposits from Beautiful Garden Centre Ltd of £1000 and from A. Dealer £19 000.

and note that loans make deposits, for what is loaned to one customer, and used by him/her, returns almost the same day as a deposit from the person to whom the cheque was given. Loans make deposits!

How is it that banks can successfully lend in this way more money than they really have. The answer is that they depend upon confidence in the banking system. Depositors have to have the confidence to leave their money with the bank sure of their ability to regain control of it at any time either as a cash withdrawal or as an ability to write cheques to settle debts at any time.

Confidence in the continued value of accounts is therefore crucial to the system, and experience has shown that confidence can be maintained by providing customers with cash whenever they ask for it.

Banks must be careful though, to strike a balance between profitability, which still primarily comes from loans, and safety – which comes from cash. If some unforeseen event occurs 5 per cent of cash may not be a sufficient reserve. There could be a call on the bank for cash which goes on for some days, weeks or even months. Because of this banks actually keep about 30 per cent of their total assets in liquid form. A liquid asset is one that is either in cash form or can be quickly turned into cash without significant capital loss. Banks have liquid assets of various maturity dates – from overnight money to three or six months. Overnight money can be called back next day, and a lot of other money is at short notice with the Discount Houses – whose part in ensuring liquidity for the banks is explained later in this chapter. 'Call' money can be called for at anytime, and 'short notice' implies less than seven days. Three month and six month money is loaned against bills of exchange, usually with the name of a reputable bank endorsed on the bank. Such a bill becomes a 'bank bill' and can always be turned into cash, if necessary by discounting it with the Bank of England. In emergencies the realisation of all these liquid assets would enable a bank to meet its obligations. In fact therefore banks do not create credit to the full extent of the theoretical possibility described in Fig. 14.1. There is a greater reserve than 5 per cent cash; about 30 per cent of cash and near-cash (money at call or short notice). There is thus a balance between liquidity and profitability.

One other factor promotes the stability of the banking system. It is called 'Keeping in step'.

Keeping in step

In the example quoted above there was one weakness which the alert student will have detected. It was assumed that A. Dealer who received the cheque for £19 000 for the car sold to A. Borrower banked at the same bank as A. Borrower. Suppose this is not the case, and Dealer banks at some other bank. Helpful Bank PLC will at once be in difficulties, losing liquidity to another bank – say – The Caring Bank PLC.

Banks work in a competitive environment. There are many other banks in the field and it would be easy for one bank to lose the cash it needs for customer

Fig. 14.2 *Keeping in step to preserve liquidity*

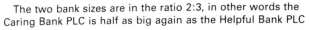

The two bank sizes are in the ratio 2:3, in other words the
Caring Bank PLC is half as big again as the Helpful Bank PLC

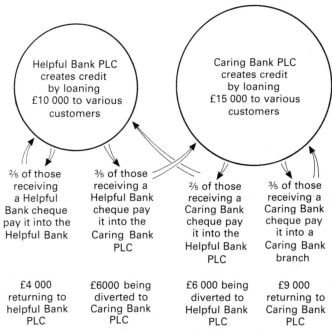

Helpful Bank PLC
creates credit
by loaning
£10 000 to various
customers

Caring Bank PLC
creates credit
by loaning
£15 000 to various
customers

⅖ of those receiving a Helpful Bank cheque pay it into the Helpful Bank	⅗ of those receiving a Helpful Bank cheque pay it into the Caring Bank PLC	⅖ of those receiving a Caring Bank cheque pay it into the Helpful Bank PLC	⅗ of those receiving a Caring Bank cheque pay it into a Caring Bank branch
£4 000 returning to helpful Bank PLC	£6000 being diverted to Caring Bank PLC	£6 000 being diverted to Helpful Bank PLC	£9 000 returning to Caring Bank PLC

Notes

1   The ratio between the sizes of the two banks is 2:3, and we are imagining they are the only two banks in the system.

2   If they keep their lending in this ratio, as shown in the example, the probability is that two fifths of any cheques paid out by customers of the Helpful Bank PLC will be received by people who also bank at Helpful Bank PLC. However, three fifths will be diverted to the Caring Bank PLC.

Now correspondingly two fifths of the cheques paid out by customers of the Caring Bank PLC will be directed to Helpful Bank PLC, and three-fifths will return to Caring Bank PLC.

3   As long as the loans by the two banks are in the same ratio as the size of the banks, both banks will receive back all they loaned out, and liquidity will be maintained.

4   Suppose Helpful Bank PLC is aggressively competitive and tries to increase its loans to customers to £20 000. Only £8000 of this will return, and £12 000 will be diverted to Caring Bank PLC. This will mean – since Caring Bank PLC has not changed its lending policies the following:

Helpful Bank: loaned £20 000 – received back £8000 + £6000 = £14000 (The bank is £6000 short)

Caring Bank: loaned £15 000 – received back £12 000 + £9000 = £21 000 (The bank has £6000 extra.)

Helpful Bank must pay Caring Bank £6000 in cash, but it does not have it to pay. Consequently it is in financial difficulties, and faces bankruptcy.

confidence to the other banks within the system. To avoid this banks have to 'keep in step'. This means that they only create credit (account money) in line with the basic sizes of their businesses. The process is outlined in Fig. 14.2 and explained in the notes below the diagram.

Banks are often accused of running a cartel, that is an arrangement where they work together to take advantage of their position to the detriment of the general public who are their customers. Much of this public misunderstanding springs from the bank's needs to keep in step. A bank cannot be more competitive than its neighbours in the long term as far as its loan policies are concerned, even if they might run temporary campaigns to attract new customers' deposits of existing money (**passive** deposits). Any excessively competitive attitude on loan policy will get the bank out of step, and into financial difficulties. Part of the new controls given to the Bank of England in the Banking Act 1987 includes the Bank's duty to review the liquidity arrangements which the management of any bank is making, to ensure that it does not get itself into an illiquid position by loaning more than its present size appears to justify. Providing banks only create *active* deposits (new deposits) in the same proportion to their passive deposits (existing deposits) as all the other banks in the system, they are in no great danger of losing the cash base which is so essential to their operations.

5 MEASURES OF MONEY SUPPLY

The preceding paragraphs should have suggested to readers that while cash is vitally important to an advanced money system from the point of view of confidence, it is less and less important in terms of actual purchases. Most 'money' in the UK is not cash at all but balances transferred by cheques, credit transfers, direct debits and other methods of payment developed by the major financial institutions – in particular the clearing banks.

Getting to grips with a definitive measure of the money supply in the UK is in fact very difficult and even the government has had eight or so measures in recent years. The main reason for this is the existence of liquid assets. If an asset can be very quickly turned into cash – so quickly and easily that most people don't normally bother to do this but exchange the asset itself – then it has claims to being regarded as money – it is performing some or all of the functions of money. The need for so many different measures of money arises from the decision to include particular liquid items – the fewer items the 'narrower' the definition of money, the more items included, the 'broader' the definition.

The government's definitions change frequently, but the full details can always be found in the current Bank of England Quarterly Bulletin. At the time of writing (1989) the Bulletin has just announced that due to changes brought about by the conversion of the Abbey National Building Society to a public company the Bank has had to review its monetary statistics. From that time on there will be six measures of money supply, called M0, N1bM1, M2, M4, M4C and M5. These are illustrated in Table 14.1 (see pages 368–9).

What is a measure of money supply?

A measure of money supply is an attempt to define the money in circulation. For example M0 is defined as notes and coins in circulation with the public, including the till money in the banks and the banks' operational deposits with the Bank of England which are used in the clearing process. That is a very narrow definition of money (it doesn't for example include the balances in people's current accounts which they might use at any minute by writing a cheque). The whole point of defining a particular measure of money supply is that we can then watch that total figure and see how it changes, and that will give us some idea how the economy is changing. M0 grew from end 1985 (£14 254 million) to end 1986 (15 188 million) to end 1987 (£16 633 million) and by end 1988 (£17 867 million).

Study Table 14.1 now and see how the other measures are arrived at.

Policies to establish control of credit

The measures of money supply give the Chancellor some idea of the quantity of money in circulation and some opportunity to introduce corrective measures if it is felt that the money supply is increasing too rapidly and is likely to produce inflation. At the time of writing the Chancellor is largely pre-occupied by the use of short-term rates of interest to control the economy. He is being strongly criticised for reducing his selection of weapons to rein-in inflation to this sole weapon. Alternative policies are:

a) **Fiscal policies**   That is changes in taxation. Since any reduction of the money in their pockets will reduce the public's demand for goods and services, any type of taxation, whether it is an increase in income tax, or in national insurance contributions, or in value added tax or in any other type of taxation must help rein-in inflation. Such changes may be more effective than an increase in interest rates, for they will be less easily avoided. A person who has no mortage and does not borrow money, is not directly affected at all by interest rate increases, though they might be affected indirectly by a turn-down in the economy resulting from the interest rate changes.

b) **Open market operations**   An open market operation is one where an official body such as the Treasury uses the money markets to influence the economic situation. For example, suppose the Treasury issues a new gilt-edged security, or even just a savings certificate, with favourable rates of interest. To the extent that this can persuade the general public to buy the security the spending power of the public will, be reduced, and this removes money from their pockets and purses which otherwise might be spent on goods and services.

c) **Bank directives**   A bank directive is an order to the banking community from the Bank of England limiting the loans they may grant for non-essential activities. Thus a directive to restrict loans to holiday makers might be sensible because it would reduce the demand for foreign travel, hotel accommodation, etc. It would not be sensible to reduce loans to new businesses, or to exporters, since they are wealth-creating activities. They are rarely used.

d) **Special deposits and the corset**   The Bank of England in its policy statement 'Monetary Control – Provisions' reserved the right to call for special deposits at the Bank of England at any time when it wished to reduce

Table 14.1 Measures of money supply

Name of measure	M0	N1BM1	M2	M4	M4C	M5 (formerly PSL2)
Purpose of measure	A very narrow definition of money supply (somewhat anomalously called 'the wide monetary base')	Non-interest bearing component of M1. M1 has now been discontinued, details below.	A slightly broader definition covering the funds available to the private sector for transactions of all types	The private sector's money M3 (old sterling M3), plus the private sector's holdings of building society shares and deposits and sterling certificates of deposit, less the building societies' holdings of bank deposits and bank certificates of deposit, notes and coin	This new measure will be introduced shortly. It will include deposits in currency other than sterling (hence the C in the title)	The same as M4 but including also private sector holdings of money market instruments, certificates of tax deposits and short-term national savings (but leaving out the building societies' holdings of these instruments)
Items included:						
a) Notes and coins in public circulation	Yes	Yes	Yes	Yes	Yes	Yes
b) Banks' till money	Yes	No	No	No	No	No
c) Banks' operational deposits at the Bank of England	Yes	No	No	No	No	No
d) Bank current accounts of private sector (adjusted for items in transit)	No	Yes, but only the non-interest-bearing current accounts	Yes (both types)	Yes	Yes	Yes
e) Bank deposit accounts in sterling, of the private sector	No	No	Yes	Yes	Yes	Yes

Measure						
f) Private sector holdings of sterling certificates of deposit	No	No	No	Yes	Yes	Yes
g) Bank deposit accounts as in both (e) and (f) but designated in foreign currencies	No	No	No	No	Yes	No
h) Private sector's holding of money market instruments (bank bills, Treasury bills and local authority deposits)	No	No	No	Yes (but not building society holdings of these)	Yes (but not building society holdings of these)	Yes (but not building society holdings of these)
i) Certificates of tax deposit	No	No	No	Yes	Yes	Yes (but not building societies' tax deposits)
j) Private savings in National Savings Bank	No	No	Yes	No	No	Yes (but not savings certificates, SAYE and other long-term deposits)
k) Private savings in building societies	No	No	Yes	No	No	Yes (but not term shares or SAYE)
Some seasonally adjusted figures for each measure:						
End 1981 (£m)	28 548	–	–	(Figures to be made available from June 1987)	–	–
End 1983 (£m)	33 490	–	–		–	–
End 1985 (£m)	37 071	14 254	148 163		–	240 036
End 1986 (£m)	41 410	15 188	169 409		–	276 283
End 1987 (£m)	49 445	16 633	187 373	303 944	–	319 375
End 1988 (£m)	50 035	17 867	216 989	357 488	–	372 649

Where gaps are shown in the figures it means that the measure concerned was only defined recently, so that earlier figures are not available.

drastically the banks' abilities to create credit. We have seen that a bank's cash is the source of its ability to create credit. If forced to deposit cash at the Bank of England a bank loses not only that amount of money but the ability to loan at least three times as much. Thus if its cash is reduced by £10 million it must reduce its loans by between £30 million and £40 million.

The corset is a particularly sharp way of reducing a bank's ability to lend. If a bank's loans grow by say 3 per cent a special deposit is called for. If they grow by 4 per cent a much bigger deposit at the Bank of England is demanded, and so on. The more a bank tries to lend the more it is squeezed – hence the term 'corset'.

SELF-ASSESSMENT QUESTIONS

1 What are the problems of barter?

2 What are the functions of money?

3 What are the essential characteristics of money?

4 Explain the process of 'creating credit'.

5 Why must banks 'keep in step'?

6   THE FRAMEWORK OF BANKING IN THE UK

Banking institutions in the UK fall into three strata. At the top is the nationalised central bank, the **Bank of England**. Below this is a broad bank of authorised deposit takers, who have been accorded recognition by the Bank of England as bodies with adequate management authorised to take deposits from the general public. A lower designation of some institutions as licensed deposit takers was disliked by the bodies concerned, since it appeared to reflect upon their status for investment purposes. It has been discontinued. All recognised institutions are now authorised deposit takers, but this does not mean that they can call themselves 'banks'. They may only use the word 'bank' in their names if they have capital or undistributable capital reserves in excess of £5 million, or if they used the word 'bank' in their names before 1979 and were forced to discontinue its use by the 1979 Act.

The third stratum is a layer of exempt institutions, which include the Central Banks of other countries, the European Investment Bank, a number of other high level institutions and the building societies.

It is not necessary in this book to go into great detail about the various institutions; those wishing for a more detailed description might like to read *Elements of Banking Made Simple*, by Julia Hoyle and Geoffrey Whitehead. A brief account of the main institutions is given in the following sections.

7 THE BANK OF ENGLAND

The Bank of England is the UK's central bank, a nationalised institution since 1946. It has a reputation which goes back to its foundation in 1694 as a bank of the highest quality. It developed over the centuries as the Government's banker, and the banker's banker, and since the Bank Charter Act of 1844 it has been charged with the duty of issuing notes in such quantities and such numbers as to meet the requirements of commerce, industry and the general public. By the most recent Act – the Banking Act 1987 – it is authorised to establish and maintain a Board of Banking Supervision to supervise the banking system in the UK. This Board has three *ex-officio* members, the Governor of the Bank of England, his/her deputy, and a director appointed to be in day-to-day charge of supervision duties. There are six other independent members appointed jointly by the Chancellor and the Governor as people able to advise the *ex-officio* members of any cause for concern in the banking system. The Bank's powers are very extensive, including the right to call for relevant statistics from all deposit takers, and to enquire into the liquidity arrangements of any institution and the prudential policies it is following.

Besides this general duty of supervising the banking system the Bank's functions are:

1 to act as banker to the government,
2 to act as advisor to the government on economic and financial matters,
3 to implement elements of government monetary policy, as required,
4 to act as banker to the banking system,
5 to supervise the note issue,
6 to manage the gilt-edged issue (gilt-edged investments are securities recognising a loan to the Government),
7 to represent the Government in international financial matters.

A word about each of these functions is desirable.

The Government's Banker

In the way in which High Street banks keep accounts for their customers so the Bank of England keeps accounts for the government. The main Government account is the Exchequer Account which accepts all receipts and makes all payments. The sums involved are enormous; in 1987 receipts exceeded £165 000 million and expenditures were £164 000 million. All this tax money is collected via the ordinary banking system, before being finally consolidated in the Exchequer Account.

A further important account is the National Loans Fund which records the loans made by the government primarily to the nationalised industries and local authorities.

Should any deficit arise in the Government's accounts the Bank of England makes an automatic loan. Similarly if a surplus arises it is invested at interest, through the money markets.

Adviser to the Government

Government monetary policy has far-reaching consequences and can be implemented in a number of different ways. For example, one way to combat inflatiion might be to increase interest rates. Although the Bank of England is entitled to publish a **minimum lending rate** it rarely does so, preferring to signal to the banks in the course of its ordinary dealings with them the rate of interest which it deems as desirable in view of the current economic situation. The Bank and the Treasury are in daily consultation about the financial state of the nation. It will advise the Treasury on the implications of any measures proposed and will convey the views of the Chancellor to the banking systems generally. It can if necessary issue directives about lending policies, either to banks in general or to particular institutions.

Implementing monetary policy

The Bank of England is the logical body to implement monetary policy. Since 1946 the Bank has had the power to compel banks to comply with its instructions. It has never used this power (and in the present climate of freedom of enterprise it is unlikely to) but the pressure of such compulsory powers in the background adds weight to its requests and suggestions.

Currently the main thrust of government monetary policy is the manipulation of short-term interest rates. This is achieved by the Bank of England through covert dealings on the primary London money market. Until 1981 the Bank of England used to announce the rate of interest it wished to see operative in the short-term market. This rate was known as the minimum lending rate (previously known as Bank Rate), and in fact the Bank reserves the right to set a minimum lending rate from time to time when the financial situation is adjudged of sufficient seriousness to warrant this.

The normal daily procedure is that the Bank of England acts in the commercial market to match the availability of short-term funds with short-dated bills of exchange seeking such liquid funds. In the process it can indicate to institutions what changes (if any) in the rate of interest it wishes to see and back up its wishes, if necessary, by allowing shortages or surpluses of cash to develop. A shortage should, of course, push up the interest rate, and a surplus of cash should reduce the interest rate.

Often, short-term interest rate changes will have little significance for medium or long-term rates, but if the short-rate changes are large enough, and persist for long enough then they can be expected to work through to longer rates – for example, the mortgage rate rises (or falls) eventually.

One other way in which the Bank of England has implemented government monetary policy in recent years is through its manipulation of the national debt but this is dealt with below.

Banker to the banking system

The Bank of England acts as banker to the clearing banks and the discount houses. The clearing banks keep what are known as 'operational balances' with the Bank of England. These are used in the clearing process – the daily inter-bank debts are settled by the Bank of England making adjustments to these balances. The discount houses find it in their interest to keep accounts with the Bank of England, since it is through these accounts that the 'lender of last resort' facility is extended. This is explained later in this chapter.

In addition, over 90 overseas central banks and bodies such as the International Monetary Fund maintain accounts with the Bank. These help to facilitate international transactions at an official level.

Supervision of the note issue

Ever since the Bank Charter Act of 1844 the Bank of England has had the responsibility of providing the nation with a sufficient volume of notes to meet current needs. In the period before 1914 almost all notes in circulation were backed by gold held at the Bank of England. The exception was a small 'fiduciary issue' – one made 'in good faith' to cover those notes temporarily out of circulation in money boxes and under matresses etc. Today the whole of the note issue is taken on trust by those holding it – the practice of backing by gold was never resumed after 1918, at least not for notes held inside the UK.

One problem with notes, especially the smaller denominations which tend to be used frequently by the population, is that they quickly wear out and have to be replaced. This is expensive, not especially from the point of view of the materials used, but rather with regard to the conditions of security required during the production and distribution of new notes, and the collection and destruction of old ones. Consequently replacement of lower denomination notes by coins has taken place, as mentioned earlier.

Management of the gilt edged issue and the gilt edged market

When the government wishes to borrow money it often does this by issuing stock (paper promises to repay at a future date) and selling them in the UK, usually to its own population. Such pieces of paper carry a rate of interest set throughout their life and a date by which they will be redeemed. The redemption date is the date the sum loaned to the government will be repaid. In this form, the paper is known as gilt-edged stock, or gilt-edged securities. The name derived from the fact that the official book in which records relating to such securities were originally entered had gilt-edges to the pages.

The bulk of the value of gilt-edged stock outstanding is dated, i.e. it has a redemption date upon it at the time of issue (e.g. three years from issue, ten years from issue, twenty-five years from issue, etc. This means that even if the government does not want extra borrowed money it must continue to borrow in order to replace existing loans as they fall due for redemption. This task of redeeming gilt-edged stock in an orderly manner when it falls due for redemption and issuing more in a controlled manner falls upon the Bank of England. It manages the gilt-edged market in order to give it as much stability as possible and make it an attractive place for individuals and businesses to continue to invest their funds.

In the mid-1980s, as an adjunct to interest rate policy, the Bank of England sometimes issued more debt than the government required to balance its books. Sometimes this was gilt-edged stock (the national savings movement was used in the same way) and the process was known as 'overfunding the national debt'. The object of the exercise was to reduce the volume of money in circulation – to reduce the money supply.

Representing the government in international financial affairs

After the end of the Second World War there were many points of contact of a financial nature between governments. Some of these are institutionalised – the International Monetary Fund, the World Bank, the European Community Monetary System, etc. Some are of a more ad hoc nature, e.g. attempts to solve the world debt crisis; short term arrangements between central banks to support a particular currency etc. The Bank of England acts as the representative of the UK government in these contacts.

More about the supervision of the banking system within the UK

In the years between its establishment in 1694 and its nationalisation in 1946, the Bank of England gradually developed its role as supervisor of the UK banking network. At first this supervision was of an informal nature – the banking system in the late nineteenth and early twentieth century in the UK was close knit and senior management was almost entirely in the City of London. This meant that Bank of England officials were in close contact with the officials and senior directors of the major banks – a few words of advice or admonishment were seen as sufficient to keep an institution behaving in a proper and prudent manner. As the twentieth century moved into its third quarter though, the small, simple structure of the UK financial institutions, and the relative simplicity of their products, became much more complex. The secondary banking crisis of 1974 signalled that the system was out of control and effectively ended informal regulation, though it took until 1979 to get the means of formal regulation – the 1979 Banking Act – on to the statute book. Even this Act proved inadequate in a rapidly changing financial world and itself was replaced by the Banking Act 1987 which sets out in detail the powers which the Bank of England has over the financial community.

Briefly, the 1987 Act has the following provisions:

a) An institution wishing to take deposits from the general public within the UK must be authorised by the Bank of England (the exceptions are the 'exempt' institutions, such as building societies, foreign National Banks etc).

b) Authorised institutions must meet certain criteria; that the directors, controllers and managers are 'fit and proper' people to hold such positions; that there is adequate capital, provision for bad debts etc; that there are suitable accounting, recording and internal control systems; and that the authorised institution has net assets of not less than £1 million.

c) Each authorised institution will have an independent firm of accountants report to the Bank of England on the internal control system, accounting system and records, and the prudential reserves of that institution.

d) There are rules relating to mergers which give the Bank of England power to intervene.

e) Notice must be given of large loans in some cases before the loan is made.

f) The Deposit Protection Scheme is enlarged to cover all authorised institutions, and the sum required from any institution may be not less than £10 000 and not more than £300 000.

A Board of Banking Supervision is established which gives advice from a team of six independent persons to the three *ex-officio* members about the Bank's handling of any of its duties. If the advice is not taken the six members may report to the Chancellor of the Exchequer and state their reasons for giving the advice which has been ignored.

8   THE DISCOUNT HOUSES

The discount houses, members of the London Discount Market Association (LDMA) form together the primary London money market. They are bill brokers, which is to say they lend money against bills of exchange. They take money from anyone who has money to spare and lend it to those in need of money against the security of a bill of exchange. Most of the funds they borrow come from the institutions, the clearing banks, merchant banks, insurance companies, and other institutions, including the Bank of England (when the Treasury has spare funds available which it wishes to use profitably). They borrow these funds at very economic rates because they borrow them 'at call' or 'short notice', which means they are liable to have to return the money either immediately or within a few days should the institution concerned get into liquidity difficulties. Under the terms of a Bank of England paper, 'Monetary Control – Provisions', all banks whose bills of exchange are eligible for discount at the Bank of England must keep funds equal to 4 per cent of their eligible liabilities with the members of the LDMA. This ensures that the Discount Market always has funds to lend. With these cheap funds the discount houses can lend money out cheaply to those in need of funds. The bills of exchange which they take as security are unconditional orders on the drawees (the people on whom the bills are drawn) to pay a sum of money on a due date which is clearly stated on the bill (or can be calculated from the bill, such as '90 days after date pay . . .'). The drawee will have signed the bill as accepting the obligation, making the drawee the 'acceptor' of the bill and fully liable on it. There will usually also be a further signature from an accepting house (a merchant bank specialising in accepting bills of exchange, for a fee). Where funds are lent to bankers (**bank bills**) the usual minimum size is £10 000; for **trade bills** they may be smaller, since the manufacturing firms who borrow in this way may need only a smaller amount. The Discount Houses take call money because it is possible to borrow it at slightly more favourable interest rates than money loaned for longer periods. This enables them to offer money for bills at competitive rates and still make a profit. Their margins are normally small – about ¼ per cent – and because of this overheads are kept to a minimum. Dealing is done by word of mouth and the motto of the discount houses is 'My word is by bond' – no written contract is needed.

The discount houses, are of course, in an exposed position – they are borrowing short term and lending longer term (by buying bills with only a few days, weeks or months to maturity). Sometimes they are caught out and then they take advantage of a special relationship they have with the Bank of England. This is called the 'Lender of Last Resort' facility. Under this arrangement the Bank will always lend funds to a Discount House which cannot balance its books at the end of the day – usually because some of the institutions from which it borrowed money have 'called' funds to balance their own books. Such a discount house is said to be 'forced into the Bank' and must ask the Bank of England for assistance.

The lender of last resort facility confers a great deal of power upon the Bank of England and is one way in which it can control short-term interest rates. The Bank will always lend, but at what rate and interest? If the bank wants to see higher rates it will charge the discount houses more for their money than they have recently been paying; if it wishes to see lower rates, less than they have recently been paying. These discount houses pass on this change in rates to their customers and help in bringing about general changes in short term interest rates.

9 MERCHANT BANKS

Merchant banks first achieved importance from the services offered to the business community in respect of foreign bills of exchange. These bills used to be the standard method of payment in international trade and traders and manufacturers in the UK and Europe were often offered bills from obscure origins. In order to be able to pass on, or 'discount' these bills, and thus get their money before the bills matured, they had to overcome this problem of 'obscurity' (the more obscure, the greater the risk and the greater the reluctance of third parties to take the bill). A way round the problem was found by the simple expedient of getting respectable institutions to put their name to the bill, thus guaranteeing payment should the original debtor default. The best people to lend their names to these bills were the great merchants who dealt in the overseas territories already, and knew of the 'obscure' people who had accepted the bills. Hence the name 'merchant' bank. These merchant banks were prepared to offer their service for a fee and thus became 'accepting houses', i.e. they 'accepted' the obligations on bills of exchange by putting their name to them.

The most important and influential accepting houses are members of the Accepting Houses Committee. They are:

Robert Fleming	Schroder
Baring Brothers	NM Rothschild
Lazard Brothers	Hill Samuel
Charterhouse Japhet	Samuel Montagu
Brown Shipley	Hambros
Guinness Mahon	SG Warburg
Singer and Friedland	Morgan Grenfell
Rea Brothers	Kleinwort Benson

A further important activity of merchant banks is the floating of loans and the handling of share issues for customers. This field of activity is known as the New Issue Market, and the issuing houses – who are not all merchant banks – raise capital for firms either by a public issue of shares or by 'placing' them with reputable investors. They also deal in the areas of corporate finance and investment management.

Merchant banks are *not* clearers, and offer no retail services to the population as a whole.

10 THE CLEARING BANKS

Clearing banks are those with which the general public are most familiar. They have a heavy high street presence and are greatly involved in retail banking, i.e. dealing with counter customers. They are called clearing banks because they are involved with the Bankers' Clearing House. The Clearing House operates a system which is designed to simplify and minimise the movement of funds between banks. Suppose that at the end of a trading day customers of Lloyds bank have made out cheques and other payments to customers of Barclays Bank to the value of £1479 million, and that Barclays' customers have made out cheques etc. to customers of Lloyds to the value of £1477 million. Rather than settle these debts by the movement of £2956 million the Clearing House will merely notify the Bank of England to settle the *difference* – £2 million, a much less cumbersome way of settling inter-bank indebtedness. We say that all that needs to be settled is the net indebtedness.

Clearing banks offer a vast range of services to both their personal and business customers, but in addition, in recent years have moved into areas previously the domain of merchant banks. They have often done this through the formation or acquisition of specialist subsidiaries, which can carry on merchant bank activities.

11   GIROBANK AND THE NATIONAL SAVINGS BANK

The Girobank was established in 1968 as a banking system designed to work through post office outlets (at that time about 20 000 units). It has nearly two million accounts and is in the process of being privatised. Generally Girobank caters for those customers who require a range of services of a more basic nature than the mainstream banks. Originally it was designed to cater for the non-banking sector of the economy – the relatively unsophisticated customers who, at that time, had banking activities that were largely catered for by the old Post Office Savings Bank. The advent of Girobank woke the ordinary clearing banks up to the fact that they had overlooked this huge area of banking business and they began to take an interest in the under-banked sector.

Also operated from Post Office outlets is the completely separate **National Savings Bank** which offers a wide variety of investment opportunities to the small saver.

12   FINANCE HOUSES

Finance houses – many of them now subsidiaries of major banks – are particularly concerned with the provision of consumer credit, especially hire purchase and personal loans linked to second mortgages. Much of their business is secured against repossessable physical assets, e.g. motor cars. In the early days of their existence 'hire purchase' companies had a reputation for dubious repossession practices, but more recently, and largely due to closer control and the involvement of larger banking institutions, the sector has become much more respectable.

In recent years they have developed their business in the field of leasing – a process whereby companies secure the use of capital assets, not by purchasing them, but by hiring them. The process of leasing has become popular partly because companies do not need to find the capital sums required to purchase the assets they need. The finance house buys and owns the asset, but makes it available to the lessee for a monthly rental. This monthly rental is a deductible expense for tax purposes, which is a benefit to the lessee, while the finance house can claim a 25 per cent deduction for the asset in the first year of its purchase, and 25 per cent of the diminishing balance each subsequent year.

13 BUILDING SOCIETIES

Building societies under the terms of the 1987 Banking Act are 'exempt institutions', i.e. they are not regulated by that Act. Building Societies are mutual organisations – originally non-profit seeking organisations set up to provide ordinary working people with the chance to purchase domestic property for their own occupation.

Gradually, building societies have extended their operations and are now real competitors to the high street banks, especially in the area of personal business. The Building Societies Act of 1986 is responsible for much of the expansion into areas outside of lending for house purchase, and also enabled building societies to abandon their mutual status and become incorporated. The Abbey National was the first Society to take advantage of this opportunity, and is now a public limited company and an authorised deposit taker, designated as a bank.

14 THE STOCK EXCHANGE

Mention was made earlier of the activities of the merchant banks in the New Issue Market. Immediately shares have been issued they can be bought and sold on the Stock Exchange, which is the market for *existing* stocks and shares. Such a market is essential, for when people invest in shares they do not anticipate keeping the shares forever, but only for so long as it is convenient, and worthwhile.

Fate knocks on someone's door every day, and when it does the people concerned need to sell their shares, either to raise funds to deal with the problem that has arisen, or in the case of death – to pay the inheritance tax due and pass the ownership of what is left to the beneficiaries under the will of the deceased. The place to buy and sell shares is the Stock Exchange.

There are two activities on the Stock Exchange; market making and stockbroking. The operators are called *broker-dealers*, and can act both as brokers (buying and selling shares for the general pubic and for their personal portfolios) or as dealers, making a market. However, they can act in only a single capacity if they wish. Market makers quote prices at which they are prepared to buy and sell shares, and feed these prices into an electronic display called **SEAQ** – the **Stock Exchange Automated Quotation**. Brokers anywhere who are on-line to the computer can place orders to buy shares, or can offer shares to market makers, at the prices quoted. They can also sell shares from their personal portfolios to customers, but if they do they must offer them at the 'best execution' price available on the screen at the moment of sale. Thus if a share in X Co. Ltd is valued at £3.56 at the moment, but a broker has bought some last week at £3.90 which he/she is anxious to dispose of, it would be unfair to sell them to the customer at £3.95 (thus making a 5p profit on each share). If the shares have fallen in value and the broker has therefore suffered a loss while they were in his/her portfolio it is wrong to pass that loss to the customer. The shares must be sold at the 'best execution' price shown on the SEAQ screen at the time of the sale, or a better price. They may not be sold at a worse price, and all sales are time-tagged so that a check-up can be made by the authorities.

The vital point about the Stock Exchange is that it lends liquidity to capital funds, which have actually been fixed into fixed capital (plant, machinery, premises, etc) by the companies who borrowed it originally. I cannot ask the Magnificent Oil Co. to give me back my capital – they have fixed it into drilling rigs. I *can* ask my broker dealer to find me someone who has cash and wants shares in the Magnificent Oil Co. I regain liquidity through the market place for stocks and shares.

How capital is raised

When a company wishes to expand production or pursue any other business activity it usually needs finance. The commonest ways of finding finance are:

1 By self-financing – ploughing back profits into the business.
2 By borrowing from a bank, either on overdraft or by a slightly more formal loan – where the funds are made available against a clear programme of repayments.
3 Temporary difficulties may be financed by a loan from the money markets, secured against bills of exchange.
4 Permanent capital may be obtained by a new issue, either of debentures (loan stock) or shares. The issue will be arranged by one of the new issue houses, usually a merchant bank, and requires the publication of a prospectus outlining the profitability over recent years, and full details of the new issue. Such debentures and shares then become the subject of dealings on the Stock Exchange, as described above.

15   THE WORLD BANK

A chapter on banking would be incomplete without mention of the World Bank. There are two parts to the World Bank; the International Bank for Reconstruction and Development (IBRD) and the International Development Association (IDA). The latter has a further subsidiary; the International Finance Corporation (IFC). Set up in 1945 the World Bank seeks to promote a more uniform world economy by assisting countries to develop by the provision of capital borrowed from the advanced nations. It also acts as a watchdog where countries are pursuing 'beggar-my-neighbour' policies by such activities as 'dumping', or manipulation of their exchange rates to the detriment of other nations (instead of putting their own economic house in order). The World Bank has done some extremely useful work, especially where the projects have been grass-roots projects linked to the development of the nation concerned at a level appropriate to its economy at the time the aid was provided. It has been less successful with prestige projects, which are capital intensive rather than labour extensive, and have in some cases proved to be inappropriate for the state of technology in the less-developed world. The Head Office of the World Bank is in Washington DC, but it does have an office in London at New Zealand House, Haymarket, London, SW1.

16   THE IMPORTANCE OF BANKING IN THE ECONOMY

We may conclude that money, credit and banking are very important elements in any economy, and an efficient monetary system is a great catalyst for the production, distribution and exchange of wealth. It provides a simple, flexible, method for meeting every requirement in the economy. It is the simplest way to reward people who are prepared to supply factors (land, labour and capital) to the production process. It is the simplest way to re-route funds from those who have a surplus of purchasing power which they do not wish to use at the moment, to those who are starved of capital but wish to show enterprise. It is the simple way to take care of all those activities which are essential to peaceful existence, defence, law and order, education, the relief of misfortune, care of the young and of the old. Paying taxes provides all the funds necessary to do these things, and wise government ensures a balance between the various claims and counterclaims. The money system is also the simplest way to arrange the myriad day to day transactions which are required when people wish to purchase a balanced basket of goods and services for the peaceful pursuit of family and personal life.

No-one pretends that the efficient maintenance of the balance in the economy is easy. We cannot allow the banks to create credit to the point where people face such a mountain of debt that suicide seems the only way out. We cannot live beyond our means (which is the wealth we have created in the form of goods and services). If too much money is created, inflation (a rise in the prices of goods and services) must occur. We must have wise government if these problems are to be avoided, but at the same time the money system is a great institution. It embodies the wisdom of countless generations since the first coins were struck in the Middle East about 700 BC.

SELF-ASSESSMENT QUESTIONS

6 List the various institutions which have a part to play in the financial arrangements of every day life.

7 What are the main elements in the Banking Act 1987?

8 Explain the activities of the discount houses?

9 Taking an ordinary family as an example, explain the importance of the money system to them.

REVISION TEST

Answers	Questions
	1 What is barter?
1 The exchange of goods or services for other goods or services.	**2** What are the problems of barter?
2 (a) The need for a coincidence of wants; (b) the need to strike equations of value; (c) the problems that arise when an item is indivisible (like a horse).	**3** What are the functions of money?
3 It is (a) a medium of exchange (b) a store of value; (c) a measure of value; (d) a standard for deferred payments.	**4** What are the forms of money?
4 (a) Coins; (b) notes; (c) cheques and other bills of exchange (d) any other instrument of payment, for example standing orders, direct debits, bank cards, credit cards, postal orders, etc.	**5** What are the characteristics of money?
5 It should be (a) universally acceptable; (b) stable in value; (c) recognisable; (d) homogeneous; (e) portable; (f) durable; (g) difficult to imitate; (h) divisable into very small units.	**6** What is the creation of credit?
6 The lending of money by banks to a greater limit than the funds they actually have available, because they know that the probability of anyone actually asking for cash is less than 5 per cent and, as long as they can always give customers cash as and when they need it, a crisis of confidence will not occur.	**7** What happens when a crisis of confidence does occur?

7 There is a run on the Bank, and it has to close. A rescue operation will be mounted by the other banks, through the Bank of England.

8 What is 'keeping in step'?

8 A requirement of the money system by which banks must not lend out more money than other banks in proportion to their present size. If they do they will have liquidity problems as some cheques drawn on them are paid into other banks, and they will be unable to match the loans made with the sums received.

9 Who supervises 'keeping in step'?

9 The Bank of England, which is entitled to monitor the prudential behaviour of all banks, and will query with top management any loss of liquidity (usually evidenced by the failure of the bank concerned to keep its agreed 4 per cent of elegible liabilities with the discount houses).

10 What are the measures of money supply?

10 They do vary from time to time as the Treasury wrestles with the problem of measuring the state of the economy. The current list is M0, NIBMI, M2, M4, M4C and M5.

11 State how the money system helps the economy to work.

11 (a) It makes possible the rewards to factors, rent, wages, interest and profits paid to landlords, workers, savers, and entrepreneurs; (b) It makes possible the provision of capital by those with funds to spare to those in need of funds; (c) It makes possible public sector activities like defence, law and order, education, health services and social security. (d) It makes possible the day-to-day transactions of personal and family life.

Go over the test until you are sure of all the answers. Then try the questions below.

ANSWERS

See Self-assessment questions on pages 370 and 381.

1 The problems of barter are as follows: (a) the need for a coincidence of wants. We must have two people, each of which wants what the other has, and has what the other wants; (b) we have to strike equations of value – is a sharp knife worth a glazed cooking pot? etc. (c) we cannot always strike a fair bargain because some things are indivisible – like a horse. We may have to carry over part of the exchange to a later date.

2   The functions of money are: (a) that it is a medium of exchange, readily exchangeable for any good or service; (b) that it is a store of value, which can be held in reserve for use in any way desired at some future time; (c) that it is a measure of value, by which we may compare any good or service with any other good or service; and (d) it is a standard for deferred payments, making it possible to postpone payment of any item to a later date, under terms and conditions acceptable to both parties.

3   The essential characteristics of money are that it should be: (a) universally acceptable; (b) stable in value; (c) easily recognisable as money (d) homogeneous (that is every unit must be exactly the same as every other unit); (e) portable; (f) durable; (g) difficult to imitate and (h) divisible into small units so that even the smallest transactions are possible.

4   A bank creates credit when it lends out more money that it really has. Because the likely proportion of any deposit made that will be demanded back in cash form is low (a cash ratio of about 5 per cent) the bank can lend out considerably more than the other 95 per cent of any deposit made. Suppose £10 000 is deposited, of which 5 per cent (£500) is likely to be asked for. The bank has £9500 spare cash, but actually can lend up to 19 times this (though it usually only lends about four times). Suppose the bank lends £38 000. This will be spent by the borrower, by writing cheques to suppliers. If these suppliers pay the cheques in to the bank again, as deposits of £38 000, they are only likely to ask for 5 per cent (£1900) in cash. As the bank has £9500 in cash it is perfectly safe, and can always meet its obligations (except in times of severe distress – like the start of the war – when the Government always closes the banks).

5   Banks must 'keep in step' – by which we mean they must only lend the same proportion of their total assets as all the other banks – because if they don't they will lose liquidity to other Banks and eventually go bankrupt. Since Banks are lending money they haven't got they must rely on getting back from those who are paid by cheque enough cheques to balance the total paid out. If they lend more than their size warrants more of their cheques will be diverted to other banks then other banks' cheques will be diverted to them. They will lose liquidity to other banks and will eventually be bankrupted. (See Fig. 14.2 for an illustration of this process.)

6   The institutions are the Bank of England, the discount houses, the merchant banks, the clearing banks, the finance houses, the building societies, Girobank, the National Savings Bank, the Stock Exchange and the New Issue Houses.

7   The main elements of the Banking Act 1987 are (a) the setting up of a Board of Banking Supervision; (b) the designation of all institutions as authorised deposit takers; (c) the restriction of the right to use the name 'bank' to those institutions

with over £5 million capital; (d) the requirements about independent reports on the prudential reserves of each institution; (e) the rules about mergers; (f) the further enlargement of the Deposit Protection Scheme.

8 The discount houses are bill brokers. They take funds from anyone who has funds to spare and lend them to borrowers in search of funds, against the security of a bill of exchange (usually a three month or six month bill). The money they borrow is chiefly 'call money' from banks, or short-notice money repayable in two or three days. They also lend money to the Treasury by tendering for the weekly Treasury Bill issue – which averages about £40 million each week. Because they are borrowing short to lend long they sometimes cannot balance their books and are put into difficulties. They are helped out of their problem by the Bank of England as 'lender of last resort', but the Bank can vary the rate it will charge and if they have been lending too freely the rate can be made a penal rate (which means they will have to pay the Bank more interest than they are getting from their customers). This makes them raise interest rates to customers next day, and reduces the demand for money.

9 To an ordinary family money is important because (a) it is the way they get rewarded for the work they do (the rewards to factors); (b) it is the way they borrow if they are short of funds for everyday use; (c) it is the way they pay for all the goods and services they need for everyday living; (d) it is the way they save (a store of value) for the future, for retirement, for holidays etc.

QUESTIONS ON CHAPTER 14

1 Explain the importance of a money system to an advanced economy.

2 Write short explanations of the following terms:
a) money as a store of value
b) growth of the national income
c) barter
d) 'real' incomes and 'money' incomes

3 What are 'measures of money supply'? What help are they in trying to control the money supply?

4 The 'Sign of the Chestnut Horse' is the place where you will find the friendliest bank manager. 'I'm sorry, you cannot possibly have an overdraft!' Why may even the friendliest bank manager be unable to lend money to a customer?

5 'Loans make deposits.' Explain this statement by reference to Miss A, who borrows £5000 to buy a car which she purchases from Valley Motors Ltd.

6 Describe the activities of the discount houses in the primary money market. Why are they occasionally 'forced into the Bank', and how do they get out again?

7 What are (a) authorised deposit takers and (b) banks?

8 What is the Deposit Protection Fund and whom is it trying to protect against what?

9 How may a government seek to control money supply in a country?

(Courtesy of the Institute of Marketing)

10 What limits the power of a commercial bank to create credit?

(Courtesy of the Institute of Commercial Management)

11 What are the chief functions of the Bank of England?

12 How can an enterprise raise finance?

(Courtesy of the association of Business Executives)

13 How can the central monetary authorities control the supply of money?

(Courtesy of the Institute of Marketing)

14 What is the effect on the money supply if the government successfully launches a new gilt-edged security which the public purchases in large quantities?

TIPS FOR STUDENTS: A SPECIMEN ANSWER TO QUESTION 12

Enterprises can raise finance by self-financing (ploughing back the profits of the business) or by borrowing from a variety of institutions. For short term loans the clearing banks are prepared to lend an overdraft to meet temporary difficulties (for example a weak cash flow situation at particular times in the year). Overdrafts are not intended to run for ever, and a permanent overdraft will usually be converted to a loan, with an agreed sum of money being put into the current account of the firm or company, repayable by agreed instalments. Finance houses will lend money against hire purchase agreements, and will arrange leasing contracts whereby they buy assets required by a firm and allow the firm to lease them for a monthly fee.

More permanent finance can be obtained by issuing debentures or shares. A debenture is a loan to a company against the security of a deed – the debenture – which is secured upon the fixed assets of the company (a fixed debenture) or on the current assets (a floating debenture). A naked debenture is one that is unsecured, hence its name – the lender of the money is rather exposed. A fixed debenture is secured on the fixed assets and prevents the borrower selling the assets without the permission of the debenture trustee (usually a local accountant). A floating debenture floats over the stock, but does not prevent the company buying and selling stock. It only crystallises over the stock if the debenture trustee detects financial difficulties ahead, and seizes the stock for sale to repay the money borrowed.

Ordinary shares and preference shares are issued in a formal manner in accordance with regulations laid down in the Companies Act 1985. The purchasers of shares become shareholders, and as such share in the ownership of the company concerned. They participate in the profits of the firm. Preference shareholders get the percentage profit named in the share name – for example 8 per cent Preference Shares. Ordinary shareholders share equally in the profits of the business and hence they are often called 'equity' shares.

15 Conclusions about economics for marketing and business

1 ECONOMICS AND PUBLIC POLICY

We are coming to the end of a long and complex book on elementary economics. Since economics embraces the study of every facet of human life and every matter on which policy needs to be laid down by anyone seeking to manage the economy, it is clear that many matters which are of great importance have not been touched upon, and it is quite impossible to cover everything. Students will realise by now that economics is a very wide subject area, and all sorts of more detailed studies of different aspects of production, distribution and marketing are necessary. This book has been about basic principles of economics, but further fields of study in applied economics lie ahead. These are not necessarily academic studies, though most young people do carry on their studies in some field of higher education to achieve both academic qualifications and membership of appropriate professional bodies. From a wider viewpoint economics is part of the study of the rich pattern of life – particularly business life – since it is concerned largely with wealth creation. It is also concerned to ensure that wealth creation is achieved in a proper manner. The early capitalists in the UK were condemned for the way they created wealth as cheaply as possible for themselves while heaping social costs upon the general public in the form of smoke, fumes, slag heaps and other forms of pollution. Today the same thing is happening in many parts of the economy, and in almost all countries. Economics will have an important part to play in seeking to correct adverse impacts on the environment by excessive wealth creation.

2 ECONOMICS – THE UNIVERSAL DISCIPLINE

When Adam Smith and his contemporaries first examined the economic state of mankind, they did not have the vision that we have today of where economics would lead mankind. They were puzzled by the paradox of capitalist society, that while the economic possibility of unlimited wealth creation was being revealed to mankind, the majority of the population were desperately poor. Forced off the land by Enclosure Acts the rural poor were driven into the industrial areas to work endlessly in the 'dark satanic mills' where wealth was created. Thomas Malthus, the son of a country squire, enunciated the Malthusian Doctrine, which held that while the food of the world was only increasing in arithmetical proportions 2, 4, 6, 8, 10, population was rising in geometric proportions 2, 4, 8, 16, 32, etc. Today the Malthusian nightmare is upon us. In the single decade of the 1990s, it is estimated that world population will rise by 1 000 000 000. This is the same increase that occurred from the dawn of history until 1830. 1830–1930 produced the next 1000 million; 1930–60 the third gigabirth explosion; 1960–75 the fourth gigabirth; 1975–90, the fifth, and AD 1990–2000 will produce as large an increase of population as took place from the earliest times to 1830. Malthus may have been right after all: population may be rising so fast that it will outstrip food production. Perhaps the checks he cited to control population are waiting to operate – 'infant mortality, infanticide, disease, epidemics, plagues, unwholesome foods, dangerous occupations, war and famine – which with one mighty blow levels the population with the food supply of the world'. We expect the year AD 2000 to see 6000 million people on the earth, and by 2025 there may be 16 000 million. Not only have huge populations been born into the world, but they have fixed their eyes on the most distant horizons. They judge their conditions not by the lot of their village neighbours, but by the condition of those who circle the world in jumbo jets. The economic problems of the next half century are likely to be enormous. Only the most concerted international effort is likely to resolve the difficulties without a major catastrophe.

The solution to these problems are almost entirely economic. This is no time for economists to be downhearted or lose confidence. Only economic life is universal, and crosses political, religious and ethnic barriers. If we are all to survive, it is economists who must provide the survival vehicle and business people who must drive it. No one else creates wealth. Art, literature, music and all the other disciplines have their merits, but only economics and business activity make them, and life itself, possible.

Index